THE COMPLETE WORKS
OF
ROBERT BROWNING

Volume 1

THE COMPLETE WORKS OF
ROBERT BROWNING

Volume 1

PAULINE, PARACELSUS, PIPPA
PASSES, ETC.

WILDSIDE PRESS

Copyright, 1899,
BY HOUGHTON, MIFFLIN & CO

All rights reserved.

CONTENTS

	PAGE
INTRODUCTION	ix
PAULINE: A FRAGMENT OF A CONFESSION	1
PARACELSUS:	
I. PARACELSUS ASPIRES	27
II. PARACELSUS ATTAINS	46
III. PARACELSUS	61
IV. PARACELSUS ASPIRES	85
V. PARACELSUS ATTAINS	101
NOTE	123
STRAFFORD: A TRAGEDY	129
SORDELLO	193
PIPPA PASSES: A DRAMA	327
KING VICTOR AND KING CHARLES: A TRAGEDY	369
NOTES	413

INTRODUCTION

BROWNING wrote *Pauline* at the age of twenty-one, when under the influence of Shelley. It was read by his parents, who saw something in it to commend, though his father criticised it severely. It was their approval of it, on the whole, however, that led an aunt to put into his hand the money with which to print it, and it appeared from the press of Saunders & Utley, in 1833. It attracted almost no attention from the press, but was reviewed by the Rev. William Johnson Fox, editor of the *Monthly Repository*. Of this friendly and appreciative notice Browning wrote: "I shall never write a line without thinking of the source of my first praise, be assured." John Stuart Mill also proposed to write in commendation of the poem, but the only periodical to which he had free access had already printed a contemptuous disapproval of it. Years later Dante Gabriel Rossetti found the poem in the British Museum and copied it in full, with the conviction that Browning was the author.

PAULINE.

This poem was intended by Browning for the introduction to an extended work, but nothing more of it was written. Five years after the publication of *Pauline* he wrote in a copy: "The only remaining crab of the Shapely Tree of Life in my Fool's Paradise, . . . written in pursuance of a foolish plan I forget or have no wish to remember." The poet permitted *Pauline* to pass into neglect until 1867, when the announcement of its republication by some one who wished to take advantage of his growing fame led him to publish it with his own name, and the following preface: —

"The first piece in the series (*Pauline*), I acknowledge and retain with extreme repugnance, indeed purely of necessity; for not long ago I inspected one, and am certified of the existence of other transcripts, intended sooner or later to be published abroad : by forestalling these, I can at least correct some misprints (no syllable is changed) and introduce a boyish work by an exculpatory word. The thing was my earliest attempt at 'poetry always dramatic in principle, and so many utterances of so many imaginary persons, not mine,' which I have since written according to a scheme less extravagant and scale less impracticable than were ventured upon in this crude preliminary sketch, — a sketch that, on reviewal, appears not altogether wide of some hint of the characteristic features of that particular *dramatis persona* it would fain have reproduced; good draughtsmanship, however, and right handling were far beyond the artist at that time. R. B.

"LONDON, *December* 25, 1867."

On making his final collective edition of his works, Browning added the following statement : —

"I preserve, in order to supplement it, the foregoing preface. I had thought, when compelled to include in my collected works the poem to which it refers, that the honest course would be to reprint, and leave mere literary errors unaltered. Twenty years' endurance of an eyesore seems more than sufficient: my faults remain duly recorded against me, and I claim permission to somewhat diminish these, so far as style is concerned, in the present and final edition, where *Pauline* must needs, first of my performances, confront the reader. I have simply removed solecisms, mended the metre a little, and endeavored to strengthen the phraseology, — experiences helping in some degree the helplessness of juvenile haste and heat in their untried adventure long ago.

"LONDON, *February* 27, 1888."

When reprinting the poem for the last time, Browning made the additional comment : —

"This introduction would appear less absurdly pretentious did it apply, as was intended, to a completed structure of which the poem was meant for only a beginning and remains a fragment."

It may be said of *Pauline* that it has no historical foundation, as did so many of Browning's later poems. The speaker is

INTRODUCTION

addressing Pauline, and confessing to her his soul experiences, therefore it is wholly subjective and introspective.

Paracelsus was written in the winter of 1834–35, and was dedicated to the young count who had suggested the subject to him. The original preface was an attempt to explain and justify the method adopted by the poet.

PARACEL-
SUS.

"I am anxious that the reader should not, at the very outset, — mistaking my performance for one of a class with which it has nothing in common, — judge it by principles on which it was never moulded, and subject it to a standard to which it was never meant to conform. I therefore anticipate his discovery that it is an attempt, probably more novel than happy, to reverse the method usually adopted by writers whose aim it is to set forth any phenomenon of the mind or the passions, by the operation of persons and events; and that, instead of having recourse to an external machinery of incidents to create and evolve the crisis I desire to produce, I have ventured to display somewhat minutely the mood itself in its rise and progress, and have suffered the agency by which it is influenced and determined to be generally discernible in its effects alone, and subordinate throughout, if not altogether excluded: and this for a reason. I have endeavored to write a poem, not a drama: the canons of the drama are well known, and I cannot but think that, inasmuch as they have immediate regard to stage representation, the peculiar advantages they hold out are really such only so long as the purpose for which they were at first instituted is kept in view. I do not very well understand what is called a Dramatic Poem, wherein all those restrictions only submitted to on account of compensating good in the original scheme are scrupulously retained, as though for some special fitness in themselves, — and all new facilities placed at an author's disposal by the vehicle he selects, as pertinaciously rejected. It is certain, however, that a work like mine depends on the intelligence and sympathy of the reader for its success, — indeed, were my scenes stars, it must be his coöperating fancy which, supplying all chasms, shall connect the scattered lights into one constellation, — a Lyre or a Crown. I trust for his indulgence towards a poem which had not been imagined six months ago; and that even should he think slightingly of the present (an experiment I am in no case likely to repeat) he will not be prejudiced against other productions which may follow in a more popular, and perhaps less difficult form.

"15*th March*, 1835."

In carrying out this purpose, Browning selected the career of Theophrastus Bombast von Hohenheim, known as Paracelsus, who was born near the city of Zurich in 1493, or not far from that date. He was early taught by his father, entered the University of Basel or Basle, but did not long remain, then studied under Johann Trithemius, a bishop, but also a famous alchemist and astrologer of the day. He seems to have given attention to chemistry and medicine, and to have become somewhat proficient in both, according to the standards of the time.

About 1512 Paracelsus set out on his scientific travels, his purpose being his own education, and the gaining of whatever knowledge was to be found anywhere. He went through Germany, Italy, France, the Netherlands, Denmark, Sweden, Russia, and probably some parts of Asia. He is said to have gone through Prussia, Austria, Turkey, Egypt, Tartary, and back again to Constantinople, where he is said to have spent some time. He is even reported to have been a captive in Tartary, and to have learned valuable medical secrets there; and it is stated that he settled in Constantinople for some years as a physician. Waite says that in Muscovy he was brought before the great Cham. "His knowledge of medicine and chemistry made him a favorite at the court of this potentate, who sent him in company with his son on an embassy to Constantinople. It was here, according to Helmont, that he was taught the supreme secret of alchemistry by a generous Arabian, who gave him the universal dissolvent, the Azoth of Western adepts, the alcohect or sophic fire."

Very little is really known about the travels of Paracelsus, and it is by no means certain that he was ever in the East. The supposition of Hartmann, that he must have acquired some of his teachings by contact with Indian or other Asiatic believers in occultism, has little to support it; and Neo-Platonism could have given him everything of this kind which he expressed in his books. Hartmann's account of his method of acquiring know-

INTRODUCTION xiii

ledge is much more to the point: "Paracelsus travelled through the countries along the Danube, and came into Italy, where he served as an army surgeon in the imperial army, and participated in many of the warlike expeditions of these times. On these occasions he collected a great deal of useful information, not only from physicians, surgeons, and alchemists, but also by his personal intercourse with executioners, barbers, shepherds, Jews, gypsies, midwives, and fortune-tellers. He collected useful information from the high and low, from the learned and from the vulgar, and it was nothing unusual to see him in the company of teamsters and vagabonds, on the highways and at public inns, — a circumstance on account of which his narrow-minded enemies heaped upon him bitter reproach and vilifications."

Having spent something more than ten years on his travels, Paracelsus returned home, and began his career as a physician and teacher. In 1526 or 1527 Paracelsus returned to Basle, and was almost at once made the town physician. He performed some remarkable cures, which brought him into notice as possessed of great knowledge and remarkable skill. One of the cures he wrought was that of Froben, who was cured by him of gout by the means of laudanum. Froben was one of the earliest of the great printers, a man of learning and skill, the intimate friend of Erasmus, and the publisher of his many works, and of the editions of the classic and Christian writers which he edited. On the recommendation of Œcolampadius, and other leaders among the Protestant reformers, Paracelsus was soon appointed by the city council of Basle to the post of professor of physic, medicine, and surgery in the university, and with a considerable salary.

Learned as Paracelsus undoubtedly was, and skilful as he must have been, he seems not to have had the discretion and sound judgment which are a better part of all wisdom. That he was a man of much originality we may admit, and that he had the boldness of the true reformer; but he was wanting in tact, and in capacity for wisely guiding other men. Very soon after he was established in Basle he came into collision with the city authorities and with the people. He asked the town council to make the apothecaries subject to him as the city physician, and that they should not be allowed to sell any medicines except at his order. This was probably a just request from the point of view of a wise physician; but the apothecaries would not submit to the control of Paracelsus, and they excited the people against the reformer. This action was construed as a direct attack upon the business of all the druggists and apothecaries in the city; and it excited the jealousy of the other physicians, who likewise turned against the innovator.

As a professor and lecturer in the university Paracelsus carried his spirit of innovation still farther than he had done as the city physician. From the very first the method of Paracelsus was boldly original, not to say egotistical. He did what had not before been undertaken in connection with university teaching, — he discarded Latin in his lectures, and spoke in the vernacular, which was Swiss-German. Then he did not reproduce the teachings of the books, did not go to Galen, Celsus, or any of the masters of the past; but he drew from his own observations, and presented theories and methods of his own. This was doing in medicine what Erasmus had done as a scholar and what Luther had done as a religious teacher. In Paracelsus, however, there was not the gravity and solidity which marked the careers of Luther and Erasmus; and he laid himself open to the charge of being a charlatan. In his lectures he denounced the teachings of Galen and Avicenna, then the great masters of medical science, and he burned their works before his pupils in a dramatic manner. He said that the physicians educated in the old way were quacks and impostors, and that in his own shoe-strings was more knowledge than in the men whose writings had been the standards of medicine for centuries. He proposed to cut wholly loose from the old medical system, and to establish this science upon a basis of its own, which he was ready to supply.

Paracelsus seems to have had an egotism which was repellent to others, rather than an aid to his own success. He said in the preface to one of his books: "I know that the monarchy of mind will belong to me, that mine will be the honor. I do not praise myself, but Nature praises me, for I am born of Nature, and follow her. She knows me and I know her."

The immediate cause of the departure of Paracelsus from Basle was the failure of the city authorities to sustain him in his rights as a physician. Having attended a certain Canon Cornelius, of Lichtenfels, as a physician, and cured him of gout, this priest refused to pay him for his services; and the authorities refused to sustain Paracelsus in his attempts to collect the fee. Many causes, however, conspired together to secure the downfall of Paracelsus. His novelties in medicine, his rejection of the methods of the schools, his careless and coarse habits of living, his pretentious and bombastic ways of speaking of himself, and his use of alchemy and magic, were among the causes that his enemies made use of to defeat his efforts. So great was the opposition to him that he was obliged to leave Basle without taking with him his instruments and his chemicals, and his property was taken charge of by Oporinus, his pupil and amanuensis. He spent a short time at Esslingen, but want drove him on, and he was for a dozen years a constant wanderer through the cities of Switzerland and southern Germany. In 1541 he was invited by Archbishop Ernst to settle in Salzburg under his protection. His privations, however, had worn him out, and he died, September 24, 1541, in the "White Horse" inn, and was buried in the graveyard of St. Sebastian.

Paracelsus was a quack without doubt, and yet he was one of the very first students to distinguish chemistry from alchemy. He was an investigator and discoverer, but his mind was under the dominion of astrological guesses and magical formulas. He was so pretentious that his name gave origin to the word "bombast" to describe an inflated and egotistical method of speech. He was a man of a fervid and erratic character, full of great purposes, which he had not the stability and persistence to realize. He had genius, but he was visionary, and wanting in sound judgment. Much doubt exists as to the real worth of his discoveries because he refused to make known his medical formulas, and kept his scientific acquisitions a secret with himself. He published many books, but they are now practically forgotten. His name is included among the great pretenders and charlatans, rather than among the originators of science.

The inconsistent elements in the character of Paracelsus are well described by Professor Ferguson: "It is not difficult to criticise Paracelsus, and to represent him as so far below the level of his time as to be utterly contemptible. It is difficult, but perhaps not impossible, to raise Paracelsus to a place among the great spirits of mankind. It is most difficult of all to ascertain what his true character really was, to appreciate aright this man of fervid imagination, of powerful and persistent convictions, of unabated honesty and love of truth, of keen insight into the errors (as he thought them) of his time, of a merciless will to lay bare these errors, and to reform the abuses to which they gave rise, who in an instant offends us by his boasting, his grossness, his want of self-respect. It is a problem how to reconcile his ignorance, his weakness, his superstition, his crude notions, his erroneous observations, his ridiculous inferences and theories, with his grasp of method, his lofty views of the true scope of medicine, his lucid statements, his incisive and epigrammatic criticisms of men and motives."

In spite of his egotism and his charlatanry in method, it is unquestionable that Paracelsus was the first of the new race of alchemists who sought not for gold, but to know how to prepare medicines. He was much of a Neo-Platonist, or a believer, perhaps, in the teachings of the Khabbalah; and he made use of these spiritualistic doctrines in his medical theories. He sought for remedies that would act upon the spiritual nature of disease, and accordingly made a large use of the doctrine of signatures, or the correspondence of the microcosm with the macrocosm. This led him to his theory of specifics, and to his arcana of medicines. He taught that nature-philosophy which had so remarkable an expression in the philosophy of Schelling. He was a theosophist, and taught much which has in recent years newly appeared under that name. He had not learned to separate these speculations from those of legitimate science; and in his writings they are almost inextricably mixed with each other, the true scientific method being employed to maintain the wildest theosophic or cabalistic speculations. This strange mixture of good and evil in his teachings is described by Erdmann, who is writing of his theory of the arcana, and says: "Here, as in general with Paracelsus, it is hard to tell where self-deception ceases and charlatanry begins. He cannot be acquitted of either; on the contrary, neither here nor in the case of the famous recipe for the production of the homunculus, is it possible to think of an ironical jest. Amid all the assertions which appear so fantastic, he is never tired of warning his readers against fantasies, and of demanding that Nature herself should be allowed to point out the way."

Charles Kingsley, Jules Andrieu, and other writers, have expressed the idea that Browning has given a better interpretation of the career of Paracelsus than have his philosophical exponents. Browning has interpreted Paracelsus as one who was a believer in intuition as a source of truth, and this he undoubtedly was. He expected to arrive at the secrets of Nature by direct apprehension or by intuition. He thought that the soul could see directly into Nature, and find truth by the special activity of the interior being. "Hidden things of the soul," he says in his *De Natura Rerum*, "which cannot be perceived by the physical senses, may be found through the sidereal body, through whose organism we may look into nature in the same way as the sun shines through a glass. The inner nature of everything may therefore be known through magic in general, and through the powers of the inner or second sight."

Browning subjected *Paracelsus* to thorough revision, and in the edition of 1888 at least one third of the lines have been in some way emended, by omission, addition, or rewriting. Among the few who read it with enthusiasm was William Macready, the actor, whom Browning first met at the house of the Rev. W. J. Fox, in November, 1835. "The actor was exceedingly charmed with the young and ardent writer, who, he said, looked more like a poet than any man he had ever met. He read *Paracelsus* with a sort of ecstasy, and cultivated Mr. Browning's acquaintance on every occasion. He asked him to spend New Year's Day with him at his country-house at Elstree, and on the last day of 1835 Mr. Browning found himself at 'The Blue Posts' waiting for the coach, in company with two or three other persons, who looked at him with curiosity. One of these, a tall, ardent, noticeable young fellow, constantly caught his eye, but no conversation passed as they drove northward. It turned out that they were all Macready's guests, while the noticeable youth was no other than John Forster. He, on being introduced to Mr. Browning, said: 'Did you see a little notice of you I wrote in the *Examiner*?' The friendship so begun lasted, with a certain interval, until the end of Forster's life."

On this occasion it probably was that Macready asked the poet to write him a play, and even named to him a subject; but Browning was not caught by the theme proposed. A year later the two met at a supper given by Macready after the successful presentation of Talfourd's *Ion*. When the guests were leaving, the actor said to the poet: "Write a play, Browning, and keep me from going to America." "Shall it be historical and English?" queried Browning. "What do you say to a drama on Strafford?" The subject was suggested by the fact that the poet had been giving his aid to John Forster in the writing of his biography of Strafford published in *Lives of Eminent British Statesmen*. It has been asserted by Dr. Furnivall that this biography was, in fact, written by Browning, though this is probably much too sweeping a statement; but the poet seems to have given considerable aid to his friend. However, whatever the service rendered, it sufficed to direct Browning's attention to this subject, which Macready accepted, and the play was written. It was produced at the Covent Garden Theatre, May 1, 1837, with a fair degree of success. It was soon after published, with the following preface: —

"I had for some time been engaged in a Poem of a very different nature, when induced to make the present attempt; and am not without apprehension that my eagerness to freshen a jaded mind, by diverting it to the healthy natures of a grand epoch, may have operated unfavorably on the represented play, which is one of Action in Character, rather than Character in Action. To remedy this, in some degree, considerable curtailment will be necessary, and, in a few instances, the supplying details not required, I suppose, by the mere reader. While a trifling success would much gratify, failure will not wholly discourage me from another effort: experience is to come; and earnest endeavor may yet remove many disadvantages.

"The portraits are, I think, faithful; and I am exceedingly fortunate in being able, in proof of this, to refer to the subtle and eloquent exposition of the characters of Eliot and Strafford, in the *Lives of Eminent British Statesmen*, now in the course of publication in Lardner's *Cyclopedia*, by a writer [John Forster] whom I am proud to call my friend; and whose biographies of Hampden, Pym, and Vane will, I am sure, fitly illustrate the

INTRODUCTION

present year — the Second Centenary of the Trial concerning Ship-Money. My Carlisle, however, is purely imaginary: I at first sketched her singular likeness roughly in, as suggested by Matthews and the memoir-writers — but it was too artificial, and the substituted outline is exclusively from Voiture and Waller."

In the introduction to Miss Emily H. Hickey's edition of *Strafford* is given a careful survey of the historical truthfulness of the tragedy from the pen of Professor Samuel R. Gardiner, the able and learned historian. "We may be sure," says Professor Gardiner, "that it was not by accident that Mr. Browning, in writing this play, decisively abandoned all attempt to be historically accurate. Only here and there does anything in the course of the drama take place as it could have taken place at the actual Court of Charles I. Not merely are there frequent minor inaccuracies, but the very roots of the situation are untrue to fact. The real Strafford was far from opposing the war with the Scots at the time when the Short Parliament was summoned. Pym never had such a friendship for Strafford as he is represented as having, and, to any one who knows anything of the habits of Charles, the idea of Pym or his friends entering into colloquies with Strafford, and even bursting in unannounced into Charles's presence, is, from the historical point of view, simply ludicrous.

"So completely does the drama proceed irrespectively of historical truth, that the critic may dispense with the thankless task of pointing out discrepancies. He will be better employed in asking what ends those discrepancies were intended to serve, and whether the neglect of truth of fact has resulted in the highest truth of character.

"There is not much difficulty in answering the first question. From the beginning to the end of the play the personal relations between the actors are exaggerated at the expense of the political. To make that dramatic which would otherwise not be dramatic, Mr. Browning has been utterly regardless even of historical probability. Whatever personal feeling may have entwined itself in the political attachment between Strafford and Charles is strengthened until it becomes the very basis of Strafford's life, and the keynote of his character. Having thus brought out the moral qualities of his hero, it remained for Mr.

Browning to impress his readers with Strafford's intellectual greatness. The historian who tries to do that will have much to say on his constitutional views and his Irish government, but a dramatist who tried to follow in such a path would only make himself ridiculous. Mr. Browning understood the force of the remark of the Greek philosopher, that Homer makes us realize Helen's beauty most by speaking of the impression which it made upon the old men who looked on her. Mr. Browning brings out Strafford's greatness by showing the impression which he made on Pym and Lady Carlisle.

"Mr. Browning took a hint from the old story, which is without any satisfactory evidence, and which is indirectly contradicted by all the evidence which has reached us, that Pym and Strafford were once intimate friends. In carrying on Pym's feeling of admiration for Charles's minister to the days of the Short and even of the Long Parliament, the dramatist has filled his play with scenes which are more hopelessly impossible than anything else in it; but they all conduce to his main object, the creation of the impression about Strafford which he wished to convey. He pursues the same object in dealing with Lady Carlisle. What he needs is her admiration of Strafford, not Strafford's admiration of her. He takes care to show that she was not, as vulgar rumor supposed, Strafford's mistress. The impression of Strafford's greatness is brought more completely home to the spectator or the reader, because of the effect which it produces upon one who has given her heart without return.

"Having thus noted the means employed in creating the impression desired, we have still to ask how far the impression is a correct one. On this point each reader must judge for himself. For myself, I can only say that, every time that I read the play, I feel more certain that Mr. Browning has seized the real Strafford, the man of critical brain, of rapid decision, and tender heart, who strove for the good of his nation without sympathy for the generation in which he lived. Charles, too, with his faults perhaps exaggerated, is nevertheless the real Charles. Of Lady Carlisle we know too little to speak with anything like certainty, but, in spite of Mr. Browning's statement that his character of her is purely imaginary, there is a wonderful parallelism between the Lady Carlisle of the play and the less noble Lady Carlisle which history conjectures rather than describes. There is the same tendency to fix the heart upon the truly great man, and to labor for him without the requital of human affection, though in the play no part is played by that vanity which seems to have been the main motive with the real personage.

"On the other hand, Pym is the most unsatisfactory, from an historical point of view, of the leading personages. It was perhaps necessary for dramatic purposes that he should appear to be larger-hearted than he was, but it imparts an unreality to his character. It must be remembered, however, that the aim of the dramatist was to place Strafford before the eyes of men, not to produce an exact representation of the statesmen of the Long Parliament."

After the publication of *Paracelsus*, Browning began another extended poem, somewhat in the same style. This he put aside in order that he might write *Strafford*, and perhaps also in order to the preparation of the earlier numbers of his *Bells and Pomegranates*. Finally, in 1840, *Sordello* was published, but without preface. The obscurity of the poem was frequently commented upon, both seriously and in a humorous manner. This led the poet to revise it in 1863, to add a commentary in the form of headlines, and to make a brief defense of it in a dedicatory letter to J. Milsland, of Dijon. At first he thought of completely rewriting the poem, but he soon saw that this was impossible. His words of interpretation of his purpose in the poem have become memorable: "The historical decoration was purposely of no more importance than a background requires; and my stress lay on the incidents in the development of a soul; little else is worth study."

SORDELLO.

Concerning the revised edition Browning wrote to a friend, protesting against the statement that he had rewritten the poem, or that he had made any essential change in it: —

"I do not understand what —— can mean by saying that *Sordello* has been 'rewritten.' I did certainly at one time intend to rewrite much of it, but changed my mind, — and the edition which I reprinted was the same in all respects as its predecessors — only with an elucidatory heading to each page, and some few alterations, presumably for the better, in the text, such as occur in most of my works. I cannot remember a single instance of any importance that is rewritten, and I only suppose that —— has taken project for performance, and set down as 'done' what was for a while intended to be done."

In the sixth canto of Dante's *Purgatorio* Sordello appears, and is made the guide of Virgil and his companion. The shade of Sordello is described as being silent and watchful: —

> "Nothing whatever did it say to us,
>   But let us go our way, eyeing us only
>   After the manner of a couchant lion;
> Still near to it Virgilius drew, entreating
>   That it would point us out the best ascent;
>   And it replied not unto his demand,
> But of our native land and of our life
>   It questioned us; and the sweet Guide began:
> 'Mantua,' — and the shade, all in itself recluse,
> Rose tow'rds him from the place where first it was,
>   Saying: 'O Mantuan, I am Sordello
>   Of thine own land!' and one embraced the other.
>   .   .   .   .
> That noble soul was so impatient, only
>   At the sweet sound of his own native land,
>   To make its citizen glad welcome there."

Dante thus honors Sordello because that poet had preceded him in the attempt to establish a vernacular Italian speech as a medium of literary expression. For the same cause he described Sordello in his *De Vulgari Eloquio* as "a man so choice in his language, that not only in his poems, but in whatever way he spoke, he abandoned the dialect of his province." Sordello lived during the first part of the thirteenth century, and he was a poet, a troubadour, a soldier by profession, and a politician of some ability. Little is now known about him, and that little is much obscured by tradition and legend. It is probable that two persons have in some way been mixed together in the accounts given of him. One of these persons was a poet, and the other was a man of action and political intrigue.

Browning evidently studied whatever was written about Sordello by the chroniclers; but he has not undertaken to unriddle the biographical difficulties which surround his name. Whatever would best serve his purpose in the traditions he has used;

INTRODUCTION xxiii

but he has not tried to be consistent with historical probability. He makes Sordello the supposed son of an archer, El Corte by name, and he has been brought up at the castle of Goïto, by Adelaide, the wife of Eccelin of Romano. In the first book the life of Sordello at Goïto is described; and his failure as a troubadour is set forth in the second. In the third book Sordello journeys to Verona, and Palma declares her love for him. He then becomes her minstrel and her devoted lover. In the fourth book the horrors of civil war are described, and their effect on Sordello in making him desert the Ghibelline cause, which had the devotion of his lady love. The fifth book discloses the true birth of Sordello, and he finds his father in Salinguerra, the great Ghibelline chief and politician. Through his connection with Palma it is now made possible for Sordello to become the head of all of Northern Italy. The last book shows him struggling between the ambition of leadership, which he can now gratify, and the conviction of his heart that the popular cause is the true one and the one he ought to support. At last he makes the sacrifice; but the attempt is too much for him, and he dies before it is fairly accomplished.

One account of Sordello is that presented by Quadrio in his *Storia d' ogni Poesia*, who says: "Sordello, native of Goïto (Sordel de Goi), a village in the Mantuan territory, was born in 1184, and was the son of a poor knight named Elcort. . . . Having afterwards returned to Italy, he governed Mantua with the title of regent and captain-general, and was opposed to the tyrant Ezzelino, being a great lover of justice, as Agnelli writes. Finally he died, very old and full of honor, about 1280. He wrote not only in Provençal, but also in our own common Italian tongue; and he was one of those poets who avoided the dialect of his own province, and used the good, choice language, as Dante affirms in his book of *De Vulgari Eloquio*."

Commenting on the accounts given of Sordello, Millot, in his *History of the Literature of the Troubadours*, says: "According to Agnelli and Platina, historians of Mantua, he was of the house of Visconti of that city; valiant in deeds of arms, famous in jousts and tournaments, he won the love of Beatrice, daughter of Ezzelin de Romano, Lord of the Marca Trevigiana, and married her; he governed Mantua as podestà and captain-general, and though son-in-law of the tyrant Ezzelin, he always opposed him, being a great lover of justice. We find these facts cited by Crescimbeni, who says that Sordello was the lord of Goïto; but as they are not applicable to our poet, we presume they refer to a warrior of the same name, and perhaps of a different family. Among the pieces of Sordello, thirty-four in number, there are some fifteen songs of gallantry, though Nostradamus says that all his pieces turn only upon philosophical subjects."

The French historians give a somewhat different account of Sordello, and they especially dwell upon his character as a troubadour. Nostradamus, in his *Lives of the Provençal Poets*, says: "Sordello was a Mantuan poet, who surpassed in Provençal song Calvo, Folchetto of Marseilles, Lanfranco Cicala, Percival Doria, and all the other Genoese and Tuscan poets, who took far greater delight in our Provençal tongue, on account of its sweetness, than in their own maternal language. This poet was very studious, and exceedingly eager to know all things, and as much as any one of his nation excellent in learning as well as in understanding and in prudence. He wrote several beautiful songs, not indeed of love, for not one of that kind is found among his works, but on philosophic subjects. Raymond Belinghieri, the last Count of Provence of that name, in the last days of his life (the poet being then but fifteen years of age) on account of the excellence of his poetry and the rare invention shown in his productions, took him into his service, as Pietro di Castelnuovo, himself a Provençal poet, informs us. He also wrote various satires in the same language, and among others one in which he reproves all the Christian princes; and it is composed in the form of a funeral song on the death of Blancasso."

Raynouard, in his *Poetry of the Troubadours*, tells the story of Sordello's life in a way of his own: "Sordello was a Mantuan of Sirier, son of a poor knight whose name was Sir El Cort. And he delighted in learning songs and in making them, and wrote love-songs and satires. And he came to the court of the Count of Saint Boniface, and the Count honored him greatly, and by way of pastime he fell in love with the wife of the Count, and she with him. And it happened that the Count quarreled with her brothers, and became estranged from her; and her brothers, Sir Icellis and Sir Albrics, persuaded Sir Sordello to run away with her, and he came to live with them in great content. And afterwards he went into Provence and received great honor from all good men, and from the Count and Countess, who gave him a good castle and a gentlewoman for his wife."

In his *Literature of Southern Europe*, Sismondi says that the poet has always been a hero to his biographer. "No one has experienced this good fortune in an equal degree with Sordello of Mantua, whose real merit consists in the harmony and sensibility of his verses. He was among the first to adopt the balladform of writing, and in one of those, which has been translated by Millot (into French) he beautifully contrasts, in the burden of his ballad, the gayeties of Nature and the ever-reviving grief of a heart devoted to love. Sordel, or Sordello, was born at Goïto, near Mantua, and was, for some time, attached to the house of Count St. Boniface, the chief of the Guelph party, in the March of Trevise. He afterwards passed into the service of Raymond Berenger, the last Count of Provence of the house of Barcelona. Although a Lombard, he had adopted, in his compositions, the Provençal language, and many of his countrymen imitated him. It was not, at that time, believed that the Italian was capable of becoming a polished language. The age of Sordello was that of the most brilliant chivalric virtues and the most atrocious crimes. He lived in the midst of heroes and monsters. The imagination of the people was still haunted by the recollection of the ferocious Ezzelino, tyrant of Verona, with whom Sordello is said to have had a contest, and who was probably often mentioned in his verses. The historical monuments of this reign of blood were, however, little known, and the people mingled the name of their favorite with every revolution which excited their terror. It was said that he had carried off the wife of the Count of St. Boniface, the sovereign of Mantua, that he had married the daughter or sister of Ezzelino, and that he had fought this monster with glory to himself. He united, according to popular report, the most brilliant military exploits to the most distinguished poetical genius. By the voice of St. Louis himself, he had been recognized, at a tourney, as the most valiant and gallant of knights; and at last the sovereignty of Mantua had been bestowed upon this noblest of the poets and warriors of his age. Histories of credit have collected, three centuries after Sordello's death, these brilliant fictions, which are, however, disproved by the testimony of contemporary writers. The reputation of Sordello is owing, very materially, to the admiration which has been expressed for him by Dante."

The period in which Sordello lived was a remarkable one. The Crusades were drawing to a close, in failure. They had given a new life to Europe, however, and out of them had grown feudalism and chivalry. In the South of France the spirit of chivalry was beginning to express itself, and it especially found utterance in Provençal poetry. Sordello was a troubadour, if we may believe some of those who have written of him; and he had some of the finer, as well as some of the coarser qualities which were associated with chivalry.

We see in the life of Sordello another remarkable movement of his time finding expression, that of the origin of the modern European languages and literatures. Until his time Latin had been the sole language of literature, science, and theology, for a period of several centuries. The new life that was springing up found utterance in the use of the common or vulgar language of the people as a medium of literary expression. The troubadours developed this movement in France, as the minnesingers did in Germany. A little later Dante wrote his great poem in Italian, and for the first time in modern history made the language in which the people spoke the medium of great and vital ideas. One of the predecessors of Dante in this work, by whose aid it became possible for him to accomplish what he did, was Sordello. This Mantuan poet wrote either in the speech of his own province or in Provençal, in either case discarding Latin, and singing of love, honor, and philosophy in a speech the people could understand.

In another direction Sordello was an actor in a great movement of his time. The struggle between the Church and the Empire — the struggle between religious and secular authority — had begun long before, and at one time appeared to have been settled in the victory of Hildebrand over Henry IV. It had been revived before the time of Sordello, and was in full activity in his day, as a fierce struggle between Guelf and Ghibelline. The Guelfs were on the side of the Church and the popes, and

INTRODUCTION

desired that the pope should exercise a spiritual authority extending over all countries, and superior to all secular rulers. Singularly enough to those who judge the Catholic Church from more recent standards, the Guelfs were the democrats of the time, and were on the side of the people as against the hard and oppressive rule of the secular authorities, from duke to emperor. It was this fact which made the cities of Northern Italy incline to the side of the Guelfs, for the cities were developing an independent life, and were as democratic as was then possible.

The Ghibellines took the side of the emperor of the German Empire, which had been known as the Holy Roman Empire. They desired that the Church should rule in all spiritual matters, and that the Empire or the state should rule through the emperor in all secular matters. On their side were the beginnings of the modern idea of the state, and of its entire separation from the church.

PIPPA PASSES

It appears that both *Paracelsus* and *Sordello* were published at the expense of Browning's father, but when they proved financially unsuccessful he was reluctant to continue this method of bringing his poems before the public. "One day," says Mr. Gosse, "as the poet was discussing the matter with Mr. Edward Moxon, the publisher, the latter remarked that at that time he was bringing out some editions of the old Elizabethan dramatists, in a comparatively cheap form, and that if Mr. Browning would consent to print his poems as pamphlets, using this cheap type, the expense would be very inconsiderable. The poet jumped at the idea, and it was agreed that each poem should form a separate brochure of just one sheet, — sixteen pages, in double columns, — the entire cost of which should not exceed twelve or fifteen pounds. In this fashion began the celebrated series of *Bells and Pomegranates*, eight numbers of which, a perfect treasury of fine poetry, came out successively between 1841 and 1846. *Pippa Passes* led the way, and was priced first at sixpence; then, the sale being inconsiderable, at a shilling, which greatly encouraged the sale; and so, slowly, up to half a crown, at which the price of each number finally rested."

xxviii   INTRODUCTION

With the first number appeared the preface to the whole series, in the following form : —

ADVERTISEMENT.

Two or three years ago I wrote a Play, about which the chief matter I much care to recollect at present is, that a Pitful of goodnatured people applauded it : ever since I have been desirous of doing something in the same way that should better reward their attention. What follows, I mean for the first of a series of Dramatical Pieces, to come out at intervals; and I amuse myself by fancying that the cheap mode in which they appear, will for once help me to a sort of Pit-audience again. Of course such a work must go on no longer than it is liked ; and to provide against a too certain and but too possible contingency, let me hasten to say now — what, if I were sure of success, I would try to say circumstantially enough at the close — that I dedicate my best intentions most admiringly to the Author of *Ion* — most affectionately to Sergeant Talfourd.

ROBERT BROWNING.

As a preface to the last issue to the series appeared the following : —

"Here ends my first series of *Bells and Pomegranates*, and I take the opportunity of explaining, in reply to inquiries, that I only meant by that title to indicate an endeavor towards something like an alternation, or mixture, of music with discoursing, sound with sense, poetry with thought ; which looks too ambitious, thus expressed, so the symbol was preferred. It is little to the purpose, that such is actually one of the most familiar of the many Rabbinical (and Patristic) acceptations of the phrase ; because I confess that, letting authority alone, I supposed the bare words, in such juxtaposition, would sufficiently convey the desired meaning. 'Faith and good works' is another fancy, for instance, and perhaps no easier to arrive at ; yet Giotto placed a pomegranate fruit in the hand of Dante, and Raffaello crowned his Theology (in the *Camera della Segnatura*) with blossoms of the same ; as if the Bellari and Vasari would be sure to come after, and explain that it was merely '*simbolo delle buone opere — il qual Pomogranato fu però usato nelle veste del Pontefice appresso gli Ebrei.*' R. B."

The title *Bells and Pomegranates* was taken from the description of the priest's robe in Exodus xxviii. 34, where it is required that the robe should have on the hem of it "pomegranates of

INTRODUCTION

blue, and of purple, and of scarlet, and bells of gold between them." Miss Elizabeth Barrett wrote to Browning asking him to inform her precisely what he meant by his *Bells and Pomegranates* title, and suggested that he give in the next number a solution of this Sphinx riddle. Under date of October 18, 1845, he replied: "I will make a note as you suggest — or, perhaps, keep it for the closing number (the next), when it will come fitly in with two or three parting words I shall have to say. The Rabbis make Bells and Pomegranates symbolical of Pleasure and Profit, the gay and the grave, the Poetry and the Prose, Singing and Sermonizing — such a mixture of effects as in the original hour (that is, a quarter of an hour) of confidence and creation, I meant the whole should prove at last." *Pippa Passes* has no historical foundation, the scene of it being the Venetian town of Asola, where Browning lived for some months, and where he died. The town was once held by Caterino Cornaro as a fief from the city of Venice, after it had deposed her as Queen of Cyprus. The poem was suggested to Browning one day as he was walking alone in a wood near Dulwich, in the neighborhood of London, when the thought flashed upon him of some one walking alone in that way through life, a person apparently too obscure to leave behind a trace of his or her character, yet unconsciously impressing all who came near with the stamp of a positive individuality of influence.

The second number of *Bells and Pomegranates*, which appeared in 1842, contained the tragedy of *King Victor and King Charles*. In the preface, which has been retained in all subsequent editions, Browning indicated the sources of his information, and also made a brief justification of his method of dealing with history. Victor Amadeus II., 1666-1732, was Duke of Savoy, but was ambitious and scheming, and succeeded, with the aid of Austria, in building up for himself an independent kingdom. The tragedy turns upon his abdication in behalf of his son, Charles Emanuel, who was of a very modest and vacillating character. This event was brought about by political complications, but was soon repented of by Victor, largely because of the schemings of his ambitious and unscrupulous wife. The poet has made good use of these materials, but without any attempt to follow the details of the historians or to keep strictly within the limits of fact. In this tragedy, as in his *Paracelsus* and *Sordello*, he does not make poetry the vehicle of history, but he uses history for the sake of plot and environment, giving to his characters such interpretation as justifies itself to his own poet's conception of truth.

(*Prefixed to the three-volume edition issued in 1863.*)

I DEDICATE THESE VOLUMES TO MY OLD FRIEND JOHN FORSTER, GLAD AND GRATEFUL THAT HE WHO, FROM THE FIRST PUBLICATION OF THE VARIOUS POEMS THEY INCLUDE, HAS BEEN THEIR PROMPTEST AND STAUNCHEST HELPER, SHOULD SEEM EVEN NEARER TO ME NOW THAN ALMOST THIRTY YEARS AGO.

R. B.

London, April 21, 1863.

PAULINE:

A FRAGMENT OF A CONFESSION.

Plus ne suis ce que j'ai été,
Et ne le sçaurois jamais être.
MAROT.

NON dubito, quin titulus libri nostri raritate sua quamplurimos alliciat ad legendum : inter quos nonnulli obliquæ opinionis, mente languidi, multi etiam maligni, et in ingenium nostrum ingrati accedent, qui temeraria sua ignorantia, vix conspecto titulo clamabunt. Nos vetita docere, hæresium semina jacere : piis auribus offendiculo, præclaris ingeniis scandalo esse : . . . adeo conscientiæ suæ consulentes, ut nec Apollo, nec Musæ omnes, neque Angelus de cœlo me ab illorum execratione vindicare queant : quibus et ego nunc consulo, ne scripta nostra legant, nec intelligant, nec meminerint : nam noxia sunt, venenosa sunt : Acherontis ostium est in hoc libro, lapides loquitur, caveant, ne cerebrum illis excutiat. Vos autem, qui æqua mente ad legendum venitis, si tantam prudentiæ discretionem adhibueritis, quantam in melle legendo apes, jam securi legite. Puto namque vos et utilitatis haud parum et voluptatis plurimum accepturos. Quod si qua repereritis, quæ vobis non placeant, mittite illa, nec utimini. NAM ET EGO VOBIS ILLA NON PROBO, SED NARRO. Cætera tamen propterea non respuite . . . Ideo, si quid liberius dictum sit, ignoscite adolescentiæ nostræ, qui minor quam adolescens hoc opus composui. — *Hen. Corn. Agrippa, De Occult. Philosoph. in Præfat.*

LONDON : *January*, 1833.
V. A. XX.

[This introduction would appear less absurdly pretentious did it apply, as was intended, to a completed structure of which the poem was meant for only a beginning and remains a fragment.]

> PAULINE, mine own, bend o'er me — thy soft breast
> Shall pant to mine — bend o'er me — thy sweet eyes,
> And loosened hair and breathing lips, and arms
> Drawing me to thee — these build up a screen
> To shut me in with thee, and from all fear ;
> So that I might unlock the sleepless brood
> Of fancies from my soul, their lurking-place,
> Nor doubt that each would pass, ne'er to return
> To one so watched, so loved and so secured.
> But what can guard thee but thy naked love ?
> Ah dearest, whoso sucks a poisoned wound
> Envenoms his own veins ! Thou art so good,
> So calm — if thou shouldst wear a brow less light
> For some wild thought which, but for me, were kept
> From out thy soul as from a sacred star !
> Yet till I have unlocked them it were vain

To hope to sing; some woe would light on me;
Nature would point at one whose quivering lip
Was bathed in her enchantments, whose brow burned
Beneath the crown to which her secrets knelt,
Who learned the spell which can call up the dead,
And then departed smiling like a fiend
Who has deceived God, — if such one should seek
Again her altars and stand robed and crowned
Amid the faithful! Sad confession first,
Remorse and pardon and old claims renewed,
Ere I can be — as I shall be no more.

I had been spared this shame if I had sat
By thee forever from the first, in place
Of my wild dreams of beauty and of good,
Or with them, as an earnest of their truth:
No thought nor hope having been shut from thee,
No vague wish unexplained, no wandering aim
Sent back to bind on fancy's wings and seek
Some strange fair world where it might be a law;
But, doubting nothing, had been led by thee,
Through youth, and saved, as one at length awaked
Who has slept through a peril. Ah vain, vain!

Thou lovest me; the past is in its grave
Though its ghost haunts us; still this much is ours,
To cast away restraint, lest a worse thing
Wait for us in the dark. Thou lovest me;
And thou art to receive not love but faith,
For which thou wilt be mine, and smile and take
All shapes and shames, and veil without a fear
That form which music follows like a slave:
And I look to thee and I trust in thee,
As in a Northern night one looks alway
Unto the East for morn and spring and joy.
Thou seest then my aimless, hopeless state,
And, resting on some few old feelings won
Back by thy beauty, wouldst that I essay
The task which was to me what now thou art:
And why should I conceal one weakness more?

Thou wilt remember one warm morn when winter
Crept aged from the earth, and spring's first breath
Blew soft from the moist hills; the black-thorn boughs,
So dark in the bare wood, when glistening
In the sunshine were white with coming buds,

Like the bright side of a sorrow, and the banks
Had violets opening from sleep like eyes.
I walked with thee who knew'st not a deep shame
Lurked beneath smiles and careless words which sought
To hide it till they wandered and were mute,
As we stood listening on a sunny mound
To the wind murmuring in the damp copse,
Like heavy breathings of some hidden thing
Betrayed by sleep; until the feeling rushed
That I was low indeed, yet not so low
As to endure the calmness of thine eyes.
And so I told thee all, while the cool breast
I leaned on altered not its quiet beating:
And long ere words like a hurt bird's complaint
Bade me look up and be what I had been,
I felt despair could never live by thee:
Thou wilt remember. Thou art not more dear
Than song was once to me; and I ne'er sung
But as one entering bright halls where all
Will rise and shout for him: sure I must own
That I am fallen, having chosen gifts
Distinct from theirs — that I am sad and fain
Would give up all to be but where I was,
Not high as I had been if faithful found,
But low and weak yet full of hope, and sure
Of goodness as of life — that I would lose
All this gay mastery of mind, to sit
Once more with them, trusting in truth and love
And with an aim — not being what I am.

O Pauline, I am ruined who believed
That though my soul had floated from its sphere
Of wild dominion into the dim orb
Of self — that it was strong and free as ever!
It has conformed itself to that dim orb,
Reflecting all its shades and shapes, and now
Must stay where it alone can be adored.
I have felt this in dreams — in dreams in which
I seemed the fate from which I fled; I felt
A strange delight in causing my decay.
I was a fiend in darkness chained forever
Within some ocean-cave; and ages rolled,
Till through the cleft rock, like a moonbeam, came
A white swan to remain with me; and ages
Rolled, yet I tired not of my first free joy
In gazing on the peace of its pure wings:

And then I said, " It is most fair to me,
Yet its soft wings must sure have suffered change
From the thick darkness, sure its eyes are dim,
Its silver pinions must be cramped and numbed
With sleeping ages here; it cannot leave me,
For it would seem, in light beside its kind,
Withered, though here to me most beautiful."
And then I was a young witch whose blue eyes,
As she stood naked by the river springs,
Drew down a god : I watched his radiant form
Growing less radiant, and it gladdened me ;
Till one morn, as he sat in the sunshine
Upon my knees, singing to me of heaven,
He turned to look at me, ere I could lose
The grin with which I viewed his perishing :
And he shrieked and departed and sat long
By his deserted throne, but sunk at last
Murmuring, as I kissed his lips and curled
Around him, " I am still a god — to thee."

Still I can lay my soul bare in its fall,
Since all the wandering and all the weakness
Will be a saddest comment on the song :
And if, that done, I can be young again,
I will give up all gained, as willingly
As one gives up a charm which shuts him out
From hope or part or care in human kind.
As life wanes, all its care and strife and toil
Seem strangely valueless, while the old trees
Which grew by our youth's home, the waving mass
Of climbing plants heavy with bloom and dew,
The morning swallows with their songs like words,
All these seem clear and only worth our thoughts :
So, aught connected with my early life,
My rude songs or my wild imaginings,
How I look on them — most distinct amid
The fever and the stir of after years !

I ne'er had ventured e'en to hope for this,
Had not the glow I felt at HIS award,
Assured me all was not extinct within :
HIS whom all honor, whose renown springs up
Like sunlight which will visit all the world,
So that e'en they who sneered at him at first,
Come out to it, as some dark spider crawls
From his foul nets which some lit torch invades,
Yet spinning still new films for his retreat.

Thou didst smile, poet, but can we forgive?
Sun-treader, life and light be thine forever!
Thou art gone from us; years go by and spring
Gladdens and the young earth is beautiful,
Yet thy songs come not, other bards arise,
But none like thee: they stand, thy majesties,
Like mighty works which tell some spirit there
Hath sat regardless of neglect and scorn,
Till, its long task completed, it hath risen
And left us, never to return, and all
Rush in to peer and praise when all in vain.
The air seems bright with thy past presence yet,
But thou art still for me as thou hast been
When I have stood with thee as on a throne
With all thy dim creations gathered round
Like mountains, and I felt of mould like them,
And with them creatures of my own were mixed,
Like things half-lived, catching and giving life.
But thou art still for me who have adored
Though single, panting but to hear thy name
Which I believed a spell to me alone,
Scarce deeming thou wast as a star to men!
As one should worship long a sacred spring
Scarce worth a moth's flitting, which long grasses cross
And one small tree embowers droopingly —
Joying to see some wandering insect won
To live in its few rushes, or some locust
To pasture on its boughs, or some wild bird
Stoop for its freshness from the trackless air:
And then should find it but the fountain-head,
Long lost, of some great river washing towns
And towers, and seeing old woods which will live
But by its banks untrod of human foot,
Which, when the great sun sinks, lie quivering
In light as some thing lieth half of life
Before God's foot, waiting a wondrous change;
Then girt with rocks which seek to turn or stay
Its course in vain, for it does ever spread
Like a sea's arm as it goes rolling on,
Being the pulse of some great country — so
Wast thou to me, and art thou to the world!
And I, perchance, half feel a strange regret
That I am not what I have been to thee:
Like a girl one has silently loved long
In her first loneliness in some retreat,
When, late emerged, all gaze and glow to view
Her fresh eyes and soft hair and lips which bloom

Like a mountain berry: doubtless it is sweet
To see her thus adored, but there have been
Moments when all the world was in our praise,
Sweeter than any pride of after hours.
Yet, sun-treader, all hail! From my heart's heart
I bid thee hail! E'en in my wildest dreams,
I proudly feel I would have thrown to dust
The wreaths of fame which seemed o'erhanging me,
To see thee for a moment as thou art.

And if thou livest, if thou lovest, spirit!
Remember me who set this final seal
To wandering thought — that one so pure as thou
Could never die. Remember me who flung
All honor from my soul, yet paused and said,
"There is one spark of love remaining yet,
For I have naught in common with him, shapes
Which followed him avoid me, and foul forms
Seek me, which ne'er could fasten on his mind;
And though I feel how low I am to him,
Yet I aim not even to catch a tone
Of harmonies he called profusely up;
So, one gleam still remains, although the last."
Remember me who praise thee e'en with tears,
For never more shall I walk calm with thee;
Thy sweet imaginings are as an air,
A melody some wondrous singer sings,
Which, though it haunt men oft in the still eve,
They dream not to essay; yet it no less
But more is honored. I was thine in shame,
And now when all thy proud renown is out,
I am a watcher whose eyes have grown dim
With looking for some star which breaks on him
Altered and worn and weak and full of tears.

Autumn has come like spring returned to us,
Won from her girlishness; like one returned
A friend that was a lover, nor forgets
The first warm love, but full of sober thoughts
Of fading years; whose soft mouth quivers yet
With the old smile, but yet so changed and still!
And here am I the scoffer, who have probed
Life's vanity, won by a word again
Into my own life — by one little word
Of this sweet friend who lives in loving me,
Lives strangely on my thoughts and looks and words.

As fathoms down some nameless ocean thing
Its silent course of quietness and joy.
O dearest, if indeed I tell the past,
May'st thou forget it as a sad sick dream!
Or if it linger — my lost soul too soon
Sinks to itself and whispers we shall be
But closer linked, two creatures whom the earth
Bears singly, with strange feelings unrevealed
Save to each other, or two lonely things
Created by some power whose reign is done,
Having no part in God or his bright world.
I am to sing whilst ebbing day dies soft,
As a lean scholar dies worn o'er his book,
And in the heaven stars steal out one by one
As hunted men steal to their mountain watch.
I must not think, lest this new impulse die
In which I trust; I have no confidence :
So, I will sing on fast as fancies come;
Rudely, the verse being as the mood it paints.

I strip my mind bare, whose first elements
I shall unveil — not as they struggled forth
In infancy, nor as they now exist,
When I am grown above them and can rule —
But in that middle stage when they were full
Yet ere I had disposed them to my will;
And then I shall show how these elements
Produced my present state, and what it is.

I am made up of an intensest life,
Of a most clear idea of consciousness
Of self, distinct from all its qualities,
From all affections, passions, feelings, powers;
And thus far it exists, if tracked, in all :
But linked, in me, to self-supremacy,
Existing as a centre to all things,
Most potent to create and rule and call
Upon all things to minister to it;
And to a principle of restlessness
Which would be all, have, see, know, taste, feel, all —
This is myself; and I should thus have been
Though gifted lower than the meanest soul.

And of my powers, one springs up to save
From utter death a soul with such desire
Confined to clay — of powers the only one

Which marks me — an imagination which
Has been a very angel, coming not
In fitful visions, but beside me ever
And never failing me; so, though my mind
Forgets not, not a shred of life forgets,
Yet I can take a secret pride in calling
The dark past up to quell it regally.

A mind like this must dissipate itself,
But I have always had one lode-star; now,
As I look back, I see that I have halted
Or hastened as I looked towards that star —
A need, a trust, a yearning after God:
A feeling I have analyzed but late,
But it existed, and was reconciled
With a neglect of all I deemed his laws,
Which yet, when seen in others, I abhorred.
I felt as one beloved, and so shut in
From fear: and thence I date my trust in signs
And omens, for I saw God everywhere;
And I can only lay it to the fruit
Of a sad after-time that I could doubt
Even his being — e'en the while I felt
His presence, never acted from myself,
Still trusted in a hand to lead me through
All danger; and this feeling ever fought
Against my weakest reason and resolve.

And I can love nothing — and this dull truth
Has come the last: but sense supplies a love
Encircling me and mingling with my life.

These make myself: I have long sought in vain
To trace how they were formed by circumstance,
Yet ever found them mould my wildest youth
Where they alone displayed themselves, converted
All objects to their use: now see their course!

They came to me in my first dawn of life
Which passed alone with wisest ancient books
All halo-girt with fancies of my own;
And I myself went with the tale — a god
Wandering after beauty, or a giant
Standing vast in the sunset — an old hunter
Talking with gods, or a high-crested chief
Sailing with troops of friends to Tenedos.

I tell you, naught has ever been so clear:
As the place, the time, the fashion of those lives:
I had not seen a work of lofty art,
Nor woman's beauty nor sweet nature's face,
Yet, I say, never morn broke clear as those
On the dim clustered isles in the blue sea,
The deep groves and white temples and wet caves,
And nothing ever will surprise me now —
Who stood beside the naked Swift-footed,
Who bound my forehead with Proserpine's hair.

And strange it is that I who could so dream
Should e'er have stooped to aim at aught beneath —
Aught low or painful; but I never doubted:
So, as I grew, I rudely shaped my life
To my immediate wants; yet strong beneath
Was a vague sense of power though folded up —
A sense that, though those shades and times were past,
Their spirit dwelt in me, with them should rule.

Then came a pause, and long restraint chained down
My soul till it was changed. I lost myself,
And were it not that I so loathe that loss,
I could recall how first I learned to turn
My mind against itself; and the effects
In deeds for which remorse were vain as for
The wanderings of delirious dream; yet thence
Came cunning, envy, falsehood, all world's wrong
That spotted me: at length I cleansed my soul.
Yet long world's influence remained; and naught
But the still life I led, apart once more,
Which left me free to seek soul's old delights,
Could e'er have brought me thus far back to peace.

As peace returned, I sought out some pursuit;
And song rose, no new impulse but the one
With which all others best could be combined.
My life has not been that of those whose heaven
Was lampless save where poesy shone out;
But as a clime where glittering mountain-tops
And glancing sea and forests steeped in light
Give back reflected the far-flashing sun;
For music (which is earnest of a heaven,
Seeing we know emotions strange by it,
Not else to be revealed,) is like a voice,
A low voice calling fancy, as a friend,

To the green woods in the gay summer time:
And she fills all the way with dancing shapes
Which have made painters pale, and they go on
Till stars look at them and winds call to them
As they leave life's path for the twilight world
Where the dead gather. This was not at first,
For I scarce knew what I would do. I had
An impulse but no yearning — only sang.

And first I sang as I in dream have seen
Music wait on a lyrist for some thought,
Yet singing to herself until it came.
I turned to those old times and scenes where all
That's beautiful had birth for me, and made
Rude verses on them all; and then I paused —
I had done nothing, so I sought to know
What other minds achieved. No fear outbroke
As on the works of mighty bards I gazed,
In the first joy at finding my own thoughts
Recorded, my own fancies justified,
And their aspirings but my very own.
With them I first explored passion and mind, —
All to begin afresh! I rather sought
To rival what I wondered at than form
Creations of my own; if much was light
Lent by the others, much was yet my own.

I paused again: a change was coming — came:
I was no more a boy, the past was breaking
Before the future and like fever worked.
I thought on my new self, and all my powers
Burst out. I dreamed not of restraint, but gazed
On all things: schemes and systems went and came,
And I was proud (being vainest of the weak)
In wandering o'er thought's world to seek some one
To be my prize, as if you wandered o'er
The White Way for a star.

                              And my choice fell
Not so much on a system as a man —
On one, whom praise of mine shall not offend,
Who was as calm as beauty, being such
Unto mankind as thou to me, Pauline, —
Believing in them and devoting all
His soul's strength to their winning back to peace

Who sent forth hopes and longings for their sake,
Clothed in all passion's melodies: such first
Caught me and set me, slave of a sweet task,
To disentangle, gather sense from song:
Since, song-inwoven, lurked there words which seemed
A key to a new world, the muttering
Of angels, something yet unguessed by man.
How my heart leapt as still I sought and found
Much there, I felt my own soul had conceived,
But there living and burning! Soon the orb
Of his conceptions dawned on me; its praise
Lives in the tongues of men, men's brows are high
When his name means a triumph and a pride,
So, my weak voice may well forbear to shame
What seemed decreed my fate: I threw myself
To meet it, I was vowed to liberty,
Men were to be as gods and earth as heaven,
And I — ah, what a life was mine to prove!
My whole soul rose to meet it. Now, Pauline,
I shall go mad, if I recall that time!

Oh let me look back ere I leave forever
The time which was an hour one fondly waits
For a fair girl that comes a withered hag!
And I was lonely, far from woods and fields,
And amid dullest sights, who should be loose
As a stag; yet I was full of bliss, who lived
With Plato and who had the key to life;
And I had dimly shaped my first attempt,
And many a thought did I build up on thought,
As the wild bee hangs cell to cell; in vain,
For I must still advance, no rest for mind.

'T was in my plan to look on real life,
The life all new to me; my theories
Were firm, so them I left, to look and learn
Mankind, its cares, hopes, fears, its woes and joys;
And, as I pondered on their ways, I sought
How best life's end might be attained — an end
Comprising every joy. I deeply mused.

And suddenly without heart-wreck I awoke
As from a dream: I said, "'T was beautiful,
Yet but a dream, and so adieu to it!"
As some world-wanderer sees in a far meadow
Strange towers and high-walled gardens thick with trees,

Where song takes shelter and delicious mirth
From laughing fairy creatures peeping over,
And on the morrow when he comes to lie
Forever 'neath those garden-trees fruit-flushed
Sung round by fairies, all his search is vain.
First went my hopes of perfecting mankind,
Next — faith in them, and then in freedom's self
And virtue's self, then my own motives, ends
And aims and loves, and human love went last.
I felt this no decay, because new powers
Rose as old feelings left — wit, mockery,
Light-heartedness; for I had oft been sad,
Mistrusting my resolves, but now I cast
Hope joyously away: I laughed and said,
"No more of this!" I must not think: at length
I looked again to see if all went well.

My powers were greater: as some temple seemed
My soul, where naught is changed and incense rolls
Around the altar, only God is gone
And some dark spirit sitteth in his seat.
So, I passed through the temple and to me
Knelt troops of shadows, and they cried, "Hail, king!
We serve thee now and thou shalt serve no more!
Call on us, prove us, let us worship thee!"
And I said, "Are ye strong? Let fancy bear me
Far from the past!" And I was borne away,
As Arab birds float sleeping in the wind,
O'er deserts, towers and forests, I being calm.
And I said, "I have nursed up energies,
They will prey on me." And a band knelt low
And cried, "Lord, we are here and we will make
Safe way for thee in thine appointed life!
But look on us!" And I said, "Ye will worship
Me; should my heart not worship too?" They shouted,
"Thyself, thou art our king!" So, I stood there
Smiling — oh, vanity of vanities!
For buoyant and rejoicing was the spirit
With which I looked out how to end my course;
I felt once more myself, my powers — all mine;
I knew while youth and health so lifted me
That, spite of all life's nothingness, no grief
Came nigh me, I must ever be light-hearted;
And that this knowledge was the only veil
Betwixt joy and despair: so, if age came,
I should be left — a wreck linked to a soul

Yet fluttering, or mind-broken and aware
Of my decay. So a long summer morn
Found me; and ere noon came, I had resolved
No age should come on me ere youth was spent,
For I would wear myself out, like that morn
Which wasted not a sunbeam; every hour
I would make mine, and die.

                      And thus I sought
To chain my spirit down which erst I freed
For flights to fame : I said, " The troubled life
Of genius, seen so gay when working forth
Some trusted end, grows sad when all proves vain —
How sad when men have parted with truth's peace
For falsest fancy's sake, which waited first
As an obedient spirit when delight
Came without fancy's call : but alters soon,
Comes darkened, seldom, hastens to depart,
Leaving a heavy darkness and warm tears.
But I shall never lose her; she will live
Dearer for such seclusion. I but catch
A hue, a glance of what I sing : so, pain
Is linked with pleasure, for I ne'er may tell
Half the bright sights which dazzle me; but now
Mine shall be all the radiance : let them fade
Untold — others shall rise as fair, as fast!
And when all's done, the few dim gleams transferred," —
(For a new thought sprang up how well it were,
Discarding shadowy hope, to weave such lays
As straight encircle men with praise and love,
So, I should not die utterly, — should bring
One branch from the gold forest, like the knight
Of old tales, witnessing I had been there) —
" And when all's done, how vain seems e'en success —
The vaunted influence poets have o'er men !
'T is a fine thing that one weak as myself
Should sit in his lone room, knowing the words
He utters in his solitude shall move
Men like a swift wind — that though dead and gone,
New eyes shall glisten when his beauteous dreams
Of love come true in happier frames than his.
Ay, the still night brings thoughts like these, but morn
Comes and the mockery again laughs out
At hollow praises, smiles allied to sneers;
And my soul's idol ever whispers me
To dwell with him and his unhonored song :

And I foreknow my spirit, that would press
First in the struggle, fail again to make
All bow enslaved, and I again should sink.

" And then know that this curse will come on us,
To see our idols perish ; we may wither,
No marvel, we are clay, but our low fate
Should not extend to those whom trustingly
We sent before into time's yawning gulf
To face what dread may lurk in darkness there.
To find the painter's glory pass and feel
Music can move us not as once, or, worst,
To weep decaying wits ere the frail body
Decays !   Naught makes me trust some love is true.
But the delight of the contented lowness
With which I gaze on him I keep forever
Above me ; I to rise and rival him ?
Feed his fame rather from my heart's best blood,
Wither unseen that he may flourish still."

Pauline, my soul's friend, thou dost pity yet
How this mood swayed me when that soul found thine
When I had set myself to live this life,
Defying all past glory.   Ere thou camest
I seemed defiant, sweet, for old delights
Had flocked like birds again ; music, my life,
Nourished me more than ever ; then the lore
Loved for itself and all it shows — that king
Treading the purple calmly to his death,
While round him, like the clouds of eve, all dusk,
The giant shades of fate, silently flitting,
Pile the dim outline of the coming doom ;
And him sitting alone in blood while friends
Are hunting far in the sunshine ; and the boy
With his white breast and brow and clustering curls
Streaked with his mother's blood, but striving hard
To tell his story ere his reason goes.
And when I loved thee as love seemed so oft,
Thou lovedst me indeed : I wondering searched
My heart to find some feeling like such love,
Believing I was still much I had been.
Too soon I found all faith had gone from me,
And the late glow of life, like change on clouds,
Proved not the morn-blush widening into day,
But eve faint-colored by the dying sun
While darkness hastens quickly.   I will tell

My state as though 'twere none of mine — despair
Cannot come near us — this it is, my state.

Souls alter not, and mine must still advance ;
Strange that I knew not, when I flung away
My youth's chief aims, their loss might lead to loss
Of what few I retained, and no resource
Be left me : for behold how changed is all !
I cannot chain my soul : it will not rest
In its clay prison, this most narrow sphere :
It has strange impulse, tendency, desire,
Which nowise I account for nor explain,
But cannot stifle, being bound to trust
All feelings equally to hear all sides :
How can my life indulge them ? yet they live,
Referring to some state of life unknown.

My selfishness is satiated not,
It wears me like a flame ; my hunger for
All pleasure, howsoe'er minute, grows pain ;
I envy — how I envy him whose soul
Turns its whole energies to some one end,
To elevate an aim, pursue success
However mean ! So, my still baffled hope
Seeks out abstractions ; I would have one joy,
But one in life, so it were wholly mine,
One rapture all my soul could fill : and this
Wild feeling places me in dream afar
In some vast country where the eye can see
No end to the far hills and dales bestrewn
With shining towers and towns, till I grow mad
Well-nigh, to know not one abode but holds
Some pleasure, while my soul could grasp the world,
But must remain this vile form's slave. I look
With hope to age at last, which quenching much,
May let me concentrate what sparks it spares.

This restlessness of passion meets in me
A craving after knowledge : the sole proof
Of yet commanding will is in that power
Repressed ; for I beheld it in its dawn,
The sleepless harpy with just-budding wings,
And I considered whether to forego
All happy ignorant hopes and fears, to live,
Finding a recompense in its wild eyes.
And when I found that I should perish so,
I bade its wild eyes close from me forever,

And I am left alone with old delights;
See! it lies in me a chained thing, still prompt
To serve me if I loose its slightest bond :
I cannot but be proud of my bright slave.

How should this earth's life prove my only sphere?
Can I so narrow sense but that in life
Soul still exceeds it? In their elements
My love outsoars my reason; but since love
Perforce receives its object from this earth
While reason wanders chainless, the few truths
Caught from its wanderings have sufficed to quell
Love chained below; then what were love, set free,
Which, with the object it demands, would pass
Reason companioning the seraphim?
No, what I feel may pass all human love
Yet fall far short of what my love should be.
And yet I seem more warped in this than aught,
Myself stands out more hideously : of old
I could forget myself in friendship, fame,
Liberty, nay, in love of mightier souls;
But I begin to know what thing hate is —
To sicken and to quiver and grow white —
And I myself have furnished its first prey.
Hate of the weak and ever-wavering will,
The selfishness, the still-decaying frame . . .
But I must never grieve whom wing can waft
Far from such thoughts — as now. Andromeda!
And she is with me : years roll, I shall change,
But change can touch her not — so beautiful
With her fixed eyes, earnest and still, and hair
Lifted and spread by the salt-sweeping breeze,
And one red beam, all the storm leaves in heaven,
Resting upon her eyes and hair, such hair,
As she awaits the snake on the wet beach
By the dark rock and the white wave just breaking
At her feet; quite naked and alone ; a thing
I doubt not, nor fear for, secure some god
To save will come in thunder from the stars.
Let it pass! Soul requires another change.
I will be gifted with a wondrous mind,
Yet sunk by error to men's sympathy,
And in the wane of life, yet only so
As to call up their fears ; and there shall come
A time requiring youth's best energies ;
And lo, I fling age, sorrow, sickness off,
And rise triumphant, triumph through decay.

And thus it is that I supply the chasm
'Twixt what I am and all I fain would be:
But then to know nothing, to hope for nothing,
To seize on life's dull joys from a strange fear
Lest, losing them, all 's lost and naught remains!

There 's some vile juggle with my reason here;
I feel I but explain to my own loss
These impulses: they live no less the same.
Liberty! what though I despair? my blood
Rose never at a slave's name proud as now.
Oh sympathies, obscured by sophistries! —
Why else have I sought refuge in myself,
But from the woes I saw and could not stay?
Love! is not this to love thee, my Pauline?
I cherish prejudice, lest I be left
Utterly loveless? witness my belief
In poets, though sad change has come there too;
No more I leave myself to follow them —
Unconsciously I measure me by them —
Let me forget it: and I cherish most
My love of England — how her name, a word
Of hers in a strange tongue makes my heart beat!

Pauline, could I but break the spell! Not now —
All 's fever — but when calm shall come again,
I am prepared: I have made life my own.
I would not be content with all the change
One frame should feel, but I have gone in thought
Through all conjuncture, I have lived all life
When it is most alive, where strangest fate
New-shapes it past surmise — the throes of men
Bit by some curse or in the grasps of doom
Half-visible and still-increasing round,
Or crowning their wide being's general aim.

These are wild fancies, but I feel, sweet friend,
As one breathing his weakness to the ear
Of pitying angel — dear as a winter flower,
A slight flower growing alone, and offering
Its frail cup of three leaves to the cold sun,
Yet joyous and confiding like the triumph
Of a child: and why am I not worthy thee?
I can live all the life of plants, and gaze
Drowsily on the bees that flit and play,
Or bare my breast for sunbeams which will kill,

Or open in the night of sounds, to look
For the dim stars; I can mount with the bird
Leaping airily his pyramid of leaves
And twisted boughs of some tall mountain tree,
Or rise cheerfully springing to the heavens;
Or like a fish breathe deep the morning air
In the misty sun-warm water; or with flower
And tree can smile in light at the sinking sun
Just as the storm comes, as a girl would look
On a departing lover — most serene.

Pauline, come with me, see how I could build
A home for us, out of the world, in thought!
I am uplifted: fly with me, Pauline!

Night, and one single ridge of narrow path
Between the sullen river and the woods
Waving and muttering, for the moonless night
Has shaped them into images of life,
Like the uprising of the giant-ghosts,
Looking on earth to know how their sons fare:
Thou art so close by me, the roughest swell
Of wind in the tree-tops hides not the panting
Of thy soft breasts. No, we will pass to morning —
Morning, the rocks and valleys and old woods.
How the sun brightens in the mist, and here,
Half in the air, like creatures of the place,
Trusting the element, living on high boughs
That swing in the wind — look at the silver spray
Flung from the foam-sheet of the cataract
Amid the broken rocks! Shall we stay here
With the wild hawks? No, ere the hot noon come,
Dive we down — safe! See this our new retreat
Walled in with a sloped mound of matted shrubs,
Dark, tangled, old and green, still sloping down
To a small pool whose waters lie asleep
Amid the trailing boughs turned water-plants:
And tall trees overarch to keep us in,
Breaking the sunbeams into emerald shafts,
And in the dreamy water one small group
Of two or three strange trees are got together
Wondering at all around, as strange beasts herd
Together far from their own land: all wildness,
No turf nor moss, for boughs and plants pave all,
And tongues of bank go shelving in the lymph,
Where the pale-throated snake reclines his head,
And old gray stones lie making eddies there,

The wild-mice cross them dry-shod. Deeper in!
Shut thy soft eyes — now look — still deeper in!
This is the very heart of the woods all round
Mountain-like heaped above us; yet even here
One pond of water gleams; far off the river
Sweeps like a sea, barred out from land; but one —
One thin clear sheet has overleaped and wound
Into this silent depth, which gained, it lies
Still, as but let by sufferance; the trees bend
O'er it as wild men watch a sleeping girl,
And through their roots long creeping plants out-stretch
Their twined hair, steeped and sparkling; farther on,
Tall rushes and thick flag-knots have combined
To narrow it; so, at length, a silver thread,
It winds, all noiselessly through the deep wood
Till through a cleft-way, through the moss and stone,
It joins its parent-river with a shout.

Up for the glowing day, leave the old woods!
See, they part, like a ruined arch: the sky!
Nothing but sky appears, so close the roots
And grass of the hill-top level with the air —
Blue sunny air, where a great cloud floats laden
With light, like a dead whale that white birds pick,
Floating away in the sun in some north sea.
Air, air, fresh life-blood, thin and searching air,
The clear, dear breath of God that loveth us,
Where small birds reel and winds take their delight!
Water is beautiful, but not like air:
See, where the solid azure waters lie
Made as of thickened air, and down below,
The fern-ranks like a forest spread themselves
As though each pore could feel the element;
Where the quick glancing serpent winds his way,
Float with me there, Pauline! — but not like air.

Down the hill! Stop — a clump of trees, see, set
On a heap of rock, which look o'er the far plain:
So, envious climbing shrubs would mount to rest
And peer from their spread boughs; wide they wave, looking
At the muleteers who whistle on their way,
To the merry chime of morning bells, past all
The little smoking cots, mid fields and banks
And copses bright in the sun. My spirit wanders:
Hedgerows for me — those living hedgerows where
The bushes close and clasp above and keep
Thought in — I am concentrated — I feel;

But my soul saddens when it looks beyond :
I cannot be immortal, taste all joy.

O God, where do they tend — these struggling aims ?[1]
What would I have ? What is this " sleep " which seems
To bound all ? can there be a " waking " point
Of crowning life ? The soul would never rule ;
It would be first in all things, it would have
Its utmost pleasure filled, but, that complete,
Commanding, for commanding, sickens it.
The last point I can trace is — rest beneath
Some better essence than itself, in weakness ;
This is " myself," not what I think should be :
And what is that I hunger for but God ?

My God, my God, let me for once look on thee
As though naught else existed, we alone !
And as creation crumbles, my soul's spark
Expands till I can say, — Even from myself
I need thee and I feel thee and I love thee.
I do not plead my rapture in thy works
For love of thee, nor that I feel as one
Who cannot die : but there is that in me
Which turns to thee, which loves or which should love.

[1] Je crains bien que mon pauvre ami ne soit pas toujours parfaitement compris dans ce qui reste à lire de cet étrange fragment, mais il est moins propre que tout autre à éclaircir ce qui de sa nature ne peut jamais être que songe et confusion. D'ailleurs je ne sais trop si en cherchant à mieux co-ordonner certaines parties l'on ne courrait pas le risque de nuire au seul mérite auquel une production si singulière peut prétendre, celui de donner une idée assez précise du genre qu'elle n'a fait qu'ébaucher. Ce début sans prétention, ce remuement des passions qui va d'abord en accroissant et puis s'apaise par degrés, ces élans de l'âme, ce retour soudain sur soi-même, et par-dessus tout, la tournure d'esprit tout particulière de mon ami, rendent les changemens presque impossibles. Les raisons qu'il fait valoir ailleurs, et d'autres encore plus puissantes, ont fait trouver grâce à mes yeux pour cet écrit qu'autrement je lui eusse conseillé de jeter au feu. Je n'en crois pas moins au grand principe de toute composition — à ce principe de Shakespeare, de Rafaelle, de Beethoven, d'où il suit que la concentration des idées est due bien plus à leur conception qu'à leur mise en exécution : j'ai tout lieu de craindre que la première de ces qualités ne soit encore étrangère à mon ami, et je doute fort qu'un redoublement de travail lui fasse acquérir la seconde. Le mieux serait de brûler ceci ; mais que faire ? Je crois que dans ce qui suit il fait allusion à un certain examen qu'il fit autrefois de l'âme, ou plutôt de son âme, pour découvrir la suite des objets auxquels il lui serait possible d'atteindre, et dont chacun une fois obtenu devait former une espèce de plateau d'où l'on pouvait apercevoir d'autres buts, d'autres projets, d'autres jouissances qui à leur tour, devaient être surmontés. Il en résultait que l'oubli et le sommeil devaient tout terminer. Cette idée, que je ne saisis pas parfaitement, lui est peut-être aussi inintelligible qu'à moi. PAULINE.

Why have I girt myself with this hell-dress?
Why have I labored to put out my life?
Is it not in my nature to adore,
And e'en for all my reason do I not
Feel him, and thank him, and pray to him — now?
Can I forego the trust that he loves me?
Do I not feel a love which only ONE . . .
O thou pale form, so dimly seen, deep-eyed!
I have denied thee calmly — do I not
Pant when I read of thy consummate power,
And burn to see thy calm pure truths out-flash
The brightest gleams of earth's philosophy?
Do I not shake to hear aught question thee?
If I am erring save me, madden me,
Take from me powers and pleasures, let me die
Ages, so I see thee! I am knit round
As with a charm by sin and lust and pride,
Yet though my wandering dreams have seen all shapes
Of strange delight, oft have I stood by thee —
Have I been keeping lonely watch with thee
In the damp night by weeping Olivet,
Or leaning on thy bosom, proudly less,
Or dying with thee on the lonely cross,
Or witnessing thine outburst from the tomb.

A mortal, sin's familiar friend, doth here
Avow that he will give all earth's reward,
But to believe and humbly teach the faith,
In suffering and poverty and shame,
Only believing he is not unloved.

And now, my Pauline, I am thine forever!
I feel the spirit which has buoyed me up
Desert me, and old shades are gathering fast;
Yet while the last light waits, I would say much,
This chiefly, it is gain that I have said
Somewhat of love I ever felt for thee
But seldom told; our hearts so beat together
That speech seemed mockery; but when dark hours come,
And joy departs, and thou, sweet, deem'st it strange
A sorrow moves me, thou canst not remove,
Look on this lay I dedicate to thee,
Which through thee I began, which thus I end,
Collecting the last gleams to strive to tell
How I am thine, and more than ever now
That I sink fast: yet though I deeplier sink,

No less song proves one word has brought me L
Another still may win bliss surely back.
Thou knowest, dear, I could not think all calm,
For fancies followed thought and bore me off,
And left all indistinct; ere one was caught
Another glanced; so, dazzled by my wealth,
I knew not which to leave nor which to choose,
For all so floated, naught was fixed and firm.
And then thou said'st a perfect bard was one
Who chronicled the stages of all life,
And so thou bad'st me shadow this first stage.
'T is done, and even now I recognize
The shift, the change from last to past — discern
Faintly how life is truth and truth is good.
And why thou must be mine is, that e'en now
In the dim hush of night, that I have done,
Despite the sad forebodings, love looks through —
Whispers, — E'en at the last I have her still,
With her delicious eyes as clear as heaven
When rain in a quick shower has beat down mist,
And clouds float white above like broods of swans.
How the blood lies upon her cheek, outspread
As thinned by kisses! only in her lips
It wells and pulses like a living thing,
And her neck looks like marble misted o'er
With love-breath, — a Pauline from heights above,
Stooping beneath me, looking up — one look
As I might kill her and be loved the more.

So, love me — me, Pauline, and naught but me,
Never leave loving! Words are wild and weak,
Believe them not, Pauline! I stained myself
But to behold thee purer by my side,
To show thou art my breath, my life, a last
Resource, an extreme want: never believe
Aught better could so look on thee; nor seek
Again the world of good thoughts left for mine!
There were bright troops of undiscovered suns,
Each equal in their radiant course; there were
Clusters of far fair isles which ocean kept
For his own joy, and his waves broke on them
Without a choice; and there was a dim crowd
Of visions, each a part of some grand whole:
And one star left his peers and came with peace
Upon a storm, and all eyes pined for him;
And one isle harbored a sea-beaten ship,

And the crew wandered in its bowers and plucked
Its fruits and gave up all their hopes of home ;
And one dream came to a pale poet's sleep,
And he said, " I am singled out by God,
No sin must touch me." Words are wild and weak,
But what they would express is, — Leave me not,
Still sit by me with beating breast and hair
Loosened, be watching earnest by my side,
Turning my books or kissing me when I
Look up — like summer wind ! Be still to me
A help to music's mystery which mind fails
To fathom, its solution, no mere clue !
O reason's pedantry, life's rule prescribed !
I hopeless, I the loveless, hope and love.
Wiser and better, know me now, not when
You loved me as I was. Smile not ! I have
Much yet to dawn on you, to gladden you.
No more of the past ! I 'll look within no more.
I have too trusted my own lawless wants,
Too trusted my vain self, vague intuition —
Draining soul's wine alone in the still night,
And seeing how, as gathering films arose,
As by an inspiration life seemed bare
And grinning in its vanity, while ends
Foul to be dreamed of, smiled at me as fixed
And fair, while others changed from fair to foul
As a young witch turns an old hag at night.
No more of this ! We will go hand in hand,
I with thee, even as a child — love's slave,
Looking no farther than his liege commands.

And thou hast chosen where this life shall be :
The land which gave me thee shall be our home,
Where nature lies all wild amid her lakes
And snow-swathed mountains and vast pines begirt
With ropes of snow — where nature lies all bare,
Suffering none to view her but a race
Or stinted or deformed, like the mute dwarfs
Which wait upon a naked Indian queen.
And there (the time being when the heavens are thick
With storm) I 'll sit with thee while thou dost sing
Thy native songs, gay as a desert bird
Which crieth as it flies for perfect joy,
Or telling me old stories of dead knights ;
Or I will read great lays to thee — how she,
The fair pale sister, went to her chill grave

With power to love and to be loved and live:
Or we will go together, like twin gods
Of the infernal world, with scented lamp
Over the dead, to call and to awake,
Over the unshaped images which lie
Within my mind's cave: only leaving all,
That tells of the past doubt. So, when spring **comes**
With sunshine back again like an old smile,
And the fresh waters and awakened birds
And budding woods await us, I shall be
Prepared, and we will question life once more,
Till its old sense shall come renewed by change,
Like some clear thought which harsh words veiled before;
Feeling God loves us, and that all which errs
Is but a dream which death will dissipate.
And then what need of longer exile? Seek
My England, and, again there, calm approach
All I once fled from, calmly look on those
The works of my past weakness, as one views
Some scene where danger met him long before.
Ah that such pleasant life should be but dreamed!

But whate'er come of it, and though it fade,
And though ere the cold morning all be gone,
As it may be; — though music wait to wile,
And strange eyes and bright wine lure, laugh **like sin**
Which steals back softly on a soul half saved,
And I the first deny, decry, despise,
With this avowal, these intents so fair, —
Still be it all my own, this moment's pride!
No less I make an end in perfect joy.
E'en in my brightest time, a lurking fear
Possessed me: I well knew my weak **resolves**,
I felt the witchery that makes mind sleep
Over its treasure, as one half afraid
To make his riches definite: but now
These feelings shall not utterly be lost,
I shall not know again that nameless care
Lest, leaving all undone in youth, some new
And undreamed end reveal itself too late:
For this song shall remain to tell forever
That when I lost all hope of such a change,
Suddenly beauty rose on me again.
No less I make an end in perfect joy,
For I, who thus again was visited,
Shall doubt not many another bliss awaits,

And, though this weak soul sink and darkness whelm,
Some little word shall light it, raise aloft,
To where I clearlier see and better love,
As I again go o'er the tracts of thought
Like one who has a right, and I shall live
With poets, calmer, purer still each time,
And beauteous shapes will come for me to seize,
And unknown secrets will be trusted me
Which were denied the waverer once ; but now
I shall be priest and prophet as of old.

Sun-treader, I believe in God and truth
And love ; and as one just escaped from death
Would bind himself in bands of friends to feel
He lives indeed, so, I would lean on thee !
Thou must be ever with me, most in gloom
If such must come, but chiefly when I die,
For I seem, dying, as one going in the dark
To fight a giant : but live thou forever,
And be to all what thou hast been to me !
All in whom this wakes pleasant thoughts of me
Know my last state is happy, free from doubt
Or touch of fear.   Love me and wish me well.

RICHMOND, *October* 22, 1832.

PAULINE

A FRAGMENT OF A CONFESSION

*Plus ne suis ce que j'ai été,
Et ne le sçaurois jamais être.*
MAROT.

NON dubito, quin titulus libri nostri raritate sua quamplurimos alliciat ad legendum: inter quos nonnulli obliquæ opinionis, mente languidi, multi etiam maligni, et in ingenium nostrum ingrati accedent, qui temeraria sua ignorantia, vix conspecto titulo clamabunt: Nos vetita docere, hæresium semina jacere: piis auribus offendiculo, præclaris ingeniis scandalo esse: . . . adeo conscientiæ suæ consulentes, ut nec Apollo, nec Musæ omnes, neque Angelus de cœlo me ab illorum execratione vindicare queant: quibus et ego nunc consulo, ne scripta nostra legant, nec intelligant, nec meminerint: nam noxia sunt, venenosa sunt: Acherontis ostium est in hoc libro, lapides loquitur, caveant, ne cerebrum illis excutiat. Vos autem, qui æqua mente ad legendum venitis, si tantam prudentiæ discretionem adhibueritis, quantam in melle legendo apes, jam securi legite. Puto namque vos et utilitatis haud parum et voluptatis plurimum accepturos. Quod si qua repereritis, quæ vobis non placeant, mittite illa, nec utimini. NAM ET EGO VOBIS ILLA NON PROBO, SED NARRO. Cætera tamen propterea non respuite . . . Ideo, si quid liberius dictum sit, ignoscite adolescentiæ nostræ, qui minor quam adolescens hoc opus composui. — *Hen. Corn. Agrippa, De Occult. Philosoph. in Prefat.*

LONDON, *January*, 1833.
V. A. XX.

PAULINE, mine own, bend o'er me — thy soft breast
Shall pant to mine — bend o'er me — thy sweet eyes,
And loosened hair and breathing lips, and arms
Drawing me to thee — these build up a screen
To shut me in with thee, and from all fear ;
So that I might unlock the sleepless brood
Of fancies from my soul, their lurking-place,
Nor doubt that each would pass, ne'er to return
To one so watched, so loved and so secured.
But what can guard thee but thy naked love ?
Ah dearest, whoso sucks a poisoned wound
Envenoms his own veins ! Thou art so good,
So calm — if thou shouldst wear a brow less light
For some wild thought which, but for me, were kept
From out thy soul as from a sacred star !
Yet till I have unlocked them it were vain

To hope to sing; some woe would light on me,
Nature would point at one whose quivering lip
Was bathed in her enchantments, whose brow burned
Beneath the crown to which her secrets knelt,
Who learned the spell which can call up the dead,
And then departed smiling like a fiend
Who has deceived God, — if such one should seek
Again her altars and stand robed and crowned
Amid the faithful: sad confession first,
Remorse and pardon and old claims renewed,
Ere I can be — as I shall be no more.

I had been spared this shame if I had sat
By thee forever from the first, in place
Of my wild dreams of beauty and of good,
Or with them, as an earnest of their truth:
No thought nor hope having been shut from thee,
No vague wish unexplained, no wandering aim
Sent back to bind on fancy's wings and seek
Some strange fair world where it might be a law;
But doubting nothing, had been led by thee,
Through youth, and saved, as one at length awaked
Who has slept through a peril. Ah vain, vain!

Thou lovest me; the past is in its grave
Though its ghost haunts us; still this much is ours,
To cast away restraint, lest a worse thing
Wait for us in the darkness. Thou lovest me;
And thou art to receive not love but faith,
For which thou wilt be mine, and smile and take
All shapes and shames, and veil without a fear
That form which music follows like a slave:
And I look to thee and I trust in thee,
As in a Northern night one looks alway
Unto the East for morn and spring and joy.
Thou seest then my aimless, hopeless state,
And, resting on some few old feelings won
Back by thy beauty, wouldst that I essay
The task which was to me what now thou art:
And why should I conceal one weakness more?

Thou wilt remember one warm morn when winter
Crept aged from the earth, and spring's first breath
Blew soft from the moist hills; the black-thorn boughs,
So dark in the bare wood, when glistening
In the sunshine were white with coming buds,

Like the bright side of a sorrow, and the banks
Had violets opening from sleep like eyes.
I walked with thee who knew'st not a deep shame
Lurked beneath smiles and careless words which sought
To hide it till they wandered and were mute,
As we stood listening on a sunny mound
To the wind murmuring in the damp copse,
Like heavy breathings of some hidden thing
Betrayed by sleep; until the feeling rushed
That I was low indeed, yet not so low
As to endure the calmness of thine eyes;
And so I told thee all, while the cool breast
I leaned on altered not its quiet beating,
And long ere words like a hurt bird's complaint
Bade me look up and be what I had been,
I felt despair could never live by thee:
Thou wilt remember. Thou art not more dear
Than song was once to me; and I ne'er sung
But as one entering bright halls where all
Will rise and shout for him: sure I must own
That I am fallen, having chosen gifts
Distinct from theirs — that I am sad and fain
Would give up all to be but where I was,
Not high as I had been if faithful found,
But low and weak yet full of hope, and sure
Of goodness as of life — that I would lose
All this gay mastery of mind, to sit
Once more with them, trusting in truth and love,
And with an aim — not being what I am.
O Pauline, I am ruined who believed
That though my soul had floated from its sphere
Of wild dominion into the dim orb
Of self — that it was strong and free as ever!
It has conformed itself to that dim orb,
Reflecting all its shades and shapes, and now
Must stay where it alone can be adored.
I have felt this in dreams — in dreams in which
I seemed the fate from which I fled; I felt
A strange delight in causing my decay;
I was a fiend in darkness chained forever
Within some ocean-cave; and ages rolled,
Till through the cleft rock, like a moonbeam, came
A white swan to remain with me; and ages
Rolled, yet I tired not of my first joy
In gazing on the peace of its pure wings:
And then I said, "It is most fair to me,

Yet its soft wings must sure have suffered change
From the thick darkness, sure its eyes are dim,
Its silver pinions must be cramped and numbed
With sleeping ages here; it cannot leave me,
For it would seem, in light beside its kind,
Withered, though here to me most beautiful."
And then I was a young witch whose blue eyes,
As she stood naked by the river springs,
Drew down a god; I watched his radiant form
Growing less radiant, and it gladdened me;
Till one morn, as he sat in the sunshine
Upon my knees, singing to me of heaven,
He turned to look at me, ere I could lose
The grin with which I viewed his perishing:
And he shrieked and departed and sat long
By his deserted throne, but sunk at last
Murmuring, as I kissed his lips and curled
Around him, " I am still a god — to thee."
Still I can lay my soul bare in its fall,
For all the wandering and all the weakness
Will be a saddest comment on the song:
And if, that done, I can be young again,
I will give up all gained, as willingly
As one gives up a charm which shuts him out
From hope or part of care in human kind.
As life wanes, all its cares and strife and toil
Seem strangely valueless, while the old trees
Which grew by our youth's home, the waving mass
Of climbing plants heavy with bloom and dew,
The morning swallows with their songs like words,
All these seem clear and only worth our thoughts:
So, aught connected with my early life,
My rude songs or my wild imaginings,
How I look on them — most distinct amid
The fever and the stir of after years!

I ne'er had ventured e'er to hope for this;
Had not the glow I felt at His award,
Assured me all was not extinct within:
His whom all honor, whose renown springs up
Like sunlight which will visit all the world,
So that e'en they who sneered at him at first,
Come out to it, as some dark spider crawls
From his foul nets which some lit torch invades,
Yet spinning still new films for his retreat.
Thou didst smile, poet, but can we forgive?

Sun-treader, life and light be thine forever!
Thou art gone from us; years go by and spring
Gladdens and the young earth is beautiful,
Yet thy songs come not, other bards arise,
But none like thee: they stand, thy majesties,
Like mighty works which tell some spirit there
Hath sat regardless of neglect and scorn,
Till, its long task completed, it hath risen
And left us, never to return, and all
Rush in to peer and praise when all in vain.
The air seems bright with thy past presence yet,
But thou art still for me as thou hast been
When I have stood with thee as on a throne
With all thy dim creations gathered round
Like mountains, and I felt of mould like them,
And creatures of my own were mixed with them,
Like things half-lived, catching and giving life.
But thou art still for me, who have adored
Though single, panting but to hear thy name
Which I believed a spell to me alone,
Scarce deeming thou wast as a star to men!
As one should worship long a sacred spring
Scarce worth a moth's flitting, which long grasses cross,
And one small tree embowers droopingly,
Joying to see some wandering insect won
To live in its few rushes, or some locust,
To pasture on its boughs, or some wild bird
Stoop for its freshness from the trackless air:
And then should find it but the fountain-head,
Long lost, of some great river washing towns
And towers, and seeing old woods which will live
But by its banks untrod of human foot,
Which, when the great sun sinks, lie quivering
In light as some thing lieth half of life
Before God's foot, waiting a wondrous change;
Then girt with rocks which seek to turn or stay
Its course in vain, for it does ever spread
Like a sea's arm as it goes rolling on,
Being the pulse of some great country — so
Wast thou to me, and art thou to the world!
And I, perchance, half feel a strange regret,
That I am not what I have been to thee:
Like a girl one has loved long silently
In her first loveliness in some retreat,
When, first emerged, all gaze and glow to view
Her fresh eyes and soft hair and lips which bleed

Like a mountain berry : doubtless it is sweet
To see her thus adored, but there have been
Moments when all the world was in his praise,
Sweeter than all the pride of after hours.
Yet, sun-treader, all hail! From my heart's heart
I bid thee hail! E'en in my wildest dreams,
I am proud to feel I would have thrown up all
The wreaths of fame which seemed o'erhanging me,
To have seen thee for a moment as thou art.
And if thou livest, if thou lovest, spirit!
Remember me who set this final seal
To wandering thought — that one so pure as thou
Could never die. Remember me who flung
All honor from my soul yet paused and said,
"There is one spark of love remaining yet,
For I have nought in common with him, shapes
Which followed him avoid me, and foul forms
Seek me, which ne'er could fasten on his mind;
And though I feel how low I am to him,
Yet I aim not even to catch a tone
Of all the harmonies which he called up;
So, one gleam still remains, although the last."
Remember me who praise thee e'en with tears,
For never more shall I walk calm with thee;
Thy sweet imaginings are as an air,
A melody some wondrous singer sings,
Which, though it haunt men oft in the still eve,
They dream not to essay; yet it no less
But more is honored. I was thine in shame,
And now when all thy proud renown is out,
I am a watcher whose eyes have grown dim
With looking for some star which breaks on him
Altered and worn and weak and full of tears.

Autumn has come like spring returned to us,
Won from her girlishness; like one returned
A friend that was a lover nor forgets
The first warm love, but full of sober thoughts
Of fading years; whose soft mouth quivers yet
With the old smile but yet so changed and still!
And here am I the scoffer, who have probed
Life's vanity, won by a word again
Into my own life — for one little word
Of this sweet friend who lives in loving me,
Lives strangely on my thoughts and looks and words,
As fathoms down some nameless ocean thing

Its silent course of quietness and joy.
O dearest, if indeed I tell the past,
Mayst thou forget it as a sad sick dream !
Or if it linger — my lost soul too soon
Sinks to itself and whispers, we shall be
But closer linked, two creatures whom the earth
Bears singly, with strange feelings unrevealed
But to each other ; or two lonely things
Created by some power whose reign is done,
Having no part in God or his bright world.
I am to sing whilst ebbing day dies soft,
As a lean scholar dies worn o'er his book,
And in the heaven stars steal out one by one
As hunted men steal to their mountain watch.
I must not think, lest this new impulse die
In which I trust ; I have no confidence :
So, I will sing on fast as fancies come ;
Rudely, the verse being as the mood it paints.

I strip my mind bare, whose first elements
I shall unveil — not as they struggled forth
In infancy, nor as they now exist,
That I am grown above them and can rule —
But in that middle stage when they were full
Yet ere I had disposed them to my will ;
And then I shall show how these elements
Produced my present state, and what it is.

I am made up of an intensest life,
Of a most clear idea of consciousness
Of self, distinct from all its qualities,
From all affections, passions, feelings, powers ;
And thus far it exists, if tracked in all :
But linked, in me, to self-supremacy,
Existing as a centre to all things,
Most potent to create and rule and call
Upon all things to minister to it ;
And to a principle of restlessness
Which would be all, have, see, know, taste, feel, all —
This is myself ; and I should thus have been
Though gifted lower than the meanest soul.

And of my powers, one springs up to save
From utter death a soul with such desire
Confined to clay — which is the only one
Which marks me — an imagination which

Has been an angel to me, coming not
In fitful visions but beside me ever
And never failing me; so, though my mind
Forgets not, not a shred of life forgets,
Yet I can take a secret pride in calling
The dark past up to quell it regally.

A mind like this must dissipate itself,
But I have always had one lode-star; now,
As I look back, I see that I have wasted
Or progressed as I looked towards that star —
A need, a trust, a yearning after God:
A feeling I have analyzed but late,
But it existed, and was reconciled
With a neglect of all I deemed his laws,
Which yet, when seen in others, I abhorred.

I felt as one beloved, and so shut in
From fear: and thence I date my trust in signs
And omens, for I saw God everywhere;
And I can only lay it to the fruit
Of a sad after-time that I could doubt
Even his being — having always felt
His presence, never acting from myself,
Still trusting in a hand that leads me through
All danger; and this feeling still has fought
Against my weakest reason and resolve.

And I can love nothing — and this dull truth
Has come the last: but sense supplies a love
Encircling me and mingling with my life.

These make myself: for I have sought in vain
To trace how they were formed by circumstance,
For I still find them turning my wild youth
Where they alone displayed themselves, converting
All objects to their use: now see their course.

They came to me in my first dawn of life
Which passed alone with wisest ancient books
All halo-girt with fancies of my own;
And I myself went with the tale — a god
Wandering after beauty, or a giant
Standing vast in the sunset — an old hunter
Talking with gods, or a high-crested chief,
Sailing with troops of friends to Tenedos.

I tell you, nought has ever been so clear
As the place, the time, the fashion of those lives:
I had not seen a work of lofty art,
Nor woman's beauty nor sweet nature's face,
Yet, I say, never morn broke clear as those
On the dim clustered isles in the blue sea,
The deep groves and white temples and wet caves:
And nothing ever will surprise me now —
Who stood beside the naked Swift-footed,
Who bound my forehead with Proserpine's hair.

And strange it is that I who could so dream
Should e'er have stooped to aim at aught beneath —
Aught low, or painful; but I never doubted,
So, as I grew, I rudely shaped my life
To my immediate wants; yet strong beneath
Was a vague sense of powers folded up —
A sense that though those shadowy times were past
Their spirit dwelt in me, and I should rule.

Then came a pause, and long restraint chained down
My soul till it was changed. I lost myself,
And were it not that I so loathe that time,
I could recall how first I learned to turn
My mind against itself; and the effects
In deeds for which remorse were vain as for
The wanderings of delirious dream; yet thence
Came cunning, envy, falsehood, which so long
Have spotted me: at length I was restored.

Yet long the influence remained; and nought
But the still life I led, apart from all,
Which left my soul to seek its old delights,
Could e'er have brought me thus far back to peace.
As peace returned, I sought out some pursuit;
And song rose, no new impulse but the one
With which all others best could be combined.
My life has not been that of those whose heaven
Was lampless save where poesy shone out;
But as a clime where glittering mountain-tops
And glancing sea and forests steeped in light
Give back reflected the far-flashing sun;
For music (which is earnest of a heaven,
Seeing we know emotions strange by it,
Not else to be revealed,) is as a voice,
A low voice calling fancy, as a friend,

To the green woods in the gay summer time:
And she fills all the way with dancing shapes
Which have made painters pale, and they go on
While stars look at them and winds call to them
As they leave life's path for the twilight world
Where the dead gather.   This was not at first,
For I scarce knew what I would do.   I had
No wish to paint, no yearning; but I sang.

And first I sang as I in dream have seen
Music wait on a lyrist for some thought,
Yet singing to herself until it came.
I turned to those old times and scenes where all
That's beautiful had birth for me, and made
Rude verses on them all; and then I paused —
I had done nothing, so I sought to know
What mind had yet achieved.   No fear was mine
As I gazed on the works of mighty bards,
In the first joy at finding my own thoughts
Recorded and my powers exemplified,
And feeling their aspirings were my own.
And then I first explored passion and mind;
And I began afresh; I rather sought
To rival what I wondered at, than form
Creations of my own; so, much was light
Lent back by others, yet much was my own.

I paused again, a change was coming on,
I was no more a boy, the past was breaking
Before the coming and like fever worked.
I first thought on myself, and here my powers
Burst out: I dreamed not of restraint but gazed
On all things: schemes and systems went and came,
And I was proud (being vainest of the weak)
In wandering o'er them to seek out some one
To be my own, as one should wander o'er
The white way for a star.

      And my choice fell
Not so much on a system as a man —
On one, whom praise of mine would not offend,
Who was as calm as beauty, being such
Unto mankind as thou to me, Pauline, —
Believing in them and devoting all
His soul's strength to their winning back to peace;
Who sent forth hopes and longings for their sake,

Clothed in all passion's melodies, which first
Caught me and set me, as to a sweet task,
To gather every breathing of his songs :
And woven with them there were words which seemed
A key to a new world, the muttering
Of angels of some thing unguessed by man.
How my heart beat as I went on and found
Much there, I felt my own mind had conceived,
But there living and burning! Soon the whole
Of his conceptions dawned on me ; their praise
Is in the tongues of men, men's brows are high
When his name means a triumph and a pride,
So, my weak hands may well forbear to dim
What then seemed my bright fate : I threw myself
To meet it, I was vowed to liberty,
Men were to be as gods and earth as heaven,
And I — ah, what a life was mine to be !
My whole soul rose to meet it. Now, Pauline,
1 shall go mad, if I recall that time !

Oh let me look back ere I leave forever
The time which was an hour that one waits
For a fair girl that comes a withered hag !
And I was lonely, far from woods and fields,
And amid dullest sights, who should be loose
As a stag ; yet I was full of joy, who lived
With Plato and who had the key to life ;
And I had dimly shaped my first attempt,
And many a thought did I build up on thought,
As the wild bee hangs cell to cell ; in vain,
For I must still go on, my mind rests not.

'T was in my plan to look on real life
Which was all new to me ; my theories
Were firm, so I left them, to look upon
Men and their cares and hopes and fears and joys ;
And as I pondered on them all I sought
How best life's end might be attained — an end
Comprising every joy. I deeply mused.

And suddenly without heart-wreck I awoke
As from a dream : I said, " 'T was beautiful
Yet but a dream, and so adieu to it ! "
As some world-wanderer sees in a far meadow
Strange towers and walled gardens thick with trees,
Where singing goes on and delicious mirth,

And laughing fairy creatures peeping over,
And on the morrow when he comes to live
Forever by those springs and trees fruit-flushed
And fairy bowers, all his search is vain.
First went my hopes of perfecting mankind,
And faith in them, then freedom in itself
And virtue in itself, and then my motives, ends
And powers and loves, and human love went last.
I felt this no decay, because new powers
Rose as old feelings left — wit, mockery
And happiness; for I had oft been sad,
Mistrusting my resolves, but now I cast
Hope joyously away: I laughed and said,
" No more of this!" I must not think: at length
I looked again to see how all went on.

My powers were greater: as some temple seemed
My soul, where nought is changed and incense rolls
Around the altar, only God is gone
And some dark spirit sitteth in his seat.
So, I passed through the temple and to me
Knelt troops of shadows, and they cried, " Hail, king!
We serve thee now and thou shalt serve no more!
Call on us, prove us, let us worship thee!"
And I said, " Are ye strong? Let fancy bear me
Far from the past!" And I was borne away,
As Arab birds float sleeping in the wind,
O'er deserts, towers and forests, I being calm;
And I said, " I have nursed up energies,
They will prey on me." And a band knelt low
And cried, " Lord, we are here and we will make
A way for thee in thine appointed life!
Oh look on us!" And I said, " Ye will worship
Me; but my heart must worship too." They shouted,
" Thyself, thou art our king!" So, I stood there
Smiling . . . .
And buoyant and rejoicing was the spirit
With which I looked out how to end my days;
I felt once more myself, my powers were mine;
I found that youth or health so lifted me
That, spite of all life's vanity, no grief
Came nigh me, I must ever be light-hearted;
And that this feeling was the only veil
Betwixt me and despair: so, if age came,
I should be as a wreck linked to a soul
Yet fluttering, or mind-broken and aware

Of my decay. So a long summer morn
Found me; and ere noon came, I had resolved
No age should come on me ere youth's hope went,
For I would wear myself out, like that morn
Which wasted not a sunbeam; every joy
I would make mine, and die. And thus I sought
To chain my spirit down which I had fed
With thoughts of fame. I said, " The troubled life
Of genius, seen so bright when working forth
Some trusted end, seems sad when all in vain —
Most sad when men have parted with all joy
For their wild fancy's sake, which waited first
As an obedient spirit when delight
Came not with her alone; but alters soon,
Comes darkened, seldom, hastening to depart,
Leaving a heavy darkness and warm tears.
But I shall never lose her; she will live
Brighter for such seclusion. I but catch
A hue, a glance of what I sing, so, pain
Is linked with pleasure, for I ne'er may tell
The radiant sights which dazzle me; but now
They shall be all my own; and let them fade
Untold — others shall rise as fair, as fast!
And when all's done, the few dim gleams transferred,"—
(For a new thought sprung up that it were well
To leave all shadowy hope, and weave such lays
As would encircle me with praise and love,
So, I should not die utterly, I should bring
One branch from the gold forest, like the knight
Of old tales, witnessing I had been there) —
" And when all's done, how vain seems e'en success
And all the influence poets have o'er men!
'T is a fine thing that one weak as myself
Should sit in his lone room, knowing the words
He utters in his solitude shall move
Men like a swift wind — that though he be forgotten,
Fair eyes shall glisten when his beauteous dreams
Of love come true in happier frames than his.
Ay, the still night brought thoughts like these, but morn
Came and the mockery again laughed out
At hollow praises, and smiles almost sneers;
And my soul's idol seemed to whisper me
To dwell with him and his unhonored name:
And I well knew my spirit, that would be
First in the struggle, and again would make
All bow to it, and I should sink again.

"And then know that this curse will come on us,
To see our idols perish; we may wither,
Nor marvel, we are clay, but our low fate
Should not extend to them, whom trustingly
We sent before into time's yawning gulf
To face whate'er might lurk in darkness there.
To see the painter's glory pass, and feel
Sweet music move us not as once, or, worst,
To see decaying wits ere the frail body
Decays! Nought makes me trust in love so really
As the delight of the contented lowness
With which I gaze on souls I'd keep forever
In beauty; I'd be sad to equal them;
I'd feed their fame e'en from my heart's best blood,
Withering unseen that they might flourish still."

Pauline, my sweet friend, thou dost not forget
How this mood swayed me when thou first wast mine,
When I had set myself to live this life,
Defying all opinion. Ere thou camest
I was most happy, sweet, for old delights
Had come like birds again; music, my life,
I nourished more than ever, and old lore
Loved for itself and all it shows — the king
Treading the purple calmly to his death,
While round him, like the clouds of eve, all dusk,
The giant shades of fate, silently flitting,
Pile the dim outline of the coming doom;
And him sitting alone in blood while friends
Are hunting far in the sunshine; and the boy
With his white breast and brow and clustering curls
Streaked with his mother's blood, and striving hard
To tell his story ere his reason goes.
And when I loved thee as I've loved so oft,
Thou lovedst me, and I wondered and looked in
My heart to find some feeling like such love,
Believing I was still what I had been;
And soon I found all faith had gone from me,
And the late glow of life, changing like clouds,
'Twas not the morn-blush widening into day,
But evening colored by the dying sun
While darkness is quick hastening. I will tell
My state as though 'twere none of mine — despair
Cannot come near me — thus it is with me.
Souls alter not, and mine must progress still;
And this I knew not when I flung away

My youth's chief aims. I ne'er supposed the loss
Of what few I retained, for no resource
Awaits me: now behold the change of all.
I cannot chain my soul, it will not rest
In its clay prison, this most narrow sphere:
It has strange powers and feelings and desires,
Which I cannot account for nor explain,
But which I stifle not, being bound to trust
All feelings equally, to hear all sides:
Yet I cannot indulge them, and they live,
Referring to some state or life unknown.

My selfishness is satiated not,
It wears me like a flame; my hunger for
All pleasure, howsoe'er minute, is pain;
I envy — how I envy him whose mind
Turns with its energies to some one end,
To elevate a sect or a pursuit
However mean! So, my still baffled hopes
Seek out abstractions; I would have but one
Delight on earth, so it were wholly mine,
One rapture all my soul could fill: and this
Wild feeling places me in dream afar
In some wild country where the eye can see
No end to the far hills and dales bestrewn
With shining towers and dwellings: I grow mad
Well-nigh, to know not one abode but holds
Some pleasure, for my soul could grasp them all
But must remain with this vile form. I look
With hope to age at last, which quenching much,
May let me concentrate the sparks it spares.

This restlessness of passion meets in me
A craving after knowledge: the sole proof
Of a commanding will is in that power
Repressed; for I beheld it in its dawn,
That sleepless harpy with its budding wings,
And I considered whether I should yield
All hopes and fears, to live alone with it,
Finding a recompense in its wild eyes;
And when I found that I should perish so,
I bade its wild eyes close from me forever,
And I am left alone with my delights;
So, it lies in me a chained thing, still ready
To serve me if I loose its slightest bond:
I cannot but be proud of my bright slave.

And thus I know this earth is not my sphere,
For I cannot so narrow me but that
I still exceed it: in their elements
My love would pass my reason; but since here
Love must receive its objects from this earth
While reason will be chainless, the few truths
Caught from its wanderings have sufficed to quell
All love below; then what must be that love
Which, with the object it demands, would quell
Reason though it soared with the seraphim?
No, what I feel may pass all human love
Yet fall far short of what my love should be.
And yet I seem more warped in this than aught,
For here myself stands out more hideously:
I can forget myself in friendship, fame,
Or liberty, or love of mighty souls;
But I begin to know what thing hate is —
To sicken and to quiver and grow white —
And I myself have furnished its first prey.
All my sad weaknesses, this wavering will,
This selfishness, this still decaying frame . . .
But I must never grieve while I can pass
Far from such thoughts — as now, Andromeda!
And she is with me: years roll, I shall change,
But change can touch her not — so beautiful
With her dark eyes, earnest and still, and hair
Lifted and spread by the salt-sweeping breeze,
And one red beam, all the storm leaves in heaven,
Resting upon her eyes and face and hair
As she awaits the snake on the wet beach
By the dark rock and the white wave just breaking
At her feet; quite naked and alone; a thing
You doubt not, nor fear for, secure that God
Will come in thunder from the stars to save her.
Let it pass! I will call another change.
I will be gifted with a wondrous soul,
Yet sunk by error to men's sympathy,
And in the wane of life, yet only so
As to call up their fears; and there shall come
A time requiring youth's best energies;
And straight I fling age, sorrow, sickness off,
And I rise triumphing over my decay.

And thus it is that I supply the chasm
'Twixt what I am and all that I would be.
But then to know nothing, to hope for nothing,

To seize on life's dull joys from a strange fear
Lest, losing them, all 's lost and nought remains!

There 's some vile juggle with my reason here;
I feel I but explain to my own loss
These impulses; they live no less the same.
Liberty! what though I despair? my blood
Rose not at a slave's name proudlier than now,
And sympathy, obscured by sophistries!
Why have not I sought refuge in myself,
But for the woes I saw and could not stay?
And love! do I not love thee, my Pauline?
I cherish prejudice, lest I be left
Utterly loveless — witness this belief
In poets, though sad change has come there too;
No more I leave myself to follow them —
Unconsciously I measure me by them —
Let me forget it: and I cherish most
My love of England — how her name, a word
Of hers in a strange tongue makes my heart beat!

Pauline, I could do anything — not now —
All 's fever — but when calm shall come again,
I am prepared: I have made life my own.
I would not be content with all the change
One frame should feel, but I have gone in thought
Through all conjuncture, I have lived all life
When it is most alive, where strangest fate
New shapes it past surmise — the tales of men
Bit by some curse or in the grasps of doom
Half-visible and still increasing round,
Or crowning their wide being's general aim.

These are wild fancies, but I feel, sweet friend,
As one breathing his weakness to the ear
Of pitying angel — dear as a winter flower,
A slight flower growing alone, and offering
Its frail cup of three leaves to the cold sun,
Yet joyous and confiding like the triumph
Of a child: and why am I not worthy thee?
I can live all the life of plants, and gaze
Drowsily on the bees that flit and play,
Or bare my breast for sunbeams which will kill,
Or open in the night of sounds, to look
For the dim stars; I can mount with the bird
Leaping airily his pyramid of leaves

And twisted boughs of some tall mountain tree,
Or rise cheerfully springing to the heavens;
Or like a fish breathe-in the morning air
In the misty sun-warm water; or with flowers
And trees can smile in light at the sinking sun
Just as the storm comes, as a girl would look
On a departing lover — most serene.

Pauline, come with me, see how I could build
A home for us, out of the world, in thought!
I am inspired: come with me, Pauline!

Night, and one single ridge of narrow path
Between the sullen river and the woods
Waving and muttering, for the moonless night
Has shaped them into images of life,
Like the upraising of the giant-ghosts,
Looking on earth to know how their sons fare :
Thou art so close by me, the roughest swell
Of wind in the tree-tops hides not the panting
Of thy soft breasts. No, we will pass to morning —
Morning, the rocks and valleys and old woods.
How the sun brightens in the mist, and here,
Half in the air, like creatures of the place,
Trusting the element, living on high boughs
That swing in the wind — look at the golden spray
Flung from the foam-sheet of the cataract
Amid the broken rocks! Shall we stay here
With the wild hawks? No; ere the hot noon come,
Dive we down — safe! See this our new retreat
Walled in with a sloped mound of matted shrubs,
Dark, tangled, old and green, still sloping down
To a small pool whose waters lie asleep
Amid the trailing boughs turned water-plants:
And tall trees over-arch to keep us in,
Breaking the sunbeams into emerald shafts,
And in the dreamy water one small group
Of two or three strange trees are got together
Wondering at all around, as strange beasts herd
Together far from their own land : all wildness,
No turf nor moss, for boughs and plants pave all,
And tongues of bank go shelving in the waters,
Where the pale-throated snake reclines his head,
And old gray stones lie making eddies there,
The wild-mice cross them dry-shod : deeper in!
Shut thy soft eyes — now look — still deeper in!

This is the very heart of the woods all round
Mountain-like heaped above us; yet even here
One pond of water gleams; far off the river
Sweeps like a sea, barred out from land; but one —
One thin clear sheet has overleaped and wound
Into this silent depth, which gained, it lies
Still, as but let by sufferance; the trees bend
O'er it as wild men watch a sleeping girl,
And through their roots long creeping plants stretch out
Their twined hair, steeped and sparkling; farther on,
Tall rushes and thick flag-knots have combined
To narrow it; so, at length, a silver thread,
It winds, all noiselessly through the deep wood
Till through a cleft-way, through the moss and stone,
It joins its parent-river with a shout.
Up for the glowing day, leave the old woods!
See, they part, like a ruined arch: the sky!
Nothing but sky appears, so close the roots
And grass of the hill-top level with the air —
Blue sunny air, where a great cloud floats laden
With light, like a dead whale that white birds pick,
Floating away in the sun in some north sea.
Air, air, fresh life-blood, thin and searching air,
The clear, dear breath of God that loveth us,
Where small birds reel and winds take their delight!
Water is beautiful, but not like air:
See, where the solid azure waters lie
Made as of thickened air, and down below,
The fern-ranks like a forest spread themselves
As though each pore could feel the element;
Where the quick glancing serpent winds his way,
Float with me there, Pauline! — but not like air.
Down the hill! Stop — a clump of trees, see, set
On a heap of rocks, which look o'er the far plains,
And envious climbing shrubs would mount to rest
And peer from their spread boughs; there they wave,
    looking
At the muleteers who whistle as they go
To the merry chime of their morning bells, and all
The little smoking cots and fields and banks
And copses bright in the sun. My spirit wanders:
Hedge-rows for me — still, living hedge-rows where
The bushes close and clasp above and keep
Thought in — I am concentrated — I feel;
But my soul saddens when it looks beyond:
I cannot be immortal nor taste all.

O God, where does this tend — these struggling aims?*
What would I have? What is this " sleep " which seems
To bound all ? can there be a " waking " point
Of crowning life ? The soul would never rule ;
It would be first in all things, it would have
Its utmost pleasure filled, but, that complete,
Commanding, for commanding, sickens it.
The last point I can trace is, rest, beneath
Some better essence than itself, in weakness ;
This is " myself," not what I think should be :
And what is that I hunger for but God ?
My God, my God, let me for once look on thee
As though nought else existed, we alone !
And as creation crumbles, my soul's spark
Expands till I can say, — Even from myself
I need thee and I feel thee and I love thee :
I do not plead my rapture in thy works
For love of thee, nor that I feel as one
Who cannot die : but there is that in me
Which turns to thee, which loves or which should love.
Why have I girt myself with this hell-dress ?
Why have I labored to put out my life ?
Is it not in my nature to adore,

* Je crains bien que mon pauvre ami ne soit pas toujours parfaitement compris dans ce qui reste à lire de cet étrange fragment, mais il est moins propre que tout autre à éclaircir ce qui de sa nature ne peut jamais être que songe et confusion. D'ailleurs je ne sais trop si en cherchant à mieux co-ordonner certaines parties l'on ne courrait pas le risque de nuire au seul mérite auquel une production si singulière peut prétendre, celui de donner une idée assez précise du genre qu'elle n'a fait qu'ébaucher. Ce début sans prétention, ce remuement des passions qui va d'abord en accroissant et puis s'appaise par degrés, ces élans de l'âme, ce retour soudain sur soi-même, et par-dessus tout, la tournure d'esprit tout particulière de mon ami, rendent les changemens presque impossibles. Les raisons qu'il fait valoir ailleurs, et d'autres encore plus puissantes, ont fait trouver grâce à mes yeux pour cet écrit qu'autrement je lui eusse conseillé de jeter au feu. Je n'en crois pas moins au grand principe de toute composition — à ce principe de Shakespeare, de Rafaelle, de Beethoven, d'où il suit que la concentration des idées est dûe bien plus à leur conception qu'à leur mise en execution : j'ai tout lieu de craindre que la première de ces qualités ne soit encore étrangère à mon ami, et je doute fort qu'un redoublement de travail lui fasse acquérir la seconde. Le mieux serait de brûler ceci ; mais que faire ?
Je crois que dans ce qui suit il fait allusion à un certain examen qu'il fit autrefois de l'âme ou plutôt de son âme, pour découvrir la suite des objets auxquels il lui serait possible d'attendre, et dont chacun une fois obtenu devait former une espèce de plateau d'où l'on pouvait apercevoir d'autres buts, d'autres projets, d'autres jouissances qui, à leur tour, devaient être surmontés. Il en résultait que l'oubli et le sommeil devaient tout terminer. Cette idée, que je ne saisis pas parfaitement, lui est peutêtre aussi inintelligible qu'à moi.   PAULINE.

And e'en for all my reason do I not
Feel him, and thank him, and pray to him — now?
Can I forego the trust that he loves me?
Do I not feel a love which only ONE . . . .
O thou pale form, so dimly seen, deep-eyed!
I have denied thee calmly — do I not
Pant when I read of thy consummate deeds,
And burn to see thy calm pure truths out-flash
The brightest gleams of earth's philosophy?
Do I not shake to hear aught question thee?
If I am erring save me, madden me,
Take from me powers and pleasures, let me die
Ages, so I see thee! I am knit round
As with a charm by sin and lust and pride,
Yet though my wandering dreams have seen all shapes
Of strange delight, oft have I stood by thee —
Have I been keeping lonely watch with thee
In the damp night by weeping Olivet,
Or leaning on thy bosom, proudly less,
Or dying with thee on the lonely cross,
Or witnessing thy bursting from the tomb.

A mortal, sin's familiar friend, doth here
Avow that he will give all earth's reward,
But to believe and humbly teach the faith,
In suffering and poverty and shame,
Only believing he is not unloved.

And now, my Pauline, I am thine forever!
I feel the spirit which has buoyed me up
Deserting me, and old shades gathering on;
Yet while its last light waits, I would say much,
And chiefly, I am glad that I have said
That love which I have ever felt for thee
But seldom told; our hearts so beat together
That speech is mockery; but when dark hours come,
And I feel sad, and thou, sweet, deem'st it strange
A sorrow moves me, thou canst not remove,
Look on this lay I dedicate to thee,
Which through thee I began, and which I end,
Collecting the last gleams to strive to tell
That I am thine, and more than ever now
That I am sinking fast: yet though I sink,
No less I feel that thou hast brought me bliss
And that I still may hope to win it back.
Thou knowest, dear friend, I could not think all calm,

For wild dreams followed me and bore me off,
And all was indistinct; ere one was caught
Another glanced; so, dazzled by my wealth,
Knowing not which to leave nor which to choose,
For all my thoughts so floated, nought was fixed.
And then thou saidst a perfect bard was one
Who shadowed out the stages of all life,
And so thou bad'st me tell this my first stage.
'T is done, and even now I feel all dim the shift
Of thought; these are my last thoughts; I discern
Faintly immortal life and truth and good.
And why thou must be mine is, that e'en now
In the dim hush of night, that I have done,
With fears and sad forebodings, I look through
And say, — E'en at the last I have her still,
With her delicious eyes as clear as heaven
When rain in a quick shower has beat down mist,
And clouds float white in the sun like broods of swans.
How the blood lies upon her cheek, all spread
As thinned by kisses! only in her lips
It wells and pulses like a living thing,
And her neck looks like marble misted o'er
With love-breath, — a dear thing to kiss and love,
Standing beneath me, looking out to me,
As I might kill her and be loved for it.

Love me — love me, Pauline, love nought but me,
Leave me not! All these words are wild and weak,
Believe them not, Pauline! I stooped so low
But to behold thee purer by my side,
To show thou art my breath, my life, a last
Resource, an extreme want: never believe
Aught better could so look to thee; nor seek
Again the world of good thoughts left for me!
There were bright troops of undiscovered suns,
Each equal in their radiant course; there were
Clusters of far fair isles which ocean kept
For his own joy, and his waves broke on them,
Without a choice; and there was a dim crowd
Of visions, each a part of the dim whole:
And one star left his peers and came with peace
Upon a storm, and all eyes pined for him;
And one isle harbored a sea-beaten ship,
And the crew wandered in its bowers and plucked
Its fruits and gave up all their hopes for home;
And one dream came to a pale poet's sleep,

And he said, " I am singled out by God,
No sin must touch me." I am very weak,
But what I would express is, — Leave me not,
Still sit by me with beating breast and hair
Loosened, be watching earnest by my side,
Turning my books or kissing me when I
Look up — like summer wind ! Be still to me
A key to music's mystery when mind fails,
A reason, a solution and a clue !
You see I have thrown off my prescribed rules :
I hope in myself — and hope and pant and love.
You 'll find me better, know me more than when
You loved me as I was. Smile not! I have
Much yet to gladden you, to dawn on you ;
No more of the past ! I 'll look within no more :
I have too trusted to my own wild wants,
Too trusted to myself, to intuition —
Draining the wine alone in the still night,
And seeing how, as gathering films arose,
As by an inspiration life seemed bare
And grinning in its vanity, and ends
Hard to be dreamed of, stared at me as fixed,
And others suddenly became all foul
As a fair witch turned an old hag at night.
No more of this ! We will go hand in hand ;
I will go with thee, even as a child,
Looking no farther than thy sweet commands,
And thou hast chosen where this life shall be :
The land which gave me thee shall be our home,
Where nature lies all wild amid her lakes
And snow-swathed mountains and vast pines all girt
With ropes of snow — where nature lies all bare,
Suffering none to view her but a race
Most stinted and deformed, like the mute dwarfs
Which wait upon a naked Indian queen.
And there (the time being when the heavens are thick
With storms) I 'll sit with thee while thou dost sing
Thy native songs, gay as a desert bird
Who crieth as he flies for perfect joy,
Or telling me old stories of dead knights ;
Or I will read old lays to thee — how she,
The fair pale sister, went to her chill grave
With power to love and to be loved and live:
Or we will go together, like twin gods
Of the infernal world, with scented lamp,
Over the dead, to call and to awake,

Over the unshaped images which lie
Within my mind's cave: only leaving all
That tells of the past doubts. So, when spring comes,
And sunshine comes again like an old smile,
And the fresh waters and awakened birds
And budding woods await us, I shall be
Prepared, and we will go and think again,
And all old loves shall come to us, but changed
As some sweet thought which harsh words veiled before:
Feeling God loves us, and that all that errs
Is a strange dream which death will dissipate.
And then when I am firm, we'll seek again
My own land, and again I will approach
My old designs, and calmly look on all
The works of my past weakness, as one views
Some scene where danger met him long before.
Ah that such pleasant life should be but dreamed!

But whate'er come of it, and though it fade,
And though ere the cold morning all be gone,
As it will be; — though music wait for me,
And fair eyes and bright wine laughing like sin
Which steals back softly on a soul half saved,
And I be first to deny all, and despise
This verse, and these intents which seem so fair, —
Still this is all my own, this moment's pride,
No less I make an end in perfect joy.
E'en in my brightest time, a lurking fear
Possessed me: I well knew my weak resolves,
I felt the witchery that makes mind sleep
Over its treasure, as one half afraid
To make his riches definite: but now
These feelings shall not utterly be lost,
I shall not know again that nameless care
Lest, leaving all undone in youth, some new
And undreamed end reveal itself too late:
For this song shall remain to tell forever
That when I lost all hope of such a change,
Suddenly beauty rose on me again.
No less I make an end in perfect joy,
For I, having thus again been visited,
Shall doubt not many another bliss awaits,
And, though this weak soul sink and darkness come,
Some little word shall light it up again,
And I shall see all clearer and love better,
I shall again go o'er the tracts of thought

As one who has a right, and I shall live
With poets, calmer, purer still each time,
And beauteous shapes will come to me again,
And unknown secrets will be trusted me
Which were not mine when wavering; but now
I shall be priest and lover as of old.

Sun-treader, I believe in God and truth
And love; and as one just escaped from death
Would bind himself in bands of friends to feel
He lives indeed, so, I would lean on thee!
Thou must be ever with me, most in gloom
When such shall come, but chiefly when I die,
For I seem, dying, as one going in the dark
To fight a giant: and live thou forever,
And be to all what thou hast been to me!
All in whom this wakes pleasant thoughts of me,
Know my last state is happy, free from doubt
Or touch of fear. Love me and wish me well!

RICHMOND, *October* 22, 1832.

PARACELSUS

INSCRIBED TO

AMÉDÉE DE RIPERT-MONCLAR

BY HIS AFFECTIONATE FRIEND

LONDON, *March* 15, 1835.   R. B.

PERSONS.

AUREOLUS PARACELSUS, a student.
FESTUS and MICHAL, his friends.
APRILE, an Italian poet.

I. PARACELSUS ASPIRES.

SCENE, *Würzburg; a garden in the environs.* 1512.

FESTUS, PARACELSUS, MICHAL.

Par. Come close to me, dear friends ; still closer ; thus!
Close to the heart which, though long time roll by
Ere it again beat quicker, pressed to yours,
As now it beats — perchance a long, long time —
At least henceforth your memories shall make
Quiet and fragrant as befits their home.
Nor shall my memory want a home in yours —
Alas, that it requires too well such free
Forgiving love as shall embalm it there !
For if you would remember me aright,
As I was born to be, you must forget
All fitful, strange and moody waywardness
Which e'er confused my better spirit, to dwell
Only on moments such as these, dear friends !
— My heart no truer, but my words and ways
More true to it : as Michal, some months hence,
Will say, " this autumn was a pleasant time,"
For some few sunny days ; and overlook
Its bleak wind, hankering after pining leaves.
Autumn would fain be sunny ; I would look

Liker my nature's truth : and both are frail,
And both beloved, for all our frailty.
  Mich.   Aureole !
  Par. Drop by drop ! she is weeping like a child !
Not so ! I am content — more than content ;
Nay, autumn wins you best by this its mute
Appeal to sympathy for its decay :
Look up, sweet Michal, nor esteem the less
Your stained and drooping vines their grapes bow down,
Nor blame those creaking trees bent with their fruit,
That apple-tree with a rare after-birth
Of peeping blooms sprinkled its wealth among !
Then for the winds — what wind that ever raved
Shall vex that ash which overlooks you both,
So proud it wears its berries ? Ah, at length,
The old smile meet for her, the lady of this
Sequestered nest ! — this kingdom, limited
Alone by one old populous green wall
Tenanted by the ever-busy flies,
Gray crickets and shy lizards and quick spiders,
Each family of the silver-threaded moss —
Which, look through near, this way, and it appears
A stubble-field or a cane-brake, a marsh
Of bulrush whitening in the sun : laugh now !
Fancy the crickets, each one in his house,
Looking out, wondering at the world — or best,
Yon painted snail with his gay shell of dew,
Travelling to see the glossy balls high up
Hung by the caterpillar, like gold lamps.
  Mich. In truth we have lived carelessly and well.
  Par. And shall, my perfect pair ! — each, trust me, born
For the other ; nay, your very hair, when mixed,
Is of one hue. For where save in this nook
Shall you two walk, when I am far away,
And wish me prosperous fortune ? Stay : that plant
Shall never wave its tangles lightly and softly,
As a queen's languid and imperial arm
Which scatters crowns among her lovers, but you
Shall be reminded to predict to me
Some great success ! Ah see, the sun sinks broad
Behind Saint Saviour's : wholly gone, at last !
  Fest. Now, Aureole, stay those wandering eyes awhile !
You are ours to-night, at least ; and while you spoke
Of Michal and her tears, I thought that none
Could willing leave what he so seemed to love :
But that last look destroys my dream — that look

As if, where'er you gazed, there stood a star!
How far was Würzburg with its church and spire
And garden-walls and all things they contain,
From that look's far alighting?
    Par.   I but spoke
And looked alike from simple joy to see
The beings I love best, shut in so well
From all rude chances like to be my lot,
That, when afar, my weary spirit, — disposed
To lose awhile its care in soothing thoughts
Of them, their pleasant features, looks and words, —
Needs never hesitate, nor apprehend
Encroaching trouble may have reached them too,
Nor have recourse to fancy's busy aid
And fashion even a wish in their behalf
Beyond what they possess already here;
But, unobstructed, may at once forget
Itself in them, assured how well they fare.
Beside, this Festus knows he holds me one
Whom quiet and its charms arrest in vain,
One scarce aware of all the joys I quit,
Too filled with airy hopes to make account
Of soft delights his own heart garners up:
Whereas behold how much our sense of all
That's beauteous proves alike! When Festus learns
That every common pleasure of the world
Affects me as himself; that I have just
As varied appetite for joy derived
From common things; a stake in life, in short,
Like his; a stake which rash pursuit of aims
That life affords not, would as soon destroy; —
He may convince himself that, this in view,
I shall act well advised. And last, because,
Though heaven and earth and all things were at stake,
Sweet Michal must not weep, our parting eve.
    Fest. True: and the eve is deepening, and we sit
As little anxious to begin our talk
As though to-morrow I could hint of it
As we paced arm-in-arm the cheerful town
At sun-dawn; or could whisper it by fits
(Trithemius busied with his class the while)
In that dim chamber where the noon-streaks peer
Half-frightened by the awful tomes around;
Or in some grassy lane unbosom all
From even-blush to midnight: but, to-morrow!
Have I full leave to tell my inmost mind?

We have been brothers, and henceforth the world
Will rise between us : — all my freest mind?
'T is the last night, dear Aureole!
  Par.   Oh, say on!
Devise some test of love, some arduous feat
To be performed for you : say on! If night
Be spent the while, the better! Recall how oft
My wondrous plans and dreams and hopes and fears
Have — never wearied you, oh no ! — as I
Recall, and never vividly as now,
Your true affection, born when Einsiedeln
And its green hills were all the world to us;
And still increasing to this night which ends
My further stay at Würzburg. Oh, one day
You shall be very proud! Say on, dear friends!
 Fest. In truth? 'T is for my proper peace, indeed,
Rather than yours; for vain all projects seem
To stay your course : I said my latest hope
Is fading even now. A story tells
Of some far embassy dispatched to win
The favor of an eastern king, and how
The gifts they offered proved but dazzling dust
Shed from the ore-beds native to his clime.
Just so, the value of repose and love,
I meant should tempt you, better far than I
You seem to comprehend ; and yet desist
No whit from projects where repose nor love
Has part.
  Par. Once more? Alas! As I foretold.
 Fest. A solitary brier the bank puts forth
To save our swan's nest floating out to sea.
 Par. Dear Festus, hear me. What is it you wish?
That I should lay aside my heart's pursuit,
Abandon the sole ends for which I live,
Reject God's great commission, and so die!
You bid me listen for your true love's sake :
Yet how has grown that love? Even in a long
And patient cherishing of the self-same spirit
It now would quell; as though a mother hoped
To stay the lusty manhood of the child
Once weak upon her knees. I was not born
Informed and fearless from the first, but shrank
From aught which marked me out apart from men :
I would have lived their life, and died their death,
Lost in their ranks, eluding destiny :
But you first guided me through doubt and fear,

Taught me to know mankind and know myself;
And now that I am strong and full of hope,
That, from my soul, I can reject all aims
Save those your earnest words made plain to me,
Now that I touch the brink of my design,
When I would have a triumph in their eyes,
A glad cheer in their voices — Michal weeps,
And Festus ponders gravely!
  Fest.   When you deign
To hear my purpose . . .
  Par.   Hear it? I can say
Beforehand all this evening's conference!
'T is this way, Michal, that he uses: first,
Or he declares, or I, the leading points
Of our best scheme of life, what is man's end
And what God's will; no two faiths e'er agreed
As his with mine. Next, each of us allows
Faith should be acted on as best we may;
Accordingly, I venture to submit
My plan, in lack of better, for pursuing
The path which God's will seems to authorize.
Well, he discerns much good in it, avows
This motive worthy, that hope plausible,
A danger here to be avoided, there
An oversight to be repaired: in fine,
Our two minds go together — all the good
Approved by him, I gladly recognize,
All he counts bad, I thankfully discard,
And nought forbids my looking up at last
For some stray comfort in his cautious brow,
When, lo! I learn that, spite of all, there lurks
Some innate and inexplicable germ
Of failure in my scheme; so that at last
It all amounts to this — the sovereign proof
That we devote ourselves to God, is seen
In living just as though no God there were;
A life which, prompted by the sad and blind
Folly of man, Festus abhors the most;
But which these tenets sanctify at once,
Though to less subtle wits it seems the same,
Consider it how they may.
  Mich.   Is it so, Festus?
He speaks so calmly and kindly: is it so?
  Par. Reject those glorious visions of God's love
And man's design; laugh loud that God should send
Vast longings to direct us; say how soon

Power satiates these, or lust, or gold; I know
The world's cry well, and how to answer it.
But this ambiguous warfare . . .
  Fest.   . . . Wearies so
That you will grant no last leave to your friend
To urge it? — for his sake, not yours? I wish
To send my soul in good hopes after you;
Never to sorrow that uncertain words
Erringly apprehended, a new creed
Ill understood, begot rash trust in you,
Had share in your undoing.
  Par.   Choose your side,
Hold or renounce: but meanwhile blame me not
Because I dare to act on your own views,
Nor shrink when they point onward, nor espy
A peril where they most ensure success.
  Fest. Prove that to me — but that! Prove you abide
Within their warrant, nor presumptuous boast
God's labor laid on you; prove, all you covet,
A mortal may expect; and, most of all,
Prove the strange course you now affect, will lead
To its attainment — and I bid you speed,
Nay, count the minutes till you venture forth!
You smile; but I had gathered from slow thought —
Much musing on the fortunes of my friend —
Matter I deemed could not be urged in vain;
But it all leaves me at my need: in shreds
And fragments I must venture what remains.
  Mich. Ask at once, Festus, wherefore he should scorn.
  Fest. Stay, Michal: Aureole, I speak guardedly
And gravely, knowing well, whate'er your error,
This is no ill-considered choice of yours,
No sudden fancy of an ardent boy.
Not from your own confiding words alone
Am I aware your passionate heart long since
Gave birth to, nourished and at length matures
This scheme. I will not speak of Einsiedeln,
Where I was born your elder by some years
Only to watch you fully from the first:
In all beside, our mutual tasks were fixed
Even then — 't was mine to have you in my view
As you had your own soul and those intents
Which filled it when, to crown your dearest wish,
With a tumultuous heart, you left with me
Our childhood's home to join the favored few
Whom, here, Trithemius condescends to teach

A portion of his lore : and not one youth
Of those so favored, whom you now despise,
Came earnest as you came, resolved, like you,
To grasp all, and retain all, and deserve
By patient toil a wide renown like his.
Now, this new ardor which supplants the old
I watched, too ; 't was significant and strange,
In one matched to his soul's content at length
With rivals in the search for wisdom's prize,
To see the sudden pause, the total change ;
From contest, the transition to repose —
From pressing onward as his fellows pressed,
To a blank idleness, yet most unlike
The dull stagnation of a soul, content,
Once foiled, to leave betimes a thriveless quest.
That careless bearing, free from all pretence
Even of contempt for what it ceased to seek —
Smiling humility, praising much, yet waiving
What it professed to praise — though not so well
Maintained but that rare outbreaks, fierce and brief,
Revealed the hidden scorn, as quickly curbed.
That ostentatious show of past defeat,
That ready acquiescence in contempt,
I deemed no other than the letting go
His shivered sword, of one about to spring
Upon his foe's throat ; but it was not thus :
Not that way looked your brooding purpose then.
For after-signs disclosed, what you confirmed,
That you prepared to task to the uttermost
Your strength, in furtherance of a certain aim
Which — while it bore the name your rivals gave
Their own most puny efforts — was so vast
In scope that it included their best flights,
Combined them, and desired to gain one prize
In place of many, — the secret of the world,
Of man, and man's true purpose, path and fate.
— That you, not nursing as a mere vague dream
This purpose, with the sages of the past,
Have struck upon a way to this, if all
You trust be true, which following, heart and soul,
You, if a man may, dare aspire to KNOW :
And that this aim shall differ from a host
Of aims alike in character and kind,
Mostly in this, — that in itself alone
Shall its reward be, not an alien end
Blending therewith ; no hope nor fear nor joy

Nor woe, to elsewhere move you, but this pure
Devotion to sustain you or betray:
Thus you aspire.
  Par. You shall not state it thus:
I should not differ from the dreamy crew
You speak of. I profess no other share
In the selection of my lot, than this
My ready answer to the will of God
Who summons me to be his organ. All
Whose innate strength supports them shall succeed
No better than the sages.
  Fest.   Such the aim, then,
God sets before you; and 't is doubtless need
That he appoint no less the way of praise
Than the desire to praise; for, though I hold,
With you, the setting forth such praise to be
The natural end and service of a man,
And hold such praise is best attained when man
Attains the general welfare of his kind —
Yet this, the end, is not the instrument.
Presume not to serve God apart from such
Appointed channel as he wills shall gather
Imperfect tributes, for that sole obedience
Valued perchance. He seeks not that his altars
Blaze, careless how, so that they do but blaze.
Suppose this, then; that God selected you
To KNOW (heed well your answers, for my faith
Shall meet implicitly what they affirm),
I cannot think you dare annex to such
Selection aught beyond a steadfast will,
An intense hope; nor let your gifts create
Scorn or neglect of ordinary means
Conducive to success, make destiny
Dispense with man's endeavor. Now, dare you search
Your inmost heart, and candidly avow
Whether you have not rather wild desire
For this distinction than security
Of its existence? whether you discern
The path to the fulfilment of your purpose
Clear as that purpose — and again, that purpose
Clear as your yearning to be singled out
For its pursuer. Dare you answer this?
  Par. (after a pause). No, I have nought to fear! Who
   will may know
The secret'st workings of my soul. What though
It be so? — if indeed the strong desire

Eclipse the aim in me? — if splendor break
Upon the outset of my path alone,
And duskest shade succeed? What fairer seal
Shall I require to my authentic mission
Than this fierce energy? — this instinct striving
Because its nature is to strive? — enticed
By the security of no broad course,
Without success forever in its eyes!
How know I else such glorious fate my own,
But in the restless irresistible force
That works within me? Is it for human will
To institute such impulses? — still less,
To disregard their promptings! What should I
Do, kept among you all; your loves, your cares,
Your life — all to be mine? Be sure that God
Ne'er dooms to waste the strength he deigns impart!
Ask the gier-eagle why she stoops at once
Into the vast and unexplored abyss,
What full-grown power informs her from the first,
Why she not marvels, strenuously beating
The silent boundless regions of the sky!
Be sure they sleep not whom God needs! Nor fear
Their holding light his charge, when every hour
That finds that charge delayed, is a new death.
This for the faith in which I trust; and hence
I can abjure so well the idle arts
These pedants strive to learn and teach; Black Arts,
Great Works, the Secret and Sublime, forsooth —
Let others prize: too intimate a tie
Connects me with our God! A sullen fiend
To do my bidding, fallen and hateful sprites
To help me — what are these, at best, beside
God helping, God directing everywhere,
So that the earth shall yield her secrets up,
And every object there be charged to strike,
Teach, gratify her master God appoints?
And I am young, my Festus, happy and free!
I can devote myself; I have a life
To give; I, singled out for this, the One!
Think, think; the wide East, where all Wisdom sprung;
The bright South, where she dwelt; the hopeful North,
All are passed o'er — it lights on me! 'T is time
New hopes should animate the world, new light
Should dawn from new revealings to a race
Weighed down so long, forgotten so long; thus shall
The heaven reserved for us at last receive

Creatures whom no unwonted splendors blind,
But ardent to confront the unclouded blaze,
Whose beams not seldom blessed their pilgrimage,
Not seldom glorified their life below.
 Fest. My words have their old fate and make faint stand
Against your glowing periods. Call this, truth —
Why not pursue it in a fast retreat,
Some one of Learning's many palaces,
After approved example ? — seeking there
Calm converse with the great dead, soul to soul,
Who laid up treasure with the like intent
— So lift yourself into their airy place,
And fill out full their unfulfilled careers,
Unravelling the knots their baffled skill
Pronounced inextricable, true ! — but left
Far less confused. A fresh eye, a fresh hand,
Might do much at their vigor's waning-point ;
Succeeding with new-breathed new-hearted force,
As at old games the runner snatched the torch
From runner still : this way success might be.
But you have coupled with your enterprise
An arbitrary self-repugnant scheme
Of seeking it in strange and untried paths.
What books are in the desert ? Writes the sea
The secret of her yearning in vast caves
Where yours will fall the first of human feet ?
Has wisdom sat there and recorded aught
You press to read ? Why turn aside from her
To visit, where her vesture never glanced,
Now — solitudes consigned to barrenness
By God's decree, which who shall dare impugn ?
Now — ruins where she paused but would not stay,
Old ravaged cities that, renouncing her,
She called an endless curse on, so it came :
Or worst of all, now — men you visit, men,
Ignoblest troops who never heard her voice
Or hate it, men without one gift from Rome
Or Athens, — these shall Aureole's teachers be !
Rejecting past example, practice, precept,
Aidless 'mid these he thinks to stand alone :
Thick like a glory round the Stagirite
Your rivals throng, the sages : here stand you !
Whatever you may protest, knowledge is not
Paramount in your love ; or for her sake
You would collect all help from every source —
Rival, assistant, friend, foe, all would merge

In the broad class of those who showed her haunts,
And those who showed them not.
 Par.   What shall I say?
Festus, from childhood I have been possessed
By a fire — by a true fire, or faint or fierce,
As from without some master, so it seemed,
Repressed or urged its current: this but ill
Expresses what I would convey: but rather
I will believe an angel ruled me thus,
Than that my soul's own workings, own high nature,
So became manifest. I knew not then
What whispered in the evening, and spoke out
At midnight. If some mortal, born too soon,
Were laid away in some great trance — the ages
Coming and going all the while — till dawned
His true time's advent; and could then record
The words they spoke who kept watch by his bed, —
Then I might tell more of the breath so light
Upon my eyelids, and the fingers light
Among my hair. Youth is confused; yet never
So dull was I but, when that spirit passed,
I turned to him, scarce consciously, as turns
A water-snake when fairies cross his sleep.
And having this within me and about me
While Einsiedeln, its mountains, lakes and woods
Confined me — what oppressive joy was mine
When life grew plain, and I first viewed the thronged,
The everlasting concourse of mankind!
Believe that ere I joined them, ere I knew
The purpose of the pageant, or the place
Consigned me in its ranks — while, just awake,
Wonder was freshest and delight most pure —
'T was then that least supportable appeared
A station with the brightest of the crowd,
A portion with the proudest of them all.
And from the tumult in my breast, this only
Could I collect, that I must thenceforth die
Or elevate myself far, far above
The gorgeous spectacle. I seemed to long
At once to trample on yet save mankind,
To make some unexampled sacrifice
In their behalf, to wring some wondrous good
From heaven or earth for them, to perish, winning
Eternal weal in the act: as who should dare
Pluck out the angry thunder from its cloud,
That, all its gathered flame discharged on him,

No storm might threaten summer's azure sleep:
Yet never to be mixed with men so much
As to have part even in my own work, share
In my own largess. Once the feat achieved,
I would withdraw from their officious praise,
Would gently put aside their profuse thanks.
Like some knight traversing a wilderness,
Who, on his way, may chance to free a tribe
Of desert-people from their dragon-foe;
When all the swarthy race press round to kiss
His feet, and choose him for their king, and yield
Their poor tents, pitched among the sand-hills, for
His realm: and he points, smiling, to his scarf
Heavy with riveled gold, his burgonet
Gay set with twinkling stones — and to the East,
Where these must be displayed!
 Fest.   Good: let us hear
No more about your nature, "which first shrank
From all that marked you out apart from men!"
 Par. I touch on that; these words but analyze
The first mad impulse: 't was as brief as fond,
For as I gazed again upon the show,
I soon distinguished here and there a shape
Palm-wreathed and radiant, forehead and full eye.
Well pleased was I their state should thus at once
Interpret my own thoughts: — " Behold the clue
To all," I rashly said, " and what I pine
To do, these have accomplished: we are peers.
They know and therefore rule: I, too, will know!"
You were beside me, Festus, as you say;
You saw me plunge in their pursuits whom fame
Is lavish to attest the lords of mind,
Not pausing to make sure the prize in view
Would satiate my cravings when obtained,
But since they strove I strove. Then came a slow
And strangling failure. We aspired alike,
Yet not the meanest plodder, Tritheim counts
A marvel, but was all-sufficient, strong,
Or staggered only at his own vast wits;
While I was restless, nothing satisfied,
Distrustful, most perplexed. I would slur over
That struggle; suffice it, that I loathed myself
As weak compared with them, yet felt somehow
A mighty power was brooding, taking shape
Within me; and this lasted till one night
When, as I sat revolving it and more,

A still voice from without said — " Seest thou not,
Desponding child, whence spring defeat and loss?
Even from thy strength. Consider : hast thou gazed
Presumptuously on wisdom's countenance,
No veil between ; and can thy faltering hands,
Unguided by the brain the sight absorbs,
Pursue their task as earnest blinkers do
Whom radiance ne'er distracted?   Live their life
If thou wouldst share their fortune, choose their eyes
Unfed by splendor. Let each task present
Its petty good to thee. Waste not thy gifts
In profitless waiting for the gods' descent,
But have some idol of thine own to dress
With their array. Know, not for knowing's sake,
But to become a star to men forever ;
Know, for the gain it gets, the praise it brings,
The wonder it inspires, the love it breeds :
Look one step onward, and secure that step ! "
And I smiled as one never smiles but once,
Then first discovering my own aim's extent,
Which sought to comprehend the works of God,
And God himself, and all God's intercourse
With the human mind ; I understood, no less,
My fellows' studies, whose true worth I saw,
But smiled not, well aware who stood by me.
And softer came the voice — " There is a way :
'T is hard for flesh to tread therein, imbued
With frailty — hopeless, if indulgence first
Have ripened inborn germs of sin to strength :
Wilt thou adventure for my sake and man's,
Apart from all reward ? "   And last it breathed —
" Be happy, my good soldier ; I am by thee,
Be sure, even to the end ! " — I answered not,
Knowing him. As he spoke, I was endued
With comprehension and a steadfast will ;
And when he ceased, my brow was sealed his own.
If there took place no special change in me,
How comes it all things wore a different hue
Thenceforward ? — pregnant with vast consequence,
Teeming with grand result, loaded with fate ?
So that when, quailing at the mighty range
Of secret truths which yearn for birth, I haste
To contemplate undazzled some one truth,
Its bearings and effects alone — at once
What was a speck expands into a star,
Asking a life to pass exploring thus,

Till I near craze. I go to prove my soul!
I see my way as birds their trackless way.
I shall arrive! what time, what circuit first,
I ask not: but unless God send his hail
Or blinding fireballs, sleet or stifling snow,
In some time, his good time, I shall arrive:
He guides me and the bird. In his good time!
  Mich. Vex him no further, Festus; it is so!
  Fest. Just thus you help me ever. This would hold
Were it the trackless air, and not a path
Inviting you, distinct with footprints yet
Of many a mighty marcher gone that way.
You may have purer views than theirs, perhaps,
But they were famous in their day — the proofs
Remain. At least accept the light they lend.
  Par. Their light! the sum of all is briefly this:
They labored and grew famous, and the fruits
Are best seen in a dark and groaning earth
Given over to a blind and endless strife
With evils, what of all their lore abates?
No; I reject and spurn them utterly
And all they teach. Shall I still sit beside
Their dry wells, with a white lip and filmed eye,
While in the distance heaven is blue above
Mountains where sleep the unsunned tarns?
  Fest.   And yet
As strong delusions have prevailed ere now.
Men have set out as gallantly to seek
Their ruin. I have heard of such: yourself
Avow all hitherto have failed and fallen.
  Mich. Nay, Festus, when but as the pilgrims faint
Through the drear way, do you expect to see
Their city dawn amid the clouds afar?
  Par. Ay, sounds it not like some old well-known tale?
For me, I estimate their works and them
So rightly, that at times I almost dream
I too have spent a life the sages' way,
And tread once more familiar paths. Perchance
I perished in an arrogant self-reliance
Ages ago; and in that act, a prayer
For one more chance went up so earnest, so
Instinct with better light let in by death,
That life was blotted out — not so completely
But scattered wrecks enough of it remain,
Dim memories, as now, when once more seems
The goal in sight again. All which, indeed,

Is foolish, and only means — the flesh I wear,
The earth I tread, are not more clear to me
Than my belief, explained to you or no.
  Fest. And who am I, to challenge and dispute
That clear belief ?   I will divest all fear.
  Mich. Then Aureole is God's commissary ! he shall
Be great and grand — and all for us !
  Par.   No, sweet !
Not great and grand. If I can serve mankind
'T is well ; but there our intercourse must end :
I never will be served by those I serve.
  Fest. Look well to this ; here is a plague-spot, here,
Disguise it how you may ! 'T is true, you utter
This scorn while by our side and loving us ;
'T is but a spot as yet : but it will break
Into a hideous blotch if overlooked ;
How can that course be safe which from the first
Produces carelessness to human love ?
It seems you have abjured the helps which men
Who overpass their kind, as you would do,
Have humbly sought ; I dare not thoroughly probe
This matter, lest I learn too much.   Let be
That popular praise would little instigate
Your efforts, nor particular approval
Reward you ; put reward aside ; alone
You shall go forth upon your arduous task,
None shall assist you, none partake your toil,
None share your triumph : still you must retain
Some one to cast your glory on, to share
Your rapture with.   Were I elect like you,
I would encircle me with love, and raise
A rampart of my fellows ; it should seem
Impossible for me to fail, so watched
By gentle friends who made my cause their own.
They should ward off fate's envy — the great gift,
Extravagant when claimed by me alone,
Being so a gift to them as well as me.
If danger daunted me or ease seduced,
How calmly their sad eyes should gaze reproach !
  Mich. O Aureole, can I sing when all alone,
Without first calling, in my fancy, both
To listen by my side — even I ! And you ?
Do you not feel this ?   Say that you feel this !
  Par. I feel 't is pleasant that my aims, at length
Allowed their weight, should be supposed to need
A further strengthening in these goodly helps !

My course allures for its own sake, its sole
Intrinsic worth; and ne'er shall boat of mine
Adventure forth for gold and apes at once.
Your sages say, " if human, therefore weak : "
If weak, more need to give myself entire
To my pursuit; and by its side, all else . . .
No matter! I deny myself but little
In waiving all assistance save its own.
Would there were some real sacrifice to make!
Your friends the sages threw their joys away,
While I must be content with keeping mine.
 Fest. But do not cut yourself from human weal!
You cannot thrive — a man that dares affect
To spend his life in service to his kind
For no reward of theirs, unbound to them
By any tie; nor do so, Aureole! No —
There are strange punishments for such. Give up
(Although no visible good flow thence) some part
Of the glory to another; hiding thus,
Even from yourself, that all is for yourself.
Say, say almost to God — " I have done all
For her, not for myself! "
 Par.   And who but lately
Was to rejoice in my success like you?
Whom should I love but both of you?
 Fest.   I know not:
But know this, you, that 't is no will of mine
You should abjure the lofty claims you make;
And this the cause — I can no longer seek
To overlook the truth, that there would be
A monstrous spectacle upon the earth,
Beneath the pleasant sun, among the trees:
— A being knowing not what love is. Hear me!
You are endowed with faculties which bear
Annexed to them as 't were a dispensation
To summon meaner spirits to do their will
And gather round them at their need; inspiring
Such with a love themselves can never feel,
Passionless 'mid their passionate votaries.
I know not if you joy in this or no,
Or ever dream that common men can live
On objects you prize lightly, but which make
Their heart's sole treasure: the affections seem
Beauteous at most to you, which we must taste
Or die: and this strange quality accords,
I know not how, with you; sits well upon

That luminous brow, though in another it scowls
An eating brand, a shame. I dare not judge you.
The rules of right and wrong thus set aside,
There's no alternative — I own you one
Of higher order, under other laws
Than bind us; therefore, curb not one bold glance!
'T is best aspire. Once mingled with us all . . .
    Mich. Stay with us, Aureole! cast those hopes away,
And stay with us! An angel warns me, too,
Man should be humble; you are very proud:
And God, dethroned, has doleful plagues for such!
— Warns me to have in dread no quick repulse,
No slow defeat, but a complete success:
You will find all you seek, and perish so!
    Par. (*after a pause*). Are these the barren first-fruits
      of my quest?
Is love like this the natural lot of all?
How many years of pain might one such hour
O'erbalance? Dearest Michal, dearest Festus,
What shall I say, if not that I desire
To justify your love; and will, dear friends,
In swerving nothing from my first resolves.
See, the great moon! and ere the mottled owls
Were wide awake, I was to go. It seems
You acquiesce at last in all save this —
If I am like to compass what I seek
By the untried career I choose; and then,
If that career, making but small account
Of much of life's delight, will yet retain
Sufficient to sustain my soul: for thus
I understand these fond fears just expressed.
And first; the lore you praise and I neglect,
The labors and the precepts of old time,
I have not lightly disesteemed. But, friends,
Truth is within ourselves; it takes no rise
From outward things, whate'er you may believe.
There is an inmost centre in us all,
Where truth abides in fulness; and around,
Wall upon wall, the gross flesh hems it in,
This perfect, clear perception — which is truth,
A baffling and perverting carnal mesh
Binds it, and makes all error: and, to KNOW,
Rather consists in opening out a way
Whence the imprisoned splendor may escape,
Than in effecting entry for a light
Supposed to be without. Watch narrowly

The demonstration of a truth, its birth,
And you trace back the effluence to its spring
And source within us; where broods radiance vast,
To be elicited ray by ray, as chance
Shall favor: chance — for hitherto, your sage
Even as he knows not how those beams are born,
As little knows he what unlocks their fount.
And men have oft grown old among their books
To die case-hardened in their ignorance,
Whose careless youth had promised what long years
Of unremitted labor ne'er performed:
While, contrary, it has chanced some idle day,
To autumn loiterers just as fancy-free
As the midges in the sun, gives birth at last
To truth — produced mysteriously as cape
Of cloud grown out of the invisible air.
Hence, may not truth be lodged alike in all,
The lowest as the highest? some slight film
The interposing bar which binds a soul
And makes the idiot, just as makes the sage
Some film removed, the happy outlet whence
Truth issues proudly? See this soul of ours!
How it strives weakly in the child, is loosed
In manhood, clogged by sickness, back compelled
By age and waste, set free at last by death:
Why is it, flesh enthralls it or enthrones?
What is this flesh we have to penetrate?
Oh, not alone when life flows still, do truth
And power emerge, but also when strange chance
Ruffles its current; in unused conjuncture,
When sickness breaks the body — hunger, watching,
Excess or languor — oftenest death's approach,
Peril, deep joy or woe. One man shall crawl
Through life surrounded with all stirring things,
Unmoved; and he goes mad: and from the wreck
Of what he was, by his wild talk alone,
You first collect how great a spirit he hid.
Therefore, set free the soul alike in all,
Discovering the true laws by which the flesh
Accloys the spirit! We may not be doomed
To cope with seraphs, but at least the rest
Shall cope with us. Make no more giants, God,
But elevate the race at once! We ask
To put forth just our strength, our human strength,
All starting fairly, all equipped alike,
Gifted alike, all eagle-eyed, true-hearted —

See if we cannot beat thine angels yet!
Such is my task. I go to gather this
The sacred knowledge, here and there dispersed
About the world, long lost ór never found.
And why should I be sad or lorn of hope?
Why ever make man's good distinct from God's,
Or, finding they are one, why dare mistrust?
Who shall succeed if not one pledged like me?
Mine is no mad attempt to build a world
Apart from his, like those who set themselves
To find the nature of the spirit they bore,
And, taught betimes that all their gorgeous dreams
Were only born to vanish in this life,
Refused to fit them to its narrow sphere,
But chose to figure forth another world
And other frames meet for their vast desires, —
And all a dream! Thus was life scorned; but life
Shall yet be crowned : twine amaranth! I am priest!
And all for yielding with a lively spirit
A poor existence, parting with a youth
Like those who squander every energy
Convertible to good, on painted toys,
Breath-bubbles, gilded dust! And though I spurn
All adventitious aims, from empty praise
To love's award, yet whoso deems such helps
Important, and concerns himself for me,
May know even these will follow with the rest —
As in the steady rolling Mayne, asleep
Yonder, is mixed its mass of schistous ore.
My own affections, laid to rest awhile,
Will waken purified, subdued alone
By all I have achieved. Till then — till then . . .
Ah, the time-wiling loitering of a page
Through bower and over lawn, till eve shall bring
The stately lady's presence whom he loves —
The broken sleep of the fisher whose rough coat
Enwraps the queenly pearl — these are faint types!
See, see they look on me : I triumph now!
But one thing, Festus, Michal! I have told
All I shall e'er disclose to mortal : say —
Do you believe I shall accomplish this?
    Fest. I do believe!
    Mich.   I ever did believe!
    Par. Those words shall never fade from out my **brain!**
This earnest of the end shall never fade!
Are there not, Festus, are there not, dear **Michal,**

Two points in the adventure of the diver,
One — when, a beggar, he prepares to plunge,
One — when, a prince, he rises with his pearl?
Festus, I plunge!
   Fest.   We wait you when you rise!

II. PARACELSUS ATTAINS.

SCENE, *Constantinople; the house of a Greek conjurer.* 1521.

PARACELSUS.

Over the waters in the vaporous West
The sun goes down as in a sphere of gold
Behind the arm of the city, which between,
With all that length of domes and minarets,
Athwart the splendor, black and crooked runs
Like a Turk verse along a scimitar.
There lie, sullen memorial, and no more
Possess my aching sight! 'T is done at last.
Strange — and the juggles of a sallow cheat
Have won me to this act! 'T is as yon cloud
Should voyage unwrecked o'er many a mountain-top
And break upon a molehill. I have dared
Come to a pause with knowledge; scan for once
The heights already reached, without regard
To the extent above; fairly compute
All I have clearly gained; for once excluding
A brilliant future to supply and perfect
All half-gains and conjectures and crude hopes:
And all because a fortune-teller wills
His credulous seekers should inscribe thus much
Their previous life's attainment, in his roll,
Before his promised secret, as he vaunts,
Make up the sum : and here, amid the scrawled
Uncouth recordings of the dupes of this
Old arch-genethliac, lie my life's results!

A few blurred characters suffice to note
A stranger wandered long through many lands
And reaped the fruit he coveted in a few
Discoveries, as appended here and there,
The fragmentary produce of much toil,
In a dim heap, fact and surmise together
Confusedly massed as when acquired; he was

Intent on gain to come too much to stay
And scrutinize the little gained : the whole
Slipt in the blank space 'twixt an idiot's gibber
And a mad lover's ditty — there it lies.

And yet those blottings chronicle a life —
A whole life, and my life! Nothing to do,
No problem for the fancy, but a life
Spent and decided, wasted past retrieve
Or worthy beyond peer. Stay, what does this
Remembrancer set down concerning "life "?
" ' Time fleets, youth fades, life is an empty dream,'
It is the echo of time; and he whose heart
Beat first beneath a human heart, whose speech
Was copied from a human tongue, can never
Recall when he was living yet knew not this.
Nevertheless long seasons pass o'er him
Till some one hour's experience shows what nothing,
It seemed, could clearer show; and ever after,
An altered brow and eye and gait and speech
Attest that now he knows the adage true,
' Time fleets, youth fades, life is an empty dream.' "

Ay, my brave chronicler, and this same hour
As well as any : now, let my time be!

Now! I can go no farther; well or ill,
'T is done. I must desist and take my chance.
I cannot keep on the stretch : 't is no back-shrinking —
For let but some assurance beam, some close
To my toil grow visible, and I proceed
At any price, though closing it, I die.
Else, here I pause. The old Greek's prophecy
Is like to turn out true : " I shall not quit
His chamber till I know what I desire!"
Was it the light wind sang it o'er the sea?

An end, a rest! strange how the notion, once
Encountered, gathers strength by moments! Rest!
Where has it kept so long? this throbbing brow
To cease, this beating heart to cease, all cruel
And gnawing thoughts to cease! To dare let down
My strung, so high-strung brain, to dare unnerve
My harassed o'ertasked frame, to know my place,
My portion, my reward, even my failure,
Assigned, made sure forever! To lose myself

Among the common creatures of the world,
To draw some gain from having been a man,
Neither to hope nor fear, to live at length!
Even in failure, rest! But rest in truth
And power and recompense . . . I hoped that once!

What, sunk insensibly so deep? Has all
Been undergone for this? This the request
My labor qualified me to present
With no fear of refusal? Had I gone
Slightingly through my task, and so judged fit
To moderate my hopes; nay, were it now
My sole concern to exculpate myself,
End things or mend them, — why, I could not choose
A humbler mood to wait for the event!
No, no, there needs not this; no, after all,
At worst I have performed my share of the task;
The rest is God's concern; mine, merely this,
To know that I have obstinately held
By my own work. The mortal whose brave foot
Has trod, unscathed, the temple-court so far
That he descries at length the shrine of shrines,
Must let no sneering of the demons' eyes,
Whom he could pass unquailing, fasten now
Upon him, fairly past their power; no, no —
He must not stagger, faint, fall down at last,
Having a charm to baffle them; behold,
He bares his front: a mortal ventures thus
Serene amid the echoes, beams and glooms!
If he be priest henceforth, if he wake up
The god of the place to ban and blast him there,
Both well! What's failure or success to me?
I have subdued my life to the one purpose
Whereto I ordained it; there alone I spy,
No doubt, that way I may be satisfied.
Yes, well have I subdued my life! beyond
The obligation of my strictest vow,
The contemplation of my wildest bond,
Which gave my nature freely up, in truth,
But in its actual state, consenting fully
All passionate impulses its soil was formed
To rear, should wither; but foreseeing not
The tract, doomed to perpetual barrenness,
Would seem one day, remembered as it was,
Beside the parched sand-waste which now it is,
Already strewn with faint blooms, viewless then.

I ne'er engaged to root up loves so frail
I felt them not; yet now, 't is very plain
Some soft spots had their birth in me at first,
If not love, say, like love : there was a time
When yet this wolfish hunger after knowledge
Set not remorselessly love's claims aside.
This heart was human once, or why recall
Einsiedeln, now, and Würzburg which the Mayne
Forsakes her course to fold as with an arm?

And Festus — my poor Festus, with his praise
And counsel and grave fears — where is he now
With the sweet maiden, long ago his bride?
I surely loved them — that last night, at least,
When we . . . gone! gone! the better. I am saved
The sad review of an ambitious youth
Choked by vile lusts, unnoticed in their birth,
But let grow up and wind around a will
Till action was destroyed. No, I have gone
Purging my path successively of aught
Wearing the distant likeness of such lusts.
I have made life consist of one idea:
Ere that was master, up till that was born,
I bear a memory of a pleasant life
Whose small events I treasure; till one morn
I ran o'er the seven little grassy fields,
Startling the flocks of nameless birds, to tell
Poor Festus, leaping all the while for joy,
To leave all trouble for my future plans,
Since I had just determined to become
The greatest and most glorious man on earth.
And since that morn all life has been forgotten;
All is one day, one only step between
The outset and the end : one tyrant all-
Absorbing aim fills up the interspace,
One vast unbroken chain of thought, kept up
Through a career apparently adverse
To its existence : life, death, light and shadow,
The shows of the world, were bare receptacles
Or indices of truth to be wrung thence,
Not ministers of sorrow or delight:
A wondrous natural robe in which she went.
For some one truth would dimly beacon me
From mountains rough with pines, and flit and wink
O'er dazzling wastes of frozen snow, and tremble
Into assured light in some branching mine

Where ripens, swathed in fire, the liquid gold —
And all the beauty, all the wonder fell
On either side the truth, as its mere robe;
I see the robe now — then I saw the form.
So far, then, I have voyaged with success,
So much is good, then, in this working sea
Which parts me from that happy strip of land:
But o'er that happy strip a sun shone, too!
And fainter gleams it as the waves grow rough,
And still more faint as the sea widens; last
I sicken on a dead gulf streaked with light
From its own putrefying depths alone.
Then, God was pledged to take me by the hand;
Now, any miserable juggle can bid
My pride depart. All is alike at length:
God may take pleasure in confounding pride
By hiding secrets with the scorned and base —
I am here, in short: so little have I paused
Throughout! I never glanced behind to know
If I had kept my primal light from wane,
And thus insensibly am — what I am!

Oh, bitter; very bitter!
     And more bitter,
To fear a deeper curse, an inner ruin,
Plague beneath plague, the last turning the first
To light beside its darkness. Let me weep
My youth and its brave hopes, all dead and gone,
In tears which burn! Would I were sure to win
Some startling secret in their stead, a tincture
Of force to flush old age with youth, or breed
Gold, or imprison moonbeams till they change
To opal shafts! — only that, hurling it
Indignant back, I might convince myself
My aims remained supreme and pure as ever!
Even now, why not desire, for mankind's sake,
That if I fail, some fault may be the cause,
That, though I sink, another may succeed?
O God, the despicable heart of us!
Shut out this hideous mockery from my heart!

'T was politic in you, Aureole, to reject
Single rewards, and ask them in the lump;
At all events, once launched, to hold straight on:
For now 't is all or nothing. Mighty profit
Your gains will bring if they stop short of such

Full consummation ! As a man, you had
A certain share of strength ; and that is gone
Already in the getting these you boast.
Do not they seem to laugh, as who should say —
"Great master, we are here indeed, dragged forth
To light ; this hast thou done: be glad ! Now, seek
The strength to use which thou hast spent in getting !"

And yet 't is much, surely 't is very much,
Thus to have emptied youth of all its gifts,
To feed a fire meant to hold out till morn
Arrived with inexhaustible light; and lo,
I have heaped up my last, and day dawns not !
And I am left with gray hair, faded hands,
And furrowed brow. Ha, have I, after all,
Mistaken the wild nursling of my breast ?
Knowledge it seemed, and power, and recompense !
Was she who glided through my room of nights,
Who laid my head on her soft knees and smoothed
The damp locks, — whose sly soothings just began
When my sick spirit craved repose awhile —
God ! was I fighting sleep off for death's sake ?

God ! Thou art mind ! Unto the master-mind
Mind should be precious. Spare my mind alone !
All else I will endure ; if, as I stand
Here, with my gains, thy thunder smite me down,
I bow me ; 't is thy will, thy righteous will ;
I o'erpass life's restrictions, and I die ;
And if no trace of my career remain
Save a thin corpse at pleasure of the wind
In these bright chambers level with the air,
See thou to it ! But if my spirit fail,
My once proud spirit forsake me at the last,
Hast thou done well by me ? So do not thou !
Crush not my mind, dear God, though I be crushed !
Hold me before the frequence of thy seraphs
And say — " I crushed him, lest he should disturb
My law. Men must not know their strength : behold,
Weak and alone, how he had raised himself !"

But if delusions trouble me, and thou,
Not seldom felt with rapture in thy help
Throughout my toils and wanderings, dost intend
To work man's welfare through my weak endeavor,
To crown my mortal forehead with a beam

From thine own blinding crown, to smile, and guide
This puny hand and let the work so wrought
Be styled my work, — hear me! I covet not
An influx of new power, an angel's soul:
It were no marvel then — but I have reached
Thus far, a man; let me conclude, a man!
Give but one hour of my first energy,
Of that invincible faith, but only one!
That I may cover with an eagle-glance
The truths I have, and spy some certain way
To mould them, and completing them, possess!

Yet God is good: I started sure of that,
And why dispute it now? I'll not believe
But some undoubted warning long ere this
Had reached me: a fire-labarum was not deemed
Too much for the old founder of these walls.
Then, if my life has not been natural,
It has been monstrous: yet, till late, my course
So ardently engrossed me, that delight,
A pausing and reflecting joy, 't is plain,
Could find no place in it. True, I am worn;
But who clothes summer, who is life itself?
God, that created all things, can renew!
And then, though after-life to please me now
Must have no likeness to the past, what hinders
Reward from springing out of toil, as changed
As bursts the flower from earth and root and stalk?
What use were punishment, unless some sin
Be first detected? let me know that first!
No man could ever offend as I have done . . .

(*A voice from within.*)

I hear a voice, perchance I heard
Long ago, but all too low,
So that scarce a care it stirred
If the voice were real or no:
I heard it in my youth when first
The waters of my life outburst:
But, now their stream ebbs faint, I hear
That voice, still low, but fatal-clear —
As if all poets, God ever meant
Should save the world, and therefore lent
Great gifts to, but who, proud, refused
To do his work, or lightly used
Those gifts, or failed through weak endeavor,

So, mourn cast off by him forever, —
As if these leaned in airy ring
To take me; this the song they sing.

"Lost, lost! yet come,
With our wan troop make thy home.
Come, come! for we
Will not breathe, so much as breathe
Reproach to thee,
Knowing what thou sink'st beneath.
So sank we in those old years,
We who bid thee, come! thou last
Who, living yet, hast life o'erpast.
And altogether we, thy peers,
Will pardon crave for thee, the last
Whose trial is done, whose lot is cast
With those who watch but work no more,
Who gaze on life but live no more.
Yet we trusted thou shouldst speak
The message which our lips, too weak,
Refused to utter, — shouldst redeem
Our fault: such trust, and all a dream!
Yet we chose thee a birthplace
Where the richness ran to flowers:
Couldst not sing one song for grace?
Not make one blossom man's and ours?
Must one more recreant to his race
Die with unexerted powers,
And join us, leaving as he found
The world, he was to loosen, bound?
Anguish! ever and forever;
Still beginning, ending never!
Yet, lost and last one, come!
How couldst understand, alas,
What our pale ghosts strove to say,
As their shades did glance and pass
Before thee night and day?
Thou wast blind as we were dumb:
Once more, therefore, come, O come!
How should we clothe, how arm the spirit
Shall next thy post of life inherit —
How guard him from thy speedy ruin?
Tell us of thy sad undoing
Here, where we sit, ever pursuing
Our weary task, ever renewing
Sharp sorrow, far from God who gave
Our powers, and man they could not save!"

(APRILE *enters.*)

Ha, ha! our king that wouldst be, here at last?
Art thou the poet who shall save the world?
Thy hand to mine! Stay, fix thine eyes on mine!
Thou wouldst be king? Still fix thine eyes on mine!
   Par. Ha, ha! why crouchest not? Am I not king?
So torture is not wholly unavailing!
Have my fierce spasms compelled thee from thy lair?
Art thou the sage I only seemed to be,
Myself of after-time, my very self
With sight a little clearer, strength more firm,
Who robes him in my robe and grasps my crown
For just a fault, a weakness, a neglect?
I scarcely trusted God with the surmise
That such might come, and thou didst hear the while!
   Apr. Thine eyes are lustreless to mine; my hair
Is soft, nay silken soft: to talk with thee
Flushes my cheek, and thou art ashy-pale.
Truly, thou hast labored, hast withstood her lips,
The siren's! Yes, 't is like thou hast attained!
Tell me, dear master, wherefore now thou comest?
I thought thy solemn songs would have their meed
In after-time; that I should hear the earth
Exult in thee and echo with thy praise,
While I was laid forgotten in my grave.
   Par. Ah fiend, I know thee, I am not thy dupe!
Thou art ordained to follow in my track,
Reaping my sowing, as I scorned to reap
The harvest sown by sages passed away.
Thou art the sober searcher, cautious striver,
As if, except through me, thou hast searched or striven!
Ay, tell the world! Degrade me after all,
To an aspirant after fame, not truth —
To all but envy of thy fate, be sure!
   Apr. Nay, sing them to me; I shall envy not:
Thou shalt be king! Sing thou, and I will sit
Beside, and call deep silence for thy songs,
And worship thee, as I had ne'er been meant
To fill thy throne: but none shall ever know!
Sing to me; for already thy wild eyes
Unlock my heart-strings, as some crystal-shaft
Reveals by some chance blaze its parent fount
After long time: so thou reveal'st my soul.
All will flash forth at last, with thee to hear!
   Par. (His secret! I shall get his secret — fool!)
I am he that aspired to KNOW: and thou?

Apr. I would LOVE infinitely, and be loved!
Par. Poor slave! I am thy king indeed.
Apr.   Thou deem'st
That — born a spirit, dowered even as thou,
Born for thy fate — because I could not curb
My yearnings to possess at once the full
Enjoyment, but neglected all the means
Of realizing even the frailest joy,
Gathering no fragments to appease my want,
Yet nursing up that want till thus I die —
Thou deem'st I cannot trace thy safe sure march
O'er perils that o'erwhelm me, triumphing,
Neglecting nought below for aught above,
Despising nothing and ensuring all —
Nor that I could (my time to come again)
Lead thus my spirit securely as thine own.
Listen, and thou shalt see I know thee well.
I would love infinitely . . . Ah, lost! lost!
    Oh ye who armed me at such cost,
    How shall I look on all of ye
    With your gifts even yet on me?
Par. (Ah, 't is some moonstruck creature after all!
Such fond fools as are like to haunt this den:
They spread contagion, doubtless: yet he seemed
To echo one foreboding of my heart
So truly, that . . . no matter! How he stands
With eve's last sunbeam staying on his hair
Which turns to it as if they were akin:
And those clear smiling eyes of saddest blue
Nearly set free, so far they rise above
The painful fruitless striving of the brow
And enforced knowledge of the lips, firm-set
In slow despondency's eternal sigh!
Has he, too, missed life's end, and learned the cause?)
I charge thee, by thy fealty, be calm!
Tell me what thou wouldst be, and what I am.
Apr. I would love infinitely, and be loved.
First: I would carve in stone, or cast in brass,
The forms of earth. No ancient hunter lifted
Up to the gods by his renown, no nymph
Supposed the sweet soul of a woodland tree
Or sapphirine spirit of a twilight star,
Should be too hard for me; no shepherd-king
Regal for his white locks; no youth who stands
Silent and very calm amid the throng,
His right hand ever hid beneath his robe

Until the tyrant pass; no lawgiver,
No swan-soft woman rubbed with lucid oils
Given by a god for love of her — too hard!
Every passion sprung from man, conceived by man,
Would I express and clothe it in its right form,
Or blend with others struggling in one form,
Or show repressed by an ungainly form.
Oh, if you marvelled at some mighty spirit
With a fit frame to execute its will —
Even unconsciously to work its will —
You should be moved no less beside some strong
Rare spirit, fettered to a stubborn body,
Endeavoring to subdue it and inform it
With its own splendor! All this I would do:
And I would say, this done, " His sprites created,
God grants to each a sphere to be its world,
Appointed with the various objects needed
To satisfy its own peculiar want;
So, I create a world for these my shapes
Fit to sustain their beauty and their strength!"
And, at the word, I would contrive and paint
Woods, valleys, rocks and plains, dells, sands and wastes,
Lakes which, when morn breaks on their quivering bed,
Blaze like a wyvern flying round the sun,
And ocean isles so small, the dog-fish tracking
A dead whale, who should find them, would swim thrice
Around them, and fare onward — all to hold
The offspring of my brain. Nor these alone:
Bronze labyrinth, palace, pyramid and crypt,
Baths, galleries, courts, temples and terraces,
Marts, theatres and wharfs — all filled with men,
Men everywhere! And this performed in turn,
When those who looked on, pined to hear the hopes
And fears and hates and loves which moved the crowd,
I would throw down the pencil as the chisel,
And I would speak; no thought which ever stirred
A human breast should be untold; all passions,
All soft emotions, from the turbulent stir
Within a heart fed with desires like mine,
To the last comfort shutting the tired lids
Of him who sleeps the sultry noon away
Beneath the tent-tree by the wayside well:
And this in language as the need should be,
Now poured at once forth in a burning flow,
Now piled up in a grand array of words.
This done, to perfect and consummate all,

Even as a luminous haze links star to star,
I would supply all chasms with music, breathing
Mysterious motions of the soul, no way
To be defined save in strange melodies.
Last, having thus revealed all I could love,
Having received all love bestowed on it,
I would die: preserving so throughout my course
God full on me, as I was full on men:
He would approve my prayer, "I have gone through
The loveliness of life; create for me
If not for men, or take me to thyself,
Eternal, infinite love!"
      If thou hast ne'er
Conceived this mighty aim, this full desire,
Thou hast not passed my trial, and thou art
No king of mine.
 Par.   Ah me!
 Apr.   But thou art here!
Thou didst not gaze like me upon that end
Till thine own powers for compassing the bliss
Were blind with glory; nor grow mad to grasp
At once the prize long patient toil should claim,
Nor spurn all granted short of that. And I
Would do as thou, a second time: nay, listen!
Knowing ourselves, our world, our task so great,
Our time so brief, 't is clear if we refuse
The means so limited, the tools so rude
To execute our purpose, life will fleet,
And we shall fade, and leave our task undone.
We will be wise in time: what though our work
Be fashioned in despite of their ill-service,
Be crippled every way? 'T were little praise
Did full resources wait on our goodwill
At every turn. Let all be as it is.
Some say the earth is even so contrived
That tree and flower, a vesture gay, conceal
A bare and skeleton framework. Had we means
Answering to our mind! But now I seem
Wrecked on a savage isle: how rear thereon
My palace? Branching palms the props shall be,
Fruit glossy mingling; gems are for the East;
Who heeds them? I can pass them. Serpents' scales,
And painted birds' down, furs and fishes' skins
Must help me; and a little here and there
Is all I can aspire to: still my art
Shall show its birth was in a gentler clime.

"Had I green jars of malachite, this way
I'd range them: where those sea-shells glisten above,
Cressets should hang, by right: this way we set
The purple carpets, as these mats are laid,
Woven of fern and rush and blossoming flag."
Or if, by fortune, some completer grace
Be spared to me, some fragment, some slight sample
Of the prouder workmanship my own home boasts,
Some trifle little heeded there, but here
The place's one perfection — with what joy
Would I enshrine the relic, cheerfully
Foregoing all the marvels out of reach!
Could I retain one strain of all the psalm
Of the angels, one word of the fiat of God,
To let my followers know what such things are!
I would adventure nobly for their sakes:
When nights were still, and still the moaning sea,
And far away I could descry the land
Whence I departed, whither I return,
I would dispart the waves, and stand once more
At home, and load my bark, and hasten back,
And fling my gains to them, worthless or true.
"Friends," I would say, "I went far, far for them,
Past the high rocks the haunt of doves, the mounds
Of red earth from whose sides strange trees grow out,
Past tracts of milk-white minute blinding sand,
Till, by a mighty moon, I tremblingly
Gathered these magic herbs, berry and bud,
In haste, not pausing to reject the weeds,
But happy plucking them at any price.
To me, who have seen them bloom in their own soil,
They are scarce lovely: plait and wear them, you!
And guess, from what they are, the springs that fed them,
The stars that sparkled o'er them, night by night,
The snakes that travelled far to sip their dew!"
Thus for my higher loves; and thus even weakness
Would win me honor. But not these alone
Should claim my care; for common life, its wants
And ways, would I set forth in beauteous hues:
The lowest hind should not possess a hope,
A fear, but I'd be by him, saying better
Than he his own heart's language. I would live
Forever in the thoughts I thus explored,
As a discoverer's memory is attached
To all he finds; they should be mine henceforth,
Imbued with me, though free to all before:

For clay, once cast into my soul's rich mine,
Should come up crusted o'er with gems. Nor this
Would need a meaner spirit than the first;
Nay, 't would be but the selfsame spirit, clothed
In humbler guise, but still the selfsame spirit:
As one spring wind unbinds the mountain snow
And comforts violets in their hermitage.

But, master, poet, who hast done all this,
How didst thou 'scape the ruin whelming me?
Didst thou, when nerving thee to this attempt,
Ne'er range thy mind's extent, as some wide hall,
Dazzled by shapes that filled its length with light,
Shapes clustered there to rule thee, not obey,
That will not wait thy summons, will not rise
Singly, nor when thy practised eye and hand
Can well transfer their loveliness, but crowd
By thee forever, bright to thy despair?
Didst thou ne'er gaze on each by turns, and ne'er
Resolve to single out one, though the rest
Should vanish, and to give that one, entire
In beauty, to the world; forgetting, so,
Its peers, whose number baffles mortal power?
And, this determined, wast thou ne'er seduced
By memories and regrets and passionate love,
To glance once more farewell? and did their eyes
Fasten thee, brighter and more bright, until
Thou couldst but stagger back unto their feet,
And laugh that man's applause or welfare ever
Could tempt thee to forsake them? Or when years
Had passed and still their love possessed thee wholly,
When from without some murmur startled thee
Of darkling mortals famished for one ray
Of thy so-hoarded luxury of light,
Didst thou ne'er strive even yet to break those spells
And prove thou couldst recover and fulfil
Thy early mission, long ago renounced,
And to that end, select some shape once more?
And did not mist-like influences, thick films,
Faint memories of the rest that charmed so long
Thine eyes, float fast, confuse thee, bear thee off,
As whirling snow-drifts blind a man who treads
A mountain ridge, with guiding spear, through storm?
Say, though I fell, I had excuse to fall;
Say, I was tempted sorely: say but this,
Dear lord, Aprile's lord!
 Par.   Clasp me not thus,

Aprile! That the truth should reach me thus!
We are weak dust. Nay, clasp not or I faint!
　　Apr. My king! and envious thoughts could outrage
　　　　thee?
Lo, I forget my ruin, and rejoice
In thy success, as thou! Let our God's praise
Go bravely through the world at last! What care
Through me or thee? I feel thy breath. Why, tears?
Tears in the darkness, and from thee to me?
　　Par. Love me henceforth, Aprile, while I learn
To love; and, merciful God, forgive us both!
We wake at length from weary dreams; but both
Have slept in fairy-land: though dark and drear
Appears the world before us, we no less
Wake with our wrists and ankles jewelled still.
I too have sought to KNOW as thou to LOVE —
Excluding love as thou refusedst knowledge.
Still thou hast beauty and I, power. We wake:
What penance canst devise for both of us?
　　Apr. I hear thee faintly. The thick darkness! Even
Thine eyes are hid. 'T is as I knew: I speak,
And now I die. But I have seen thy face!
O poet, think of me, and sing of me!
But to have seen thee and to die so soon!
　　Par. Die not, Aprile! We must never part.
Are we not halves of one dissevered world,
Whom this strange chance unites once more? Part?
　　　　never!
Till thou the lover, know; and I, the knower,
Love — until both are saved. Aprile, hear!
We will accept our gains, and use them — now!
God, he will die upon my breast! Aprile!
　　Apr. To speak but once, and die! yet by his side.
Hush! hush!
　　　　　　Ha! go you ever girt about
With phantoms, powers? I have created such,
But these seem real as I.
　　Par.　　　　Whom can you see
Through the accursed darkness?
　　Apr.　　　　　　Stay; I know,
I know them: who should know them well as I?
White brows, lit up with glory; poets all!
　　Par. Let him but live, and I have my reward!
　　Apr. Yes; I see now. God is the perfect poet,
Who in his person acts his own creations.
Had you but told me this at first! Hush! hush!

Par. Live! for my sake, because of my great sin,
To help my brain, oppressed by these wild words
And their deep import. Live! 't is not too late.
I have a quiet home for us, and friends.
Michal shall smile on you. Hear you? Lean thus,
And breathe my breath. I shall not lose one word
Of all your speech, one little word, Aprile!
   Apr. No, no. Crown me? I am not one of you!
'T is he, the king, you seek. I am not one.
   Par. Thy spirit, at least, Aprile! Let me love.

I have attained, and now I may depart.

III. PARACELSUS.

SCENE, *Basel; a chamber in the house of Paracelsus.* 1526.

PARACELSUS, FESTUS.

   Par. Heap logs and let the blaze laugh out!
   Fest.   True, true!
'T is very fit all, time and chance and change
Have wrought since last we sat thus, face to face
And soul to soul — all cares, far-looking fears,
Vague apprehensions, all vain fancies bred
By your long absence, should be cast away,
Forgotten in this glad unhoped renewal
Of our affections.
   Par.   Oh, omit not aught
Which witnesses your own and Michal's own
Affection: spare not that! Only forget
The honors and the glories and what not,
It pleases you to tell profusely out.
   Fest. Nay, even your honors, in a sense, I waive:
The wondrous Paracelsus, life's dispenser,
Fate's commissary, idol of the schools
And courts, shall be no more than Aureole still,
Still Aureole and my friend as when we parted
Some twenty years ago, and I restrained
As best I could the promptings of my spirit
Which secretly advanced you, from the first,
To the pre-eminent rank which, since, your own
Adventurous ardor, nobly triumphing,
Has won for you.
   Par.   Yes, yes. And Michal's face
Still wears that quiet and peculiar light
Like the dim circlet floating round a pearl?

Fest. Just so.

Par. And yet her calm sweet countenance,
Though saintly, was not sad ; for she would sing
Alone. Does she still sing alone, bird-like,
Not dreaming you are near? Her carols dropt
In flakes through that old leafy bower built under
The sunny wall at Würzburg, from her lattice
Among the trees above, while I, unseen,
Sat conning some rare scroll from Tritheim's shelves,
Much wondering notes so simple could divert
My mind from study. Those were happy days.
Respect all such as sing when all alone !

Fest. Scarcely alone : her children, you may guess,
Are wild beside her.

Par. Ah, those children quite
Unsettle the pure picture in my mind :
A girl, she was so perfect, so distinct :
No change, no change! Not but this added grace
May blend and harmonize with its compeers,
And Michal may become her motherhood ;
But 't is a change, and I detest all change,
And most a change in aught I loved long since.
So, Michal — you have said she thinks of me?

Fest. O very proud will Michal be of you !
Imagine how we sat, long winter-nights,
Scheming and wondering, shaping your presumed
Adventure, or devising its reward;
Shutting out fear with all the strength of hope.
For it was strange how, even when most secure
In our domestic peace, a certain dim
And flitting shade could sadden all ; it seemed
A restlessness of heart, a silent yearning,
A sense of something wanting, incomplete —
Not to be put in words, perhaps avoided
By mute consent — but, said or unsaid, felt
To point to one so loved and so long lost.
And then the hopes rose and shut out the fears —
How you would laugh should I recount them now !
I still predicted your return at last
With gifts beyond the greatest of them all,
All Tritheim's wondrous troop ; did one of which
Attain renown by any chance, I smiled,
As well aware of who would prove his peer.
Michal was sure some woman, long ere this,
As beautiful as you were sage, had loved . . .

Par. Far-seeing, truly, to discern so much

In the fantastic projects and day-dreams
Of a raw restless boy!
    Fest.   Oh, no: the sunrise
Well warranted our faith in this full noon!
Can I forget the anxious voice which said,
" Festus, have thoughts like these e'er shaped themselves
In other brains than mine? have their possessors
Existed in like circumstance? were they weak
As I, or ever constant from the first,
Despising youth's allurements and rejecting
As spider-films the shackles I endure?
Is there hope for me?" — and I answered gravely
As an acknowledged elder, calmer, wiser,
More gifted mortal. O you must remember,
For all your glorious . . .
    Par.   Glorious? ay, this hair,
These hands — nay, touch them, they are mine! Recall
With all the said recallings, times when thus
To lay them by your own ne'er turned you pale
As now. Most glorious, are they not?
    Fest.   Why — why —
Something must be subtracted from success
So wide, no doubt. He would be scrupulous, truly,
Who should object such drawbacks. Still, still, Aureole,
You are changed, very changed! 'T were losing nothing
To look well to it: you must not be stolen
From the enjoyment of your well-won meed.
    Par. My friend! you seek my pleasure, past a doubt:
You will best gain your point, by talking, not
Of me, but of yourself.
    Fest.   Have I not said
All touching Michal and my children? Sure
You know, by this, full well how Aennchen looks
Gravely, while one disparts her thick brown hair;
And Aureole's glee when some stray gannet builds
Amid the birch-trees by the lake. Small hope
Have I that he will honor (the wild imp)
His namesake. Sigh not! 't is too much to ask
That all we love should reach the same proud fate.
But you are very kind to humor me
By showing interest in my quiet life;
You, who of old could never tame yourself
To tranquil pleasures, must at heart despise . . .
    Par. Festus, strange secrets are let out by death
Who blabs so oft the follies of this world:
And I am death's familiar, as you know.

I helped a man to die, some few weeks since,
Warped even from his go-cart to one end —
The living on princes' smiles, reflected from
A mighty herd of favorites. No mean trick
He left untried, and truly well-nigh wormed
All traces of God's finger out of him:
Then died, grown old. And just an hour before,
Having lain long with blank and soulless eyes,
He sat up suddenly, and with natural voice
Said that in spite of thick air and closed doors
God told him it was June; and he knew well,
Without such telling, harebells grew in June;
And all that kings could ever give or take
Would not be precious as those blooms to him.
Just so, allowing I am passing sage,
It seems to me much worthier argument
Why pansies,* eyes that laugh, bear beauty's prize
From violets, eyes that dream — (your Michal's choice) —
Than all fools find to wonder at in me
Or in my fortunes. And be very sure
I say this from no prurient restlessness,
No self-complacency, itching to turn,
Vary and view its pleasure from all points,
And, in this instance, willing other men
May be at pains, demonstrate to itself
The realness of the very joy it tastes.
What should delight me like the news of friends
Whose memories were a solace to me oft,
As mountain-baths to wild fowls in their flight?
Ofter than you had wasted thought on me
Had you been wise, and rightly valued bliss.
But there's no taming nor repressing hearts:
God knows I need such! — So, you heard me speak?
    Fest. Speak? when?
    Par. When but this morning at my class?
There was noise and crowd enough. I saw you not.
Surely you know I am engaged to fill
The chair here? — that 't is part of my proud fate
To lecture to as many thick-skulled youths
As please, each day, to throng the theatre,
To my great reputation, and no small
Danger of Basel's benches long unused
To crack beneath such honor?
    Fest. I was there;
I mingled with the throng: shall I avow

---

* Citrinula (flammula) herba Paracelso multum familiaris. —

Small care was mine to listen? — too intent
On gathering from the murmurs of the crowd
A full corroboration of my hopes!
What can I learn about your powers? but they
Know, care for nought beyond your actual state,
Your actual value; yet they worship you,
Those various natures whom you sway as one!
But ere I go, be sure I shall attend . . .
    Par. Stop, o' God's name: the thing's by no means yet
Past remedy! Shall I read this morning's labor
— At least in substance? Nought so worth the gaining
As an apt scholar! Thus then, with all due
Precision and emphasis — you, beside, are clearly
Guiltless of understanding more, a whit,
The subject than your stool — allowed to be
A notable advantage.
    Fest.   Surely, Aureole,
You laugh at me!
    Par.   I laugh? Ha, ha! thank heaven,
I charge you, if 't be so! for I forget
Much, and what laughter should be like. No less,
However, I forego that luxury
Since it alarms the friend who brings it back.
True, laughter like my own must echo strangely
To thinking men; a smile were better far;
So, make me smile! If the exulting look
You wore but now be smiling, 't is so long
Since I have smiled! Alas, such smiles are born
Alone of hearts like yours, or herdsmen's souls
Of ancient time, whose eyes, calm as their flocks,
Saw in the stars mere garnishry of heaven,
And in the earth a stage for altars only.
Never change, Festus: I say, never change!
    Fest. My God, if he be wretched after all!
    Par. When last we parted, Festus, you declared,
— Or Michal, yes, her soft lips whispered words
I have preserved. She told me she believed
I should succeed (meaning, that in the search
I then engaged in, I should meet success)
And yet be wretched: now, she augured false.
    Fest. Thank heaven! but you spoke strangely: could I
      venture
To think bare apprehension lest your friend,
Dazzled by your resplendent course, might find
Henceforth less sweetness in his own, could move
Such earnest mood in you? Fear not, dear friend,

That I shall leave you, inwardly repining
Your lot was not my own!
  Par.   And this forever!
Forever! gull who may, they will be gulled!
They will not look nor think; 't is nothing new
In them: but surely he is not of them!
My Festus, do you know, I reckoned, you —
Though all beside were sand-blind — you, my friend,
Would look at me, once close, with piercing eye
Untroubled by the false glare that confounds
A weaker vision: would remain serene,
Though singular amid a gaping throng.
I feared you, or I had come, sure, long ere this,
To Einsiedeln. Well, error has no end,
And Rhasis is a sage, and Basel boasts
A tribe of wits, and I am wise and blest
Past all dispute! 'T is vain to fret at it.
I have vowed long ago my worshippers
Shall owe to their own deep sagacity
All further information, good or bad.
Small risk indeed my reputation runs,
Unless perchance the glance now searching me
Be fixed much longer; for it seems to spell
Dimly the characters a simpler man
Might read distinct enough. Old eastern books
Say, the fallen prince of morning some short space
Remained unchanged in semblance; nay, his brow
Was hued with triumph: every spirit then
Praising, *his* heart on flame the while: — a tale!
Well, Festus, what discover you, I pray?
  Fest. Some foul deed sullies then a life which else
Were raised supreme?
  Par.   Good: I do well, most well!
Why strive to make men hear, feel, fret themselves
With what is past their power to comprehend?
I should not strive now: only, having nursed
The faint surmise that one yet walked the earth,
One, at least, not the utter fool of show,
Not absolutely formed to be the dupe
Of shallow plausibilities alone:
One who, in youth, found wise enough to choose
The happiness his riper years approve,
Was yet so anxious for another's sake,
That, ere his friend could rush upon a mad
And ruinous course, the converse of his own,
His gentle spirit essayed, prejudged for him

The perilous path, foresaw its destiny,
And warned the weak one in such tender words,
Such accents — his whole heart in every tone —
That oft their memory comforted that friend
When it by right should have increased despair:
— Having believed, I say, that this one man
Could never lose the light thus from the first
His portion — how should I refuse to grieve
At even my gain if it disturb our old
Relation, if it make me out more wise?
Therefore, once more reminding him how well
He prophesied, I note the single flaw
That spoils his prophet's title. In plain words,
You were deceived, and thus were you deceived —
I have not been successful, and yet am
Most miserable; 't is said at last; nor you
Give credit, lest you force me to concede
That common sense yet lives upon the world!
   Fest. You surely do not mean to banter me?
   Par. You know, or — if you have been wise enough
To cleanse your memory of such matters — knew,
As far as words of mine could make it clear,
That 't was my purpose to find joy or grief
Solely in the fulfilment of my plan
Or plot or whatsoe'er it was; rejoicing
Alone as it proceeded prosperously,
Sorrowing then only when mischance retarded
Its progress. That was in those Würzburg days!
Not to prolong a theme I thoroughly hate,
I have pursued this plan with all my strength;
And having failed therein most signally,
Cannot object to ruin utter and drear
As all-excelling would have been the prize
Had fortune favored me. I scarce have right
To vex your frank good spirit late so glad
In my supposed prosperity, I know,
And, were I lucky in a glut of friends,
Would well agree to let your error live,
Nay, strengthen it with fables of success.
But mine is no condition to refuse
The transient solace of so rare a godsend,
My solitary luxury, my one friend:
Accordingly I venture to put off
The wearisome vest of falsehood galling me,
Secure when he is by. I lay me bare,
Prone at his mercy — but he is my friend!

Not that he needs retain his aspect grave;
That answers not my purpose; for 't is like,
Some sunny morning — Basel being drained
Of its wise population, every corner
Of the amphitheatre crammed with learned clerks,
Here Œcolampadius, looking worlds of wit,
Here Castellanus, as profound as he,
Munsterus here, Frobenius there, all squeezed
And staring, — that the zany of the show,
Even Paracelsus, shall put off before them
His trappings with a grace but seldom judged
Expedient in such cases : — the grim smile
That will go round! Is it not therefore best
To venture a rehearsal like the present
In a small way? Where are the signs I seek,
The first-fruits and fair sample of the scorn
Due to all quacks? Why, this will never do!
 Fest. These are foul vapors, Aureole; nought beside!
The effect of watching, study, weariness.
Were there a spark of truth in the confusion
Of these wild words, you would not outrage thus
Your youth's companion. I shall ne'er regard
These wanderings, bred of faintness and much study.
'T is not thus you would trust a trouble to me,
To Michal's friend.
 Par.   I have said it, dearest Festus!
For the manner, 't is ungracious probably;
You may have it told in broken sobs, one day,
And scalding tears, ere long: but I thought best
To keep that off as long as possible.
Do you wonder still?
 Fest.   No; it must oft fall out
That one whose labor perfects any work,
Shall rise from it with eye so worn that he
Of all men least can measure the extent
Of what he has accomplished. He alone
Who, nothing tasked, is nothing weary too,
May clearly scan the little he effects:
But we, the bystanders, untouched by toil,
Estimate each aright.
 Par.   This worthy Festus
Is one of them, at last! 'T is so with all!
First, they set down all progress as a dream;
And next, when he whose quick discomfiture
Was counted on, accomplishes some few
And doubtful steps in his career, — behold,

They look for every inch of ground to vanish
Beneath his tread, so sure they spy success!
   Fest. Few doubtful steps? when death retires before
Your presence — when the noblest of mankind,
Broken in body or subdued in soul,
May through your skill renew their vigor, raise
The shattered frame to pristine stateliness?
When men in racking pain may purchase dreams
Of what delights them most, swooning at once
Into a sea of bliss or rapt along
As in a flying sphere of turbulent light?
When we may look to you as one ordained
To free the flesh from fell disease, as frees
Our Luther's burning tongue the fettered soul?
When . . .
   Par. When and where, the devil, did you get
This notable news?
   Fest. Even from the common voice;
From those whose envy, daring not dispute
The wonders it decries, attributes them
To magic and such folly.
   Par. Folly? Why not
To magic, pray? You find a comfort doubtless
In holding, God ne'er troubles him about
Us or our doings: once we were judged worth
The devil's tempting . . . I offend: forgive me,
And rest content. Your prophecy on the whole
Was fair enough as prophesyings go;
At fault a little in detail, but quite
Precise enough in the main; and hereupon
I pay due homage: you guessed long ago
(The prophet!) I should fail — and I have failed.
   Fest. You mean to tell me, then, the hopes which fed
Your youth have not been realized as yet?
Some obstacle has barred them hitherto?
Or that their innate . . .
   Par. As I said but now,
You have a very decent prophet's fame,
So you but shun details here. Little matter
Whether those hopes were mad, — the aims they sought,
Safe and secure from all ambitious fools;
Or whether my weak wits are overcome
By what a better spirit would scorn: I fail.
And now methinks 't were best to change a theme
I am a sad fool to have stumbled on.
I say confusedly what comes uppermost;

But there are times when patience proves at fault,
As now: this morning's strange encounter — you
Beside me once again! you, whom I guessed
Alive, since hitherto (with Luther's leave)
No friend have I among the saints at peace,
To judge by any good their prayers effect.
I knew you would have helped me — why not he,
My strange competitor in enterprise,
Bound for the same end by another path,
Arrived, or ill or well, before the time,
At our disastrous journey's doubtful close?
How goes it with Aprile? Ah, they miss
Your lone sad sunny idleness of heaven,
Our martyrs for the world's sake; heaven shuts fast:
The poor mad poet is howling by this time!
Since you are my sole friend then, here or there,
I could not quite repress the varied feelings
This meeting wakens; they have had their vent,
And now forget them. Do the rear-mice still
Hang like a fretwork on the gate (or what
In my time was a gate) fronting the road
From Einsiedeln to Lachen?
  Fest.   Trifle not:
Answer me, for my sake alone! You smiled
Just now, when I supposed some deed, unworthy
Yourself, might blot the else so bright result;
Yet if your motives have continued pure,
Your will unfaltering, and in spite of this,
You have experienced a defeat, why then
I say not you would cheerfully withdraw
From contest — mortal hearts are not so fashioned —
But surely you would ne'ertheless withdraw.
You sought not fame nor gain nor even love,
No end distinct from knowledge, — I repeat
Your very words: once satisfied that knowledge
Is a mere dream, you would announce as much,
Yourself the first. But how is the event?
You are defeated — and I find you here!
  Par. As though "here" did not signify defeat!
I spoke not of my little labors here,
But of the break-down of my general aims:
For you, aware of their extent and scope,
To look on these sage lecturings, approved
By beardless boys, and bearded dotards worse,
As a fit consummation of such aims,
Is worthy notice. A professorship

At Basel! Since you see so much in it,
And think my life was reasonably drained
Of life's delights to render me a match
For duties arduous as such post demands, —
Be it far from me to deny my power
To fill the petty circle lotted out
Of infinite space, or justify the host
Of honors thence accruing. So, take notice,
This jewel dangling from my neck preserves
The features of a prince, my skill restored
To plague his people some few years to come:
And all through a pure whim. He had eased the earth
For me, but that the droll despair which seized
The vermin of his household, tickled me.
I came to see. Here, drivelled the physician,
Whose most infallible nostrum was at fault;
There quaked the astrologer, whose horoscope
Had promised him interminable years;
Here a monk fumbled at the sick man's mouth
With some undoubted relic — a sudary
Of the Virgin; while another piebald knave
Of the same brotherhood (he loved them ever)
Was actively preparing 'neath his nose
Such a suffumigation as, once fired,
Had stunk the patient dead ere he could groan.
I cursed the doctor and upset the brother,
Brushed past the conjurer, vowed that the first gust
Of stench from the ingredients just alight
Would raise a cross-grained devil in my sword,
Not easily laid: and ere an hour the prince
Slept as he never slept since prince he was.
A day — and I was posting for my life,
Placarded through the town as one whose spite
Had near availed to stop the blessed effects
Of the doctor's nostrum which, well seconded
By the sudary, and most by the costly smoke —
Not leaving out the strenuous prayers sent up
Hard by in the abbey — raised the prince to life:
To the great reputation of the seer
Who, confident, expected all along
The glad event — the doctor's recompense —
Much largess from his highness to the monks —
And the vast solace of his loving people,
Whose general satisfaction to increase,
The prince was pleased no longer to defer
The burning of some dozen heretics

Remanded till God's mercy should be shown
Touching his sickness: last of all were joined
Ample directions to all loyal folk
To swell the complement by seizing me
Who — doubtless some rank sorcerer — endeavored
To thwart these pious offices, obstruct
The prince's cure, and frustrate heaven by help
Of certain devils dwelling in his sword.
By luck, the prince in his first fit of thanks
Had forced this bauble on me as an earnest
Of further favors. This one case may serve
To give sufficient taste of many such,
So, let them pass. Those shelves support a pile
Of patents, licenses, diplomas, titles
From Germany, France, Spain, and Italy;
They authorize some honor; ne'ertheless,
I set more store by this Erasmus sent;
He trusts me; our Frobenius is his friend,
And him " I raised " (nay, read it) " from the dead."
I weary you, I see. I merely sought
To show, there's no great wonder after all
That, while I fill the class-room and attract
A crowd to Basel, I get leave to stay,
And therefore need not scruple to accept
The utmost they can offer, if I please:
For 't is but right the world should be prepared
To treat with favor e'en fantastic wants
Of one like me, used up in serving her.
Just as the mortal, whom the gods in part
Devoured, received in place of his lost limb
Some virtue or other — cured disease, I think;
You mind the fables we have read together.
   Fest. You do not think I comprehend a word.
The time was, Aureole, you were apt enough
To clothe the airiest thoughts in specious breath;
But surely you must feel how vague and strange
These speeches sound.
   Par.   Well, then: you know my hopes
I am assured, at length, those hopes were vain;
That truth is just as far from me as ever;
That I have thrown my life away; that sorrow
On that account is idle, and further effort
To mend and patch what's marred beyond repairing,
As useless: and all this was taught your friend
By the convincing good old-fashioned method
Of force — by sheer compulsion. Is that plain?

Fest. Dear Aureole, can it be my fears were just?
God wills not . . .
    Par.   Now, 't is this I most admire —
The constant talk men of your stamp keep up
Of God's will, as they style it; one would swear
Man had but merely to uplift his eye,
And see the will in question charactered
On the heaven's vault. 'T is hardly wise to moot
Such topics: doubts are many and faith is weak.
I know as much of any will of God
As knows some dumb and tortured brute what Man,
His stern lord, wills from the perplexing blows
That plague him every way; but there, of course,
Where least he suffers, longest he remains —
My case; and for such reasons I plod on,
Subdued but not convinced. I know as little
Why I deserve to fail, as why I hoped
Better things in my youth. I simply know
I am no master here, but trained and beaten
Into the path I tread; and here I stay,
Until some further intimation reach me,
Like an obedient drudge. Though I prefer
To view the whole thing as a task imposed
Which, whether dull or pleasant, must be done —
Yet, I deny not, there is made provision
Of joys which tastes less jaded might affect;
Nay, some which please me too, for all my pride —
Pleasures that once were pains: the iron ring
Festering about a slave's neck grows at length
Into the flesh it eats. I hate no longer
A host of petty vile delights, undreamed of
Or spurned before; such now supply the place
Of my dead aims: as in the autumn woods
Where tall trees used to flourish, from their roots
Springs up a fungous brood sickly and pale,
Chill mushrooms colored like a corpse's cheek.
    Fest. If I interpret well your words, I own
It troubles me but little that your aims,
Vast in their dawning and most likely grown
Extravagantly since, have baffled you.
Perchance I am glad; you merit greater praise;
Because they are too glorious to be gained,
You do not blindly cling to them and die;
You fell, but have not sullenly refused
To rise, because an angel worsted you
In wrestling, though the world holds not your peer;

And though too harsh and sudden is the change
To yield content as yet, still you pursue
The ungracious path as though 't were rosy-strewn.
'T is well: and your reward, or soon or late,
Will come from him whom no man serves in vain.
 Par. Ah, very fine! For my part, I conceive
The very pausing from all further toil,
Which you find heinous, would become a seal
To the sincerity of all my deeds.
To be consistent I should die at once;
I calculated on no after-life;
Yet (how crept in, how fostered, I know not)
Here am I with as passionate regret
For youth and health and love so vainly lavished,
As if their preservation had been first
And foremost in my thoughts; and this strange **fact**
Humbled me wondrously, and had due force
In rendering me the less averse to follow
A certain counsel, a mysterious warning —
You will not understand — but 't was a man
With aims not mine and yet pursued like mine,
With the same fervor and no more success,
Perishing in my sight; who summoned me,
As I would shun the ghastly fate I saw,
To serve my race at once; to wait no longer
That God should interfere in my behalf,
But to distrust myself, put pride away,
And give my gains, imperfect as they were,
To men. I have not leisure to explain
How, since, a singular series of events
Has raised me to the station you behold,
Wherein I seem to turn to most account
The mere wreck of the past, — perhaps receive
Some feeble glimmering token that God views
And may approve my penance: therefore here
You find me, doing most good or least harm.
And if folks wonder much and profit little
'T is not my fault; only, I shall rejoice
When my part in the farce is shuffled through,
And the curtain falls: I must hold out till then.
 Fest. Till when, dear Aureole?
 Par.   Till I 'm fairly **thrust**
From my proud eminence. Fortune is fickle
And even professors fall: should that arrive,
I see no sin in ceding to my bent.
You little fancy what rude shocks apprise us

We sin ; God's intimations rather fail
In clearness than in energy : 't were well
Did they but indicate the course to take
Like that to be forsaken. I would fain
Be spared a further sample. Here I stand,
And here I stay, be sure, till forced to flit.
  Fest. Be you but firm on that head ! long ere then
All I expect will come to pass, I trust:
The cloud that wraps you will have disappeared.
Meantime, I see small chance of such event :
They praise you here as one whose lore, already
Divulged, eclipses all the past can show,
But whose achievements, marvellous as they be,
Are faint anticipations of a glory
About to be revealed. When Basel's crowds
Dismiss their teacher, I shall be content
That he depart.
  Par. This favor at their hands
I look for earlier than your view of things
Would warrant. Of the crowd you saw to-day,
Remove the full half sheer amazement draws,
Mere novelty, nought else ; and next, the tribe
Whose innate blockish dulness just perceives
That unless miracles (as seem my works)
Be wrought in their behalf, their chance is slight
To puzzle the devil ; next, the numerous set
Who bitterly hate established schools, and help
The teacher that oppugns them, till he once
Have planted his own doctrine, when the teacher
May reckon on their rancor in his turn ;
Take, too, the sprinkling of sagacious knaves
Whose cunning runs not counter to the vogue,
But seeks, by flattery and crafty nursing,
To force my system to a premature
Short-lived development. Why swell the list ?
Each has his end to serve, and his best way
Of serving it : remove all these, remains
A scantling, a poor dozen at the best,
Worthy to look for sympathy and service,
And likely to draw profit from my pains.
  Fest. 'T is no encouraging picture : still these few
Redeem their fellows. Once the germ implanted,
Its growth, if slow, is sure.
  Par.   God grant it so !
I would make some amends : but if I fail,
The luckless rogues have this excuse to urge,

That much is in my method and my manner,
My uncouth habits, my impatient spirit,
Which hinders of reception and result
My doctrine : much to say, small skill to speak!
These old aims suffered not a looking-off
Though for an instant; therefore, only when
I thus renounced them and resolved to reap
Some present fruit — to teach mankind some truth
So dearly purchased — only then I found
Such teaching was an art requiring cares
And qualities peculiar to itself :
That to possess was one thing — to display
Another. With renown first in my thoughts,
Or popular praise, I had soon discovered it:
One grows but little apt to learn these things.
  Fest. If it be so, which nowise I believe,
There needs no waiting fuller dispensation
To leave a labor of so little use.
Why not throw up the irksome charge at once ?
  Par. A task, a task !
                    But wherefore hide the whole
Extent of degradation, once engaged
In the confessing vein ? Despite of all
My fine talk of obedience and repugnance,
Docility and what not, 't is yet to learn
If when the task shall really be performed,
My inclination free to choose once more,
I shall do aught but slightly modify
The nature of the hated task I quit.
In plain words, I am spoiled ; my life still tends
As first it tended ; I am broken and trained
To my old habits: they are part of me.
I know, and none so well, my darling ends
Are proved impossible : no less, no less,
Even now what humors me, fond fool, as when
Their faint ghosts sit with me and flatter me
And send me back content to my dull round ?
How can I change this soul ? — this apparatus
Constructed solely for their purposes,
So well adapted to their every want,
To search out and discover, prove and perfect;
This intricate machine whose most minute
And meanest motions have their charm to me
Though to none else — an aptitude I seize,
An object I perceive, a use, a meaning,
A property, a fitness, I explain

And I alone: — how can I change my soul?
And this wronged body, worthless save when tasked
Under that soul's dominion — used to care
For its bright master's cares and quite subdue
Its proper cravings — not to ail nor pine
So he but prosper — whither drag this poor
Tried patient body? God! how I essayed
To live like that mad poet, for a while,
To love alone; and how I felt too warped
And twisted and deformed! What should I do,
Even though released from drudgery, but return
Faint, as you see, and halting, blind and sore,
To my old life and die as I began?
I cannot feed on beauty for the sake
Of beauty only, nor can drink in balm
From lovely objects for their loveliness;
My nature cannot lose her first imprint;
I still must hoard and heap and class all truths
With one ulterior purpose: I must know!
Would God translate me to his throne, believe
That I should only listen to his word
To further my own aim! For other men,
Beauty is prodigally strewn around,
And I were happy could I quench as they
This mad and thriveless longing, and content me
With beauty for itself alone: alas,
I have addressed a frock of heavy mail
Yet may not join the troop of sacred knights;
And now the forest-creatures fly from me,
The grass-banks cool, the sunbeams warm no more.
Best follow, dreaming that ere night arrive,
I shall o'ertake the company and ride
Glittering as they!
    Fest.   I think I apprehend
What you would say: if you, in truth, design
To enter once more on the life thus left,
Seek not to hide that all this consciousness
Of failure is assumed!
    Par.   My friend, my friend,
I toil, you listen; I explain, perhaps
You understand: there our communion ends.
Have you learnt nothing from to-day's discourse?
When we would thoroughly know the sick man's state
We feel awhile the fluttering pulse, press soft
The hot brow, look upon the languid eye,
And thence divine the rest. Must I lay bare

My heart, hideous and beating, or tear up
My vitals for your gaze, ere you will deem
Enough made known? You! who are you, forsooth?
That is the crowning operation claimed
By the arch-demonstrator — heaven the hall,
And earth the audience. Let Aprile and you
Secure good places: 't will be worth the while.
 Fest. Are you mad, Aureole? What can I have said
To call for this? I judged from your own words.
 Par. Oh, doubtless! A sick wretch describes the ape
That mocks him from the bed-foot, and all gravely
You thither turn at once: or he recounts
The perilous journey he has late performed,
And you are puzzled much how that could be!
You find me here, half stupid and half mad;
It makes no part of my delight to search
Into these matters, much less undergo
Another's scrutiny; but so it chances
That I am led to trust my state to you:
And the event is, you combine, contrast
And ponder on my foolish words as though
They thoroughly conveyed all hidden here —
Here, loathsome with despair and hate and rage!
Is there no fear, no shrinking and no shame?
Will you guess nothing? will you spare me nothing?
Must I go deeper? Ay or no?
 Fest.   Dear friend . . .
 Par. True: I am brutal — 't is a part of it;
The plague's sign — you are not a lazar-haunter,
How should you know? Well then, you think it strange
I should profess to have failed utterly,
And yet propose an ultimate return
To courses void of hope: and this, because
You know not what temptation is, nor how
'T is like to ply men in the sickliest part.
You are to understand that we who make
Sport for the gods, are hunted to the end:
There is not one sharp volley shot at us,
Which 'scaped with life, though hurt, we slacken pace
And gather by the wayside herbs and roots
To stanch our wounds, secure from further harm:
We are assailed to life's extremest verge.
It will be well indeed if I return,
A harmless busy fool, to my old ways!
I would forget hints of another fate,
Significant enough, which silent hours
Have lately scared me with.

Fest.   Another! and what?
Par.   After all, Festus, you say well: I am
A man yet: I need never humble me.
I would have been — something, I know not what;
But though I cannot soar, I do not crawl.
There are worse portions than this one of mine.
You say well!
    Fest.   Ah!
    Par.   And deeper degradation!
If the mean stimulants of vulgar praise,
If vanity should become the chosen food
Of a sunk mind, should stifle even the wish
To find its early aspirations true,
Should teach it to breathe falsehood like life-breath —
An atmosphere of craft and trick and lies;
Should make it proud to emulate, surpass
Base natures in the practices which woke
Its most indignant loathing once . . . No, no!
Utter damnation is reserved for hell!
I had immortal feelings; such shall never
Be wholly quenched: no, no!
                         My friend, you wear
A melancholy face, and certain 't is
There's little cheer in all this dismal work.
But was it my desire to set abroach
Such memories and forebodings? I foresaw
Where they would drive. 'T were better we discuss
News from Lucerne or Zurich; ask and tell
Of Egypt's flaring sky or Spain's cork-groves.
    Fest. I have thought: trust me, this mood will pass away!
I know you and the lofty spirit you bear,
And easily ravel out a clue to all.
These are the trials meet for such as you,
Nor must you hope exemption: to be mortal
Is to be plied with trials manifold.
Look round! The obstacles which kept the rest
From your ambition, have been spurned by you;
Their fears, their doubts, the chains that bind them all,
Were flax before your resolute soul, which nought
Avails to awe save these delusions bred
From its own strength, its selfsame strength disguised,
Mocking itself. Be brave, dear Aureole! Since
The rabbit has his shade to frighten him,
The fawn a rustling bough, mortals their cares,
And higher natures yet would slight and laugh

At these entangling fantasies, as you
At trammels of a weaker intellect, —
Measure your mind's height by the shade it casts!
I know you.
  Par. And I know you, dearest Festus!
And how you love unworthily; and how
All admiration renders blind.
  Fest.   You hold
That admiration blinds?
  Par.   Ay and alas!
  Fest. Nought blinds you less than admiration, friend:
Whether it be that all love renders wise
In its degree; from love which blends with love —
Heart answering heart — to love which spends itself
In silent mad idolatry of some
Pre-eminent mortal, some great soul of souls,
Which ne'er will know how well it is adored.
I say, such love is never blind; but rather
Alive to every the minutest spot
Which mars its object, and which hate (supposed
So vigilant and searching) dreams not of.
Love broods on such: what then? When first perceived
Is there no sweet strife to forget, to change,
To overflush those blemishes with all
The glow of general goodness they disturb?
— To make those very defects an endless source
Of new affection grown from hopes and fears?
And, when all fails, is there no gallant stand
Made even for much proved weak? no shrinking-back
Lest, since all love assimilates the soul
To what it loves, it should at length become
Almost a rival of its idol? Trust me,
If there be fiends who seek to work our hurt,
To ruin and drag down earth's mightiest spirits
Even at God's foot, 't will be from such as love,
Their zeal will gather most to serve their cause;
And least from those who hate, who most essay
By contumely and scorn to blot the light
Which forces entrance even to their hearts:
For thence will our defender tear the veil
And show within each heart, as in a shrine,
The giant image of perfection, grown
In hate's despite, whose calumnies were spawned
In the untroubled presence of its eyes.
True admiration blinds not; nor am I
So blind. I call your sin exceptional;

It springs from one whose life has passed the bounds
Prescribed to life. Compound that fault with God!
I speak of men; to common men like me
The weakness you reveal endears you more,
Like the far traces of decay in suns.
I bid you have good cheer!
  Par.   *Præclare! Optime!*
Think of a quiet mountain-cloistered priest
Instructing Paracelsus! yet 't is so.
Come, I will show you where my merit lies.
'T is in the advance of individual minds
That the slow crowd should ground their expectation
Eventually to follow; as the sea
Waits ages in its bed till some one wave
Out of the multitudinous mass, extends
The empire of the whole, some feet perhaps,
Over the strip of sand which could confine
Its fellows so long time: thenceforth the rest,
Even to the meanest, hurry in at once,
And so much is clear gained. I shall be glad
If all my labors, failing of aught else,
Suffice to make such inroad and procure
A wider range for thought: nay, they do this;
For, whatsoe'er my notions of true knowledge
And a legitimate success, may be,
I am not blind to my undoubted rank
When classed with others: I precede my age:
And whoso wills is very free to mount
These labors as a platform whence his own
May have a prosperous outset. But, alas!
My followers — they are noisy as you heard;
But, for intelligence, the best of them
So clumsily wield the weapons I supply
And they extol, that I begin to doubt
Whether their own rude clubs and pebble-stones
Would not do better service than my arms
Thus vilely swayed — if error will not fall
Sooner before the old awkward batterings
Than my more subtle warfare, not half learned.
 Fest. I would supply that art, then, or withhold
New arms until you teach their mystery.
 Par. Content you, 't is my wish; I have recourse
To the simplest training. Day by day I seek
To wake the mood, the spirit which alone
Can make those arms of any use to men.
Of course they are for swaggering forth at once

Graced with Ulysses' bow, Achilles' shield —
Flash on us, all in armor, thou Achilles!
Make our hearts dance to thy resounding step!
A proper sight to scare the crows away!
  Fest. Pity you choose not then some other method
Of coming at your point. The marvellous art
At length established in the world bids fair
To remedy all hindrances like these:
Trust to Frobenius' press the precious lore
Obscured by uncouth manner, or unfit
For raw beginners; let his types secure
A deathless monument to after-time;
Meanwhile wait confidently and enjoy
The ultimate effect: sooner or later
You shall be all-revealed.
  Par.   The old dull question
In a new form; no more. Thus: I possess
Two sorts of knowledge; one, — vast, shadowy,
Hints of the unbounded aim I once pursued:
The other consists of many secrets, caught
While bent on nobler prize, — perhaps a few
Prime principles which may conduct to much:
These last I offer to my followers here.
Now, bid me chronicle the first of these,
My ancient study, and in effect you bid
Revert to the wild courses just abjured:
I must go find them scattered through the world.
Then, for the principles, they are so simple
(Being chiefly of the overturning sort),
That one time is as proper to propound them
As any other — to-morrow at my class,
Or half a century hence embalmed in print.
For if mankind intend to learn at all,
They must begin by giving faith to them
And acting on them: and I do not see
But that my lectures serve indifferent well:
No doubt these dogmas fall not to the earth,
For all their novelty and rugged setting.
I think my class will not forget the day
I let them know the gods of Israel,
Aëtius, Oribasius, Galen, Rhasis,
Serapion, Avicenna, Averroës,
Were blocks!
  Fest. And that reminds me, I heard something
About your waywardness: you burned their books,
It seems, instead of answering those sages.

Par. And who said that?
Fest. Some I met yesternight
With Œcolampadius. As you know, the purpose
Of this short stay at Basel was to learn
His pleasure touching certain missives sent
For our Zuinglius and himself. 'T was he
Apprised me that the famous teacher here
Was my old friend.
Par. Ah, I forgot: you went . . .
Fest. From Zurich with advices for the ear
Of Luther, now at Wittenberg — (you know,
I make no doubt, the differences of late
With Carolostadius) — and returning sought
Basel and . . .
Par. I remember. Here's a case, now,
Will teach you why I answer not, but burn
The books you mention. Pray, does Luther dream
His arguments convince by their own force
The crowds that own his doctrine? No, indeed!
His plain denial of established points
Ages had sanctified and men supposed
Could never be oppugned while earth was under
And heaven above them — points which chance or time
Affected not — did more than the array
Of argument which followed. Boldly deny!
There is much breath-stopping, hair-stiffening
Awhile; then, amazed glances, mute awaiting
The thunderbolt which does not come; and next,
Reproachful wonder and inquiry: those
Who else had never stirred, are able now
To find the rest out for themselves, perhaps
To outstrip him who set the whole at work,
— As never will my wise class its instructor.
And you saw Luther?
Fest. 'T is a wondrous soul!
Par. True: the so-heavy chain which galled mankind
Is shattered, and the noblest of us all
Must bow to the deliverer — nay, the worker
Of our own project — we who long before
Had burst our trammels, but forgot the crowd,
We should have taught, still groaned beneath the load:
This he has done and nobly. Speed that may!
Whatever be my chance or my mischance,
What benefits mankind must glad me too;
And men seem made, though not as I believed,
For something better than the times produce.

Witness these gangs of peasants your new lights
From Suabia have possessed, whom Münzer leads,
And whom the duke, the landgrave and the elector
Will calm in blood! Well, well; 't is not my world!
  Fest. Hark!
  Par.   'T is the melancholy wind astir
Within the trees; the embers too are gray:
Morn must be near.
  Fest.   Best ope the casement: see,
The night, late strewn with clouds and flying stars,
Is blank and motionless: how peaceful sleep
The tree-tops altogether! Like an asp,
The wind slips whispering from bough to bough.
  Par. Ay; you would gaze on a wind-shaken tree
By the hour, nor count time lost.
  Fest.   So you shall gaze:
Those happy times will come again.
  Par.   Gone, gone,
Those pleasant times! Does not the moaning wind
Seem to bewail that we have gained such gains
And bartered sleep for them?
  Fest.   It is our trust
That there is yet another world to mend
All error and mischance.
  Par.   Another world!
And why this world, this common world, to be
A make-shift, a mere foil, how fair soever,
To some fine life to come? Man must be fed
With angels' food, forsooth; and some few traces
Of a diviner nature which look out
Through his corporeal baseness, warrant him
In a supreme contempt of all provision
For his inferior tastes — some straggling marks
Which constitute his essence, just as truly
As here and there a gem would constitute
The rock, their barren bed, one diamond.
But were it so — were man all mind — he gains
A station little enviable. From God
Down to the lowest spirit ministrant,
Intelligence exists which casts our mind
Into immeasurable shade. No, no:
Love, hope, fear, faith — these make humanity;
These are its sign and note and character,
And these I have lost! — gone, shut from me forever,
Like a dead friend safe from unkindness more!
See, morn at length. The heavy darkness seems

Diluted, gray and clear without the stars;
The shrubs bestir and rouse themselves, as if
Some snake, that weighed them down all night, let go
His hold; and from the East, fuller and fuller
Day, like a mighty river, flowing in;
But clouded, wintry, desolate and cold.
Yet see how that broad prickly star-shaped plant,
Half-down in the crevice, spreads its woolly leaves
All thick and glistering with diamond dew.
And you depart for Einsiedeln this day,
And we have spent all night in talk like this!
If you would have me better for your love,
Revert no more to these sad themes.
 Fest.   One favor,
And I have done. I leave you, deeply moved;
Unwilling to have fared so well, the while
My friend has changed so sorely. If this mood
Shall pass away, if light once more arise
Where all is darkness now, if you see fit
To hope and trust again, and strive again,
You will remember — not our love alone —
But that my faith in God's desire that man
Should trust on his support, (as I must think
You trusted) is obscured and dim through you:
For you are thus, and this is no reward.
Will you not call me to your side, dear Aureole?

IV. PARACELSUS ASPIRES.

SCENE, *Colmar in Alsatia; an Inn.* 1528.

PARACELSUS, FESTUS.

Par. (*to* JOHANNES OPORINUS, *his secretary*). *Sic itur
 ad astra!* Dear Von Visenburg
Is scandalized, and poor Torinus paralyzed,
And every honest soul that Basel holds
Aghast; and yet we live, as one may say,
Just as though Liechtenfels had never set
So true a value on his sorry carcass,
And learned Pütter had not frowned us dumb.
We live; and shall as surely start to-morrow
For Nuremberg, as we drink speedy scathe
To Basel in this mantling wine, suffused

A delicate blush, no fainter tinge is born
I' the shut heart of a bud. Pledge me, good John —
" Basel ; a hot plague ravage it, and Pütter
Oppose the plague ! " Even so ? Do you too share
Their panic, the reptiles ? Ha, ha ; faint through these,
Desist for these ! They manage matters so
At Basel, 't is like : but others may find means
To bring the stoutest braggart of the tribe
Once more to crouch in silence — means to breed
A stupid wonder in each fool again,
Now big with admiration at the skill
Which stript a vain pretender of his plumes :
And, that done, — means to brand each slavish brow
So deeply, surely, ineffaceably,
That henceforth flattery shall not pucker it
Out of the furrow ; there that stamp shall stay
To show the next they fawn on, what they are,
This Basel with its magnates, — fill my cup, —
Whom I curse soul and limb. And now dispatch,
Dispatch, my trusty John ; and what remains
To do, whate'er arrangements for our trip
Are yet to be completed, see you hasten
This night ; we'll weather the storm at least : to-morrow
For Nuremberg ! Now leave us ; this grave clerk
Has divers weighty matters for my ear :
[OPORINUS *goes out.*
And spare my lungs. At last, my gallant Festus,
I am rid of this arch-knave that dogs my heels
As a gaunt crow a gasping sheep ; at last
May give a loose to my delight. How kind,
How very kind, my first best only friend !
Why, this looks like fidelity. Embrace me !
Not a hair silvered yet ? Right ! you shall live
Till I am worth your love ; you shall be proud,
And I — but let time show ! Did you not wonder ?
I sent to you because our compact weighed
Upon my conscience — (you recall the night
At Basel, which the gods confound !) — because
Once more I aspire. I call you to my side :
You come. You thought my message strange ?
 Fest.   So strange
That I must hope, indeed, your messenger
Has mingled his own fancies with the words
Purporting to be yours.
 Par.   He said no more,
'T is probable, than the precious folk I leave

Said fiftyfold more roughly. Well-a-day,
'T is true! poor Paracelsus is exposed
At last; a most egregious quack he proves:
And those he overreached must spit their hate
On one who, utterly beneath contempt,
Could yet deceive their topping wits. You heard
Bare truth; and at my bidding you come here
To speed me on my enterprise, as once
Your lavish wishes sped me, my own friend!
  Fest. What is your purpose, Aureole?
  Par.   Oh, for purpose,
There is no lack of precedents in a case
Like mine; at least, if not precisely mine,
The case of men cast off by those they sought
To benefit.
  Fest.   They really cast you off?
I only heard a vague tale of some priest,
Cured by your skill, who wrangled at your claim,
Knowing his life's worth best; and how the judge
The matter was referred to, saw no cause
To interfere, nor you to hide your full
Contempt of him; nor he, again, to smother
His wrath thereat, which raised so fierce a flame
That Basel soon was made no place for you.
  Par. The affair of Liechtenfels? the shallowest fable,
The last and silliest outrage — mere pretence!
I knew it, I foretold it from the first,
How soon the stupid wonder you mistook
For genuine loyalty — a cheering promise
Of better things to come — would pall and pass;
And every word comes true. Saul is among
The prophets! Just so long as I was pleased
To play off the mere antics of my art,
Fantastic gambols leading to no end,
I got huge praise: but one can ne'er keep down
Our foolish nature's weakness. There they flocked,
Poor devils, jostling, swearing and perspiring,
Till the walls rang again; and all for me!
I had a kindness for them, which was right;
But then I stopped not till I tacked to that
A trust in them and a respect — a sort
Of sympathy for them; I must needs begin
To teach them, not amaze them, "to impart
The spirit which should instigate the search
Of truth," just what you bade me! I spoke out.
Forthwith a mighty squadron, in disgust,

Filed off — " the sifted chaff of the sack," I said,
Redoubling my endeavors to secure
The rest. When lo ! one man had tarried so long
Only to ascertain if I supported
This tenet of his, or that; another loved
To hear impartially before he judged,
And having heard, now judged; this bland disciple
Passed for my dupe, but all along, it seems,
Spied error where his neighbors marvelled most ;
That fiery doctor who had hailed me friend,
Did it because my by-paths, once proved wrong
And beaconed properly, would commend again
The good old ways our sires jogged safely o'er,
Though not their squeamish sons ; the other worthy
Discovered divers verses of St. John,
Which, read successively, refreshed the soul,
But, muttered backwards, cured the gout, the stone,
The colic and what not. *Quid multa?* The end
Was a clear class-room, and a quiet leer
From grave folk, and a sour reproachful glance
From those in chief who, cap in hand, installed
The new professor scarce a year before ;
And a vast flourish about patient merit
Obscured awhile by flashy tricks, but sure
Sooner or later to emerge in splendor —
Of which the example was some luckless wight
Whom my arrival had discomfited,
But now, it seems, the general voice recalled
To fill my chair and so efface the stain
Basel had long incurred. I sought no better,
Only a quiet dismissal from my post,
And from my heart I wished them better suited
And better served. Good night to Basel, then !
But fast as I proposed to rid the tribe
Of my obnoxious back, I could not spare them
The pleasure of a parting kick.
    Fest.   You smile :
Despise them as they merit !
    Par.   If I smile,
'T is with as very contempt as ever turned
Flesh into stone. This courteous recompense,
This grateful . . . Festus, were your nature fit
To be defiled, your eyes the eyes to ache
At gangrene-blotches, eating poison-blains,
The ulcerous barky scurf of leprosy
Which finds — a man, and leaves — a hideous thing

That cannot but be mended by hell-fire,
— I would lay bare to you the human heart
Which God cursed long ago, and devils make since
Their pet nest and their never-tiring home.
Oh, sages have discovered we are born
For various ends — to love, to know: has ever
One stumbled, in his search, on any signs
Of a nature in us formed to hate? To hate?
If that be our true object which evokes
Our powers in fullest strength, be sure 't is hate!
Yet men have doubted if the best and bravest
Of spirits can nourish him with hate alone.
I had not the monopoly of fools,
It seems, at Basel.
    Fest.   But your plans, your plans!
I have yet to learn your purpose, Aureole!
    Par. Whether to sink beneath such ponderous shame,
To shrink up like a crushed snail, undergo
In silence and desist from further toil,
And so subside into a monument
Of one their censure blasted? or to bow
Cheerfully as submissively, to lower
My old pretensions even as Basel dictates,
To drop into the rank her wits assign me
And live as they prescribe, and make that use
Of my poor knowledge which their rules allow,
Proud to be patted now and then, and careful
To practise the true posture for receiving
The amplest benefit from their hoofs' appliance
When they shall condescend to tutor me?
Then, one may feel resentment like a flame
Within, and deck false systems in truth's garb,
And tangle and entwine mankind with error,
And give them darkness for a dower and falsehood
For a possession, ages: or one may mope
Into a shade through thinking, or else drowse
Into a dreamless sleep and so die off.
But I, — now Festus shall divine! — but I
Am merely setting out once more, embracing
My earliest aims again! What thinks he now?
    Fest. Your aims? the aims? — to Know? and where
       is found
The early trust . . .
    Par.   Nay, not so fast; I say,
The aims — not the old means. You know they made me
A laughing-stock; I was a fool; you know

The when and the how : hardly those means again !
Not but they had their beauty ; who should know
Their passing beauty, if not I ?   Still, dreams
They were, so let them vanish, yet in beauty
If that may be.   Stay : thus they pass in song !
              [*He sings.*

 Heap cassia, sandal-buds and stripes
  Of labdanum, and aloe-balls,
 Smeared with dull nard an Indian wipes
  From out her hair : such balsam falls
  Down sea-side mountain pedestals,
 From tree-tops where tired winds are fain,
 Spent with the vast and howling main,
 To treasure half their island-gain.

 And strew faint sweetness from some old
  Egyptian's fine worm-eaten shroud
 Which breaks to dust when once unrolled ;
  Or shredded perfume, like a cloud
  From closet long to quiet vowed,
 With mothed and dropping arras hung,
 Mouldering her lute and books among,
 As when a queen, long dead, was young.

Mine, every word !   And on such pile shall die
My lovely fancies, with fair perished things,
Themselves fair and forgotten ; yes, forgotten,
Or why abjure them ?   So, I made this rhyme
That fitting dignity might be preserved ;
No little proud was I ; though the list of drugs
Smacks of my old vocation, and the verse
Halts like the best of Luther's psalms.
 Fest.   But, Aureole,
Talk not thus wildly and madly.   I am here —
Did you know all !   I have travelled far, indeed,
To learn your wishes.   Be yourself again !
For in this mood I recognize you less
Than in the horrible despondency
I witnessed last.   You may account this, joy ;
But rather let me gaze on that despair
Than hear these incoherent words and see
This flushed cheek and intensely-sparkling eye.
 Par.   Why, man, I was light-hearted in my prime,
I am light-hearted now ; what would you have ?
Aprile was a poet, I make songs —

'T is the very augury of success I want!
Why should I not be joyous now as then?
   Fest. Joyous! and how? and what remains for joy?
You have declared the ends (which I am sick
Of naming) are impracticable.
   Par.   Ay,
Pursued as I pursued them — the arch-fool!
Listen: my plan will please you not, 't is like,
But you are little versed in the world's ways.
This is my plan — (first drinking its good luck) —
I will accept all helps; all I despised
So rashly at the outset, equally
With early impulses, late years have quenched:
I have tried each way singly: now for both!
All helps! no one sort shall exclude the rest.
I seek to know and to enjoy at once,
Not one without the other as before.
Suppose my labor should seem God's own cause
Once more, as first I dreamed, — it shall not balk me
Of the meanest earthliest sensualest delight
That may be snatched; for every joy is gain,
And gain is gain, however small. My soul
Can die then, nor be taunted — " what was gained?"
Nor, on the other hand, should pleasure follow
As though I had not spurned her hitherto,
Shall she o'ercloud my spirit's rapt communion
With the tumultuous past, the teeming future,
Glorious with visions of a full success.
   Fest. Success!
   Par.   And wherefore not? Why not prefer
Results obtained in my best state of being,
To those derived alone from seasons dark
As the thoughts they bred? When I was best, my youth
Unwasted, seemed success not surest too?
It is the nature of darkness to obscure.
I am a wanderer: I remember well
One journey, how I feared the track was missed,
So long the city I desired to reach
Lay hid; when suddenly its spires afar
Flashed through the circling clouds; you may conceive
My transport. Soon the vapors closed again,
But I had seen the city, and one such glance
No darkness could obscure: nor shall the present —
A few dull hours, a passing shame or two,
Destroy the vivid memories of the past.
I will fight the battle out; a little spent

Perhaps, but still an able combatant.
You look at my gray hair and furrowed brow?
But I can turn even weakness to account:
Of many tricks I know, 't is not the least
To push the ruins of my frame, whereon
The fire of vigor trembles scarce alive,
Into a heap, and send the flame aloft.
What should I do with age? So, sickness lends
An aid; it being, I fear, the source of all
We boast of: mind is nothing but disease,
And natural health is ignorance.
  Fest.   I see
But one good symptom in this notable scheme.
I feared your sudden journey had in view
To wreak immediate vengeance on your foes.
'T is not so: I am glad.
  Par.   And if I please
To spit on them, to trample them, what then?
'T is sorry warfare truly, but the fools
Provoke it. I would spare their self-conceit
But if they must provoke me, cannot suffer
Forbearance on my part, if I may keep
No quality in the shade, must needs put forth
Power to match power, my strength against their strength,
And teach them their own game with their own arms —
Why, be it so and let them take their chance!
I am above them like a god, there 's no
Hiding the fact: what idle scruples, then,
Were those that ever bade me soften it,
Communicate it gently to the world,
Instead of proving my supremacy,
Taking my natural station o'er their head,
Then owning all the glory was a man's!
— And in my elevation man's would be.
But live and learn, though life 's short, learning hard!
And therefore, though the wreck of my past self,
I fear, dear Pütter, that your lecture-room
Must wait awhile for its best ornament,
The penitent empiric, who set up
For somebody, but soon was taught his place;
Now, but too happy to be let confess
His error, snuff the candles, and illustrate
(*Fiat experientia corpore vili*)
Your medicine's soundness in his person. Wait,
Good Pütter!
  Fest.   He who sneers thus, is a god!

Par. Ay, ay, laugh at me! I am very glad
You are not gulled by all this swaggering; you
Can see the root of the matter! — how I strive
To put a good face on the overthrow
I have experienced, and to bury and hide
My degradation in its length and breadth;
How the mean motives I would make you think
Just mingle as is due with nobler aims,
The appetites I modestly allow
May influence me as being mortal still —
Do goad me, drive me on, and fast supplant
My youth's desires. You are no stupid dupe:
You find me out! Yes, I had sent for you
To palm these childish lies upon you, Festus!
Laugh — you shall laugh at me!
 Fest.   The past, then, Aureole,
Proves nothing? Is our interchange of love
Yet to begin? Have I to swear I mean
No flattery in this speech or that? For you,
Whate'er you say, there is no degradation;
These low thoughts are no inmates of your mind,
Or wherefore this disorder? You are vexed
As much by the intrusion of base views,
Familiar to your adversaries, as they
Were troubled should your qualities alight
Amid their murky souls; not otherwise,
A stray wolf which the winter forces down
From our bleak hills, suffices to affright
A village in the vales — while foresters
Sleep calm, though all night long the famished troop
Snuff round and scratch against their crazy huts.
These evil thoughts are monsters, and will flee.
 Par. May you be happy, Festus, my own friend!
 Fest. Nay, further; the delights you fain would think
The superseders of your nobler aims,
Though ordinary and harmless stimulants,
Will ne'er content you. . . .
 Par.   Hush! I once despised them,
But that soon passes. We are high at first
In our demand, nor will abate a jot
Of toil's strict value; but time passes o'er,
And humbler spirits accept what we refuse:
In short, when some such comfort is doled out
As these delights, we cannot long retain
Bitter contempt which urges us at first
To hurl it back, but hug it to our breast

And thankfully retire. This life of mine
Must be lived out and a grave thoroughly earned:
I am just fit for that and nought beside.
I told you once, I cannot now enjoy,
Unless I deem my knowledge gains through joy;
Nor can I know, but straight warm tears reveal
My need of linking also joy to knowledge:
So, on I drive, enjoying all I can,
And knowing all I can. I speak, of course,
Confusedly; this will better explain — feel here!
Quick beating, is it not? — a fire of the heart
To work off some way, this as well as any.
So, Festus sees me fairly launched; his calm
Compassionate look might have disturbed me once,
But now, far from rejecting, I invite
What bids me press the closer, lay myself
Open before him, and be soothed with pity;
I hope, if he command hope, and believe
As he directs me — satiating myself
With his enduring love. And Festus quits me
To give place to some credulous disciple
Who holds that God is wise, but Paracelsus
Has his peculiar merits: I suck in
That homage, chuckle o'er that admiration,
And then dismiss the fool; for night is come,
And I betake myself to study again,
Till patient searchings after hidden lore
Half wring some bright truth from its prison; my frame
Trembles, my forehead's veins swell out, my hair
Tingles for triumph. Slow and sure the morn
Shall break on my pent room and dwindling lamp
And furnace dead, and scattered earths and ores;
When, with a failing heart and throbbing brow,
I must review my captured truth, sum up
Its value, trace what ends to what begins,
Its present power with its eventual bearings,
Latent affinities, the views it opens,
And its full length in perfecting my scheme.
I view it sternly circumscribed, cast down
From the high place my fond hopes yielded it,
Proved worthless — which, in getting, yet had cost
Another wrench to this fast-falling frame.
Then, quick, the cup to quaff, that chases sorrow!
I lapse back into youth, and take again
My fluttering pulse for evidence that God
Means good to me, will make my cause his own.

See! I have cast off this remorseless care
Which clogged a spirit born to soar so free,
And my dim chamber has become a tent,
Festus is sitting by me, and his Michal . . .
Why do you start? I say, she listening here,
(For yonder — Würzburg through the orchard-bough!)
Motions as though such ardent words should find
No echo in a maiden's quiet soul,
But her pure bosom heaves, her eyes fill fast
With tears, her sweet lips tremble all the while!
Ha, ha!
    Fest. It seems, then, you expect to reap
No unreal joy from this your present course,
But rather . . .
    Par.   Death! To die! I owe that much
To what, at least, I was. I should be sad
To live contented after such a fall,
To thrive and fatten after such reverse!
The whole plan is a makeshift, but will last
My time.
    Fest.   And you have never mused and said,
" I had a noble purpose, and the strength
To compass it; but I have stopped half-way,
And wrongly given the first-fruits of my toil
To objects little worthy of the gift.
Why linger round them still? why clench my fault?
Why seek for consolation in defeat,
In vain endeavors to derive a beauty
From ugliness? why seek to make the most
Of what no power can change, nor strive instead
With mighty effort to redeem the past
And, gathering up the treasures thus cast down,
To hold a steadfast course till I arrive
At their fit destination and my own?"
You have never pondered thus?
    Par.   Have I, you ask?
Often at midnight, when most fancies come,
Would some such airy project visit me:
But ever at the end . . . or will you hear
The same thing in a tale, a parable?
You and I, wandering over the world wide,
Chance to set foot upon a desert coast.
Just as we cry, " No human voice before
Broke the inveterate silence of these rocks!"
— Their querulous echo startles us; we turn:
What ravaged structure still looks o'er the sea?

Some characters remain, too! While we read,
The sharp salt wind, impatient for the last
Of even this record, wistfully comes and goes,
Or sings what we recover, mocking it.
This is the record; and my voice, the wind's.
                                    [*He sings.*

   Over the sea our galleys went,
With cleaving prows in order brave
To a speeding wind and a bounding wave,
   A gallant armament:
Each bark built out of a forest-tree
   Left leafy and rough as first it grew,
And nailed all over the gaping sides,
Within and without, with black bull-hides,
Seethed in fat and suppled in flame,
To bear the playful billows' game:
So, each good ship was rude to see,
Rude and bare to the outward view,
   But each upbore a stately tent
Where cedar pales in scented row
Kept out the flakes of the dancing brine,
And an awning drooped the mast below,
In fold on fold of the purple fine,
That neither noontide nor starshine
Nor moonlight cold which maketh mad,
   Might pierce the regal tenement.
When the sun dawned, oh, gay and glad
We set the sail and plied the oar;
But when the night-wind blew like breath,
For joy of one day's voyage more,
We sang together on the wide sea,
Like men at peace on a peaceful shore;
Each sail was loosed to the wind so free,
Each helm made sure by the twilight star,
And in a sleep as calm as death,
We, the voyagers from afar,
   Lay stretched along, each weary crew
In a circle round its wondrous tent
Whence gleamed soft light and curled rich scent,
   And with light and perfume, music too:
So the stars wheeled round, and the darkness past,
And at morn we started beside the mast,
And still each ship was sailing fast.

   Now, one morn, land appeared — a speck
Dim trembling betwixt sea and sky:

"Avoid it," cried our pilot, "check
  The shout, restrain the eager eye!"
But the heaving sea was black behind
For many a night and many a day,
And land, though but a rock, drew nigh;
So, we broke the cedar pales away,
Let the purple awning flap in the wind,
  And a statue bright was on every deck!
We shouted, every man of us,
And steered right into the harbor thus,
With pomp and pæan glorious.

A hundred shapes of lucid stone!
  All day we built its shrine for each,
A shrine of rock for every one,
  Nor paused till in the westering sun
  We sat together on the beach
To sing because our task was done.
When lo! what shouts and merry songs!
What laughter all the distance stirs!
A loaded raft with happy throngs
  Of gentle islanders!
"Our isles are just at hand," they cried,
  "Like cloudlets faint in even sleeping.
Our temple-gates are opened wide,
  Our olive-groves thick shade are keeping
For these majestic forms " — they cried.
Oh, then we awoke with sudden start
From our deep dream, and knew, too late,
How bare the rock, how desolate,
Which had received our precious freight:
  Yet we called out — " Depart!
Our gifts, once given, must here abide.
  Our work is done; we have no heart
To mar our work," — we cried.

Fest. In truth?
Par.   Nay, wait: all this in tracings faint
On rugged stones strewn here and there, but piled
In order once: then follows — mark what follows!
"The sad rhyme of the men who proudly clung
To their first fault, and withered in their pride."
Fest. Come back then, Aureole; as you fear God, come!
This is foul sin; come back! Renounce the past,
Forswear the future; look for joy no more,
But wait death's summons amid holy sights,

And trust me for the event — peace, if not joy.
Return with me to Einsiedeln, dear Aureole!
    Par. No way, no way! it would not turn to good.
A spotless child sleeps on the flowering moss —
'T is well for him; but when a sinful man,
Envying such slumber, may desire to put
His guilt away, shall he return at once
To rest by lying there? Our sires knew well
(Spite of the grave discoveries of their sons)
The fitting course for such: dark cells, dim lamps,
A stone floor one may writhe on like a worm:
No mossy pillow blue with violets!
    Fest. I see no symptom of these absolute
And tyrannous passions. You are calmer now.
This verse-making can purge you well enough
Without the terrible penance you describe.
You love me still: the lusts you fear will never
Outrage your friend. To Einsiedeln, once more!
Say but the word!
    Par. No, no; those lusts forbid:
They crouch, I know, cowering with half-shut eye
Beside you; 't is their nature. Thrust yourself
Between them and their prey; let some fool style me
Or king or quack, it matters not — then try
Your wisdom, urge them to forego their treat!
No, no; learn better and look deeper, Festus!
If you knew how a devil sneers within me
While you are talking now of this, now that,
As though we differed scarcely save in trifles!
    Fest. Do we so differ? True, change must proceed,
Whether for good or ill; keep from me, which!
Do not confide all secrets: I was born
To hope, and you . . .
    Par. To trust: you know the fruits!
    Fest. Listen: I do believe, what you call trust
Was self-delusion at the best: for, see!
So long as God would kindly pioneer
A path for you, and screen you from the world,
Procure you full exemption from man's lot,
Man's common hopes and fears, on the mere pretext
Of your engagement in his service — yield you
A limitless license, make you God, in fact,
And turn your slave — you were content to say
Most courtly praises! What is it, at last,
But selfishness without example? None
Could trace God's will so plain as you, while yours

Remained implied in it; but now you fail,
And we, who prate about that will, are fools!
In short, God's service is established here
As he determines fit, and not your way,
And this you cannot brook. Such discontent
Is weak. Renounce all creatureship at once!
Affirm an absolute right to have and use
Your energies; as though the rivers should say —
" We rush to the ocean; what have we to do
With feeding streamlets, lingering in the vales,
Sleeping in lazy pools?" Set up that plea,
That will be bold at least!
  Par.   'T is like enough.
The serviceable spirits are those, no doubt,
The East produces: lo, the master bids,—
They wake, raise terraces and garden-grounds
In one night's space; and, this done, straight begin
Another century's sleep, to the great praise
Of him that framed them wise and beautiful,
Till a lamp's rubbing, or some chance akin,
Wake them again. I am of different mould.
I would have soothed my lord, and slaved for him
And done him service past my narrow bond,
And thus I get rewarded for my pains!
Beside, 't is vain to talk of forwarding
God's glory otherwise; this is alone
The sphere of its increase, as far as men
Increase it; why, then, look beyond this sphere?
We are his glory; and if we be glorious,
Is not the thing achieved?
  Fest.   Shall one like me
Judge hearts like yours? Though years have changed yon
  much,
And you have left your first love, and retain
Its empty shade to veil your crooked ways,
Yet I still hold that you have honored God.
And who shall call your course without reward?
For, wherefore this repining at defeat
Had triumph ne'er inured you to high hopes?
I urge you to forsake the life you curse,
And what success attends me? — simply talk
Of passion, weakness and remorse; in short,
Anything but the naked truth — you choose
This so-despised career, and cheaply hold
My happiness, or rather other men's.
Once more, return!

  Par.   And quickly. John the thief
Has pilfered half my secrets by this time:
And we depart by daybreak. I am weary,
I know not how; not even the wine-cup soothes
My brain to-night . . .
Do you not thoroughly despise me, Festus?
No flattery! One like you needs not be told
We live and breathe deceiving and deceived.
Do you not scorn me from your heart of hearts,
Me and my cant, each petty subterfuge,
My rhymes and all this frothy shower of words,
My glozing self-deceit, my outward crust
Of lies which wrap, as tetter, morphew, furfair
Wrap the sound flesh? — so, see you flatter not!
Even God flatters: but my friend, at least,
Is true. I would depart, secure henceforth
Against all further insult, hate and wrong
From puny foes; my one friend's scorn shall brand ɪ
No fear of sinking deeper!
  Fest.   No, dear Aureole!
No, no; I came to counsel faithfully.
There are old rules, made long ere we were born,
By which I judge you. I, so fallible,
So infinitely low beside your mighty
Majestic spirit! — even I can see
You own some higher law than ours which call
Sin, what is no sin — weakness, what is strength.
But I have only these, such as they are,
To guide me; and I blame you where they bid,
Only so long as blaming promises
To win peace for your soul: the more, that sorrow
Has fallen on me of late, and they have helped me
So that I faint not under my distress.
But wherefore should I scruple to avow
In spite of all, as brother judging brother,
Your fate is most inexplicable to me?
And should you perish without recompense
And satisfaction yet — too hastily
I have relied on love: you may have sinned,
But you have loved. As a mere human matter —
As I would have God deal with fragile men
In the end — I say that you will triumph yet!
  Par. Have you felt sorrow, Festus? — 't is because
You love me. Sorrow, and sweet Michal yours!
Well thought on: never let her know this last
Dull winding-up of all: these miscreants dared
Insult me — me she loved: — so, grieve her not!

Fest. Your ill success can little grieve her now.
Par. Michal is dead! pray Christ we do not craze!
Fest. Aureole, dear Aureole, look not on me thus!
Fool, fool! this is the heart grown sorrow-proof —
I cannot bear those eyes.
 Par.   Nay, really dead?
 Fest. 'T is scarce a month.
 Par.   Stone dead! — then you have laid her
Among the flowers ere this. Now, do you know,
I can reveal a secret which shall comfort
Even you. I have no julep, as men think,
To cheat the grave; but a far better secret.
Know, then, you did not ill to trust your love
To the cold earth: I have thought much of it:
For I believe we do not wholly die.
 Fest. Aureole!
 Par.   Nay, do not laugh; there is a reason
For what I say: I think the soul can never
Taste death. I am, just now, as you may see,
Very unfit to put so strange a thought
In an intelligible dress of words;
But take it as my trust, she is not dead.
 Fest. But not on this account alone? you surely,
— Aureole, you have believed this all along?
 Par. And Michal sleeps among the roots and dews,
While I am moved at Basel, and full of schemes
For Nuremberg, and hoping and despairing,
As though it mattered how the farce plays out,
So it be quickly played. Away, away!
Have your will, rabble! while we fight the prize,
Troop you in safety to the snug back-seats
And leave a clear arena for the brave
About to perish for your sport! — Behold!

V. PARACELSUS ATTAINS.

SCENE, *Salzburg; a cell in the Hospital of St. Sebastian.* 1541.

FESTUS, PARACELSUS.

 Fest. No change! The weary night is well-nigh spent,
The lamp burns low, and through the casement-bars
Gray morning glimmers feebly: yet no change!
Another night, and still no sigh has stirred
That fallen discolored mouth, no pang relit
Those fixed eyes, quenched by the decaying body,
Like torch-flame choked in dust. While all beside

Was breaking, to the last they held out bright,
As a stronghold where life intrenched itself;
But they are dead now — very blind and dead:
He will drowse into death without a groan.

My Aureole — my forgotten, ruined Aureole!
The days are gone, are gone! How grand thou wast!
And now not one of those who struck thee down —
Poor glorious spirit — concerns him even to stay
And satisfy himself his little hand
Could turn God's image to a livid thing.

Another night, and yet no change! 'T is much
That I should sit by him, and bathe his brow,
And chafe his hands; 't is much: but he will sure
Know me, and look on me, and speak to me
Once more — but only once! His hollow cheek
Looked all night long as though a creeping laugh
At his own state were just about to break
From the dying man: my brain swam, my throat swelled,
And yet I could not turn away. In truth,
They told me how, when first brought here, he seemed
Resolved to live, to lose no faculty;
Thus striving to keep up his shattered strength,
Until they bore him to this stifling cell:
When straight his features fell, an hour made white
The flushed face, and relaxed the quivering limb,
Only the eye remained intense awhile
As though it recognized the tomb-like place,
And then he lay as here he lies.
       Ay, here!
Here is earth's noblest, nobly garlanded —
Her bravest champion with his well-won prize —
Her best achievement, her sublime amends
For countless generations fleeting fast
And followed by no trace; — the creature-god
She instances when angels would dispute
The title of her brood to rank with them.
Angels, this is our angel! Those bright forms
We clothe with purple, crown and call to thrones,
Are human, but not his; those are but men
Whom other men press round and kneel before;
Those palaces are dwelt in by mankind;
Higher provision is for him you seek
Amid our pomps and glories: see it here!
Behold earth's paragon! Now, raise thee, clay!

God! Thou art love! I build my faith on that
Even as I watch beside thy tortured child
Unconscious whose hot tears fall fast by him,
So doth thy right hand guide us through the world
Wherein we stumble. God! what shall we say?
How has he sinned? How else should he have done?
Surely he sought thy praise — thy praise, for all
He might be busied by the task so much
As half forget awhile its proper end.
Dost thou well, Lord? Thou canst not but prefer
That I should range myself upon his side —
How could he stop at every step to set
Thy glory forth? Hadst thou but granted him
Success, thy honor would have crowned success,
A halo round a star. Or, say he erred, —
Save him, dear God; it will be like thee: bathe him
In light and life! Thou art not made like us;
We should be wroth in such a case; but thou
Forgivest — so, forgive these passionate thoughts
Which come unsought and will not pass away!
I know thee, who hast kept my path, and made
Light for me in the darkness, tempering sorrow
So that it reached me like a solemn joy;
It were too strange that I should doubt thy love.
But what am I? Thou madest him and knowest
How he was fashioned. I could never err
That way: the quiet place beside thy feet,
Reserved for me, was ever in my thoughts:
But he — thou shouldst have favored him as well!

Ah! he wakens! Aureole, I am here! 'tis Festus!
I cast away all wishes save one wish —
Let him but know me, only speak to me!
He mutters; louder and louder; any other
Than I, with brain less laden, could collect
What he pours forth. Dear Aureole, do but look!
Is it talking or singing, this he utters fast?
Misery that he should fix me with his eye,
Quick talking to some other all the while!
If he would husband this wild vehemence
Which frustrates its intent! — I heard, I know
I heard my name amid those rapid words.
Oh, he will know me yet! Could I divert
This current, lead it somehow gently back
Into the channels of the past! — His eye
Brighter than ever! It must recognize me!

I am Erasmus : I am here to pray
That Paracelsus use his skill for me.
The schools of Paris and of Padua send
These questions for your learning to resolve.
We are your students, noble master: leave
This wretched cell, what business have you here?
Our class awaits you; come to us once more!
(O agony! the utmost I can do
Touches him not; how else arrest his ear?)
I am commissioned . . . I shall craze like him.
Better be mute and see what God shall send.
 Par. Stay, stay with me!
 Fest.   I will; I am come here
To stay with you — Festus, you loved of old;
Festus, you know, you must know!
 Par.   Festus! Where's
Aprile, then? Has he not chanted softly
The melodies I heard all night? I could not
Get to him for a cold hand on my breast,
But I made out his music well enough,
O well enough! If they have filled him full
With magical music, as they freight a star
With light, and have remitted all his sin,
They will forgive me too, I too shall know!
 Fest. Festus, your Festus!
 Par.   Ask him if Aprile
Knows as he Loves — if I shall Love and Know?
I try; but that cold hand, like lead — so cold!
 Fest. My hand, see!
 Par.   Ah, the curse, Aprile, Aprile!
We get so near — so very, very near!
'T is an old tale: Jove strikes the Titans down,
Not when they set about their mountain-piling
But when another rock would crown the work.
And Phaeton — doubtless his first radiant plunge
Astonished mortals, though the gods were calm,
And Jove prepared his thunder: all old tales!
 Fest. And what are these to you?
 Par.   Ay, fiends must laugh
So cruelly, so well! most like I never
Could tread a single pleasure underfoot,
But they were grinning by my side, were chuckling
To see me toil and drop away by flakes!
Hell-spawn! I am glad, most glad, that thus I fail!
Your cunning has o'ershot its aim. One year,
One month, perhaps, and I had served your turn!

You should have curbed your spite awhile. But now,
Who will believe 't was you that held me back?
Listen: there's shame and hissing and contempt,
And none but laughs who names me, none but spits
Measureless scorn upon me, me alone,
The quack, the cheat, the liar, — all on me!
And thus your famous plan to sink mankind
In silence and despair, by teaching them
One of their race had probed the inmost truth,
Had done all man could do, yet failed no less —
Your wise plan proves abortive. Men despair?
Ha, ha! why, they are hooting the empiric,
The ignorant and incapable fool who rushed
Madly upon a work beyond his wits;
Nor doubt they but the simplest of themselves
Could bring the matter to triumphant issue.
So, pick and choose among them all, accursed!
Try now, persuade some other to slave for you,
To ruin body and soul to work your ends!
No, no; I am the first and last, I think.
   Fest. Dear friend, who are accursed? who has done . . .
   Par. What have I done? Fiends dare ask that? or you,
Brave men? Oh, you can chime in boldly, backed
By the others! What had you to do, sage peers?
Here stand my rivals; Latin, Arab, Jew,
Greek, join dead hands against me: all I ask
Is, that the world enroll my name with theirs,
And even this poor privilege, it seems,
They range themselves, prepared to disallow.
Only observe! why, fiends may learn from them!
How they talk calmly of my throes, my fierce
Aspirings, terrible watchings, each one claiming
Its price of blood and brain; how they dissect
And sneeringly disparage the few truths
Got at a life's cost; they too hanging the while
About my neck, their lies misleading me
And their dead names browbeating me! Gray crew,
Yet steeped in fresh malevolence from hell,
Is there a reason for your hate? My truths
Have shaken a little the palm about each prince?
Just think, Aprile, all these leering dotards
Were bent on nothing less than to be crowned
As we! That yellow blear-eyed wretch in chief
To whom the rest cringe low with feigned respect,
Galen of Pergamos and hell — nay speak
The tale, old man! We met there face to face:

I said the crown should fall from thee. Once more
We meet as in that ghastly vestibule :
Look to my brow ! Have I redeemed my pledge ?
 Fest. Peace, peace ; ah, see !
 Par.   Oh, emptiness of fame !
O Persic Zoroaster, lord of stars !
— Who said these old renowns, dead long ago,
Could make me overlook the living world
To gaze through gloom at where they stood, indeed,
But stand no longer ? What a warm light life
After the shade ! In truth, my delicate witch,
My serpent-queen, you did but well to hide
The juggles I had else detected. Fire
May well run harmless o'er a breast like yours !
The cave was not so darkened by the smoke
But that your white limbs dazzled me : oh, white,
And panting as they twinkled, wildly dancing !
I cared not for your passionate gestures then,
But now I have forgotten the charm of charms,
The foolish knowledge which I came to seek,
While I remember that quaint dance ; and thus
I am come back, not for those mummeries,
But to love you, and to kiss your little feet
Soft as an ermine's winter coat !
 Fest.   A light
Will struggle through these thronging words at last,
As in the angry and tumultuous West
A soft star trembles through the drifting clouds.
These are the strivings of a spirit which hates
So sad a vault should coop it, and calls up
The past to stand between it and its fate.
Were he at Einsiedeln — or Michal here !
 Par. Cruel ! I seek her now — I kneel — I shriek —
I clasp her vesture — but she fades, still fades ;
And she is gone ; sweet human love is gone !
'T is only when they spring to heaven that angels
Reveal themselves to you ; they sit all day
Beside you, and lie down at night by you
Who care not for their presence, muse or sleep,
And all at once they leave you, and you know them !
We are so fooled, so cheated ! Why, even now
I am not too secure against foul play ;
The shadows deepen and the walls contract :
No doubt some treachery is going on.
'T is very dusk. Where are we put, Aprile ?
Have they left us in the lurch ? This murky loathsome

Death-trap, this slaughter-house, is not the hall
In the golden city! Keep by me, Aprile!
There is a hand groping amid the blackness
To catch us. Have the spider-fingers got you,
Poet? Hold on me for your life! If once
They pull you! — Hold!
     'T is but a dream — no more!
I have you still; the sun comes out again;
Let us be happy: all will yet go well!
Let us confer: is it not like, Aprile,
That spite of trouble, this ordeal passed,
The value of my labors ascertained,
Just as some stream foams long among the rocks
But after glideth glassy to the sea,
So, full content shall henceforth be my lot?
What think you, poet? Louder! Your clear voice
Vibrates too like a harp-string. Do you ask
How could I still remain on earth, should God
Grant me the great approval which I seek?
I, you, and God can comprehend each other,
But men would murmur, and with cause enough;
For when they saw me, stainless of all sin,
Preserved and sanctified by inward light,
They would complain that comfort, shut from them,
I drank thus unespied; that they live on,
Nor taste the quiet of a constant joy,
For ache and care and doubt and weariness,
While I am calm; help being vouchsafed to me,
And hid from them. — 'T were best consider that!
You reason well, Aprile; but at least
Let me know this, and die! Is this too much?
I will learn this, if God so please, and die!

If thou shalt please, dear God, if thou shalt please!
We are so weak, we know our motives least
In their confused beginning. If at first
I sought . . . but wherefore bare my heart to thee?
I know thy mercy; and already thoughts
Flock fast about my soul to comfort it,
And intimate I cannot wholly fail,
For love and praise would clasp me willingly
Could I resolve to seek them. Thou art good,
And I should be content. Yet — yet first show
I have done wrong in daring! Rather give
The supernatural consciousness of strength
Which fed my youth! Only one hour of that,
With thee to help — O what should bar me then!

Lost, lost! Thus things are ordered here! God's crea‑
 tures,
And yet he takes no pride in us! — none, none!
Truly there needs another life to come!
If this be all — (I must tell Festus that)
And other life await us not — for one,
I say 't is a poor cheat, a stupid bungle,
A wretched failure. I, for one, protest
Against it, and I hurl it back with scorn.

Well, onward though alone! Small time remains,
And much to do: I must have fruit, must reap
Some profit from my toils. I doubt my body
Will hardly serve me through; while I have labored
It has decayed; and now that I demand
Its best assistance, it will crumble fast:
A sad thought, a sad fate! How very full
Of wormwood 't is, that just at altar-service,
The rapt hymn rising with the rolling smoke,
When glory dawns and all is at the best,
The sacred fire may flicker and grow faint
And die for want of a wood-piler's help!
Thus fades the flagging body, and the soul
Is pulled down in the overthrow. Well, well —
Let men catch every word, let them lose nought
Of what I say; something may yet be done.

They are ruins! Trust me who am one of you!
All ruins, glorious once, but lonely now.
It makes my heart sick to behold you crouch
Beside your desolate fane: the arches dim,
The crumbling columns grand against the moon,
Could I but rear them up once more — but that
May never be, so leave them! Trust me, friends,
Why should you linger here when I have built
A far resplendent temple, all your own?
Trust me, they are but ruins! See, Aprile,
Men will not heed! Yet were I not prepared
With better refuge for them, tongue of mine
Should ne'er reveal how blank their dwelling is:
I would sit down in silence with the rest.

Ha, what? you spit at me, you grin and shriek
Contempt into my ear — my ear which drank
God's accents once? you curse me? Why men, men,
I am not formed for it! Those hideous eyes

Will be before me sleeping, waking, praying,
They will not let me even die. Spare, spare me,
Sinning or no, forget that, only spare me
The horrible scorn! You thought I could support it.
But now you see what silly fragile creature
Cowers thus. I am not good nor bad enough,
Not Christ nor Cain, yet even Cain was saved
From Hate like this. Let me but totter back!
Perhaps I shall elude those jeers which creep
Into my very brain, and shut these scorched
Eyelids and keep those mocking faces out.

Listen, Aprile! I am very calm:
Be not deceived, there is no passion here
Where the blood leaps like an imprisoned thing:
I am calm: I will exterminate the race!
Enough of that: 't is said and it shall be.
And now be merry: safe and sound am I
Who broke through their best ranks to get at you.
And such a havoc, such a rout, Aprile!
    Fest. Have you no thought, no memory for me,
Aureole? I am so wretched — my pure Michal
Is gone, and you alone are left me now,
And even you forget me. Take my hand —
Lean on me thus. Do you not know me, Aureole?
    Par. Festus, my own friend, you are come at last?
As you say, 't is an awful enterprise;
But you believe I shall go through with it:
'T is like you, and I thank you. Thank him for me,
Dear Michal! See how bright St. Saviour's spire
Flames in the sunset; all its figures quaint
Gay in the glancing light: you might conceive them
A troop of yellow-vested white-haired Jews
Bound for their own land where redemption dawns.
    Fest. Not that blest time — not our youth's time, dear
        God!
    Par. Ha — stay! true, I forget — all is done since,
And he is come to judge me. How he speaks,
How calm, how well! yes, it is true, all true;
All quackery; all deceit; myself can laugh
The first at it, if you desire : but still
You know the obstacles which taught me tricks
So foreign to my nature — envy and hate,
Blind opposition, brutal prejudice,
Bald ignorance — what wonder if I sunk
To humor men the way they most approved?
My cheats were never palmed on such as you,

Dear Festus! I will kneel if you require me,
Impart the meagre knowledge I possess,
Explain its bounded nature, and avow
My insufficiency — whate'er you will:
I give the fight up: let there be an end,
A privacy, an obscure nook for me.
I want to be forgotten even by God.
But if that cannot be, dear Festus, lay me,
When I shall die, within some narrow grave,
Not by itself — for that would be too proud —
But where such graves are thickest; let it look
Nowise distinguished from the hillocks round,
So that the peasant at his brother's bed
May tread upon my own and know it not;
And we shall all be equal at the last,
Or classed according to life's natural ranks,
Fathers, sons, brothers, friends — not rich, nor wise,
Nor gifted: lay me thus, then say, " He lived
Too much advanced before his brother men;
They kept him still in front: 't was for their good
But yet a dangerous station. It were strange
That he should tell God he had never ranked
With men : so, here at least he is a man."

   Fest. That God shall take thee to his breast, dear spirit,
Unto his breast, be sure! and here on earth
Shall splendor sit upon thy name forever.
Sun! all the heaven is glad for thee : what care
If lower mountains light their snowy phares
At thine effulgence, yet acknowledge not
The source of day? Their theft shall be their bale:
For after-ages shall retrack thy beams,
And put aside the crowd of busy ones
And worship thee alone — the master-mind,
The thinker, the explorer, the creator!
Then, who should sneer at the convulsive throes
With which thy deeds were born, would scorn as well
The sheet of winding subterraneous fire
Which, pent and writhing, sends no less at last
Huge islands up amid the simmering sea.
Behold thy might in me! thou hast infused
Thy soul in mine; and I am grand as thou,
Seeing I comprehend thee — I so simple,
Thou so august. I recognize thee first;
I saw thee rise, I watched thee early and late,
And though no glance reveal thou dost accept
My homage — thus no less I proffer it,
And bid thee enter gloriously thy rest.

Par. Festus!
Fest. I am for noble Aureole, God!
I am upon his side, come weal or woe.
His portion shall be mine. He has done well.
I would have sinned, had I been strong enough,
As he has sinned. Reward him or I waive
Reward! If thou canst find no place for him,
He shall be king elsewhere, and I will be
His slave forever. There are two of us.
Par. Dear Festus!
Fest. Here, dear Aureole! ever by you!
Par. Nay, speak on, or I dream again. Speak on!
Some story, anything — only your voice.
I shall dream else. Speak on! ay, leaning so!
Fest. Thus the Mayne glideth
 Where my Love abideth.
 Sleep 's no softer : it proceeds
 On through lawns, on through meads,
 On and on, whate'er befall,
 Meandering and musical,
 Though the niggard pasturage
 Bears not on its shaven ledge
 Aught but weeds and waving grasses
 To view the river as it passes,
 Save here and there a scanty patch
 Of primroses too faint to catch
 A weary bee.
Par. More, more; say on!
Fest. And scarce it pushes
 Its gentle way through strangling rushes
 Where the glossy kingfisher
 Flutters when noon-heats are near,
 Glad the shelving banks to shun,
 Red and steaming in the sun,
 Where the shrew-mouse with pale throat
 Burrows, and the speckled stoat;
 Where the quick sandpipers flit
 In and out the marl and grit
 That seems to breed them, brown as they:
 Nought disturbs its quiet way,
 Save some lazy stork that springs,
 Trailing it with legs and wings,
 Whom the shy fox from the hill
 Rouses, creep he ne'er so still.
Par. My heart! they loose my heart, those simple words;
Its darkness passes, which nought else could touch:

Like some dark snake that force may not expel,
Which glideth out to music sweet and low.
What were you doing when your voice broke through
A chaos of ugly images? You, indeed!
Are you alone here?
  Fest.   All alone: you know me?
This cell?
  Par. An unexceptionable vault:
Good brick and stone: the bats kept out, the rats
Kept in: a snug nook: how should I mistake it?
  Fest. But wherefore am I here?
  Par.   Ah, well remembered!
Why, for a purpose — for a purpose, Festus!
'T is like me: here I trifle while time fleets,
And this occasion, lost, will ne'er return.
You are here to be instructed. I will tell
God's message; but I have so much to say,
I fear to leave half out. All is confused
No doubt; but doubtless you will learn in time.
He would not else have brought you here: no doubt
I shall see clearer soon.
  Fest.   Tell me but this —
You are not in despair?
  Par.   I? and for what?
  Fest. Alas, alas! he knows not, as I feared!
  Par. What is it you would ask me with that earnest
Dear searching face?
  Fest.   How feel you, Aureole?
  Par.   Well:
Well. 'T is a strange thing: I am dying, Festus,
And now that fast the storm of life subsides,
I first perceive how great the whirl has been.
I was calm then, who am so dizzy now —
Calm in the thick of the tempest, but no less
A partner of its motion and mixed up
With its career. The hurricane is spent,
And the good boat speeds through the brightening weather
But is it earth or sea that heaves below?
The gulf rolls like a meadow-swell, o'erstrewn
With ravaged boughs and remnants of the shore;
And now some islet, loosened from the land,
Swims past with all its trees, sailing to ocean;
And now the air is full of uptorn canes,
Light strippings from the fan-trees, tamarisks
Unrooted, with their birds still clinging to them,
All high in the wind. Even so my varied life

Drifts by me; I am young, old, happy, sad,
Hoping, desponding, acting, taking rest,
And all at once: that is, those past conditions
Float back at once on me. If I select
Some special epoch from the crowd, 't is but
To will, and straight the rest dissolve away,
And only that particular state is present
With all its long-forgotten circumstance
Distinct and vivid as at first — myself
A careless looker-on and nothing more,
Indifferent and amused, but nothing more.
And this is death: I understand it all.
New being waits me; new perceptions must
Be born in me before I plunge therein;
Which last is Death's affair; and while I speak,
Minute by minute he is filling me
With power; and while my foot is on the threshold
Of boundless life — the doors unopened yet,
All preparations not complete within —
I turn new knowledge upon old events,
And the effect is . . . but I must not tell;
It is not lawful. Your own turn will come
One day. Wait, Festus! You will die like me.
 Fest. 'T is of that past life that I burn to hear.
 Par. You wonder it engages me just now?
In truth, I wonder too. What 's life to me?
Where'er I look is fire, where'er I listen
Music, and where I tend bliss evermore.
Yet how can I refrain? 'T is a refined
Delight to view those chances, — one last view.
I am so near the perils I escape,
That I must play with them and turn them over,
To feel how fully they are past and gone.
Still, it is like, some further cause exists
For this peculiar mood — some hidden purpose;
Did I not tell you something of it, Festus?
I had it fast, but it has somehow slipt
Away from me; it will return anon.
 Fest. (Indeed his cheek seems young again, his voice
Complete with its old tones: that little laugh
Concluding every phrase, with upturned eye,
As though one stooped above his head to whom
He looked for confirmation and approval,
Where was it gone so long, so well preserved?
Then, the forefinger pointing as he speaks,
Like one who traces in an open book

The matter he declares; 't is many a year
Since I remarked it last: and this in him,
But now a ghastly wreck!)
       And can it be,
Dear Aureole, you have then found out at last
That worldly things are utter vanity?
That man is made for weakness, and should wait
In patient ignorance, till God appoint . . .
 Par. Ha, the purpose : the true purpose: that is it!
How could I fail to apprehend! You here,
I thus ! But no more trifling : I see all,
I know all : my last mission shall be done
If strength suffice. No trifling ! Stay; this posture
Hardly befits one thus about to speak :
I will arise.
 Fest. Nay, Aureole, are you wild ?
You cannot leave your couch.
 Par.   No help; no help;
Not even your hand. So ! there, I stand once more !
Speak from a couch ? I never lectured thus.
My gown — the scarlet lined with fur ; now put
The chain about my neck ; my signet-ring
Is still upon my hand, I think — even so ;
Last, my good sword ; ah, trusty Azoth, leapest
Beneath thy master's grasp for the last time ?
This couch shall be my throne : I bid these walls
Be consecrate, this wretched cell become
A shrine, for here God speaks to men through me.
Now, Festus, I am ready to begin.
 Fest. I am dumb with wonder.
 Par.   Listen, therefore, Festus!
There will be time enough, but none to spare.
I must content myself with telling only
The most important points. You doubtless feel
That I am happy, Festus ; very happy.
 Fest. 'T is no delusion which uplifts him thus!
Then you are pardoned, Aureole, all your sin ?
 Par. Ay, pardoned : yet why pardoned ?
 Fest.   'T is God's praise
That man is bound to seek, and you . . .
 Par.   Have lived!
We have to live alone to set forth well
God's praise. 'T is true, I sinned much, as I thought,
And in effect need mercy, for I strove
To do that very thing ; but, do your best
Or worst, praise rises, and will rise forever.

Pardon from him, because of praise denied —
Who calls me to himself to exalt himself?
He might laugh as I laugh!
    Fest.   But all comes
To the same thing. 'T is fruitless for mankind
To fret themselves with what concerns them not;
They are no use that way: they should lie down
Content as God has made them, nor go mad
In thriveless cares to better what is ill.
    Par. No, no; mistake me not; let me not work
More harm than I have worked! This is my case:
If I go joyous back to God, yet bring
No offering, if I render up my soul
Without the fruits it was ordained to bear,
If I appear the better to love God
For sin, as one who has no claim on him, —
Be not deceived! It may be surely thus
With me, while higher prizes still await
The mortal persevering to the end.
Beside I am not all so valueless:
I have been something, though too soon I left
Following the instincts of that happy time.
    Fest. What happy time? For God's sake, for man's
        sake,
What time was happy? All I hope to know
That answer will decide. What happy time?
    Par. When but the time I vowed myself to man?
    Fest. Great God, thy judgments are inscrutable!
    Par. Yes, it was in me; I was born for it —
I, Paracelsus: it was mine by right.
Doubtless a searching and impetuous soul
Might learn from its own motions that some task
Like this awaited it about the world;
Might seek somewhere in this blank life of ours
For fit delights to stay its longings vast;
And, grappling Nature, so prevail on her
To fill the creature full she dared thus frame
Hungry for joy; and, bravely tyrannous,
Grow in demand, still craving more and more,
And make each joy conceded prove a pledge
Of other joy to follow — bating nought
Of its desires, still seizing fresh pretence
To turn the knowledge and the rapture wrung
As an extreme, last boon, from destiny,
Into occasion for new covetings,
New strifes, new triumphs: — doubtless a strong soul,

Alone, unaided might attain to this,
So glorious is our nature, so august
Man's inborn uninstructed impulses,
His naked spirit so majestical!
But this was born in me; I was made so;
Thus much time saved: the feverish appetites,
The tumult of unproved desire, the unaimed
Uncertain yearnings, aspirations blind,
Distrust, mistake, and all that ends in tears
Were saved me; thus I entered on my course.
You may be sure I was not all exempt
From human trouble; just so much of doubt
As bade me plant a surer foot upon
The sun-road, kept my eye unruined 'mid
The fierce and flashing splendor, set my heart
Trembling so much as warned me I stood there
On sufferance — not to idly gaze, but cast
Light on a darkling race; save for that doubt,
I stood at first where all aspire at last
To stand: the secret of the world was mine.
I knew, I felt, (perception unexpressed,
Uncomprehended by our narrow thought,
But somehow felt and known in every shift
And change in the spirit, — nay, in every pore
Of the body, even,) — what God is, what we are,
What life is — how God tastes an infinite joy
In infinite ways — one everlasting bliss,
From whom all being emanates, all power
Proceeds; in whom is life forevermore,
Yet whom existence in its lowest form
Includes; where dwells enjoyment there is he:
With still a flying point of bliss remote,
A happiness in store afar, a sphere
Of distant glory in full view; thus climbs
Pleasure its heights forever and forever.
The centre-fire heaves underneath the earth,
And the earth changes like a human face;
The molten ore bursts up among the rocks,
Winds into the stone's heart, outbranches bright
In hidden mines, spots barren river-beds,
Crumbles into fine sand where sunbeams bask —
God joys therein. The wroth sea's waves are edged
With foam, white as the bitten lip of hate,
When, in the solitary waste, strange groups
Of young volcanos come up, cyclops-like,
Staring together with their eyes on flame —

God tastes a pleasure in their uncouth pride.
Then all is still; earth is a wintry clod:
But spring-wind, like a dancing psaltress, passes
Over its breast to waken it, rare verdure
Buds tenderly upon rough banks, between
The withered tree-roots and the cracks of frost,
Like a smile striving with a wrinkled face;
The grass grows bright, the boughs are swoln with blooms
Like chrysalids impatient for the air,
The shining dorrs are busy, beetles run
Along the furrows, ants make their ado;
Above, birds fly in merry flocks, the lark
Soars up and up, shivering for very joy;
Afar the ocean sleeps; white fishing-gulls
Flit where the strand is purple with its tribe
Of nested limpets; savage creatures seek
Their loves in wood and plain — and God renews
His ancient rapture. Thus he dwells in all,
From life's minute beginnings, up at last
To man — the consummation of this scheme
Of being, the completion of this sphere
Of life: whose attributes had here and there
Been scattered o'er the visible world before,
Asking to be combined, dim fragments meant
To be united in some wondrous whole,
Imperfect qualities throughout creation,
Suggesting some one creature yet to make,
Some point where all those scattered rays should meet
Convergent in the faculties of man.
Power — neither put forth blindly, nor controlled
Calmly by perfect knowledge; to be used
At risk, inspired or checked by hope and fear:
Knowledge — not intuition, but the slow
Uncertain fruit of an enhancing toil,
Strengthened by love: love — not serenely pure,
But strong from weakness, like a chance-sown plant
Which, cast on stubborn soil, puts forth changed buds
And softer stains, unknown in happier climes;
Love which endures and doubts and is oppressed
And cherished, suffering much and much sustained,
And blind, oft-failing, yet believing love,
A half-enlightened, often-checkered trust: —
Hints and previsions of which faculties,
Are strewn confusedly everywhere about
The inferior natures, and all lead up higher,
All shape out dimly the superior race,

The heir of hopes too fair to turn out false,
And man appears at last. So far the seal
Is put on life; one stage of being complete,
One scheme wound up: and from the grand result
A supplementary reflux of light,
Illustrates all the inferior grades, explains
Each back step in the circle. Not alone
For their possessor dawn those qualities,
But the new glory mixes with the heaven
And earth; man, once descried, imprints forever
His presence on all lifeless things: the winds
Are henceforth voices, wailing or a shout,
A querulous mutter or a quick gay laugh,
Never a senseless gust now man is born.
The herded pines commune and have deep thoughts,
A secret they assemble to discuss
When the sun drops behind their trunks which glare
Like grates of hell: the peerless cup afloat
Of the lake-lily is an urn, some nymph
Swims bearing high above her head: no bird
Whistles unseen, but through the gaps above
That let light in upon the gloomy woods,
A shape peeps from the breezy forest-top,
Arch with small puckered mouth and mocking eye.
The morn has enterprise, deep quiet droops
With evening, triumph takes the sunset hour,
Voluptuous transport ripens with the corn
Beneath a warm moon like a happy face:
— And this to fill us with regard for man,
With apprehension of his passing worth,
Desire to work his proper nature out,
And ascertain his rank and final place,
For these things tend still upward, progress is
The law of life, man is not Man as yet.
Nor shall I deem his object served, his end
Attained, his genuine strength put fairly forth,
While only here and there a star dispels
The darkness, here and there a towering mind
O'erlooks its prostrate fellows: when the host
Is out at once to the despair of night,
When all mankind alike is perfected,
Equal in full-blown powers — then, not till then,
I say, begins man's general infancy.
For wherefore make account of feverish starts
Of restless members of a dormant whole,
Impatient nerves which quiver while the body

Slumbers as in a grave ? Oh, long ago
The brow was twitched, the tremulous lids astir,
The peaceful mouth disturbed ; half-uttered speech
Ruffled the lip, and then the teeth were set,
The breath drawn sharp, the strong right-hand clenched
    stronger,
As it would pluck a lion by the jaw ;
The glorious creature laughed out even in sleep!
But when full roused, each giant-limb awake,
Each sinew strung, the great heart pulsing fast,
He shall start up and stand on his own earth,
Then shall his long triumphant march begin,
Thence shall his being date, — thus wholly roused,
What he achieves shall be set down to him.
When all the race is perfected alike
As man, that is ; all tended to mankind,
And, man produced, all has its end thus far :
But in completed man begins anew
A tendency to God. Prognostics told
Man's near approach ; so in man's self arise
August anticipations, symbols, types
Of a dim splendor ever on before
In that eternal circle life pursues.
For men begin to pass their nature's bound,
And find new hopes and cares which fast supplant
Their proper joys and griefs ; they grow too great
For narrow creeds of right and wrong, which fade
Before the unmeasured thirst for good : while peace
Rises within them ever more and more.
Such men are even now upon the earth,
Serene amid the half-formed creatures round
Who should be saved by them and joined with them.
Such was my task, and I was born to it —
Free, as I said but now, from much that chains
Spirits, high-dowered but limited and vexed
By a divided and delusive aim,
A shadow mocking a reality
Whose truth avails not wholly to disperse
The flitting mimic called up by itself,
And so remains perplexed and nigh put out
By its fantastic fellow's wavering gleam.
I, from the first, was never cheated thus ;
I never fashioned out a fancied good
Distinct from man's ; a service to be done,
A glory to be ministered unto
With powers put forth at man's expense, withdrawn

From laboring in his behalf; a strength
Denied that might avail him. I cared not
Lest his success ran counter to success
Elsewhere: for God is glorified in man,
And to man's glory vowed I soul and limb.
Yet, constituted thus, and thus endowed,
I failed: I gazed on power till I grew blind.
Power; I could not take my eyes from that:
That only, I thought, should be preserved, increased
At any risk, displayed, struck out at once —
The sign and note and character of man.
I saw no use in the past: only a scene
Of degradation, ugliness and tears,
The record of disgraces best forgotten,
A sullen page in human chronicles
Fit to erase. I saw no cause why man
Should not stand all-sufficient even now,
Or why his annals should be forced to tell
That once the tide of light, about to break
Upon the world, was sealed within its spring:
I would have had one day, one moment's space,
Change man's condition, push each slumbering claim
Of mastery o'er the elemental world
At once to full maturity, then roll
Oblivion o'er the work, and hide from man
What night had ushered morn. Not so, dear child
Of after-days, wilt thou reject the past
Big with deep warnings of the proper tenure
By which thou hast the earth: for thee the present
Shall have distinct and trembling beauty, seen
Beside that past's own shade when, in relief,
Its brightness shall stand out: nor yet on thee
Shall burst the future, as successive zones
Of several wonder open on some spirit
Flying secure and glad from heaven to heaven:
But thou shalt painfully attain to joy,
While hope and fear and love shall keep thee man!
All this was hid from me: as one by one
My dreams grew dim, my wide aims circumscribed,
As actual good within my reach decreased,
While obstacles sprung up this way and that
To keep me from effecting half the sum,
Small as it proved; as objects, mean within
The primal aggregate, seemed, even the least,
Itself a match for my concentred strength —
What wonder if I saw no way to shun

Despair? The power I sought for man, seemed God's.
In this conjuncture, as I prayed to die,
A strange adventure made me know, one sin
Had spotted my career from its uprise;
I saw Aprile — my Aprile there!
And as the poor melodious wretch disburdened
His heart, and moaned his weakness in my ear,
I learned my own deep error; love's undoing
Taught me the worth of love in man's estate,
And what proportion love should hold with power
In his right constitution; love preceding
Power, and with much power, always much more love;
Love still too straitened in his present means,
And earnest for new power to set love free.
I learned this, and supposed the whole was learned:
And thus, when men received with stupid wonder
My first revealings, would have worshipped me,
And I despised and loathed their proffered praise —
When, with awakened eyes, they took revenge
For past credulity in casting shame
On my real knowledge, and I hated them —
It was not strange I saw no good in man,
To overbalance all the wear and waste
Of faculties, displayed in vain, but born
To prosper in some better sphere: and why?
In my own heart love had not been made wise
To trace love's faint beginnings in mankind,
To know even hate is but a mask of love's,
To see a good in evil, and a hope
In ill-success; to sympathize, be proud
Of their half-reasons, faint aspirings, dim
Struggles for truth, their poorest fallacies,
Their prejudice and fears and cares and doubts;
All with a touch of nobleness, despite
Their error, upward tending all though weak,
Like plants in mines which never saw the sun,
But dream of him, and guess where he may be,
And do their best to climb and get to him.
All this I knew not, and I failed. Let men
Regard me, and the poet dead long ago
Who loved too rashly; and shape forth a third
And better-tempered spirit, warned by both:
As from the over-radiant star too mad
To drink the life-springs, beamless thence itself —
And the dark orb which borders the abyss,
Ingulfed in icy night, — might have its course,

A temperate and equidistant world.
Meanwhile, I have done well, though not all well.
As yet men cannot do without contempt;
'T is for their good, and therefore fit awhile
That they reject the weak, and scorn the false,
Rather than praise the strong and true, in me:
But after, they will know me. If I stoop
Into a dark tremendous sea of cloud,
It is but for a time; I press God's lamp
Close to my breast; its splendor, soon or late,
Will pierce the gloom: I shall emerge one day.
You understand me? I have said enough!
   Fest. Now die, dear Aureole!
   Par.   Festus, let my hand —
This hand, lie in your own, my own true friend!
Aprile! Hand in hand with you, Aprile!

   Fest. And this was Paracelsus!

NOTE

THE liberties I have taken with my subject are very trifling; and the reader may slip the foregoing scenes between the leaves of any memoir of Paracelsus he pleases, by way of commentary. To prove this, I subjoin a popular account, translated from the *Biographie Universelle*, Paris, 1822, which I select, not as the best, certainly, but as being at hand, and sufficiently concise for my purpose. I also append a few notes, in order to correct those parts which do not bear out my own view of the character of Paracelsus; and have incorporated with them a notice or two, illustrative of the poem itself.

"PARACELSUS (Philippus Aureolus Theophrastus Bombastus ab Hohenheim) was born in 1493 at Einsiedeln,[1] a little town in the canton of Schwyz, some leagues distant from Zurich. His father, who exercised the profession of medicine at Villach in Carinthia, was nearly related to George Bombast de Hohenheim, who became afterward Grand Prior of the Order of Malta: consequently Paracelsus could not spring from the dregs of the people, as Thomas Erastus, his sworn enemy, pretends.* It appears that his elementary education was much neglected, and that he spent part of his youth in pursuing the life common to the travelling *literati* of the age; that is to say, in wandering from country to country, predicting the future by astrology and cheiromancy, evoking apparitions, and practising the different operations of magic and alchemy, in which he had been initiated whether by his father or by various ecclesiastics, among the number of whom he particularizes the Abbot Tritheim,[2] and many German bishops.

"As Paracelsus displays everywhere an ignorance of the rudiments of the most ordinary knowledge, it is not probable that he ever studied seriously in the schools: he contented himself with visiting the universities of Germany, France, and Italy; and in spite of his boasting himself to have been the ornament of those institutions, there is no proof of his having legally acquired the title of Doctor, which he assumes. It is only known that he applied himself long, under the direction of the wealthy Sigismond Fugger of Schwatz, to the discovery of the Magnum Opus.

"Paracelsus travelled among the mountains of Bohemia, in the East, and in Sweden, in order to inspect the labors of the miners, to be initiated in the mysteries of the oriental adepts, and to observe the secrets of nature and the famous mountain of loadstone.[8] He professes also to have visited Spain, Portugal, Prussia, Poland, and Transylvania; everywhere communicating freely, not merely with the physicians, but the old women, charlatans, and conjurers of these several lands. It is even believed that he extended his journeyings as far as Egypt and Tartary, and that he accompanied the son of the Khan of the Tartars to Constantinople, for the

---

* I shall disguise M. Renauldin's next sentence a little. "Hic (Erastus sc.) Paracelsum trimum a milite quodam, alii a sue exectum ferunt: constat imberbem illum, mulierumque osorem fuisse." A standing High-Dutch joke in those days at the expense of a number of learned men, as may be seen by referring to such rubbish as Melander's *Jocoseria*, etc. In the prints from his portrait by Tintoretto, painted a year before his death, Paracelsus is *barbatulus*, at all events. But Erastus was never without a good reason for his faith — *e. g.*, "Helvetium fuisse (Paracelsum) vix credo, vix enim ea regio tale monstrum ediderit." (*De Medicina Nova.*)

purpose of obtaining the secret of the tincture of Trismegistus from a Greek who inhabited that capital.

"The period of his return to Germany is unknown: it is only certain that, at about the age of thirty-three, many astonishing cures which he wrought on eminent personages procured him such a celebrity, that he was called in 1526, on the recommendation of Œcolampadius,[4] to fill a chair of physic and surgery at the University of Basil. There Paracelsus began by burning publicly in the amphitheatre the works of Avicenna and Galen, assuring his auditors that the latchets of his shoes were more instructed than those two physicians; that all universities, all writers put together, were less gifted than the hairs of his beard and of the crown of his head; and that, in a word, he was to be regarded as the legitimate monarch of medicine. 'You shall follow me,' cried he, 'you, Avicenna, Galen, Rhasis, Montagnana, Mesues, you, gentlemen of Paris, Montpellier, Germany, Cologne, Vienna,* and whomsoever the Rhine and Danube nourish; you who inhabit the isles of the sea; you, likewise, Dalmatians, Athenians; thou, Arab; thou, Greek; thou, Jew: all shall follow me, and the monarchy shall be mine.' †

"But at Basil it was speedily perceived that the new Professor was no better than an egregious quack. Scarcely a year elapsed before his lectures had fairly driven away an audience incapable of comprehending their emphatic jargon. That which above all contributed to sully his reputation was the debauched life he led. According to the testimony of Oporinus, who lived two years in his intimacy, Paracelsus scarcely ever ascended the lecture-desk unless half drunk, and only dictated to his secretaries when in a state of intoxication: if summoned to attend the sick, he rarely proceeded thither without previously drenching himself with wine. He was accustomed to retire to bed without changing his clothes; sometimes he spent the night in pot-houses with peasants, and in the morning knew no longer what he was about; and, nevertheless, up to the age of twenty-five his only drink had been water.[5]

"At length, fearful of being punished for a serious outrage on a magistrate,[6] he fled from Basil towards the end of the year 1527, and took refuge in Alsatia, whither he caused Oporinus to follow with his chemical apparatus.

"He then entered once more upon the career of ambulatory theosophist.‡ Accordingly we find him at Colmar in 1528; at Nuremberg in 1529; at St. Gall in 1531; at Pfeffers in 1535; and at Augsburg in 1536: he next made some stay in Moravia, where he still further compromised his reputation by the loss of many distinguished patients, which compelled him to betake himself to Vienna; from thence he passed into Hungary; and in 1538 was at Villach, where he dedicated his *Chronicle* to the States of Carinthia, in gratitude for the many kindnesses with which they had honored his

---

* Erastus, who relates this, here oddly remarks, "mirum quod non et Garamantos, Indos et *Anglos* adjunxit." Not so wonderful neither, if we believe what another adversary "had heard somewhere," — that all Paracelsus' system came of his pillaging "Anglum quendam, Rogerium Bacchonem."

† See his works, *passim*. I must give one specimen:— Somebody had been styling him "Luther alter." "And why not?" (he asks, as he well might.) "Luther is abundantly learned, therefore you hate him and me; but we are at least a match for you. — Nam et contra vos et vestros universos principes Avicennam, Galenum, Aristotelem, etc. me satis superque munitum esse novi. Et vertex iste meus calvus ac depilis multo plura et sublimiora novit quam vester vel Avicenna vel universæ academiæ. Prodite, et signum date, qui viri sitis, quid roboris habeatis? quid autem sitis? Doctores et magistri, pediculos pectentes et fricantes podicem." (*Frag. Med.*)

‡ "So migratory a life could afford Paracelsus but little leisure for application to books, and accordingly he informs us that for the space of ten years he never opened a single volume, and that his whole medical library was not composed of six sheets: in effect, the inventory drawn up after his death states that the only books which he left were the Bible, the New Testament, the Commentaries of St. Jerome on the Gospels, a printed volume on Medicine, and seven manuscripts."

father. Finally, from Mindelheim, which he visited in 1540, Paracelsus proceeded to Salzburg, where he died in the Hospital of St. Stephen (*Sebastian* is meant), Sept. 24, 1541."— (Here follows a criticism on his writings, which I omit.)

[1] *Paracelsus* would seem to be a fantastic version of *Von Hohenheim;* Einsiedeln is the Latinized Eremus, whence Paracelsus is sometimes called, as in the correspondence of Erasmus, Eremita. Bombast, his proper name, probably acquired, from the characteristic phraseology of his lectures, that unlucky signification which it has ever since retained.

[2] Then Bishop of Spanheim, and residing at Würzburg in Franconia; a town situated in a grassy fertile country, whence its name, Herbipolis. He was much visited there by learned men, as may be seen by his *Epistolæ Familiares*, Hag. 1536: among others, by his stanch friend Cornelius Agrippa, to whom he dates thence, in 1510, a letter in answer to the dedicatory epistle prefixed to the treatise *De Occult. Philosoph.*, which last contains the following ominous allusion to Agrippa's sojourn: "Quum nuper tecum, R. P. in cœnobio tuo apud Herbipolim aliquamdiu conversatus, multa de chymicis, multa de magicis, multa de cabalisticis, cæterisque quæ adhuc in occulto delitescunt, arcanis scientiis atque artibus una contulissemus," etc.

[3] "Inexplebilis illa aviditas naturæ perscrutandi secreta et reconditarum supellectile scientiarum animum locupletandi, uno eodemque loco diu persistere non patiebatur, sed Mercurii instar, omnes terras, nationes et urbes perlustrandi igniculos supponebat, ut cum viris naturæ scrutatoribus, chymicis præsertim, ore tenus conferret, et quæ diurturnis laboribus nocturnisque vigiliis invenerant una vel altera communicatione obtineret." (Bitiskius in *Præfat.*) "Patris auxilio primum, deinde propria industria doctissimos viros in Germania, Italia, Gallia, Hispania, aliisque Europæ regionibus, nactus est præceptores; quorum liberali doctrina, et potissimum propria inquisitione ut qui esset ingenio acutissimo ac fere divino, tantum profecit, ut multi testati sint, in universa philosophia, tam ardua, tam arcana et abdita eruisse mortalium neminem." (Melch. Adam, in *Vit. Germ. Medic.*) "Paracelsus qui in intima naturæ viscera sic penitus introierit, metallorum stirpiumque vires et facultates tam incredibili ingenii acumine exploraverit ac perviderit, ad morbos omnes vel desperatos et opinione hominum insanabiles percurandum; ut cum Theophrasto nata primum medicina perfectaque videtur." (Petri Rami *Orat. de Basilea.*) His passion for wandering is best described in his own words: "Ecce amatorem adolescentem difficillimi itineris haud piget, ut venustam saltem puellam vel fœminam aspiciat: quanto minus nobilissimarum artium amore laboris ac cujuslibet tædii pigebit?" etc. (*Defensiones Septem adversus æmulos suos.* 1573. Def. 4ta. "De peregrinationibus et exilio.")

[4] The reader may remember that it was in conjunction with Œcolampadius, then Divinity Professor at Basil, that Zuinglius published in 1528 an answer to Luther's Confession of Faith; and that both proceeded in company to the subsequent conference with Luther and Melancthon at Marburg. Their letters fill a large volume. — "*D. D. Johannis Œcolampadii et Huldrichi Zuinglii Epistolarum lib. quatuor.*" Bas. 1536. It must be also observed that Zuinglius began to preach in 1516, and at Zurich in 1519, and that in 1525 the Mass was abolished in the cantons. The tenets of Œcolampadius were supposed to be more evangelical than those up to that period maintained by the glorious German, and our brave Bishop Fisher attacked them as the fouler heresy : — "About this time arose out of Luther's school one Œcolampadius, like a mighty and fierce

giant; who, as his master had gone beyond the Church, went beyond his master (or else it had been impossible he could have been reputed the better scholar), who denied the real presence; him, this worthy champion (the Bishop) sets upon, and with five books (like so many smooth stones taken out of the river that doth always run with living water) slays the Philistine; which five books were written in the year of our Lord 1526, at which time he had governed the See of Rochester twenty years." (Life of Bishop Fisher, 1655.) Now, there is no doubt of the Protestantism of Paracelsus, Erasmus, Agrippa, etc., but the nonconformity of Paracelsus was always scandalous. L. Crasso (*Elogj d'Huomini Letterati*. Ven. 1666) informs us that his books were excommunicated by the Church. Quenstedt (*de Patr. Doct.*) affirms "nec tantum novæ medicinæ, verum etiam novæ theologiæ autor est." Delrio, in his *Disquisit. Magicar.*, classes him among those "partim atheos, partim hæreticos" (lib. I. cap. 3). "Omnino tamen multa theologica in ejusdem scriptis plane atheismum olent, ac duriuscule sonant in auribus vere Christiani." (D. Gabrielis Clauderi Schediasma *de Tinct. Univ. Norimb.* 1736.) I shall only add one more authority: — "Oporinus dicit se (Paracelsum) aliquando Lutherum et Papam, non minus quam nunc Galenum et Hippocratem redacturum in ordinem minabatur, neque enim eorum qui hactenus in scripturam sacram scripsissent, sive veteres, sive recentiores, quenquam scripturæ nucleum recte eruisse, sed circa corticem et quasi membranam tantum hærere." (Th. Erastus, *Disputat. de Med. Nova.*) These and similar notions had their due effect on Oporinus, who, says Zuingerus, in his *Theatrum*, "longum vale dixit ei (Paracelso), ne ob præceptoris, alioqui amicissimi, horrendas blasphemias ipse quoque aliquando pœnas Deo Opt. Max. lueret."

⁵ His defenders allow the drunkenness. Take a sample of their excuses: "Gentis hoc, non viri vitiolum est, a Taciti seculo ad nostrum usque non interrupto filo devolutum, sinceritati forte Germanæ coævum, et nescio an aliquo consanguinitatis vinculo junctum." (Bitiskius.) The other charges were chiefly trumped up by Oporinus : "Domi, quod Oporinus amanuensis ejus sæpe narravit, nunquam nisi potus ad explicanda sua accessit, atque in medio conclavi ad columnam τετυφωμένος adsistens, apprehenso manibus capulo ensis, cujus κοίλωμα hospitium præbuit, ut aiunt, spiritui familiari, imaginationes aut concepta sua protulit : — alii illud quod in capulo habuit, ab ipso Azoth appellatum, medicinam fuisse præstantissimam aut lapidem Philosophicum putant." (Melch. Adam.) This famous sword was no laughing-matter in those days, and it is now a material feature in the popular idea of Paracelsus. I recollect a couple of allusions to it in our own literature, at the moment.

Ne had been known the Danish Gonswart,
Or Paracelsus with his long sword.
Volpone, Act ii. Scene 2.

Bumbastus kept a devil's bird
Shut in the pummel of his sword,
That taught him all the cunning pranks
Of past and future mountebanks.
Hudibras, Part ii. Cant. 3.

This Azoth was simply "*laudanum suum.*" But in his time he was commonly believed to possess the double tincture — the power of curing diseases and transmuting metals. Oporinus often witnessed, as he declares, both these effects, as did also Franciscus, the servant of Paracelsus, who describes, in a letter to Neander, a successful projection at which he was present, and the results of which, good golden ingots, were confided to his keeping. For the other quality, let the following notice vouch

NOTE

among many others: — "Degebat Theophrastus Norimbergæ procitus a medentibus illius urbis, et vaniloquus deceptorque proclamatus, qui, ut laboranti famæ subveniat, viros quosdam authoritatis summæ in Republica illa adit, et infamiæ amoliendæ, artique suæ asserendæ, specimen ejus pollicetur editurum, nullo stipendio vel accepto pretio, horum faciles præbentium aures jussu elephantiacos aliquot, a communione hominum cæterorum segregatos, et in valetudinarium detrusos, alieno arbitrio eliguntur, quos virtute singulari remediorum suorum Theophrastus a fœda Græcorum lepra mundat, pristinæque sanitati restituit; conservat illustre harum curationum urbs in archivis suis testimonium." (Bitiskius.)* It is to be remarked that Oporinus afterwards repented of his treachery: "Sed resipuit tandem, et quem vivum convitiis insectatus fuerat defunctum veneratione prosequutus, infames famæ præceptoris morsus in remorsus conscientiæ conversi pœnitentia, heu nimis tarda, vulnera clausere exanimi quæ spiranti inflixerant." For these "bites" of Oporinus, see Disputat. Erasti, and Andreæ Jocisci *Oratio de Vit. ob. Opor^i;* for the "remorse," *Mic. Toxita in pref. Testamenti,* and Conringius (otherwise an enemy of Paracelsus), who says it was contained in a letter from Oporinus to Doctor Vegerus.†

Whatever the moderns may think of these marvellous attributes, the title of Paracelsus to be considered the father of modern chemistry is indisputable. Gerardus Vossius, *De Philos^a et Philos^{um} sectis,* thus prefaces the ninth section of cap. 9, *De Chymia*—"Nobilem hanc medicinæ partem, diu sepultam avorum ætate, quasi ab orco revocavit Th. Paracelsus." I suppose many hints lie scattered in his neglected books, which clever appropriators have since developed with applause. Thus, it appears from his treatise *De Phlebotomia,* and elsewhere, that he had discovered the circulation of the blood and the sanguification of the heart; as did after him Realdo Colombo, and still more perfectly Andrea Cesalpino of Arezzo, as Bayle and Bartoli observe. Even Lavater quotes a passage from his work *De Natura Rerum,* on practical Physiognomy, in which the definitions and axioms are precise enough: he adds, "though an astrological enthusiast, a man of prodigious genius." See Holcroft's Translation, vol. iii. p. 179 — "The Eyes." While on the subject of the writings of Paracelsus, I may explain a passage in the third part of the Poem. He was, as I have said, unwilling to publish his works, but in effect did publish a vast number. Valentius (*in Præfat. in Paramyr.*) declares "quod ad librorum Paracelsi copiam attinet, audio, a Germanis prope trecentos recenseri." "O fœcunditas ingenii!" adds he, appositely. Many of these were, however, spurious; and Fred. Bitiskius gives his good edition (3 vols. fol. Gen. 1658) "rejectis suppositis solo ipsius nomine superbientibus quorum ingens circumfertur numerus." The rest were "charissimum et pretiosissimum authoris pignus, extorsum potius ab illo quam obtentum." "Jam minime eo volente atque jubente hæc ipsius scripta in lucem prodisse videntur; quippe quæ muro inclusa ipso absente, servi cujusdam indicio, furto surrepta atque sublata sunt," says Valentius. These have been the study of a host of commentators, amongst whose labors are most notable, Petri Severini, *Idea Medicinæ Philosophiæ.* Bas. 1571; Mic. Toxetis, *Onomastica.* Arg. 1574; Dornei, *Dict. Parac.* Franc.

---

* The premature death of Paracelsus casts no manner of doubt on the fact of his having possessed the Elixir Vitæ: the alchemists have abundant reasons to adduce, from which I select the following, as explanatory of a property of the Tincture not calculated on by its votaries:—" Objectionem illam, quod Paracelsus non fuerit longævus, nonnulli quoque solvunt per rationes physicas: vitæ nimirum abbreviationem fortasse talibus accidere posse, ob Tincturam frequentiore ac largiore dosi sumtam, dum a summe efficaci et penetrabili hujus virtute calor innatus quasi suffocatur." (*Gabrielis Clauderi Schediasma.*)

† For a good defence of Paracelsus I refer the reader to Olaus Borrichius' treatise — *Hermetis etc. Sapientia vindicata*, 1674. Or, if he is no more learned than myself in such matters, I mention simply that Paracelsus introduced the use of Mercury and Laudanum.

1584 ; and P^t Philos^æ Compendium cum scholiis auctore Leone Suavio. Paris. (This last, a good book.)

6 A disgraceful affair. One Liechtenfels, a canon, having been rescued *in extremis* by the "*laudanum*" of Paracelsus, refused the stipulated fee, and was supported in his meanness by the authorities, whose interference Paracelsus would not brook. His own liberality was allowed by his bitterest foes, who found a ready solution of his indifference to profit in the aforesaid sword-handle and its guest. His freedom from the besetting sin of a profession he abhorred — (as he curiously says somewhere, "Quis quæso deinceps honorem deferat professione tali, quæ a tam facinorosis nebulonibus obitur et administratur?") — is recorded in his epitaph, which affirms — "Bona sua in pauperes distribuenda collocandaque erogavit," *honoravit*, or *ordinavit* — for accounts differ.

STRAFFORD

A TRAGEDY

DEDICATED, IN ALL AFFECTIONATE ADMIRATION,

TO

WILLIAM C. MACREADY.

LONDON, *April* 23, 1837.

PERSONS.

CHARLES I.
Earl of HOLLAND.
Lord SAVILE.
Sir HENRY VANE.
WENTWORTH, Viscount WENTWORTH, Earl of STRAFFORD.
JOHN PYM.
JOHN HAMPDEN.
The younger VANE.
DENZIL HOLLIS.
BENJAMIN RUDYARD.
NATHANIEL FIENNES.
Earl of LOUDON.
MAXWELL, *Usher of the Black Rod.*
BALFOUR, *Constable of the Tower.*
A Puritan.
Queen HENRIETTA.
LUCY PERCY, *Countess of Carlisle.*
Presbyterians, Scots Commissioners, Adherents of Strafford, Secretaries, Officers of the Court, etc. Two of Strafford's children.

ACT I.

SCENE I. *A House near Whitehall.* HAMPDEN, HOLLIS, *the younger* VANE, RUDYARD, FIENNES *and many of the Presbyterian Party:* LOUDON *and other Scots Commissioners.*

Vane. I say, if he be here —
Rud. (And he is here!) —
Hol. For England's sake let every man be still
Nor speak of him, so much as say his name,
Till Pym rejoin us! Rudyard! Henry Vane!
One rash conclusion may decide our course
And with it England's fate — think — England's fate!
Hampden, for England's sake they should be still!
Vane. You say so, Hollis? Well, I must be still.
It is indeed too bitter that one man,

     Any one man's mere presence, should suspend
England's combined endeavor: little need
To name him!
  Rud.   For you are his brother, Hollis!
  Hamp. Shame on you, Rudyard! time to tell him that
When he forgets the Mother of us all.
  Rud. Do I forget her?
  Hamp.   You talk idle hate
Against her foe : is that so strange a thing?
Is hating Wentworth all the help she needs?
  A Puritan. The Philistine strode, cursing as he went:
But David — five smooth pebbles from the brook
Within his scrip . . .
  Rud.   Be you as still as David!
  Fien. Here's Rudyard not ashamed to wag a tongue
Stiff with ten years' disuse of Parliaments;
Why, when the last sat, Wentworth sat with us!
  Rud. Let's hope for news of them now he returns —
He that was safe in Ireland, as we thought!
— But I'll abide Pym's coming.
  Vane.   Now, by Heaven,
Then may be cool who can, silent who will —
Some have a gift that way! Wentworth is here,
Here, and the King's safe closeted with him
Ere this. And when I think on all that's past
Since that man left us, how his single arm
Rolled the advancing good of England back
And set the woful past up in its place,
Exalting Dagon where the Ark should be, —
How that man has made firm the fickle King
(Hampden, I will speak out!) — in aught he feared
To venture on before; taught tyranny
Her dismal trade, the use of all her tools,
To ply the scourge yet screw the gag so close
That strangled agony bleeds mute to death —
How he turns Ireland to a private stage
For training infant villanies, new ways
Of wringing treasure out of tears and blood,
Unheard oppressions nourished in the dark
To try how much man's nature can endure
— If he dies under it, what harm? if not,
Why, one more trick is added to the rest
Worth a king's knowing, and what Ireland bears
England may learn to bear : — how all this while
That man has set himself to one dear task,
The bringing Charles to relish more and more

Power, power without law, power and blood too
— Can I be still?
  Hamp.   For that you should be still.
  Vane. Oh Hampden, then and now! The year he left us,
The People in full Parliament could wrest
The Bill of Rights from the reluctant King;
And now, he'll find in an obscure small room
A stealthy gathering of great-hearted men
That take up England's cause: England is here!
  Hamp. And who despairs of England?
  Rud.   That do I,
If Wentworth comes to rule her. I am sick
To think her wretched masters, Hamilton,
The muckworm Cottington, the maniac Laud,
May yet be longed-for back again. I say,
I do despair.
  Vane.   And, Rudyard, I'll say this —
Which all true men say after me, not loud
But solemnly and as you 'd say a prayer!
This King, who treads our England underfoot,
Has just so much . . . it may be fear or craft,
As bids him pause at each fresh outrage; friends,
He needs some sterner hand to grasp his own,
Some voice to ask, " Why shrink? Am I not by?"
Now, one whom England loved for serving her,
Found in his heart to say, " I know where best
The iron heel shall bruise her, for she leans
Upon me when you trample." Witness, you!
So Wentworth heartened Charles, so England fell.
But inasmuch as life is hard to take
From England . . .
  Many Voices. Go on, Vane! 'T is well said, Vane!
  Vane. — Who has not so forgotten Runnymead! —
  Voices. 'T is well and bravely spoken, Vane! Go on!
  Vane. — There are some little signs of late she knows
The ground no place for her. She glances round,
Wentworth has dropped the hand, is gone his way
On other service: what if she arise?
No! the King beckons, and beside him stands
The same bad man once more, with the same smile
And the same gesture. Now shall England crouch.
Or catch at us and rise?
  Voices.   The Renegade!
Haman! Ahithophel!
  Hamp.   Gentlemen of the North,
It was not thus the night your claims were urged,

And we pronounced the League and Covenant,
The cause of Scotland, England's cause as well:
Vane there, sat motionless the whole night through.
 Vane. Hampden!
 Fien.   Stay, Vane!
 Lou.   Be just and patient, Vane!
 Vane. Mind how you counsel patience, Loudon! you
Have still a Parliament, and this your League
To back it; you are free in Scotland still:
While we are brothers, hope's for England yet.
But know you wherefore Wentworth comes? to quench
This last of hopes? that he brings war with him?
Know you the man's self? what he dares?
 Lou.   We know,
All know — 't is nothing new.
 Vane.   And what's new, then,
In calling for his life? Why, Pym himself —
You must have heard — ere Wentworth dropped our cause
He would see Pym first; there were many more
Strong on the people's side and friends of his,
Eliot that's dead, Rudyard and Hampden here,
But for these Wentworth cared not; only, Pym
He would see — Pym and he were sworn, 't is said,
To live and die together; so, they met
At Greenwich. Wentworth, you are sure, was long,
Specious enough, the devil's argument
Lost nothing on his lips; he 'd have Pym own
A patriot could not play a purer part
Than follow in his track; they two combined
Might put down England. Well, Pym heard him out;
One glance — you know Pym's eye — one word was all:
"You leave us, Wentworth! while your head is on,
I 'll not leave you."
 Hamp.   Has he left Wentworth, then?
Has England lost him? Will you let him speak,
Or put your crude surmises in his mouth?
Away with this! Will you have Pym or Vane?
 Voices. Wait Pym's arrival! Pym shall speak.
 Hamp.   Meanwhile
Let Loudon read the Parliament's report
From Edinburgh: our last hope, as Vane says,
Is in the stand it makes. Loudon!
 Vane.   No, no!
Silent I can be: not indifferent!
 Hamp. Then each keep silence, praying God to spare
His anger, cast not England quite away
In this her visitation!

A Puritan. Seven years long
The Midianite drove Israel into dens
And caves. Till God sent forth a mighty man,
(PYM *enters.*)
Even Gideon!
Pym. Wentworth's come : nor sickness, care,
The ravaged body nor the ruined soul,
More than the winds and waves that beat his ship,
Could keep him from the King. He has not reached
Whitehall : they've hurried up a Council there
To lose no time and find him work enough.
Where's Loudon? your Scots' Parliament . . .
Lou. Holds firm :
We were about to read reports.
Pym. The King
Has just dissolved your Parliament.
Lou. and other Scots. Great God!
An oath-breaker! Stand by us, England, then!
Pym. The King's too sanguine; doubtless Wentworth's here;
But still some little form might be kept up.
Hamp. Now speak, Vane! Rudyard, you had much to say!
Hol. The rumor's false, then . . .
Pym. Ay, the Court gives out
His own concerns have brought him back : I know
'Tis the King calls him. Wentworth supersedes
The tribe of Cottingtons and Hamiltons
Whose part is played ; there's talk enough, by this, —
Merciful talk, the King thinks : time is now
To turn the record's last and bloody leaf
Which, chronicling a nation's great despair,
Tells they were long rebellious, and their lord
Indulgent, till, all kind expedients tried,
He drew the sword on them and reigned in peace.
Laud's laying his religion on the Scots
Was the last gentle entry : the new page
Shall run, the King thinks, " Wentworth thrust it down
At the sword's point."
A Puritan. I'll do your bidding, Pym,
England's and God's — one blow!
Pym. A goodly thing —
We all say, friends, it is a goodly thing
To right that England. Heaven grows dark above :
Let's snatch one moment ere the thunder fall,
To say how well the English spirit comes out
Beneath it! All have done their best, indeed,

From lion Eliot, that grand Englishman,
To the least here: and who, the least one here,
When she is saved (for her redemption dawns
Dimly, most dimly, but it dawns — it dawns)
Who'd give at any price his hope away
Of being named along with the Great Men?
We would not — no, we would not give that up!
   Hamp. And one name shall be dearer than all names,
When children, yet unborn, are taught that name
After their fathers', — taught what matchless man . . .
   Pym. . . . Saved England? What if Wentworth's should be still
That name?
   Rud. and others. We have just said it, Pym! His death
Saves her! We said it — there's no way beside!
I'll do God's bidding, Pym! They struck down Joab
And purged the land.
   Vane.   No villanous striking-down!
   Rud. No, a calm vengeance: let the whole land rise
And shout for it. No Feltons!
   Pym.   Rudyard, no!
England rejects all Feltons; most of all
Since Wentworth . . . Hampden, say the trust again
Of England in her servants — but I'll think
You know me, all of you. Then, I believe,
Spite of the past, Wentworth rejoins you, friends!
   Vane and others. Wentworth? Apostate! Judas! Double-dyed
A traitor! Is it Pym, indeed . . .
   Pym.   . . . Who says
Vane never knew that Wentworth, loved that man,
Was used to stroll with him, arm locked in arm,
Along the streets to see the people pass,
And read in every island-countenance
Fresh argument for God against the King, —
Never sat down, say, in the very house
Where Eliot's brow grew broad with noble thoughts,
(You've joined us, Hampden — Hollis, you as well,)
And then left talking over Gracchus' death . . .
   Vane. To frame, we know it well, the choicest clause
In the Petition of Right: he framed such clause
One month before he took at the King's hand
His Northern Presidency, which that Bill
Denounced.
   Pym. Too true! Never more, never more
Walked we together! Most alone I went.

I have had friends — all here are fast my friends —
But I shall never quite forget that friend.
And yet it could not but be real in him!
You, Vane, — you, Rudyard, have no right to trust
To Wentworth: but can no one hope with me?
Hampden, will Wentworth dare shed English blood
Like water?
    Hamp.   Ireland is Aceldama.
    Pym. Will he turn Scotland to a hunting-ground
To please the King, now that he knows the King?
The People or the King? and that King, Charles!
    Hamp. Pym, all here know you: you'll not set your heart
On any baseless dream. But say one deed
Of Wentworth's, since he left us . . .   [*Shouting without*
    Vane.   There! he comes,
And they shout for him! Wentworth's at Whitehall,
The King embracing him, now, as we speak,
And he, to be his match in courtesies,
Taking the whole war's risk upon himself,
Now, while you tell us here how changed he is!
Hear you?
    Pym.   And yet if 't is a dream, no more,
That Wentworth chose their side, and brought the King
To love it as though Laud had loved it first,
And the Queen after; — that he led their cause
Calm to success, and kept it spotless through,
So that our very eyes could look upon
The travail of our souls, and close content
That violence, which something mars even right
Which sanctions it, had taken off no grace
From its serene regard. Only a dream!
    Hamp. We meet here to accomplish certain good
By obvious means, and keep tradition up
Of free assemblages, else obsolete,
In this poor chamber: nor without effect
Has friend met friend to counsel and confirm,
As, listening to the beats of England's heart,
We spoke its wants to Scotland's prompt reply
By these her delegates. Remains alone
That word grow deed, as with God's help it shall —
But with the devil's hindrance, who doubts too?
Looked we or no that tyranny should turn
Her engines of oppression to their use?
Whereof, suppose the worst be Wentworth here —
Shall we break off the tactics which succeed
In drawing out our formidablest foe,

Let bickering and disunion take their place?
Or count his presence as our conquest's proof,
And keep the old arms at their steady play?
Proceed to England's work! Fiennes, read the list!
  Fiennes. Ship-money is refused or fiercely paid
In every county, save the northern parts
Where Wentworth's influence . . .   [*Shouting.*
  Vane.   I, in England's name,
Declare her work, this way, at end! Till now,
Up to this moment, peaceful strife was best.
We English had free leave to think; till now,
We had a shadow of a Parliament
In Scotland. But all's changed: they change the first,
They try brute-force for law, they, first of all . . .
  Voices. Good! Talk enough! The old true hearts with Vane!
  Vane. Till we crush Wentworth for her, there's no act
Serves England!
  Voices.   Vane for England!
  Pym.   Pym should be
Something to England. I seek Wentworth, friends.

Scene II. *Whitehall.*

Lady CARLISLE *and* WENTWORTH.

  Went. And the King?
  Lady Car.   Wentworth, lean on me! Sit then!
I'll tell you all; this horrible fatigue
Will kill you.
  Went.   No;— or, Lucy, just your arm;
I'll not sit till I've cleared this up with him:
After that, rest. The King?
  Lady Car.   Confides in you.
  Went. Why? or, why now?— They have kind throats, the
        knaves!
Shout for me— they!
  Lady Car.   You come so strangely soon:
Yet we took measures to keep off the crowd —
Did they shout for you?
  Went.   Wherefore should they not?
Does the King take such measures for himself?
Beside, there's such a dearth of malcontents,
You say!
  Lady Car. I said but few dared carp at you.
  Went. At me? at us, I hope! The King and I!

He's surely not disposed to let me bear
The fame away from him of these late deeds
In Ireland? I am yet his instrument
Be it for well or ill? He trusts me, too!
 Lady Car. The King, dear Wentworth, purposes, I said,
To grant you, in the face of all the Court . . . .
 Went. All the Court! Evermore the Court about us!
Savile and Holland, Hamilton and Vane
About us, — then the King will grant me — what?
That he for once put these aside and say —
" Tell me your whole mind, Wentworth!"
 Lady Car.   You professed
You would be calm.
 Went.   Lucy, and I am calm!
How else shall I do all I come to do,
Broken, as you may see, body and mind,
How shall I serve the King? Time wastes meanwhile,
You have not told me half. His footstep! No.
Quick, then, before I meet him, — I am calm —
Why does the King distrust me?
 Lady Car.   He does not
Distrust you.
 Went. Lucy, you can help me; you
Have even seemed to care for me: one word!
Is it the Queen?
 Lady Car. No, not the Queen: the party
That poisons the Queen's ear, Savile and Holland.
 Went. I know, I know: old Vane, too, he's one too?
Go on — and he's made Secretary. Well?
Or leave them out and go straight to the charge;
The charge!
 Lady Car. Oh, there's no charge, no precise charge:
Only they sneer, make light of — one may say,
Nibble at what you do.
 Went.   I know! but, Lucy,
I reckoned on you from the first! — Go on!
— Was sure could I once see this gentle friend
When I arrived, she'd throw an hour away
To help her . . . what am I?
 Lady Car.   You thought of me,
Dear Wentworth?
 Went.   But go on! The party here!
 Lady Car. They do not think your Irish government
Of that surpassing value . . .
 Went.   The one thing
Of value! The one service that the crown

May count on! All that keeps these very Vanes
In power, to vex me — not that they do vex,
Only it might vex some to hear that service
Decried, the sole support that's left the King!
  Lady Car. So the Archbishop says.
  Went.   Ah? well, perhaps
The only hand held up in my defence
May be old Laud's! These Hollands then, these Saviles
Nibble? They nibble? — that's the very word!
  Lady Car. Your profit in the Customs, Bristol says,
Exceeds the due proportion: while the tax . . .
  Went. Enough! 'tis too unworthy, — I am not
So patient as I thought! What's Pym about?
  Lady Car. Pym?
  Went.   Pym and the People.
  Lady Car.   Oh, the Faction!
Extinct — of no account: there'll never be
Another Parliament.
  Went.   Tell Savile that!
You may know — (ay, you do — the creatures here
Never forget!) that in my earliest life
I was not . . . much that I am now! The King
May take my word on points concerning Pym
Before Lord Savile's, Lucy, or if not,
I bid them ruin their wise selves, not me,
These Vanes and Hollands! I'll not be their tool
Who might be Pym's friend yet.
         But there's the King!
Where is he?
  Lady Car. Just apprised that you arrive.
  Went. And why not here to meet me? I was told
He sent for me, nay, longed for me.
  Lady Car.   Because, —
He is now . . . I think a Council's sitting now
About this Scots affair.
  Went.   A Council sits?
They have not taken a decided course
Without me in the matter?
  Lady Car.   I should say . . .
  Went. The war? They cannot have agreed to that?
Not the Scots' war? — without consulting me —
Me, that am here to show how rash it is,
How easy to dispense with? — Ah, you too
Against me! well, — the King may take his time.
— Forget it, Lucy! Cares make peevish: mine
Weigh me (but 't is a secret) to my grave.

STRAFFORD

Lady Car. For life or death I am your own, dear friend!
[*Goes out.*
Went. Heartless! but all are heartless here. Go now,
Forsake the People! I did not forsake
The People: they shall know it, when the King
Will trust me! — who trusts all beside at once,
While I have not spoke Vane and Savile fair,
And am not trusted: have but saved the throne:
Have not picked up the Queen's glove prettily,
And am not trusted. But he'll see me now.
Weston is dead: the Queen's half English now —
More English: one decisive word will brush
These insects from . . . the step I know so well!
The King! But now, to tell him . . . no — to ask
What's in me he distrusts: — or, best begin
By proving that this frightful Scots affair
Is just what I foretold. So much to say,
And the flesh fails, now, and the time is come,
And one false step no way to be repaired.
You were avenged, Pym, could you look on me.

(PYM *enters.*)

Went. I little thought of you just then.
Pym. No? I
Think always of you, Wentworth.
Went. The old voice!
I wait the King, sir.
Pym. True — you look so pale!
A Council sits within; when that breaks up
He'll see you.
Went. Sir, I thank you.
Pym. Oh, thank Laud!
You know when Laud once gets on Church affairs
The case is desperate: he'll not be long
To-day: he only means to prove, to-day,
We English all are mad to have a hand
In butchering the Scots for serving God
After their fathers' fashion: only that!
Went. Sir, keep your jests for those who relish them!
(Does he enjoy their confidence?) 'T is kind
To tell me what the Council does.
Pym. You grudge
That I should know it had resolved on war
Before you came? no need: you shall have all
The credit, trust me!
Went. Have the Council dared —

They have not dared . . . that is — I know you not.
Farewell, sir : times are changed.
  Pym.   — Since we two met
At Greenwich ? Yes : poor patriots though we be,
You cut a figure, makes some slight return
For your exploits in Ireland ! Changed indeed,
Could our friend Eliot look from out his grave !
Ah, Wentworth, one thing for acquaintance' sake,
Just to decide a question ; have you, now,
Felt your old self since you forsook us ?
  Went.   Sir !
  Pym. Spare me the gesture ! you misapprehend.
Think not I mean the advantage is with me.
I was about to say that, for my part,
I never quite held up my head since then —
Was quite myself since then : for first, you see,
I lost all credit after that event
With those who recollect how sure I was
Wentworth would outdo Eliot on our side.
Forgive me : Savile, old Vane, Holland here,
Eschew plain-speaking : 't is a trick I keep.
  Went. How, when, where, Savile, Vane, and Holland speak,
Plainly or otherwise, would have my scorn,
All of my scorn, sir . . .
  Pym.   . . . Did not my poor thoughts
Claim somewhat ?
  Went.   Keep your thoughts ! believe the King
Mistrusts me for their prattle, all these Vanes
And Saviles ! make your mind up, o' God's love,
That I am discontented with the King !
  Pym. Why, you may be : I should be, that I know,
Were I like you.
  Went.   Like me ?
  Pym.   I care not much
For titles : our friend Eliot died no lord,
Hampden's no lord, and Savile is a lord ;
But you care, since you sold your soul for one.
I can't think, therefore, your soul's purchaser
Did well to laugh you to such utter scorn
When you twice prayed so humbly for its price,
The thirty silver pieces . . . I should say,
The Earldom you expected, still expect,
And may. Your letters were the movingest !
Console yourself : I 've borne him prayers just now
From Scotland not to be oppressed by Laud,

Words moving in their way : he'll pay, be sure,
As much attention as to those you sent.
  Went. False, sir! Who showed them you? Suppose it so,
The King did very well . . . nay, I was glad
When it was shown me : I refused, the first!
John Pym, you were my friend — forbear me once!
  Pym. Oh, Wentworth, ancient brother of my soul,
That all should come to this!
  Went.   Leave me!
  Pym.   My friend,
Why should I leave you?
  Went.   To tell Rudyard this,
And Hampden this!
  Pym.   Whose faces once were bright
At my approach, now sad with doubt and fear,
Because I hope in you — yes, Wentworth, you
Who never mean to ruin England — you
Who shake off, with God's help, an obscene dream
In this Ezekiel chamber, where it crept
Upon you first, and wake, yourself, your true
And proper self, our Leader, England's Chief,
And Hampden's friend!
                  This is the proudest day!
Come, Wentworth! Do not even see the King!
The rough old room will seem itself again!
We'll both go in together : you've not seen
Hampden so long: come: and there's Fiennes: you'll have
To know young Vane. This is the proudest day!
        [*The* KING *enters.* WENTWORTH *lets fall* PYM'S *hand.*
  Cha. Arrived, my lord? — This gentleman, we know
Was your old friend.
                The Scots shall be informed
What we determine for their happiness.
                                     [PYM *goes out.*
You have made haste, my lord.
  Went.   Sir, I am come . . .
  Cha. To see an old familiar — nay, 't is well ;
Aid us with his experience: this Scots' League
And Covenant spreads too far, and we have proofs
That they intrigue with France : the Faction too,
Whereof your friend there is the head and front,
Abets them, — as he boasted, very like.
  Went. Sir, trust me! but for this once, trust me, sir!
  Cha. What can you mean?
  Went.   That you should trust me, sir!
Oh — not for my sake! but 't is sad, so sad

That for distrusting me, you suffer — you
Whom I would die to serve : sir, do you think
That I would die to serve you ?
 Cha.   But rise, Wentworth !
 Went. What shall convince you ? What does Savile do
To prove him . . . Ah, one can't tear out one's heart
And show it, how sincere a thing it is !
 Cha. Have I not trusted you ?
 Went.   Say aught but that !
There is my comfort, mark you : all will be
So different when you trust me — as you shall !
It has not been your fault, — I was away,
Mistook, maligned, how was the King to know ?
I am here, now — he means to trust me, now —
All will go on so well !
 Cha. Be sure I do —
I 've heard that I should trust you : as you came,
Your friend, the Countess, told me . . .
 Went.   No, — hear nothing —
Be told nothing about me ! — you 're not told
Your right-hand serves you, or your children love you !
 Cha. You love me, Wentworth : rise !
 Went.   I can speak now.
I have no right to hide the truth. 'T is I
Can save you : only I. Sir, what must be ?
 Cha. Since Laud 's assured (the minutes are within)
— Loath as I am to spill my subjects' blood . . .
 Went. That is, he 'll have a war : what 's done is done !
 Cha. They have intrigued with France ; that 's clear to Laud.
 Went. Has Laud suggested any way to meet
The war's expense ?
 Cha.   He 'd not decide so far
Until you joined us.
 Went.   Most considerate !
He 's certain they intrigue with France, these Scots ?
The People would be with us.
 Cha.   Pym should know.
 Went. The People for us — were the People for us !
Sir, a great thought comes to reward your trust :
Summon a Parliament ! in Ireland first,
Then, here.
 Cha. In truth ?
 Went.   That saves us ! that puts off
The war, gives time to right their grievances —
To talk with Pym. I know the Faction — Laud
So styles it — tutors Scotland : all their plans

Suppose no Parliament: in calling one
You take them by surprise. Produce the proofs
Of Scotland's treason; then bid England help:
Even Pym will not refuse.
Cha. You would begin
With Ireland?
Went. Take no care for that: that's sure
To prosper.
Cha. You shall rule me. You were best
Return at once: but take this ere you go!
Now, do I trust you? You're an Earl: my Friend
Of Friends: yes, while . . . You hear me not!
Went. Say it all o'er again — but once again:
The first was for the music : once again!
Cha. Strafford, my friend, there may have been **reports,**
Vain rumors. Henceforth touching Strafford is
To touch the apple of my sight: why gaze
So earnestly?
Went. I am grown young again,
And foolish. What was it we spoke of?
Cha. Ireland,
The Parliament, —
Went. I may go when I will?
— Now?
Cha. Are you tired so soon of us?
Went. My King!
But you will not so utterly abhor
A Parliament? I'd serve you any way.
Cha. You said just now this was the only way.
Went. Sir, I will serve you!
Cha. Strafford, spare yourself:
You are so sick, they tell me.
Went. 'T is my soul
That's well and prospers now.
This Parliament —
We'll summon it, the English one — I'll care
For everything. You shall not need them much.
Cha. If they prove restive . . .
Went. I shall be with you.
Cha. Ere they assemble?
Went. I will come, or else
Deposit this infirm humanity
I' the dust. My whole heart stays with you, my King!
[*As* WENTWORTH *goes out, the* QUEEN *enters.*
Cha. That man must love me.
Queen. Is it over then?

Why, he looks yellower than ever! Well,
At least we shall not hear eternally
Of service — services: he's paid at least.
 Cha. Not done with: he engages to surpass
All yet performed in Ireland.
 Queen.   I had thought
Nothing beyond was ever to be done.
The war, Charles — will he raise supplies enough?
 Cha. We've hit on an expedient; he . . . that is,
I have advised . . . we have decided on
The calling — in Ireland — of a Parliament.
 Queen. O truly! You agree to that? Is that
The first-fruit of his counsel? But I guessed
As much.
 Cha. This is too idle, Henriette!
I should know best. He will strain every nerve,
And once a precedent established . . .
 Queen.   Notice
How sure he is of a long term of favor!
He'll see the next, and the next after that;
No end to Parliaments!
 Cha. Well, it is done.
He talks it smoothly, doubtless. If, indeed,
The Commons here . . .
 Queen.   Here! you will summon them
Here? Would I were in France again to see
A King!
 Cha. But, Henriette . . .
 Queen.   Oh, the Scots see clear!
Why should they bear your rule?
 Cha.   But listen, sweet!
 Queen. Let Wentworth listen — you confide in him!
 Cha. I do not, love, — I do not so confide!
The Parliament shall never trouble us!
. . Nay, hear me! I have schemes, such schemes: we'll buy
The leaders off: without that, Wentworth's counsel
Had ne'er prevailed on me. Perhaps I call it
To have excuse for breaking it forever,
And whose will then the blame be? See you not?
Come, dearest! — look, the little fairy, now,
That cannot reach my shoulder! Dearest, come!

ACT II.

Scene I. (As in Act I. Scene I.)

The same Party enters.

Rud. Twelve subsidies!
Vane. O Rudyard, do not laugh
At least!
Rud. True: Strafford called the Parliament—
'T is he should laugh!
A Puritan. Out of the serpent's root
Comes forth a cockatrice.
Fien. — A stinging one,
If that's the Parliament: twelve subsidies!
A stinging one! but, brother, where's your word
For Strafford's other nest-egg, the Scots' war?
The Puritan. His fruit shall be a fiery flying serpent.
Fien. Shall be? It chips the shell, man; peeps abroad.
Twelve subsidies! — Why, how now, Vane?
Rud. Peace, Fiennes!
Fien. Ah? — But he was not more a dupe than I,
Or you, or any here, the day that Pym
Returned with the good news. Look up, friend Vane!
We all believed that Strafford meant us well
In summoning the Parliament.

(Hampden *enters.*)

Vane. Now, Hampden,
Clear me! I would have leave to sleep again:
I'd look the People in the face again:
Clear me from having, from the first, hoped, dreamed
Better of Strafford!
Hamp. You may grow one day
A steadfast light to England, Henry Vane!
Rud. Meantime, by flashes I make shift to see
Strafford revived our Parliaments; before,
War was but talked of; there's an army, now:
Still, we've a Parliament! Poor Ireland bears
Another wrench (she dies the hardest death!) —
Why, speak of it in Parliament! and lo,
'T is spoken, so console yourselves!
Fien. The jest!
We clamored, I suppose, thus long, to win
The privilege of laying on our backs
A sorer burden than the King dares lay!

Rud. Mark now : we meet at length, complaints pour in
From every county, all the land cries out
On loans and levies, curses ship-money,
Calls vengeance on the Star Chamber ; we lend
An ear. " Ay, lend them all the ears you have ! "
Puts in the King ; " my subjects, as you find,
Are fretful, and conceive great things of you.
Just listen to them, friends ; you 'll sanction me
The measures they most wince at, make them yours,
Instead of mine, I know : and, to begin,
They say my levies pinch them, — raise me straight
Twelve subsidies ! "
 Fien.   All England cannot furnish
Twelve subsidies !
 Hol.   But Strafford, just returned
From Ireland — what has he to do with that ?
How could he speak his mind ? He left before
The Parliament assembled. Pym, who knows
Strafford . . .
 Rud. Would I were sure we know ourselves !
What is for good, what, bad — who friend, who foe !
 Hol. Do you count Parliaments no gain ?
 Rud.   A gain ?
While the King's creatures overbalance us ?
— There 's going on, beside, among ourselves
A quiet, slow, but most effectual course
Of buying over, sapping, leavening
The lump till all is leaven. Glanville 's gone.
I 'll put a case ; had not the Court declared
That no sum short of just twelve subsidies
Will be accepted by the King — our House,
I say, would have consented to that offer
To let us buy off ship-money !
 Hol.   Most like,
If, say, six subsidies will buy it off,
The House . . .
 Rud. Will grant them ! Hampden, do you hear ?
Congratulate with me ! the King 's the king,
And gains his point at last — our own assent
To that detested tax ! All 's over, then !
There 's no more taking refuge in this room,
Protesting, " Let the King do what he will,
We, England, are no party to our shame :
Our day will come ! " Congratulate with me !

(PYM *enters.*)

Vane. Pym, Strafford called this Parliament, you say,
But we'll not have our Parliaments like those
In Ireland, Pym!
  Rud.   Let him stand forth, your friend!
One doubtful act hides far too many sins;
It can be stretched no more, and, to my mind,
Begins to drop from those it covered.
  Other Voices.   Good!
Let him avow himself! No fitter time!
We wait thus long for you.
  Rud.   Perhaps, too long!
Since nothing but the madness of the Court,
In thus unmasking its designs at once,
Has saved us from betraying England. Stay —
This Parliament is Strafford's: let us vote
Our list of grievances too black by far
To suffer talk of subsidies: or best,
That ship-money's disposed of long ago
By England: any vote that's broad enough:
And then let Strafford, for the love of it,
Support his Parliament!
  Vane.   And vote as well
No war to be with Scotland! Hear you, Pym?
We'll vote, no war! No part nor lot in it
For England!
  Many Voices. Vote, no war! Stop the new levies!
No Bishops' war! At once! When next we meet!
  Pym. Much more when next we meet! Friends, which of
    you
Since first the course of Strafford was in doubt,
Has fallen the most away in soul from me?
  Vane. I sat apart, even now under God's eye,
Pondering the words that should denounce you, Pym,
In presence of us all, as one at league
With England's enemy.
  Pym.   You are a good
And gallant spirit, Henry. Take my hand
And say you pardon me for all the pain
Till now! Strafford is wholly ours.
  Many Voices.   Sure? sure?
  Pym. Most sure: for Charles dissolves the Parliament
While I speak here.
        — And I must speak, friends, now!
Strafford is ours. The King detects the change,

148   STRAFFORD

Casts Strafford off forever, and resumes
His ancient path: no Parliament for us,
No Strafford for the King!
                    Come, all of you,
To bid the King farewell, predict success
To his Scots' expedition, and receive
Strafford, our comrade now.   The next will be
Indeed a Parliament!
        Vane.   Forgive me, Pym!
        Voices. This looks like truth: Strafford can have, indeed,
No choice.
        Pym.   Friends, follow me!   He's with the King.
Come, Hampden, and come, Rudyard, and come, Vane!
This is no sullen day for England, sirs!
Strafford shall tell you!
        Voices.   To Whitehall then!   Come!

SCENE II. *Whitehall.*

CHARLES *and* STRAFFORD.

        Cha. Strafford!
        Straf.   Is it a dream? my papers, here —
Thus, as I left them, all the plans you found
So happy — (look! the track you pressed my hand
For pointing out) — and in this very room,
Over these very plans, you tell me, sir,
With the same face, too — tell me just one thing
That ruins them!   How's this?   What may this mean?
Sir, who has done this?
        Cha.   Strafford, who but I?
You bade me put the rest away: indeed
You are alone.
        Straf.   Alone, and like to be!
No fear, when some unworthy scheme grows ripe,
Of those, who hatched it, leaving me to loose
The mischief on the world!   Laud hatches war,
Falls to his prayers, and leaves the rest to me,
And I'm alone.
        Cha.   At least, you knew as much
When first you undertook the war.
        Straf.   My liege,
Was this the way?   I said, since Laud would lap
A little blood, 't were best to hurry over
The loathsome business, not to be whole months

At slaughter — one blow, only one, then, peace,
Save for the dreams. I said, to please you both
I'd lead an Irish army to the West,
While in the South an English . . . but you look
As though you had not told me fifty times
'T was a brave plan! My army is all raised,
I am prepared to join it . . .
  Cha.   Hear me, Strafford!
 Straf. . . . When, for some little thing, my whole design
Is set aside — (where is the wretched paper?)
I am to lead — (ay, here it is) — to lead
The English army: why? Northumberland
That I appointed, chooses to be sick —
Is frightened: and, meanwhile, who answers for
The Irish Parliament? or army, either?
Is this my plan?
  Cha. So disrespectful, sir?
 Straf. My liege, do not believe it! I am yours,
Yours ever: 't is too late to think about:
To the death, yours. Elsewhere, this untoward step
Shall pass for mine; the world shall think it mine.
But here! But here! I am so seldom here,
Seldom with you, my King! I, soon to rush
Alone upon a giant in the dark!
  Cha. My Strafford!
 Straf. [*examines papers awhile.*] "Seize the passes of the
  Tyne!"
But, sir, you see — see all I say is true?
My plan was sure to prosper, so, no cause
To ask the Parliament for help; whereas
We need them frightfully.
  Cha.   Need the Parliament?
 Straf. Now, for God's sake, sir, not one error more!
We can afford no error; we draw, now,
Upon our last resource: the Parliament
Must help us!
  Cha. I 've undone you, Strafford!
  Straf.   Nay —
Nay — why despond, sir, 't is not come to that!
I have not hurt you? Sir, what have I said
To hurt you? I unsay it! Don't despond!
Sir, do you turn from me?
  Cha.   My friend of friends!
 Straf. We'll make a shift. Leave me the Parliament!
Help they us ne'er so little and I'll make
Sufficient out of it. We'll speak them fair.

They're sitting, that's one great thing; that half gives
Their sanction to us; that's much: don't despond!
Why, let them keep their money, at the worst!
The reputation of the People's help
Is all we want: we'll make shift yet!
  Cha.   Good Strafford!
Straf. But meantime, let the sum be ne'er so small
They offer, we'll accept it: any sum —
For the look of it: the least grant tells the Scots
The Parliament is ours — their stanch ally
Turned ours: that told, there's half the blow to strike!
What will the grant be? What does Glanville think?
  Cha. Alas!
  Straf. My liege?
  Cha.   Strafford!
  Straf.   But answer me!
Have they . . . O surely not refused us half?
Half the twelve subsidies? We never looked
For all of them. How many do they give?
  Cha. You have not heard . . .
  Straf.   (What has he done?) — Heard what?
But speak at once, sir, this grows terrible!
        [*The King continuing silent.*
You have dissolved them! — I'll not leave this man.
  Cha. 'T was old Vane's ill-judged vehemence.
  Straf.   Old Vane?
  Cha. He told them, just about to vote the half,
That nothing short of all twelve subsidies
Would serve our turn, or be accepted.
  Straf.   Vane!
Vane! Who, sir, promised me, that very Vane . . .
O God, to have it gone, quite gone from me,
The one last hope — I that despair, my hope —
That I should reach his heart one day, and cure
All bitterness one day, be proud again
And young again, care for the sunshine too,
And never think of Eliot any more, —
God, and to toil for this, go far for this,
Get nearer, and still nearer, reach this heart
And find Vane there!
 [*Suddenly taking up a paper, and continuing with a forced calmness.*
      Northumberland is sick:
Well, then, I take the army: Wilmot leads
The horse, and he, with Conway, must secure
The passes of the Tyne: Ormond supplies
My place in Ireland. Here, we'll try the City:

If they refuse a loan — debase the coin
And seize the bullion! we've no other choice.
Herbert . . .
    And this while I am here! with you!
And there are hosts such, hosts like Vane! I go,
And, I once gone, they'll close around you, sir,
When the least pique, pettiest mistrust, is sure
To ruin me — and you along with me!
Do you see that? And you along with me!
— Sir, you 'll not ever listen to these men,
And I away, fighting your battle? Sir,
If they — if She — charge me, no matter how —
Say you, "At any time when he returns
His head is mine!" Don't stop me there! You know
My head is yours, but never stop me there!
 Cha. Too shameful, Strafford! You advised the war.
And . . .
 Straf. I! I! that was never spoken with
Till it was entered on! That loathe the war!
That say it is the maddest, wickedest . . .
Do you know, sir, I think within my heart,
That you would say I did advise the war;
And if, through your own weakness, or, what's worse,
These Scots, with God to help them, drive me back,
You will not step between the raging People
And me, to say . . .
    I knew it! from the first
I knew it! Never was so cold a heart!
Remember that I said it — that I never
Believed you for a moment!
    — And, you loved me?
You thought your perfidy profoundly hid
Because I could not share the whisperings
With Vane, with Savile? What, the face was masked?
I had the heart to see, sir! Face of flesh,
But heart of stone — of smooth cold frightful stone!
Ay, call them! Shall I call for you? The Scots
Goaded to madness? Or the English — Pym —
Shall I call Pym, your subject? Oh, you think
I'll leave them in the dark about it all?
They shall not know you? Hampden, Pym shall not?

   (PYM, HAMPDEN, VANE, *etc., enter.*)

[*Dropping on his knee.*] Thus favored with your gracious
 countenance
What shall a rebel League avail against

Your servant, utterly and ever yours?
So, gentlemen, the King's not even left
The privilege of bidding me farewell
Who haste to save the People — that you style
Your People — from the mercies of the Scots
And France their friend?
[*To* CHARLES.]   Pym's grave gray eyes are fixed
Upon you, sir!
                Your pleasure, gentlemen.
Hamp. The King dissolved us — 't is the King we seek
And not Lord Strafford.
   Straf.   — Strafford, guilty too
Of counselling the measure. [*To* CHARLES.] (Hush . . . you
   know —
You have forgotten — sir, I counselled it)
A heinous matter, truly! But the King
Will yet see cause to thank me for a course
Which now, perchance . . . (Sir, tell them so!) — he blames.
Well, choose some fitter time to make your charge:
I shall be with the Scots, you understand?
Then yelp at me!
            Meanwhile, your Majesty
Binds me, by this fresh token of your trust . . .

[*Under the pretence of an earnest farewell,* STRAFFORD *conducts* CHARLES *to the door, in such a manner as to hide his agitation from the rest: as the King disappears, they turn as by one impulse to* PYM, *who has not changed his original posture of surprise.*]

Hamp. Leave we this arrogant strong wicked man!
Vane and others. Hence, Pym! Come out of this unworthy
   place
To our old room again! He's gone.
            [STRAFFORD, *just about to follow the King, looks back.*
Pym.   Not gone!
[*To* STRAFFORD.] Keep tryst! the old appointment's made
   anew:
Forget not we shall meet again!
   Straf.   So be it!
And if an army follows me?
   Vane.   His friends
Will entertain your army!
   Pym.   I 'll not say
You have misreckoned, Strafford: time shows.
                        Perish
Body and spirit! Fool to feign a doubt,
Pretend the scrupulous and nice reserve

Of one whose prowess shall achieve the feat!
What share have I in it? Do I affect
To see no dismal sign above your head
When God suspends his ruinous thunder there?
Strafford is doomed. Touch him no one of you!
[PYM, HAMPDEN, *etc.*, *go out.*
 Straf. Pym, we shall meet again!
   (Lady CARLISLE *enters.*)
        You here, child?
 Lady Car.   Hush —
I know it all: hush, Strafford!
 Straf.   Ah! you know?
Well. I shall make a sorry soldier, Lucy!
All knights begin their enterprise, we read,
Under the best of auspices; 't is morn,
The Lady girds his sword upon the Youth
(He 's always very young) — the trumpets sound,
Cups pledge him, and, why, the King blesses him —
You need not turn a page of the romance
To learn the Dreadful Giant's fate. Indeed,
We 've the fair Lady here; but she apart, —
A poor man, rarely having handled lance,
And rather old, weary, and far from sure
His Squires are not the Giant's friends. All 's one:
Let us go forth!
 Lady Car. Go forth?
 Straf.   What matters it?
We shall die gloriously — as the book says.
 Lady Car. To Scotland? not to Scotland?
 Straf.   Am I sick
Like your good brother, brave Northumberland?
Beside, these walls seem falling on me.
 Lady Car.   Strafford,
The wind that saps these walls can undermine
Your camp in Scotland, too. Whence creeps the wind?
Have you no eyes except for Pym? Look here!
A breed of silken creatures lurk and thrive
In your contempt. You 'll vanquish Pym? Old Vane
Can vanquish you. And Vane you think to fly?
Rush on the Scots! Do nobly! Vane's slight sneer
Shall test success, adjust the praise, suggest
The faint result: Vane's sneer shall reach you there.
— You do not listen!
 Straf.   Oh, — I give that up!
There 's fate in it: I give all here quite up.

Care not what old Vane does or Holland does
Against me! 'T is so idle to withstand!
In no case tell me what they do!
    Lady Car.   But, Strafford . . .
    Straf. I want a little strife, beside; real strife;
This petty palace-warfare does me harm:
I shall feel better, fairly out of it.
    Lady Car. Why do you smile?
    Straf.   I got to fear them, child!
I could have torn his throat at first, old Vane's,
As he leered at me on his stealthy way
To the Queen's closet. Lord, one loses heart!
I often found it on my lips to say,
" Do not traduce me to her!"
    Lady Car.   But the King . . .
    Straf. The King stood there, 't is not so long ago,
— There; and the whisper, Lucy, " Be my friend
Of friends!" — My King! I would have . . .
    Lady Car.   . . . Died for him?
    Straf. Sworn him true, Lucy: I can die for him.
    Lady Car. But go not, Strafford! But you must renounce
This project on the Scots! Die, wherefore die?
Charles never loved you.
    Straf.   And he never will.
He 's not of those who care the more for men
That they 're unfortunate.
    Lady Car.   Then wherefore die
For such a master?
    Straf.   You that told me first
How good he was — when I must leave true friends
To find a truer friend! — that drew me here
From Ireland, — " I had but to show myself,
And Charles would spurn Vane, Savile, and the rest " —
You, child, to ask me this?
    Lady Car.   (If he have set
His heart abidingly on Charles!)
                               Then, friend,
I shall not see you any more.
    Straf.   Yes, Lucy.
There 's one man here I have to meet.
    Lady Car.   (The King!
What way to save him from the King?
                                   My soul —
That lent from its own store the charmed disguise
Which clothes the King — he shall behold my soul!)
Strafford, — I shall speak best if you 'll not gaze

Upon me: I had never thought, indeed,
To speak, but you would perish too, so sure!
Could you but know what 't is to bear, my friend,
One image stamped within you, turning blank
The else imperial brilliance of your mind, —
A weakness, but most precious, — like a flaw
I' the diamond, which should shape forth some sweet face
Yet to create, and meanwhile treasured there
Lest nature lose her gracious thought forever!
 Straf. When could it be? no! Yet . . . was it the day
We waited in the anteroom, till Holland
Should leave the presence-chamber?
 Lady Car.   What?
 Straf.   — That I
Described to you my love for Charles?
 Lady Car.   (Ah, no —
One must not lure him from a love like that!
Oh, let him love the King and die! 'T is past.
I shall not serve him worse for that one brief
And passionate hope, silent forever now!)
And you are really bound for Scotland then?
I wish you well: you must be very sure
Of the King's faith, for Pym and all his crew
Will not be idle — setting Vane aside!
 Straf. If Pym is busy, — you may write of Pym.
 Lady Car. What need, since there's your King to take your
  part?
He may endure Vane's counsel; but for Pym —
Think you he 'll suffer Pym to . . .
 Straf.   Child, your hair
Is glossier than the Queen's!
 Lady Car.   Is that to ask
A curl of me?
 Straf.   Scotland — the weary way!
 Lady Car. Stay, let me fasten it.
         — A rival's, Strafford?
 Straf. [*showing the George.*] He hung it there: twine yours
  around it, child!
 Lady Car. No — no — another time — I trifle so!
And there's a masque on foot. Farewell. The Court
Is dull; do something to enliven us
In Scotland: we expect it at your hands.
 Straf. I shall not fail in Scotland.
 Lady Car.   Prosper — if
You 'll think of me sometimes!
 Straf.   How think of him

And not of you? of you, the lingering streak
(A golden one) in my good fortune's eve.
   Lady Car. Strafford . . . Well, when the eve has its last
    streak
The night has its first star.   [*She goes out.*
  Straf.   That voice of hers —
You'd think she had a heart sometimes! His voice
Is soft too.
    Only God can save him now.
Be Thou about his bed, about his path!
His path! Where's England's path? Diverging wide,
And not to join again the track my foot
Must follow — whither? All that forlorn way
Among the tombs! Far — far — till . . . What, they do
Then join again, these paths? For, huge in the dusk,
There's — Pym to face!
      Why then, I have a foe
To close with, and a fight to fight at last
Worthy my soul! What, do they beard the King,
And shall the King want Strafford at his need?
Am I not here?
     Not in the market-place,
Pressed on by the rough artisans, so proud
To catch a glance from Wentworth! They lie down
Hungry yet smile, "Why, it must end some day:
Is he not watching for our sake?" Not there!
But in Whitehall, the whited sepulchre,
The . . .
    Curse nothing to-night! Only one name
They'll curse in all those streets to-night. Whose fault?
Did I make kings? set up, the first, a man
To represent the multitude, receive
All love in right of them — supplant them so,
Until you love the man and not the king —
The man with the mild voice and mournful eyes
Which send me forth.
     — To breast the bloody sea
That sweeps before me: with one star for guide.
Night has its first, supreme, forsaken star.

ACT III.

Scene I. *Opposite Westminster Hall.*

Sir Henry Vane, Lord Savile, Lord Holland *and others of the Court.*

Sir H. Vane. The Commons thrust you out?
Savile.   And what kept you
From sharing their civility?
Sir H. Vane.   Kept me?
Fresh news from Scotland, sir! worse than the last,
If that may be. All's up with Strafford there:
Nothing to bar the mad Scots marching hither
Next Lord's-day morning. That detained me, sir!
Well now, before they thrust you out, — go on, —
Their Speaker — did the fellow Lenthal say
All we set down for him?
Hol.   Not a word missed.
Ere he began, we entered, Savile, I
And Bristol and some more, with hope to breed
A wholesome awe in the new Parliament.
But such a gang of graceless ruffians, Vane,
As glared at us!
Vane.   So many?
Savile.   Not a bench
Without its complement of burly knaves;
Your hopeful son among them: Hampden leant
Upon his shoulder — think of that!
Vane.   I'd think
On Lenthal's speech, if I could get at it.
Urged he, I ask, how grateful they should prove
For this unlooked-for summons from the King?
Hol. Just as we drilled him.
Vane.   That the Scots will march
On London?
Hol.   All, and made so much of it,
A dozen subsidies at least seemed sure
To follow, when . . .
Vane.   Well?
Hol.   'T is a strange thing now!
I've a vague memory of a sort of sound,
A voice, a kind of vast unnatural voice —
Pym, sir, was speaking! Savile, help me out:
What was it all?
Sav.   Something about " a matter "—
No, — " work for England."

Hol. "England's great revenge"
He talked of.
Sav. How should I get used to Pym
More than yourselves?
Hol. However that may be,
'T was something with which we had nought to do,
For we were "strangers," and 't was "England's work"—
(All this while looking us straight in the face)
In other words, our presence might be spared.
So, in the twinkling of an eye, before
I settled to my mind what ugly brute
Was likest Pym just then, they yelled us out,
Locked the doors after us; and here are we.
Vane. Eliot's old method . . .
Sav. Prithee, Vane, a truce
To Eliot and his times, and the great Duke,
And how to manage Parliaments! 'T was you
Advised the Queen to summon this: why, Strafford
(To do him justice) would not hear of it.
Vane. Say rather, you have done the best of turns
To Strafford: he's at York, we all know why.
I would you had not set the Scots on Strafford
Till Strafford put down Pym for us, my lord!
Sav. Was it I altered Strafford's plans? did I . . .

(*A* Messenger *enters.*)

Mes. The Queen, my lords — she sends me: follow me
At once; 't is very urgent! she requires
Your counsel: something perilous and strange
Occasions her command.
Sav. We follow, friend!
Now, Vane;— your Parliament will plague us all!
Vane. No Strafford here beside!
Sav. If you dare hint
I had a hand in his betrayal, sir . . .
Hol. Nay, find a fitter time for quarrels — Pym
Will overmatch the best of you; and, think,
The Queen!
Vane. Come on, then: understand, I loathe
Strafford as much as any — but his use!
To keep off Pym, to screen a friend or two,
I would we had reserved him yet awhile.

SCENE II. *Whitehall.*

The QUEEN *and* Lady CARLISLE.

Queen. It cannot be.
Lady Car. It is so.
Queen. Why, the House
Have hardly met.
Lady Car. They met for that.
Queen. No, no!
Meet to impeach Lord Strafford? 'T is a jest.
Lady Car. A bitter one.
Queen. Consider! 'T is the House
We summoned so reluctantly, which nothing
But the disastrous issue of the war
Persuaded us to summon. They 'll wreak all
Their spite on us, no doubt; but the old way
Is to begin by talk of grievances:
They have their grievances to busy them.
Lady Car. Pym has begun his speech.
Queen. Where 's Vane? — That is,
Pym will impeach Lord Strafford if he leaves
His Presidency; he 's at York, we know,
Since the Scots beat him: why should he leave York?
Lady Car. Because the King sent for him.
Queen. Ah — but if
The King did send for him, he let him know
We had been forced to call a Parliament —
A step which Strafford, now I come to think,
Was vehement against.
Lady Car. The policy
Escaped him, of first striking Parliaments
To earth, then setting them upon their feet
And giving them a sword: but this is idle.
Did the King send for Strafford? He will come.
Queen. And what am I to do?
Lady Car. What do? Fail, madam!
Be ruined for his sake! what matters how,
So it but stand on record that you made
An effort, only one?
Queen. The King away
At Theobald's!
Lady Car. Send for him at once: he must
Dissolve the House.
Queen. Wait till Vane finds the truth
Of the report: then . . .

Lady Car. —It will matter little
What the King does. Strafford that lends his arm
And breaks his heart for you!

(Sir H. VANE *enters.*)

Vane. The Commons, madam,
Are sitting with closed doors. A huge debate,
No lack of noise; but nothing, I should guess,
Concerning Strafford: Pym has certainly
Not spoken yet.
   Queen. [*To* Lady CARLISLE.] You hear?
   Lady Car. I do not hear
That the King's sent for!
   Sir H. Vane. Savile will be able
To tell you more.

(HOLLAND *enters.*)

   Queen. The last news, Holland?
   Hol. Pym
Is raging like a fire. The whole House means
To follow him together to Whitehall
And force the King to give up Strafford.
   Queen. Strafford?
   Hol. If they content themselves with Strafford! Laud
Is talked of, Cottington and Windebank too.
Pym has not left out one of them — I would
You heard Pym raging!
   Queen. Vane, go find the King!
Tell the King, Vane, the People follow Pym
To brave us at Whitehall!

(SAVILE *enters.*)

   Savile. Not to Whitehall —
'T is to the Lords they go: they seek redress
On Strafford from his peers — the legal way,
They call it.
   Queen. (Wait, Vane!)
   Sav. But the adage gives
Long life to threatened men. Strafford can save
Himself so readily: at York, remember,
In his own county: what has he to fear?
The Commons only mean to frighten him
From leaving York. Surely, he will not come.
   Queen. Lucy, he will not come!
   Lady Car. Once more, the King
Has sent for Strafford. He will come.

Vane. Oh doubtless!
And bring destruction with him: that's his way.
What but his coming spoilt all Conway's plan?
The King must take his counsel, choose his friends,
Be wholly ruled by him! What's the result?
The North that was to rise, Ireland to help, —
What came of it? In my poor mind, a fright
Is no prodigious punishment.
    Lady Car. A fright?
Pym will fail worse than Strafford if he thinks
To frighten him. [*To the* QUEEN.] You will not save him
    then?
    Sav. When something like a charge is made, the King
Will best know how to save him: and 't is clear,
While Strafford suffers nothing by the matter,
The King may reap advantage: this in question,
No dinning you with ship-money complaints!
    Queen. [*To* Lady CARLISLE.] If we dissolve them, who will
    pay the army?
Protect us from the insolent Scots?
    Lady Car. In truth,
I know not, madam. Strafford's fate concerns
Me little: you desired to learn what course
Would save him: I obey you.
    Vane. Notice, too,
There can't be fairer ground for taking full
Revenge — (Strafford's revengeful) — than he'll have
Against his old friend Pym.
    Queen. Why, he shall claim
Vengeance on Pym!
    Vane. And Strafford, who is he
To 'scape unscathed amid the accidents
That harass all beside? I, for my part,
Should look for something of discomfiture
Had the King trusted me so thoroughly
And been so paid for it.
    Hol. He'll keep at York:
All will blow over: he'll return no worse,
Humbled a little, thankful for a place
Under as good a man. Oh, we'll dispense
With seeing Strafford for a month or two!
               (STRAFFORD *enters.*)
    Queen. You here!
    Straf. The King sends for me, madam.
    Queen. Sir,
The King . . .

Straf. An urgent matter that imports the King!
[*To* Lady CARLISLE.] Why, Lucy, what's in agitation now,
That all this muttering and shrugging, see,
Begins at me? They do not speak!
    Lady Car. 'T is welcome!
For we are proud of you — happy and proud
To have you with us, Strafford! You were stanch
At Durham: you did well there! Had you not
Been stayed, you might have . . . . we said, even now,
Our hope's in you!
    Sir H. Vane. [*To* Lady CARLISLE.] The Queen would speak
    with you.
    Straf. Will one of you, his servants here, vouchsafe
To signify my presence to the King?
    Sav. An urgent matter?
    Straf. None that touches you,
Lord Savile! Say, it were some treacherous
Sly pitiful intriguing with the Scots —
You would go free, at least! (They half divine
My purpose!) Madam, shall I see the King?
The service I would render, much concerns
His welfare.
    Queen. But his Majesty, my lord,
May not be here, may . . .
    Straf. Its importance, then,
Must plead excuse for this withdrawal, madam,
And for the grief it gives Lord Savile here.
    Queen. [*Who has been conversing with* VANE *and* HOL-
    LAND.] The King will see you, sir!
[*To* Lady CARLISLE.] Mark me: Pym's worst
Is done by now: he has impeached the Earl,
Or found the Earl too strong for him, by now.
Let us not seem instructed! We should work
No good to Strafford, but deform ourselves
With shame in the world's eye. [*To* STRAFFORD.] His Ma-
    jesty
Has much to say with you.
    Straf. Time fleeting, too!
[*To* Lady CARLISLE.] No means of getting them away? And
    She —
What does she whisper? Does she know my purpose?
What does she think of it? Get them away!
    Queen. [*To* Lady CARLISLE.] He comes to baffle Pym —
    he thinks the danger
Far off: tell him no word of it! a time
For help will come; we'll not be wanting then.

Keep him in play, Lucy — you, self-possessed
And calm! [*To* STRAFFORD.] To spare your lordship some delay
I will myself acquaint the King. [*To* Lady CARLISLE.] Beware!
[*The* QUEEN, VANE, HOLLAND, *and* SAVILE *go out.*
Straf. She knows it?
Lady Car. Tell me, Strafford!
Straf. Afterward!
This moment's the great moment of all time.
She knows my purpose?
Lady Car. Thoroughly: just now
She bade me hide it from you.
Straf. Quick, dear child,
The whole o' the scheme?
Lady Car. (Ah, he would learn if they
Connive at Pym's procedure! Could they but
Have once apprised the King! But there's no time
For falsehood, now.) Strafford, the whole is known.
Straf. Known and approved?
Lady Car. Hardly discountenanced.
Straf. And the King — say, the King consents as well?
Lady Car. The King's not yet informed, but will not dare
To interpose.
Straf. What need to wait him, then?
He'll sanction it! I stayed, child, tell him, long!
It vexed me to the soul — this waiting here.
You know him, there's no counting on the King.
Tell him I waited long!
Lady Car. (What can he mean?
Rejoice at the King's hollowness?)
Straf. I knew
They would be glad of it, — all over once,
I knew they would be glad: but he'd contrive,
The Queen and he, to mar, by helping it,
An angel's making.
Lady Car. (Is he mad?) Dear Strafford,
You were not wont to look so happy.
Straf. Sweet,
I tried obedience thoroughly. I took
The King's wild plan: of course, ere I could reach
My army, Conway ruined it. I drew
The wrecks together, raised all heaven and earth,
And would have fought the Scots: the King at once
Made truce with them. Then, Lucy, then, dear child,
God put it in my mind to love, serve, die

For Charles, but never to obey him more!
While he endured their insolence at Ripon
I fell on them at Durham. But you'll tell
The King I waited? All the anteroom
Is filled with my adherents.
    Lady Car.   Strafford — Strafford,
What daring act is this you hint?
    Straf.   No, no!
'T is here, not daring if you knew! all here!
            [*Drawing papers from his breast*
Full proof; see, ample proof — does the Queen know
I have such damning proof? Bedford and Essex,
Brooke, Warwick, Savile (did you notice Savile?
The simper that I spoilt?) Saye, Mandeville —
Sold to the Scots, body and soul, by Pym!
    Lady Car. Great heaven!
    Straf.   From Savile and his lords, to Pym
And his losels, crushed! — Pym shall not ward the blow
Nor Savile creep aside from it! The Crew
And the Cabal — I crush them!
    Lady Car.   And you go —
Strafford, — and now you go? —
    Straf.   — About no work
In the background, I promise you! I go
Straight to the House of Lords to claim these knaves.
Mainwaring!
    Lady Car. Stay — stay, Strafford!
    Straf.   She'll return,
The Queen — some little project of her own!
No time to lose: the King takes fright perhaps.
    Lady Car. Pym's strong, remember!
    Straf.   Very strong, as fits
The Faction's head — with no offence to Hampden,
Vane, Rudyard, and my loving Hollis: one
And all they lodge within the Tower to-night
In just equality. Bryan! Mainwaring!
            [*Many of his Adherents enter.*
The Peers debate just now (a lucky chance)
On the Scots' war; my visit's opportune.
When all is over, Bryan, you proceed
To Ireland: these despatches, mark me, Bryan,
Are for the Deputy, and these for Ormond:
We want the army here — my army, raised
At such a cost, that should have done such good,
And was inactive all the time! no matter,
We'll find a use for it. Willis . . . or, no — you!

You, friend, make haste to York : bear this, at once . . .
Or, — better stay for form's sake, see yourself
The news you carry. You remain with me
To execute the Parliament's command,
Mainwaring! Help to seize these lesser knaves,
Take care there's no escaping at backdoors :
I'll not have one escape, mind me — not one!
I seem revengeful, Lucy? Did you know
What these men dare!
 Lady Car.   It is so much they dare!
 Straf. I proved that long ago ; my turn is now.
Keep sharp watch, Goring, on the citizens!
Observe who harbors any of the brood
That scramble off : be sure they smart for it!
Our coffers are but lean.
      And you, child, too,
Shall have your task ; deliver this to Laud.
Laud will not be the slowest in my praise :
"Thorough," he'll cry! — Foolish, to be so glad!
This life is gay and glowing, after all :
'T is worth while, Lucy, having foes like mine
Just for the bliss of crushing them. To-day
Is worth the living for.
 Lady Car.   That reddening brow!
You seem . . .
 Straf. Well — do I not? I would be well —
I could not but be well on such a day!
And, this day ended, 't is of slight import
How long the ravaged frame subjects the soul
In Strafford.
 Lady Car. Noble Strafford!
 Straf.   No farewell!
I'll see you anon, to-morrow — the first thing.
— If She should come to stay me!
 Lady Car.   Go — 't is nothing —
Only my heart that swells : it has been thus
Ere now : go, Strafford!
 Straf.   To-night, then, let it be.
I must see Him : you, the next after Him.
I'll tell you how Pym looked. Follow me, friends!
You, gentlemen, shall see a sight this hour
To talk of all your lives. Close after me!
" My friend of friends!"
      [STRAFFORD *and the rest go out.*
 Lady Car. The King — ever the King!
No thought of one beside, whose little word

Unveils the King to him — one word from me,
Which yet I do not breathe!
                    Ah, have I spared
Strafford a pang, and shall I seek reward
Beyond that memory? Surely too, some way
He is the better for my love. No, no —
He would not look so joyous — I'll believe
His very eye would never sparkle thus,
Had I not prayed for him this long, long while.

SCENE III. *The Antechamber of the House of Lords.*
Many of the Presbyterian Party. The Adherents of STRAFFORD, *etc.*

A Group of Presbyterians. — 1. I tell you he struck Maxwell: Maxwell sought
To stay the Earl: he struck him and passed on.
    2. Fear as you may, keep a good countenance
Before these rufflers.
    3.   Strafford here the first,
With the great army at his back!
    4.   No doubt.
I would Pym had made haste: that's Bryan, hush —
The gallant pointing.
    Strafford's Followers. — 1. Mark these worthies, now!
    2. A goodly gathering! "Where the carcass is
There shall the eagles" — What's the rest?
    3.   For eagles
Say crows.
    A Presbyterian. Stand back, sirs!
    One of Strafford's Followers.   Are we in Geneva?
    A Presbyterian. No, nor in Ireland; we have leave to
        breathe.
    One of Strafford's Followers. Truly? Behold how privileged we be
That serve "King Pym"! There's Some-one at Whitehall
Who skulks obscure; but Pym struts . . .
    The Presbyterian.   Nearer.
    A Follower of Strafford.   Higher,
We look to see him. [*To his* Companions.] I'm to have St
    John
In charge; was he among the knaves just now
That followed Pym within there?
    Another.   The gaunt man
Talking with Rudyard. Did the Earl expect
Pym at his heels so fast? I like it not.

(MAXWELL *enters.*)

Another. Why, man, they rush into the net! Here's Maxwell —
Ha, Maxwell? How the brethren flock around
The fellow! Do you feel the Earl's hand yet
Upon your shoulder, Maxwell?
  Max. Gentlemen,
Stand back! a great thing passes here.
  A Follower of Strafford. [*To another.*] The Earl
Is at his work! [*To* M.] Say, Maxwell, what great thing!
Speak out! [*To a* Presbyterian.] Friend, I've a kindness for
    you! Friend,
I've seen you with St. John: O stockishness!
Wear such a ruff, and never call to mind
St. John's head in a charger? How, the plague,
Not laugh?
  Another. Say, Maxwell, what great thing!
  Another. Nay, wait:
The jest will be to wait.
  First. And who's to bear
These demure hypocrites? You'd swear they came . . .
Came . . . just as we come!
    [*A Puritan enters hastily and without observing* STRAFFORD'S
      Followers.
  The Puritan. How goes on the work?
Has Pym . . .
  A Follower of Strafford. The secret's out at last. Aha,
The carrion's scented! Welcome, crow the first!
Gorge merrily, you with the blinking eye!
" King Pym has fallen! "
  The Puritan. Pym?
  A Strafford. Pym!
  A Presbyterian. Only Pym?
  Many of Strafford's Followers. No, brother, not Pym only;
    Vane as well,
Rudyard as well, Hampden, St. John as well!
  A Presbyterian. My mind misgives: can it be true?
  Another. Lost! lost!
  A Strafford. Say we true, Maxwell?
  The Puritan. Pride before destruction,
A haughty spirit goeth before a fall.
  Many of Strafford's Followers. Ah now! The very thing!
    A word in season!
A golden apple in a silver picture,
To greet Pym as he passes!

[*The doors at the back begin to open, noise and light issuing.*
Max. Stand back, all!
Many of the Presbyterians. I hold with Pym! And I!
Strafford's Followers. Now for the text!
He comes! Quick!
The Puritan. How hath the oppressor ceased!
The Lord hath broken the staff of the wicked!
The sceptre of the rulers, he who smote
The people in wrath with a continual stroke,
That ruled the nations in his anger — he
Is persecuted and none hindereth!
[*The doors open, and* STRAFFORD *issues in the greatest disorder, and amid cries from within of* " Void the House!"
Straf. Impeach me! Pym! I never struck, I think,
The felon on that calm insulting mouth
When it proclaimed — Pym's mouth proclaimed me . . . God!
Was it a word, only a word that held
The outrageous blood back on my heart — which beats!
Which beats! Some one word — " Traitor," did he say,
Bending that eye, brimful of bitter fire,
Upon me?
Max. In the Commons' name, their servant
Demands Lord Strafford's sword.
Straf. What did you say?
Max. The Commons bid me ask your lordship's sword.
Straf. Let us go forth: follow me, gentlemen!
Draw your swords too: cut any down that bar us.
On the King's service! Maxwell, clear the way!
[*The* Presbyterians *prepare to dispute his passage.*
Straf. I stay: the King himself shall see me here.
Your tablets, fellow!
[*To* MAINWARING.] Give that to the King!
Yes, Maxwell, for the next half-hour, let be!
Nay, you shall take my sword!
[MAXWELL *advances to take it.*
Or, no — not that!
Their blood, perhaps, may wipe out all thus far,
All up to that — not that! Why, friend, you see
When the King lays your head beneath my foot
It will not pay for that. Go, all of you!
Max. I dare, my lord, to disobey: none stir!
Straf. This gentle Maxwell! — Do not touch him, Bryan!
[*To the* Presbyterians.] Whichever cur of you will carry this
Escapes his fellow's fate. None saves his life?
None?
[*Cries from within of* "STRAFFORD!"

Slingsby, I've loved you at least: make haste!
Stab me! I have not time to tell you why.
You then, my Bryan! Mainwaring, you then!
Is it because I spoke so hastily
At Allerton? The King had vexed me.
[*To the* Presbyterians.] You!
— Not even you? If I live over this,
The King is sure to have your heads, you know!
But what if I can't live this minute through?
Pym, who is there with his pursuing smile!
[*Louder cries of* "STRAFFORD!"]
The King! I troubled him, stood in the way
Of his negotiations, was the one
Great obstacle to peace, the Enemy
Of Scotland: and he sent for me, from York,
My safety guaranteed — having prepared
A Parliament — I see! And at Whitehall
The Queen was whispering with Vane — I see
The trap! [*Tearing off the George.*
I tread a gewgaw underfoot,
And cast a memory from me. One stroke, now!
[*His own Adherents disarm him. Renewed cries of* "STRAFFORD!"]
England! I see thy arm in this, and yield.
Pray you now — Pym awaits me — pray you now!

[STRAFFORD *reaches the doors: they open wide.* HAMPDEN *and a crowd discovered, and, at the bar,* PYM *standing apart. As* STRAFFORD *kneels, the scene shuts.*

ACT IV.

SCENE I. *Whitehall.*

The KING, *the* QUEEN, HOLLIS, Lady CARLISLE. (VANE, HOLLAND, SAVILE, *in the background.*)

Lady Car. Answer them, Hollis, for his sake! One word!
Cha. [*To* HOLLIS.] You stand, silent and cold, as though I were.
Deceiving you — my friend, my playfellow
Of other times. What wonder after all?
Just so, I dreamed my People loved me.
Hol. Sir,
It is yourself that you deceive, not me.
You'll quit me comforted, your mind made up

That, since you 've talked thus much and grieved thus much,
All you can do for Strafford has been done.
  Queen. If you kill Strafford — (come, we grant you leave,
Suppose) —
  Hol. I may withdraw, sir?
  Lady Car.   Hear them out!
'T is the last chance for Strafford! Hear them out!
  Hol. " If we kill Strafford " — on the eighteenth day
Of Strafford's trial — " We! "
  Cha.   Pym, my good Hollis —
Pym, I should say!
  Hol. Ah, true — sir, pardon me!
You witness our proceedings every day;
But the screened gallery, I might have guessed,
Admits of such a partial glimpse at us,
Pym takes up all the room, shuts out the view.
Still, on my honor, sir, the rest of the place
Is not unoccupied. The Commons sit
— That 's England; Ireland sends, and Scotland too,
Their representatives; the Peers that judge
Are easily distinguished; one remarks
The People here and there: but the close curtain
Must hide so much!
  Queen. Acquaint your insolent crew,
This day the curtain shall be dashed aside!
It served a purpose.
  Hol.   Think! This very day?
Ere Strafford rises to defend himself?
  Cha. I will defend him, sir! — sanction the past
This day: it ever was my purpose. Rage
At me, not Strafford!
  Lady Car. Nobly! — will he not
Do nobly?
  Hol. Sir, you will do honestly;
And, for that deed, I too would be a king.
  Cha. Only, to do this now! — " deaf " (in your style)
" To subjects' prayers," — I must oppose them now.
It seems their will the trial should proceed, —
So palpably their will!
  Hol.   You peril much,
But it were no bright moment save for that.
Strafford, your prime support, the sole roof-tree
Which props this quaking House of Privilege,
(Floods come, winds beat, and see — the treacherous sand!)
Doubtless, if the mere putting forth an arm
Could save him, you 'd save Strafford.

Cha. And they dare
Consummate calmly this great wrong! No hope?
This ineffaceable wrong! No pity then?
Hol. No plague in store for perfidy? — Farewell!
You called me, sir — [*To* Lady CARLISLE.] You, lady, bade
    me come
To save the Earl: I came, thank God for it,
To learn how far such perfidy can go!
You, sir, concert with me on saving him
Who have just ruined Strafford!
    Cha. I? — and how?
    Hol. Eighteen days long he throws, one after one,
Pym's charges back: a blind moth-eaten law!
— He'll break from it at last: and whom to thank?
The mouse that gnawed the lion's net for him
Got a good friend, — but he, the other mouse,
That looked on while the lion freed himself —
Fared he so well, does any fable say?
    Cha. What can you mean?
    Hol. Pym never could have proved
Strafford's design of bringing up the troops
To force this kingdom to obedience: Vane —
Your servant, not our friend, has proved it.
    Cha. Vane?
    Hol. This day. Did Vane deliver up or no
Those notes which, furnished by his son to Pym,
Seal Strafford's fate?
    Cha. Sir, as I live, I know
Nothing that Vane has done! What treason next?
I wash my hands of it. Vane, speak the truth!
Ask Vane himself!
    Hol. I will not speak to Vane,
Who speak to Pym and Hampden every day.
    Queen. Speak to Vane's master then! What gain to him
Were Strafford's death?
    Hol. Ha? Strafford cannot turn
As you, sir, sit there — bid you forth, demand
If every hateful act were not set down
In his commission? — whether you contrived
Or no, that all the violence should seem
His work, the gentle ways — your own, — his part,
To counteract the King's kind impulses —
While . . . but you know what he could say! And then
He might produce, — mark, sir! — a certain charge
To set the King's express command aside,
If need were, and be blameless. He might add . . .

Cha. Enough!
Hol. — Who bade him break the Parliament,
Find some pretence for setting up sword-law!
Queen. Retire!
Cha. Once more, whatever Vane dared do,
I know not: he is rash, a fool — I know
Nothing of Vane!
Hol. Well — I believe you. Sir,
Believe me, in return, that . . .
[*Turning to* Lady CARLISLE.] Gentle lady,
The few words I would say, the stones might hear
Sooner than these, — I rather speak to you,
You, with the heart! The question, trust me, takes
Another shape, to-day: not, if the King
Or England shall succumb, — but, who shall pay
The forfeit, Strafford or his master. Sir,
You loved me once: think on my warning now! [*Goes out.*
Cha. On you and on your warning both! — Carlisle!
That paper!
Queen. But consider!
Cha. Give it me!
There, signed — will that content you? Do not speak!
You have betrayed me, Vane! See! any day,
According to the tenor of that paper,
He bids your brother bring the army up,
Strafford shall head it and take full revenge.
Seek Strafford! Let him have the same, before
He rises to defend himself!
Queen. In truth?
That your shrewd Hollis should have worked a change
Like this! You, late reluctant . . .
Cha. Say, Carlisle,
Your brother Percy brings the army up,
Falls on the Parliament — (I'll think of you,
My Hollis!) say, we plotted long — 't is mine,
The scheme is mine, remember! Say, I cursed
Vane's folly in your hearing! If the Earl
Does rise to do us shame, the fault shall lie
With you, Carlisle!
Lady Car. Nay, fear not me! but still
That's a bright moment, sir, you throw away.
Tear down the veil and save him!
Queen. Go, Carlisle!
Lady Car. (I shall see Strafford — speak to him: my heart
Must never beat so, then! And if I tell
The truth? What's gained by falsehood? There they stand

Whose trade it is, whose life it is! How vain
To gild such rottenness! Strafford shall know,
Thoroughly know them!)
    Queen.   Trust to me! [*To* CARLISLE.] Carlisle,
You seem inclined, alone of all the Court,
To serve poor Strafford: this bold plan of yours
Merits much praise, and yet . . .
    Lady Car.   Time presses, madam.
    Queen. Yet — may it not be something premature?
Strafford defends himself to-day — reserves
Some wondrous effort, one may well suppose!
    Lady Car. Ay, Hollis hints as much.
    Cha.   Why linger then?
Haste with the scheme — my scheme: I shall be there
To watch his look. Tell him I watch his look!
    Queen. Stay, we'll precede you!
    Lady Car.   At your pleasure.
    Cha.   Say —
Say, Vane is hardly ever at Whitehall!
I shall be there, remember!
    Lady Car.   Doubt me not.
    Cha. On our return, Carlisle, we wait you here!
    Lady Car. I 'll bring his answer. Sir, I follow you.
(Prove the King faithless, and I take away
All Strafford cares to live for: let it be —
'T is the King's scheme!
                        My Strafford, I can save,
Nay, I have saved you, yet am scarce content,
Because my poor name will not cross your mind.
Strafford, how much I am unworthy you!)

        SCENE II. *A passage adjoining Westminster Hall.*

Many groups of Spectators *of the Trial.* Officers *of the Court, etc.*

    1st Spec. More crowd than ever! Not know Hampden, man?
That's he, by Pym, Pym that is speaking now.
No, truly, if you look so high you'll see
Little enough of either!
    2d Spec.   Stay: Pym's arm
Points like a prophet's rod.
    3d Spec.   Ay, ay, we 've heard
Some pretty speaking: yet the Earl escapes.
    4th Spec. I fear it: just a foolish word or two
About his children — and we see, forsooth,
Not England's foe in Strafford, but the man
Who, sick, half-blind . . .

2d Spec. What's that Pym's saying now
Which makes the curtains flutter? look! A hand
Clutches them. Ah! The King's hand!
5th Spec. I had thought
Pym was not near so tall. What said he, friend?
2d Spec. " Nor is this way a novel way of blood,"
And the Earl turns as if to . . . Look! look!
Many Spectators. There!
What ails him? No — he rallies, see — goes on,
And Strafford smiles. Strange!
An Officer. Haselrig!
Many Spectators. Friend? Friend?
The Officer. Lost, utterly lost: just when we looked for
  Pym
To make a stand against the ill effects
Of the Earl's speech! Is Haselrig without?
Pym's message is to him.
3d Spec. Now, said I true?
Will the Earl leave them yet at fault or no?
1st Spec. Never believe it, man! These notes of Vane's
Ruin the Earl.
5th Spec. A brave end: not a whit
Less firm, less Pym all over. Then, the trial
Is closed. No — Strafford means to speak again?
An Officer. Stand back, there!
5th Spec. Why, the Earl is coming hither!
Before the court breaks up! His brother, look, —
You'd say he'd deprecated some fierce act
In Strafford's mind just now.
An Officer. Stand back, I say!
2d Spec. Who's the veiled woman that he talks with?
Many Spectators. Hush —
The Earl! the Earl!

[*Enter* STRAFFORD, SLINGSBY, *and other* Secretaries, HOLLIS, Lady
 CARLISLE, MAXWELL, BALFOUR, *etc.* STRAFFORD *converses with*
 Lady CARLISLE.

Hol. So near the end! Be patient —
Return!
Straf. [*To his* Secretaries.] Here — anywhere — or, 't is
  freshest here!
To spend one's April here, the blossom-month:
Set it down here!
            [*They arrange a table, papers, etc.*
     So, Pym can quail, can cower
Because I glance at him, yet more 's to do.
What 's to be answered, Slingsby? Let us end!

[*To* Lady CARLISLE.] Child, I refuse his offer; whatsoe'er
It be! Too late! Tell me no word of him!
'T is something, Hollis, I assure you that —
To stand, sick as you are, some eighteen days
Fighting for life and fame against a pack
Of very curs, that lie through thick and thin,
Eat flesh and bread by wholesale, and can't say
"Strafford" if it would take my life!
 Lady Car.   Be moved!
Glance at the paper!
 Straf.   Already at my heels!
Pym's faulting bloodhounds scent the track again.
Peace, child! Now, Slingsby!
[Messengers *from* LANE *and other of* STRAFFORD'S Counsel *within the Hall are coming and going during the Scene.*
 Straf. [*setting himself to write and dictate.*] I shall beat
  you, Hollis!
Do you know that? In spite of St. John's tricks,
In spite of Pym — your Pym who shrank from me!
Eliot would have contrived it otherwise.
[*To a* Messenger.] In truth? This slip, tell Lane, contains as
  much
As I can call to mind about the matter.
Eliot would have disdained . . .
[*Calling after the* Messenger.] And Radcliffe, say,
The only person who could answer Pym,
Is safe in prison, just for that.
       Well, well!
It had not been recorded in that case,
I baffled you.
 [*To* Lady CARLISLE.] Nay, child, why look so grieved?
All's gained without the King! You saw Pym quail?
What shall I do when they acquit me, think you,
But tranquilly resume my task as though
Nothing had intervened since I proposed
To call that traitor to account! Such tricks,
Trust me, shall not be played a second time,
Not even against Laud, with his gray hair —
Your good work, Hollis! Peace! To make amends,
You, Lucy, shall be here when I impeach
Pym and his fellows.
 Hol.   Wherefore not protest
Against our whole proceeding, long ago?
Why feel indignant now? Why stand this while
Enduring patiently?
 Straf.   Child, I'll tell you —

You, and not Pym — you, the slight graceful girl
Tall for a flowering lily, and not Hollis —
Why I stood patient! I was fool enough
To see the will of England in Pym's will;
To fear, myself had wronged her, and to wait
Her judgment: when, behold, in place of it . . .
[*To a* Messenger *who whispers.*] Tell Lane to answer no such
    question! Law, —
I grapple with their law! I'm here to try
My actions by their standard, not my own!
Their law allowed that levy : what's the rest
To Pym, or Lane, any but God and me?
    Lady Car. The King's so weak! Secure this chance!
'T was Vane,
Never forget, who furnished Pym the notes . . .
    Straf. Fit, — very fit, those precious notes of Vane,
To close the Trial worthily! I feared
Some spice of nobleness might linger yet
And spoil the character of all the past.
Vane eased me . . . and I will go back and say
As much — to Pym, to England! Follow me,
I have a word to say! There, my defence
Is done!
    Stay! why be proud? Why care to own
My gladness, my surprise? — Nay, not surprise!
Wherefore insist upon the little pride
Of doing all myself, and sparing him
The pain? Child, say the triumph is my King's!
When Pym grew pale, and trembled, and sank down,
One image was before me: could I fail?
Child, care not for the past, so indistinct,
Obscure — there's nothing to forgive in it,
'T is so forgotten! From this day begins
A new life, founded on a new belief
In Charles.
    Hol. In Charles? Rather believe in Pym!
And here he comes in proof! Appeal to Pym!
Say how unfair . . .
    Straf. To Pym? I would say nothing!
I would not look upon Pym's face again.
    Lady Car. Stay, let me have to think I pressed your hand!
                              [STRAFFORD *and his* Friends *go out*
        (*Enter* HAMPDEN *and* VANE.)
    Vane. O Hampden, save the great misguided man!
Plead Strafford's cause with Pym! I have remarked
He moved no muscle when we all declaimed

Against him: you had but to breathe — he turned
Those kind calm eyes upon you.
        [*Enter* PYM, *the* Solicitor-General ST. JOHN, *the* Managers *of*
            the Trial, FIENNES, RUDYARD, *etc.*
    Rud.   Horrible!
Till now all hearts were with you: I withdraw
For one.   Too horrible!   But we mistake
Your purpose, Pym: you cannot snatch away
The last spar from the drowning man.
    Fien.   He talks
With St. John of it — see, how quietly!
[*To other* Presbyterians.] You 'll join us?   Strafford may de-
        serve the worst:
But this new course is monstrous.   Vane, take heart!
This Bill of his Attainder shall not have
One true man's hand to it.
    Vane.   Consider, Pym!
Confront your Bill, your own Bill: what is it?
You cannot catch the Earl on any charge, —
No man will say the law has hold of him
On any charge; and therefore you resolve
To take the general sense on his desert,
As though no law existed, and we met
To found one.   You refer to Parliament
To speak its thought upon the abortive mass
Of half-borne-out assertions, dubious hints
Hereafter to be cleared, distortions — ay,
And wild inventions.   Every man is saved
The task of fixing any single charge
On Strafford: he has but to see in him
The enemy of England.
    Pym.   A right scruple!
I have heard some called England's enemy
With less consideration.
    Vane.   Pity me!
Indeed you made me think I was your friend!
I who have murdered Strafford, how remove
That memory from me?
    Pym.   I absolve you, Vane.
Take you no care for aught that you have done!
    Vane. John Hampden, not this Bill! Reject this Bill!
He staggers through the ordeal: let him go,
Strew no fresh fire before him!   Plead for us!
When Strafford spoke, your eyes were thick with tears!
    Hamp. England speaks louder: who are we, to play
The generous pardoner at her expense,

Magnanimously waive advantages,
And, if he conquer us, applaud his skill?
  Vane. He was your friend.
  Pym.   I have heard that before.
  Fien. And England trusts you.
  Hamp.   Shame be his, who turns
The opportunity of serving her
She trusts him with, to his own mean account —
Who would look nobly frank at her expense!
  Fien. I never thought it could have come to this.
  Pym. But I have made myself familiar, Fiennes,
With this one thought — have walked, and sat, and slept,
This thought before me. I have done such things,
Being the chosen man that should destroy
The traitor. You have taken up this thought
To play with, for a gentle stimulant,
To give a dignity to idler life
By the dim prospect of emprise to come,
But ever with the softening, sure belief,
That all would end some strange way right at last.
  Fien. Had we made out some weightier charge!
  Pym.   You say
That these are petty charges: can we come
To the real charge at all? There he is safe
In tyranny's stronghold. Apostasy
Is not a crime, treachery not a crime:
The cheek burns, the blood tingles, when you speak
The words, but where's the power to take revenge
Upon them? We must make occasion serve, —
The oversight shall pay for the main sin
That mocks us.
  Rud.   But this unexampled course,
This Bill!
  Pym. By this, we roll the clouds away
Of precedent and custom, and at once
Bid the great beacon-light God sets in all,
The conscience of each bosom, shine upon
The guilt of Strafford: each man lay his hand
Upon his breast, and judge!
  Vane.   I only see
Strafford, nor pass his corpse for all beyond!
  Rud. and others. Forgive him! He would join us, now he finds
What the King counts reward! The pardon, too,
Should be your own. Yourself should bear to Strafford
The pardon of the Commons.

Pym.   Meet him?   Strafford?
Have we to meet once more, then?   Be it so!
And yet — the prophecy seemed half fulfilled
When, at the Trial, as he gazed, my youth,
Our friendship, divers thoughts came back at once
And left me, for a time . . . 'T is very sad!
To-morrow we discuss the points of law
With Lane — to-morrow?
   Vane.   Not before to-morrow —
So, time enough!   I knew you would relent!
   Pym. The next day, Haselrig, you introduce
The Bill of his Attainder.   Pray for me!

Scene III.   *Whitehall.*
The King.

Cha. My loyal servant!   To defend himself
Thus irresistibly, — withholding aught
That seemed to implicate us!
                          We have done
Less gallantly by Strafford.   Well, the future
Must recompense the past.
                          She tarries long.
I understand you, Strafford, now!
                          The scheme —
Carlisle's mad scheme — he 'll sanction it, I fear,
For love of me.   'T was too precipitate :
Before the army 's fairly on its march,
He 'll be at large : no matter.
                          Well, Carlisle?

(*Enter* Pym.)

   Pym. Fear me not, sir : — my mission is to save,
This time.
   Cha.   To break thus on me!   unannounced!
   Pym. It is of Strafford I would speak.
   Cha.   No more
Of Strafford!   I have heard too much from you.
   Pym. I spoke, sir, for the People; will you hear
A word upon my own account?
   Cha.   Of Strafford?
(So turns the tide already?   Have we tamed
The insolent brawler? — Strafford's eloquence
Is swift in its effect.)   Lord Strafford, sir,
Has spoken for himself.

Pym.   Sufficiently.
I would apprise you of the novel course
The People take: the Trial fails.
    Cha.   Yes, yes:
We are aware, sir: for your part in it
Means shall be found to thank you.
    Pym.   Pray you, read
This schedule! I would learn from your own mouth
— (It is a matter much concerning me) —
Whether, if two Estates of us concede
The death of Strafford, on the grounds set forth
Within that parchment, you, sir, can resolve
To grant your own consent to it. This Bill
Is framed by me. If you determine, sir,
That England's manifested will should guide
Your judgment, ere another week such will
Shall manifest itself. If not, — I cast
Aside the measure.
    Cha.   You can hinder, then,
The introduction of this Bill?
    Pym.   I can.
    Cha. He is my friend, sir: I have wronged him: mark you,
Had I not wronged him, this might be. You think
Because you hate the Earl . . . (turn not away,
We know you hate him) — no one else could love
Strafford: but he has saved me, some affirm.
Think of his pride! And do you know one strange,
One frightful thing? We all have used the man
As though a drudge of ours, with not a source
Of happy thoughts except in us; and yet
Strafford has wife and children, household cares,
Just as if we had never been. Ah, sir,
You are moved, even you, a solitary man
Wed to your cause — to England if you will!
    Pym. Yes — think, my soul — to England! Draw not back!
    Cha. Prevent that Bill, sir! All your course seems fair
Till now. Why, in the end, 't is I should sign
The warrant for his death! You have said much
I ponder on; I never meant, indeed,
Strafford should serve me any more. I take
The Commons' counsel; but this Bill is yours —
Nor worthy of its leader: care not, sir,
For that, however! I will quite forget
You named it to me. You are satisfied?
    Pym. Listen to me, sir! Eliot laid his hand,
Wasted and white, upon my forehead once;

Wentworth — he's gone now! — has talked on, whole nights,
And I beside him; Hampden loves me: sir,
How can I breathe and not wish England well,
And her King well?
    Cha.   I thank you, sir, who leave
That King his servant. Thanks, sir!
    Pym.   Let me speak!
— Who may not speak again; whose spirit yearns
For a cool night after this weary day:
— Who would not have my soul turn sicker yet
In a new task, more fatal, more august,
More full of England's utter weal or woe.
I thought, sir, could I find myself with you,
After this trial, alone, as man to man —
I might say something, warn you, pray you, save —
Mark me, King Charles, save — you!
But God must do it. Yet I warn you, sir —
(With Strafford's faded eyes yet full on me)
As you would have no deeper question moved
— "How long the Many must endure the One,"
Assure me, sir, if England give assent
To Strafford's death, you will not interfere!
Or —
    Cha. God forsakes me. I am in a net
And cannot move. Let all be as you say!

    (*Enter* Lady CARLISLE.)

    Lady Car. He loves you — looking beautiful with joy
Because you sent me! he would spare you all
The pain! he never dreamed you would forsake
Your servant in the evil day — nay, see
Your scheme returned! That generous heart of his!
He needs it not — or, needing it, disdains
A course that might endanger you — you, sir,
Whom Strafford from his inmost soul . . .
    [*Seeing* PYM.]   Well met!
No fear for Strafford! All that's true and brave
On your own side shall help us: we are now
Stronger than ever.
    Ha — what, sir, is this?
All is not well! What parchment have you there?
    Pym. Sir, much is saved us both.
    Lady Car.   This Bill! Your lip
Whitens — you could not read one line to me
Your voice would falter so!

Pym. No recreant yet!
The great word went from England to my soul,
And I arose. The end is very near.
    Lady Car. I am to save him! All have shrunk beside;
'T is only I am left. Heaven will make strong
The hand now as the heart. Then let both die!

ACT V.

Scene I. *Whitehall.*

Hollis, Lady Carlisle.

Hol. Tell the King then! Come in with me!
    Lady Car.   Not so!
He must not hear till it succeeds.
    Hol.   Succeed?
No dream was half so vain — you 'd rescue Strafford
And outwit Pym! I cannot tell you . . . lady,
The block pursues me, and the hideous show.
To-day . . . is it to-day? And all the while
He 's sure of the King's pardon. Think, I have
To tell this man he is to die. The King
May rend his hair, for me! I 'll not see Strafford!
    Lady Car. Only, if I succeed, remember — Charles
Has saved him. He would hardly value life
Unless his gift. My stanch friends wait. Go in —
You must go in to Charles!
    Hol.   And all beside
Left Strafford long ago. The King has signed
The warrant for his death! the Queen was sick
Of the eternal subject. For the Court, —
The Trial was amusing in its way,
Only too much of it: the Earl withdrew
In time. But you, fragile, alone, so young,
Amid rude mercenaries — you devise
A plan to save him! Even though it fails,
What shall reward you?
    Lady Car.   I may go, you think,
To France with him? And you reward me, friend,
Who lived with Strafford even from his youth
Before he set his heart on state-affairs
And they bent down that noble brow of his.
I have learned somewhat of his latter life,
And all the future I shall know: but, Hollis,

I ought to make his youth my own as well,
Tell me, — when he is saved!
  Hol.   My gentle friend,
He should know all and love you, but 't is vain!
  Lady Car. Love? no — too late now! Let him love the
    King!
'T is the King's scheme! I have your word, remember!
We 'll keep the old delusion up. But, quick!
Quick! Each of us has work to do, beside!
Go to the King! I hope — Hollis — I hope!
Say nothing of my scheme! Hush, while we speak
Think where he is! Now for my gallant friends!
  Hol. Where he is? Calling wildly upon Charles,
Guessing his fate, pacing the prison-floor.
Let the King tell him! I 'll not look on Strafford.

     Scene II. *The Tower.*
   Strafford *sitting with his* Children. *They sing.*
      O bell' andare
      Per barca in mare,
      Verso la sera
      Di Primavera!

William. The boat's in the broad moonlight all this while —
      Verso la sera
      Di Primavera!

And the boat shoots from underneath the moon
Into the shadowy distance; only still
You hear the dipping oar —
      Verso la sera,

And faint, and fainter, and then all 's quite gone,
Music and light and all, like a lost star.
  Anne. But you should sleep, father: you were to sleep.
  Straf. I do sleep, Anne.; or if not — you must know
There 's such a thing as . . .
  Wil.   You 're too tired to sleep.
  Straf. It will come by-and-by and all day long,
In that old quiet house I told you of:
We sleep safe there.
  Anne.   Why not in Ireland?
  Straf.   No!
Too many dreams! — That song's for Venice, William:
You know how Venice looks upon the map —
Isles that the mainland hardly can let go?

Wil. You've been to Venice, father?
Straf. I was young, then.
Wil. A city with no King; that's why I like
Even a song that comes from Venice.
Straf. William!
Wil. Oh, I know why! Anne, do you love the King?
But I'll see Venice for myself one day.
Straf. See many lands, boy — England last of all, —
That way you'll love her best.
Wil. Why do men say
You sought to ruin her, then?
Straf. Ah, — they say that.
Wil. Why?
Straf. I suppose they must have words to say,
As you to sing.
Anne. But they make songs beside:
Last night I heard one, in the street beneath,
That called you . . . Oh, the names!
Wil. Don't mind her, father!
They soon left off when I cried out to them.
Straf. We shall so soon be out of it, my boy!
'T is not worth while: who heeds a foolish song?
Wil. Why, not the King.
Straf. Well: it has been the fate
Of better; and yet, — wherefore not feel sure
That time, who in the twilight comes to mend
All the fantastic day's caprice, consign
To the low ground once more the ignoble Term,
And raise the Genius on his orb again, —
That time will do me right?
Anne. (Shall we sing, William?
He does not look thus when we sing.)
Straf. For Ireland,
Something is done: too little, but enough
To show what might have been.
Wil. (I have no heart
To sing now! Anne, how very sad he looks!
Oh, I so hate the King for all he says!)
Straf. Forsook them! What, the common songs will run
That I forsook the People? Nothing more?
Ay, fame, the busy scribe, will pause, no doubt,
Turning a deaf ear to her thousand slaves
Noisy to be enrolled, — will register
The curious glosses, subtle notices,
Ingenious clearings-up one fain would see

Beside that plain inscription of The Name —
The Patriot Pym, or the Apostate Strafford!
        [*The* Children *resume their song timidly, but break off.*
        (*Enter* HOLLIS *and an* Attendant.)
  Straf. No, — Hollis? in good time! — Who is he?
  Hol.   One
That must be present.
  Straf.   Ah — I understand.
They will not let me see poor Laud alone.
How politic! They'd use me by degrees
To solitude: and, just as you came in,
I was solicitous what life to lead
When Strafford's "not so much as Constable
In the King's service." Is there any means
To keep one's self awake? What would you do
After this bustle, Hollis, in my place?
  Hol. Strafford!
  Straf.   Observe, not but that Pym and you
Will find me news enough — news I shall hear
Under a quince-tree by a fish-pond side
At Wentworth. Garrard must be re-engaged
My newsman. Or, a better project now —
What if when all's consummated, and the Saints
Reign, and the Senate's work goes swimmingly, —
What if I venture up, some day, unseen,
To saunter through the Town, notice how Pym,
Your Tribune, likes Whitehall, drop quietly
Into a tavern, hear a point discussed,
As, whether Strafford's name were John or James —
And be myself appealed to — I, who shall
Myself have near forgotten!
  Hol.   I would speak . . .
  Straf. Then you shall speak, — not now. I want just now,
To hear the sound of my own tongue. This place
Is full of ghosts.
  Hol.   Nay, you must hear me, Strafford!
  Straf. Oh, readily! Only, one rare thing more, —
The minister! Who will advise the King,
Turn his Sejanus, Richelieu and what not,
And yet have health — children, for aught I know —
My patient pair of traitors! Ah, — but, William —
Does not his cheek grow thin?
  Wil.   'T is you look thin,
Father!
  Straf. A scamper o'er the breezy wolds
Sets all to-rights.

Hol. You cannot sure forget
A prison-roof is o'er you, Strafford?
Straf. No,
Why, no. I would not touch on that, the first.
I left you that. Well, Hollis? Say at once,
The King can find no time to set me free!
A mask at Theobald's?
Hol. Hold: no such affair
Detains him.
Straf. True: what needs so great a matter?
The Queen's lip may be sore. Well: when he pleases,—
Only, I want the air: it vexes flesh
To be pent up so long.
Hol. The King—I bear
His message, Strafford: pray you, let me speak!
Straf. Go, William! Anne, try o'er your song again!
[*The* Children *retire*
They shall be loyal, friend, at all events.
I know your message: you have nothing new
To tell me: from the first I guessed as much.
I know, instead of coming here himself,
Leading me forth in public by the hand,
The King prefers to leave the door ajar
As though I were escaping — bids me trudge
While the mob gapes upon some show prepared
On the other side of the river! Give at once
His order of release! I've heard, as well
Of certain poor manœuvres to avoid
The granting pardon at his proper risk;
First, he must prattle somewhat to the Lords,
Must talk a trifle with the Commons first,
Be grieved I should abuse his confidence,
And far from blaming them, and . . . Where's the order?
Hol. Spare me!
Straf. Why, he'd not have me steal away?
With an old doublet and a steeple hat
Like Prynne's? Be smuggled into France, perhaps?
Hollis, 't is for my children! 'T was for them
I first consented to stand day by day
And give your Puritans the best of words,
Be patient, speak when called upon, observe
Their rules, and not return them prompt their lie!
What's in that boy of mine that he should prove
Son to a prison-breaker? I shall stay
And he'll stay with me. Charles should know as much,
He too has children!

[*Turning to* Hollis's *companion.*] Sir, you feel for me!
No need to hide that face! Though it have looked
Upon me from the judgment-seat . . . I know
Strangely, that somewhere it has looked on me . . .
Your coming has my pardon, nay, my thanks:
For there is one who comes not.
  Hol.   Whom forgive,
As one to die!
  Straf. True, all die, and all need
Forgiveness: I forgive him from my soul.
  Hol. 'T is a world's wonder: Strafford, you must die!
  Straf. Sir, if your errand is to set me free
This heartless jest mars much. Ha! Tears in truth?
We 'll end this! See this paper, warm — feel — warm
With lying next my heart! Whose hand is there?
Whose promise? Read, and loud for God to hear!
" Strafford shall take no hurt "— read it, I say!
" In person, honor, nor estate "—
  Hol.   The King . . .
  Straf. I could unking him by a breath! You sit
Where Loudon sat, who came to prophesy
The certain end, and offer me Pym's grace
If I 'd renounce the King: and I stood firm
On the King's faith. The King who lives . . .
  Hol.   To sign
The warrant for your death.
  Straf.   " Put not your trust
In princes, neither in the sons of men,
In whom is no salvation!"
  Hol.   Trust in God!
The scaffold is prepared: they wait for you:
He has consented. Cast the earth behind!
  Cha. You would not see me, Strafford, at your foot!
It was wrung from me! Only, curse me not!
  Hol. [*To* Strafford.] As you hope grace and pardon in
  your need,
Be merciful to this most wretched man.
            [*Voices from within.*
     Verso la sera
     Di Primavera.

  Straf. You 'll be good to those children, sir? I know
You 'll not believe her, even should the Queen
Think they take after one they rarely saw.
I had intended that my son should live
A stranger to these matters: but you are

So utterly deprived of friends! He too
Must serve you — will you not be good to him?
Or, stay, sir, do not promise — do not swear!
You, Hollis — do the best you can for me!
I've not a soul to trust to: Wandesford's dead,
And you've got Radcliffe safe, Laud's turn comes next:
I've found small time of late for my affairs,
But I trust any of you, Pym himself —
No one could hurt them: there's an infant, too —
These tedious cares! Your Majesty could spare them.
Nay — pardon me, my King! I had forgotten
Your education, trials, much temptation,
Some weakness: there escaped a peevish word —
'Tis gone: I bless you at the last. You know
All's between you and me: what has the world
To do with it? Farewell!
    Cha. [*at the door.*]   Balfour! Balfour!

(*Enter* BALFOUR.)

The Parliament! — go to them: I grant all
Demands. Their sittings shall be permanent:
Tell them to keep their money if they will:
I'll come to them for every coat I wear
And every crust I eat: only I choose
To pardon Strafford. As the Queen shall choose!
— You never heard the People howl for blood,
Beside!
    Bal. Your Majesty may hear them now:
The walls can hardly keep their murmurs out:
Please you retire!
    Cha.   Take all the troops, Balfour!
    Bal. There are some hundred thousand of the crowd.
    Cha. Come with me, Strafford! You'll not fear, at least
    Straf. Balfour, say nothing to the world of this!
I charge you, as a dying man, forget
You gazed upon this agony of one . . .
Of one . . . or if . . . why you may say, Balfour,
The King was sorry: 'tis no shame in him:
Yes, you may say he even wept, Balfour,
And that I walked the lighter to the block
Because of it. I shall walk lightly, sir!
Earth fades, heaven breaks on me: I shall stand next
Before God's throne: the moment's close at hand
When man the first, last time, has leave to lay
His whole heart bare before its Maker, leave
To clear up the long error of a life

And choose one happiness for evermore.
With all mortality about me, Charles,
The sudden wreck, the dregs of violent death —
What if, despite the opening angel-song,
There penetrate one prayer for you? Be saved
Through me! Bear witness, no one could prevent
My death! Lead on! ere he awake — best, now!
All must be ready: did you say, Balfour,
The crowd began to murmur? They'll be kept
Too late for sermon at St. Antholin's!
Now! But tread softly — children are at play
In the next room. Precede! I follow —
   (*Enter* Lady CARLISLE, *with many* Attendants.)
 Lady Car.   Me!
Follow me, Strafford, and be saved! The King?
[*To the* KING.] Well — as you ordered, they are ranged with-
 out,
The convoy . . . [*seeing the* KING's *state.*]
[*To* STRAFFORD.] You know all, then! Why, I thought
It looked best that the King should save you, — Charles
Alone; 'tis a shame that you should owe me aught.
Or no, not shame! Strafford, you'll not feel shame
At being saved by me?
 Hol.   All true! Oh Strafford,
She saves you! all her deed! this lady's deed!
And is the boat in readiness? You, friend,
Are Billingsley, no doubt. Speak to her, Strafford!
See how she trembles, waiting for your voice!
The world's to learn its bravest story yet.
 Lady Car. Talk afterward! Long nights in France enough
To sit beneath the vines and talk of home.
 Straf. You love me, child? Ah, Strafford can be loved
As well as Vane! I could escape, then?
 Lady Car.   Haste!
Advance the torches, Bryan!
 Straf.   I will die.
They call me proud: but England had no right,
When she encountered me — her strength to mine —
To find the chosen foe a craven. Girl,
I fought her to the utterance, I fell,
I am hers now, and I will die. Beside,
The lookers-on! Eliot is all about
This place, with his most uncomplaining brow.
 Lady Car. Strafford!
 Straf.   I think if you could know how much
I love you, you would be repaid, my friend!

Lady Car. Then, for my sake!
Straf.   Even for your sweet sake,
I stay.
Hol. For *their* sake!
Straf.   To bequeath a stain?
Leave me! Girl, humor me and let me die!
Lady Car. Bid him escape — wake, King! Bid him escape!
Straf. True, I will go! Die, and forsake the King?
I'll not draw back from the last service.
Lady Car. Strafford!
Straf.   And, after all, what is disgrace to me?
Let us come, child! That it should end this way,
Lead then! but I feel strangely: it was not
To end this way.
Lady Car. Lean — lean on me!
Straf.   My King!
Oh, had he trusted me — his friend of friends!
Lady Car. I can support him, Hollis!
Straf.   Not this way!
This gate — I dreamed of it, this very gate.
Lady Car. It opens on the river: our good boat
Is moored below, our friends are there.
Straf.   The same:
Only with something ominous and dark,
Fatal, inevitable.
Lady Car. Strafford! Strafford!
Straf. Not by this gate! I feel what will be there!
I dreamed of it, I tell you: touch it not!
Lady Car. To save the King, — Strafford, to save the King!
[*As* STRAFFORD *opens the door,* PYM *is discovered with* HAMPDEN, VANE, *etc.* STRAFFORD *falls back;* PYM *follows slowly and confronts him.*
Pym. Have I done well? Speak, England! Whose sole sake
I still have labored for, with disregard
To my own heart, — for whom my youth was made
Barren, my manhood waste, to offer up
Her sacrifice — this friend, this Wentworth here —
Who walked in youth with me, loved me, it may be,
And whom, for his forsaking England's cause,
I hunted by all means (trusting that she
Would sanctify all means) even to the block
Which waits for him. And saying this, I feel
No bitterer pang than first I felt, the hour
I swore that Wentworth might leave us, but I
Would never leave him: I do leave him now.

I render up my charge (be witness, God!)
To England who imposed it. I have done
Her bidding — poorly, wrongly, — it may be,
With ill effects — for I am weak, a man:
Still, I have done my best, my human best,
Not faltering for a moment. It is done.
And this said, if I say . . . yes, I will say
I never loved but one man — David not
More Jonathan! Even thus, I love him now:
And look for my chief portion in that world
Where great hearts led astray are turned again,
(Soon it may be, and, certes, will be soon:
My mission over, I shall not live long,) —
Ay, here I know I talk — I dare and must,
Of England, and her great reward, as all
I look for there; but in my inmost heart,
Believe, I think of stealing quite away
To walk once more with Wentworth — my youth's friend
Purged from all error, gloriously renewed,
And Eliot shall not blame us. Then indeed . . .
This is no meeting, Wentworth! Tears increase
Too hot. A thin mist — is it blood? — enwraps
The face I loved once. Then, the meeting be!
 Straf. I have loved England too; we'll meet then, **Pym;**
As well die now! Youth is the only time
To think and to decide on a great course:
Manhood with action follows; but 't is dreary
To have to alter our whole life in age —
The time past, the strength gone! As well die now.
When we meet, Pym, I 'd be set right — not now!
Best die. Then if there 's any fault, fault too
Dies, smothered up. Poor gray old little Laud
May dream his dream out, of a perfect Church,
In some blind corner. And there 's no one left.
I trust the King now wholly to you, Pym!
And yet, I know not: I shall not be there:
Friends fail — if he have any. And he 's weak,
And loves the Queen, and . . . Oh, my fate is nothing —
Nothing! But not that awful head — not that!
 Pym. If England shall declare such will to me . . .
 Straf. Pym, you help England! I, that am to die,
What I must see! 't is here — all here! My God,
Let me but gasp out, in one word of fire,
How thou wilt plague him, satiating hell!
What? England that you help, become through you
A green and putrefying charnel, left

Our children . . . some of us have children, Pym —
Some who, without that, still must ever wear
A darkened brow, an over-serious look,
And never properly be young ! No word ?
What if I curse you ? Send a strong curse forth
Clothed from my heart, lapped round with horror till
She 's fit with her white face to walk the world
Scaring kind natures from your cause and you —
Then to sit down with you at the board-head,
The gathering for prayer . . . O speak, but speak !
. . . Creep up, and quietly follow each one home,
You, you, you, be a nestling care for each
To sleep with, — hardly moaning in his dreams,
She gnaws so quietly, — till, lo he starts,
Gets off with half a heart eaten away !
Oh, shall you 'scape with less if she 's my child ?
You will not say a word — to me — to Him ?

Pym. If England shall declare such will to me . . .

Straf. No, not for England now, not for Heaven now, —
See, Pym, for my sake, mine who kneel to you !
There, I will thank you for the death, my friend !
This is the meeting : let me love you well !

Pym. England, — I am thine own ! Dost thou exact
That service ? I obey thee to the end.

Straf. O God, I shall die first — I shall die first !

SORDELLO

1840

TO J. MILSAND, OF DIJON.

DEAR FRIEND: Let the next poem be introduced by your name, therefore remembered along with one of the deepest of my affections, and so repay all trouble it ever cost me. I wrote it twenty-five years ago for only a few, counting even in these on somewhat more care about its subject than they really had. My own faults of expression were many; but with care for a man or book such would be surmounted, and without it what avails the faultlessness of either? I blame nobody, least of all myself, who did my best then and since; for I lately gave time and pains to turn my work into what the many might — instead of what the few must — like; but after all, I imagined another thing at first, and therefore leave as I find it. The historical decoration was purposely of no more importance than a background requires; and my stress lay on the incidents in the development of a soul: little else is worth study. I, at least, always thought so; you, with many known and unknown to me, think so; others may one day think so; and whether my attempt remain for them or not, I trust, though away and past it, to continue ever yours,

R. B.

LONDON, *June* 9, 1863.

BOOK THE FIRST.

WHO will, may hear Sordello's story told:
His story? Who believes me shall behold
The man, pursue his fortunes to the end,
Like me: for as the friendless-people's friend
Spied from his hill-top once, despite the din
And dust of multitudes, Pentapolin
Named o' the Naked Arm, I single out
Sordello, compassed murkily about
With ravage of six long sad hundred years.
Only believe me. Ye believe?
       Appears
Verona . . . Never, I should warn you first,
Of my own choice had this, if not the worst
Yet not the best expedient, served to tell

A story I could body forth so well
By making speak, myself kept out of view,
The very man as he was wont to do,
And leaving you to say the rest for him.
Since, though I might be proud to see the dim
Abysmal past divide its hateful surge,
Letting of all men this one man emerge
Because it pleased me, yet, that moment past,
I should delight in watching first to last
His progress as you watch it, not a whit
More in the secret than yourselves who sit
Fresh-chapleted to listen. But it seems
Your setters-forth of unexampled themes,
Makers of quite new men, producing them,
Would best chalk broadly on each vesture's hem
The wearer's quality ; or take their stand,
Motley on back and pointing-pole in hand,
Beside him. So, for once I face ye, friends,
Summoned together from the world's four ends,
Dropped down from heaven or cast up from hell,
To hear the story I propose to tell.
Confess now, poets know the dragnet's trick,
Catching the dead, if fate denies the quick,
And shaming her ; 't is not for fate to choose
Silence or song because she can refuse
Real eyes to glisten more, real hearts to ache
Less oft, real brows turn smoother for our sake :
I have experienced something of her spite ;
But there's a realm wherein she has no right
And I have many lovers. Say, but few
Friends fate accords me ? Here they are : now view
The host I muster ! Many a lighted face
Foul with no vestige of the grave's disgrace ;
What else should tempt them back to taste our air
Except to see how their successors fare ?
My audience ! and they sit, each ghostly man
Striving to look as living as he can,
Brother by breathing brother ; thou art set,
Clear-witted critic, by . . . but I 'll not fret
A wondrous soul of them, nor move death's spleen
Who loves not to unlock them. Friends ! I mean
The living in good earnest — ye elect
Chiefly for love — suppose not I reject
Judicious praise, who contrary shall peep,
Some fit occasion, forth, for fear ye sleep,
To glean your bland approvals. Then, appear,

Verona! stay — thou, spirit, come not near
Now — not this time desert thy cloudy place
To scare me, thus employed, with that pure face!
I need not fear this audience, I make free
With them, but then this is no place for thee!
The thunder-phrase of the Athenian, grown
Up out of memories of Marathon,
Would echo like his own sword's griding screech
Braying a Persian shield, — the silver speech
Of Sidney's self, the starry paladin,
Turn intense as a trumpet sounding in
The knights to tilt, — wert thou to hear! What heart
Have I to play my puppets, bear my part
Before these worthies?
                  Lo, the past is hurled
In twain : up-thrust, out-staggering on the world,
Subsiding into shape, a darkness rears
Its outline, kindles at the core, appears
Verona. 'T is six hundred years and more
Since an event. The Second Friedrich wore
The purple, and the Third Honorius filled
The holy chair. That autumn eve was stilled :
A last remains of sunset dimly burned
O'er the far forests, like a torch-flame turned
By the wind back upon its bearer's hand
In one long flare of crimson ; as a brand,
The woods beneath lay black. A single eye
From all Verona cared for the soft sky.
But, gathering in its ancient market-place,
Talked group with restless group ; and not a face
But wrath made livid, for among them were
Death's stanch purveyors, such as have in care
To feast him. Fear had long since taken root
In every breast, and now these crushed its fruit,
The ripe hate, like a wine : to note the way
It worked while each grew drunk! Men grave and gray
Stood, with shut eyelids, rocking to and fro,
Letting the silent luxury trickle slow
About the hollows where a heart should be ;
But the young gulped with a delirious glee
Some foretaste of their first debauch in blood
At the fierce news : for, be it understood,
Envoys apprised Verona that her prince
Count Richard of Saint Boniface, joined since
A year with Azzo, Este's Lord, to thrust
Taurello Salinguerra, prime in trust

With Ecelin Romano, from his seat
Ferrara, — over-zealous in the feat
And stumbling on a peril unaware,
Was captive, trammelled in his proper snare,
They phrase it, taken by his own intrigue.
Immediate succor from the Lombard League
Of fifteen cities that affect the Pope,
For Azzo, therefore, and his fellow-hope
Of the Guelf cause, a glory overcast!
Men's faces, late agape, are now aghast.
" Prone is the purple pavis; Este makes
Mirth for the devil when he undertakes
To play the Ecelin; as if it cost
Merely your pushing-by to gain a post
Like his! The patron tells ye, once for all,
There be sound reasons that preferment fall
On our beloved " . . .
     " Duke o' the Rood, why not? "
Shouted an Estian, " grudge ye such a lot?
The hill-cat boasts some cunning of her own,
Some stealthy trick to better beasts unknown,
That quick with prey enough her hunger blunts,
And feeds her fat while gaunt the lion hunts."
" Taurello," quoth an envoy, " as in wane
Dwelt at Ferrara. Like an osprey fain
To fly but forced the earth his couch to make
Far inland, till his friend the tempest wake,
Waits he the Kaiser's coming; and as yet
That fast friend sleeps, and he too sleeps: but let
Only the billow freshen, and he snuffs
The aroused hurricane ere it enroughs
The sea it means to cross because of him.
Sinketh the breeze? His hope-sick eye grows dim;
Creep closer on the creature! Every day
Strengthens the Pontiff; Ecelin, they say,
Dozes now at Oliero, with dry lips
Telling upon his perished finger-tips
How many ancestors are to depose
Ere he be Satan's Viceroy when the doze
Deposits him in hell. So, Guelfs rebuilt
Their houses; not a drop of blood was spilt
When Cino Bocchimpane chanced to meet
Buccio Virtù — God's wafer, and the street
Is narrow! Tutti Santi, think, a-swarm
With Ghibellins, and yet he took no harm!
This could not last. Off Salinguerra went

To Padua, Podestà, 'with pure intent,'
Said he, ' my presence, judged the single bar
To permanent tranquillity, may jar
No longer ' — so ! his back is fairly turned ?
The pair of goodly palaces are burned,
The gardens ravaged, and our Guelfs laugh, drunk
A week with joy. The next, their laughter sunk
In sobs of blood, for they found, some strange way,
Old Salinguerra back again — I say,
Old Salinguerra in the town once more
Uprooting, overturning, flame before,
Blood fetlock-high beneath him. Azzo fled ;
Who 'scaped the carnage followed ; then the dead
Were pushed aside from Salinguerra's throne,
He ruled once more Ferrara, all alone.
Till Azzo, stunned awhile, revived, would pounce
Coupled with Boniface, like lynx and ounce,
On the gorged bird. The burghers ground their teeth
To see troop after troop encamp beneath
I' the standing corn thick o'er the scanty patch
It took so many patient months to snatch
Out of the marsh ; while just within their walls
Men fed on men. At length Taurello calls
A parley : ' let the Count wind up the war ! '
Richard, light-hearted as a plunging star,
Agrees to enter for the kindest ends
Ferrara, flanked with fifty chosen friends,
No horse-boy more, for fear your timid sort
Should fly Ferrara at the bare report.
Quietly through the town they rode, jog-jog ;
' Ten, twenty, thirty, — curse the catalogue
Of burnt Guelf houses ! Strange, Taurello shows
Not the least sign of life ' — whereat arose
A general growl : ' How ? With his victors by ?
I and my Veronese ? My troops and I ?
Receive us, was your word ? ' So jogged they on,
Nor laughed their host too openly : once gone
Into the trap ! " —
            Six hundred years ago !
Such the time's aspect and peculiar woe
(Yourselves may spell it yet in chronicles,
Albeit the worm, our busy brother, drills
His sprawling path through letters anciently
Made fine and large to suit some abbot's eye)
When the new Hohenstauffen dropped the mask,
Flung John of Brienne's favor from his casque,

Forswore crusading, had no mind to leave
Saint Peter's proxy leisure to retrieve
Losses to Otho and to Barbaross,
Or make the Alps less easy to recross;
And, thus confirming Pope Honorius' fear,
Was excommunicate that very year.
" The triple-bearded Teuton come to life!"
Groaned the Great League; and, arming for the strife,
Wide Lombardy, on tiptoe to begin,
Took up, as it was Guelf or Ghibellin,
Its cry; what cry?
     " The Emperor to come!"
His crowd of feudatories, all and some,
That leapt down with a crash of swords, spears, shields,
One fighter on his fellow, to our fields,
Scattered anon, took station here and there,
And carried it, till now, with little care —
Cannot but cry for him; how else rebut
Us longer? Cliffs, an earthquake suffered jut
In the mid-sea, each domineering crest
Which naught save such another throe can wrest
From out (conceive) a certain chokeweed grown
Since o'er the waters, twine and tangle thrown
Too thick, too fast accumulating round,
Too sure to over-riot and confound
Ere long each brilliant islet with itself
Unless a second shock save shoal and shelf,
Whirling the sea-drift wide : alas, the bruised
And sullen wreck! Sunlight to be diffused
For that! Sunlight, 'neath which, a scum at first,
The million fibres of our chokeweed nurst
Dispread themselves, mantling the troubled main,
And, shattered by those rocks, took hold again,
So kindly blazed it — that same blaze to brood
O'er every cluster of the multitude
Still hazarding new clasps, ties, filaments,
An emulous exchange of pulses, vents
Of nature into nature ; till some growth
Unfancied yet, exuberantly clothe
A surface solid now, continuous, one :
" The Pope, for us the People, who begun
The People, carries on the People thus,
To keep that Kaiser off and dwell with us!"
See you?
   Or say, Two Principles that live
Each fitly by its Representative.

"Hill-cat" — who called him so? — the gracefullest
Adventurer, the ambiguous stranger-guest
Of Lombardy (sleek but that ruffling fur,
Those talons to their sheath!) whose velvet purr
Soothes jealous neighbors when a Saxon scout
— Arpo or Yoland, is it? — one without
A country or a name, presumes to couch
Beside their noblest; until men avouch
That, of all Houses in the Trevisan,
Conrad descries no fitter, rear or van,
Than Ecelo! They laughed as they enrolled
That name at Milan on the page of gold,
Godego's lord, — Ramon, Marostica,
Cartiglion, Bassano, Loria,
And every sheep-cote on the Suabian's fief!
No laughter when his son, "the Lombard Chief"
Forsooth, as Barbarossa's path was bent
To Italy along the Vale of Trent,
Welcomed him at Roncaglia! Sadness now —
The hamlets nested on the Tyrol's brow,
The Asolan and Euganean hills,
The Rhetian and the Julian, sadness fills
Them all, for Ecelin vouchsafes to stay
Among and care about them; day by day
Choosing this pinnacle, the other spot,
A castle building to defend a cot,
A cot built for a castle to defend,
Nothing but castles, castles, nor an end
To boasts how mountain ridge may join with ridge
By sunken gallery and soaring bridge.
He takes, in brief, a figure that beseems
The grisliest nightmare of the Church's dreams,
— A Signory firm-rooted, unestranged
From its old interests, and nowise changed
By its new neighborhood: perchance the vaunt
Of Otho, "my own Este shall supplant
Your Este," come to pass. The sire led in
A son as cruel; and this Ecelin
Had sons, in turn, and daughters sly and tall
And curling and compliant; but for all
Romano (so they styled him) throve, that neck
Of his so pinched and white, that hungry cheek
Proved 't was some fiend, not him, the man's-flesh went
To feed: whereas Romano's instrument,
Famous Taurello Salinguerra, sole
I' the world, a tree whose boughs were slipt the bole

Successively, why should not he shed blood
To further a design? Men understood
Living was pleasant to him as he wore
His careless surcoat, glanced some missive o'er,
Propped on his truncheon in the public way,
While his lord lifted writhen hands to pray,
Lost at Oliero's convent.
      Hill-cats, face
Our Azzo, our Guelf-Lion! Why disgrace
A worthiness conspicuous near and far
(Atii at Rome while free and consular,
Este at Padua who repulsed the Hun)
By trumpeting the Church's princely son?
— Styled Patron of Rovigo's Polesine,
Ancona's march, Ferrara's . . . ask, in fine,
Our chronicles, commenced when some old monk
Found it intolerable to be sunk
(Vexed to the quick by his revolting cell)
Quite out of summer while alive and well:
Ended when by his mat the Prior stood,
'Mid busy promptings of the brotherhood,
Striving to coax from his decrepit brains
The reason Father Porphyry took pains
To blot those ten lines out which used to stand
First on their charter drawn by Hildebrand.

 The same night wears. Verona's rule of yore
Was vested in a certain Twenty-four;
And while within his palace these debate
Concerning Richard and Ferrara's fate,
Glide we by clapping doors, with sudden glare
Of cressets vented on the dark, nor care
For aught that's seen or heard until we shut
The smother in, the lights, all noises but
The carroch's booming: safe at last! Why strange
Such a recess should lurk behind a range
Of banquet-rooms? Your finger — thus — you push
A spring, and the wall opens, would you rush
Upon the banqueters, select your prey,
Waiting (the slaughter-weapons in the way
Strewing this very bench) with sharpened ear
A preconcerted signal to appear;
Or if you simply crouch with beating heart,
Bearing in some voluptuous pageant part
To startle them. Nor mutes nor masquers now;
Nor any . . . does that one man sleep whose brow
The dying lamp-flame sinks and rises o'er?

What woman stood beside him? not the more
Is he unfastened from the earnest eyes
Because that arras fell between! Her wise
And lulling words are yet about the room,
Her presence wholly poured upon the gloom
Down even to her vesture's creeping stir.
And so reclines he, saturate with her,
Until an outcry from the square beneath
Pierces the charm: he springs up, glad to breathe,
Above the cunning element, and shakes
The stupor off as (look you) morning breaks
On the gay dress, and, near concealed by it,
The lean frame like a half-burnt taper, lit
Erst at some marriage-feast, then laid away
Till the Armenian bridegroom's dying day,
In his wool wedding-robe.
                         For he — for he,
Gate-vein of this hearts' blood of Lombardy,
(If I should falter now) — for he is thine!
Sordello, thy forerunner, Florentine!
A herald-star I know thou didst absorb
Relentless into the consummate orb
That scared it from its right to roll along
A sempiternal path with dance and song
Fulfilling its allotted period,
Serenest of the progeny of God —
Who yet resigns it not! His darling stoops
With no quenched lights, desponds with no blank troops
Of disenfranchised brilliances, for, blent
Utterly with thee, its shy element
Like thine upburneth prosperous and clear,
Still, what if I approach the august sphere
Named now with only one name, disentwine
That under-current soft and argentine
From its fierce mate in the majestic mass
Leavened as the sea whose fire was mixt with glass
In John's transcendent vision, — launch once more
That lustre? Dante, pacer of the shore
Where glutted hell disgorgeth filthiest gloom,
Unbitten by its whirring sulphur-spume —
Or whence the grieved and obscure waters slope
Into a darkness quieted by hope;
Plucker of amaranths grown beneath God's eye
In gracious twilights where his chosen lie,
I would do this! If I should falter now!
  In Mantua territory half is slough,

Half pine-tree forest; maples, scarlet-oaks
Breed o'er the river-beds; even Mincio chokes
With sand the summer through : but 't is morass
In winter up to Mantua walls. There was,
Some thirty years before this evening's coil,
One spot reclaimed from the surrounding spoil,
Goito; just a castle built amid
A few low mountains; firs and larches hid
Their main defiles, and rings of vineyard bound
The rest. Some captured creature in a pound,
Whose artless wonder quite precludes distress,
Secure beside in its own loveliness,
So peered with airy head, below, above,
The castle at its toils, the lapwings love
To glean among at grape-time. Pass within.
A maze of corridors contrived for sin,
Dusk winding-stairs, dim galleries got past,
You gain the inmost chambers, gain at last
A maple-panelled room: that haze which seems
Floating about the panel, if there gleams
A sunbeam over it, will turn to gold
And in light-graven characters unfold
The Arab's wisdom everywhere; what shade
Marred them a moment, those slim pillars made,
Cut like a company of palms to prop
The roof, each kissing top entwined with top,
Leaning together; in the carver's mind
Some knot of bacchanals, flushed cheek combined
With straining forehead, shoulders purpled, hair
Diffused between, who in a goat-skin bear
A vintage; graceful sister-palms! But quick
To the main wonder, now. A vault, see; thick
Black shade about the ceiling, though fine slits
Across the buttress suffer light by fits
Upon a marvel in the midst. Nay, stoop —
A dullish gray-streaked cumbrous font, a group
Round it, — each side of it, where'er one sees, —
Upholds it; shrinking Caryatides
Of just-tinged marble like Eve's lilied flesh
Beneath her maker's finger when the fresh
First pulse of life shot brightening the snow.
The font's edge burthens every shoulder, so
They muse upon the ground, eyelids half closed;
Some, with meek arms behind their backs disposed,
Some, crossed above their bosoms, some, to veil
Their eyes, some, propping chin and cheek so pale,

Some, hanging slack an utter helpless length
Dead as a buried vestal whose whole strength
Goes when the grate above shuts heavily.
So dwell these noiseless girls, patient to see,
Like priestesses because of sin impure
Penanced forever, who resigned endure,
Having that once drunk sweetness to the dregs.
And every eve, Sordello's visit begs
Pardon for them: constant as eve he came
To sit beside each in her turn, the same
As one of them, a certain space: and awe
Made a great indistinctness till he saw
Sunset slant cheerful through the buttress-chinks,
Gold seven times globed; surely our maiden shrinks
And a smile stirs her as if one faint grain
Her load were lightened, one shade less the stain
Obscured her forehead, yet one more bead slipt
From off the rosary whereby the crypt
Keeps count of the contritions of its charge?
Then with a step more light, a heart more large,
He may depart, leave her and every one
To linger out the penance in mute stone.
Ah, but Sordello? 'T is the tale I mean
To tell you.
    In this castle may be seen,
On the hill-tops, or underneath the vines,
Or eastward by the mound of firs and pines
That shuts out Mantua, still in loneliness,
A slender boy in a loose page's dress,
Sordello: do but look on him awhile
Watching ('t is autumn) with an earnest smile
The noisy flock of thievish birds at work
Among the yellowing vineyards; see him lurk
('T is winter with its sullenest of storms)
Beside that arras-length of broidered forms,
On tiptoe, lifting in both hands a light
Which makes yon warrior's visage flutter bright
— Ecelo, dismal father of the brood,
And Ecelin, close to the girl he wooed,
Auria, and their Child, with all his wives
From Agnes to the Tuscan that survives,
Lady of the castle, Adelaide. His face
— Look, now he turns away! Yourselves shall trace
(The delicate nostril swerving wide and fine,
A sharp and restless lip, so well combine
With that calm brow) a soul fit to receive

Delight at every sense; you can believe
Sordello foremost in the regal class
Nature has broadly severed from her mass
Of men, and framed for pleasure, as she frames
Some happy lands, that have luxurious names,
For loose fertility; a footfall there
Suffices to upturn to the warm air
Half-germinating spices; mere decay
Produces richer life; and day by day
New pollen on the lily-petal grows,
And still more labyrinthine buds the rose.
You recognize at once the finer dress
Of flesh that amply lets in loveliness
At eye and ear, while round the rest is furled
(As though she would not trust them with her world)
A veil that shows a sky not near so blue,
And lets but half the sun look fervid through.
How can such love? — like souls on each full-fraught
Discovery brooding, blind at first to aught
Beyond its beauty, till exceeding love
Becomes an aching weight; and, to remove
A curse that haunts such natures — to preclude
Their finding out themselves can work no good
To what they love nor make it very blest
By their endeavor, — they are fain invest
The lifeless thing with life from their own soul,
Availing it to purpose, to control,
To dwell distinct and have peculiar joy
And separate interests that may employ
That beauty fitly, for its proper sake.
Nor rest they here; fresh births of beauty wake
Fresh homage, every grade of love is past,
With every mode of loveliness: then cast
Inferior idols off their borrowed crown
Before a coming glory. Up and down
Runs arrowy fire, while earthly forms combine
To throb the secret forth; a touch divine —
And the scaled eyeball owns the mystic rod;
Visibly through his garden walketh God.

So fare they. Now revert. One character
Denotes them through the progress and the stir, —
A need to blend with each external charm,
Bury themselves, the whole heart wide and warm, —
In something not themselves; they would belong
To what they worship — stronger and more strong
Thus prodigally fed — which gathers shape

And feature, soon imprisons past escape
The votary framed to love and to submit
Nor ask, as passionate he kneels to it,
Whence grew the idol's empery. So runs
A legend ; light had birth ere moons and suns,
Flowing through space a river and alone,
Till chaos burst and blank the spheres were strown
Hither and thither, foundering and blind :
When into each of them rushed light — to find
Itself no place, foiled of its radiant chance.
Let such forego their just inheritance!
For there's a class that eagerly looks, too,
On beauty, but, unlike the gentler crew,
Proclaims each new revealment born a twin
With a distinctest consciousness within
Referring still the quality, now first
Revealed, to their own soul — its instinct nursed
In silence, now remembered better, shown
More thoroughly, but not the less their own ;
A dream come true ; the special exercise
Of any special function that implies
The being fair, or good, or wise, or strong,
Dormant within their nature all along —
Whose fault ? So homage, other souls direct
Without, turns inward. "How should this deject
Thee, soul ?" they murmur; "wherefore strength be quelled
Because, its trivial accidents withheld,
Organs are missed that clog the world, inert,
Wanting a will, to quicken and exert,
Like thine — existence cannot satiate,
Cannot surprise?   Laugh thou at envious fate,
Who, from earth's simplest combination stampt
With individuality — uncrampt
By living its faint elemental life,
Dost soar to heaven's complexest essence, rife
With grandeurs, unaffronted to the last,
Equal to being all !"
                In truth?   Thou hast
Life, then — wilt challenge life for us : our race
Is vindicated so, obtains its place
In thy ascent, the first of us ; whom we
May follow, to the meanest, finally,
With our more bounded wills?
                      Ah, but to find
A certain mood enervate such a mind,
Counsel it slumber in the solitude

Thus reached, nor, stooping, task for mankind's good
Its nature just as life and time accord
"— Too narrow an arena to reward
Emprise — the world's occasion worthless since
Not absolutely fitted to evince
Its mastery!" Or if yet worse befall,
And a desire possess it to put all
That nature forth, forcing our straitened sphere
Contain it, — to display completely here
The mastery another life should learn,
Thrusting in time eternity's concern, —
So that Sordello . . .
               Fool, who spied the mark
Of leprosy upon him, violet-dark
Already as he loiters? Born just now,
With the new century, beside the glow
And efflorescence out of barbarism;
Witness a Greek or two from the abysm
That stray through Florence-town with studious air,
Calming the chisel of that Pisan pair:
If Nicolo should carve a Christus yet!
While at Siena is Guidone set,
Forehead on hand; a painful birth must be
Matured ere Saint Eufemia's sacristy
Or transept gather fruits of one great gaze
At the moon: look you! The same orange haze, —
The same blue stripe round that — and, in the midst
Thy spectral whiteness, Mother-maid, who didst
Pursue the dizzy painter!
               Woe, then, worth
Any officious babble letting forth
The leprosy confirmed and ruinous
To spirit lodged in a contracted house!
Go back to the beginning, rather; blend
It gently with Sordello's life; the end
Is piteous, you may see, but much between
Pleasant enough. Meantime, some pyx to screen
The full-grown pest, some lid to shut upon
'the goblin! So they found at Babylon,
(Colleagues, mad Lucius and sage Antonine)
Sacking the city, by Apollo's shrine,
In rummaging among the rarities,
A certain coffer; he who made the prize
Opened it greedily; and out there curled
Just such another plague, for half the world
Was stung. Crawl in then, hag, and couch asquat,

Keeping that blotchy bosom thick in spot
Until your time is ripe! The coffer-lid
Is fastened, and the coffer safely hid
Under the Loxian's choicest gifts of gold.
  Who will may hear Sordello's story told,
And how he never could remember when
He dwelt not at Goito. Calmly, then,
About this secret lodge of Adelaide's
Glided his youth away; beyond the glades
On the fir-forest border, and the rim
Of the low range of mountain, was for him
No other world: but this appeared his own
To wander through at pleasure and alone.
The castle too seemed empty; far and wide
Might he disport; only the northern side
Lay under a mysterious interdict —
Slight, just enough remembered to restrict
His roaming to the corridors, the vault
Where those font-bearers expiate their fault,
The maple-chamber, and the little nooks
And nests, and breezy parapet that looks
Over the woods to Mantua: there he strolled.
Some foreign women-servants, very old,
Tended and crept about him — all his clue
To the world's business and embroiled ado
Distant a dozen hill-tops at the most.
  And first a simple sense of life engrossed
Sordello in his drowsy Paradise;
The day's adventures for the day suffice —
Its constant tribute of perceptions strange,
With sleep and stir in healthy interchange,
Suffice, and leave him for the next at ease
Like the great palmer-worm that strips the trees,
Eats the life out of every luscious plant,
And, when September finds them sere or scant,
Puts forth two wondrous winglets, alters quite,
And hies him after unforeseen delight.
So fed Sordello, not a shard disheathed;
As ever, round each new discovery, wreathed
Luxuriantly the fancies infantine
His admiration, bent on making fine
Its novel friend at any risk, would fling
In gay profusion forth: a ficklest king,
Confessed those minions! — eager to dispense
So much from his own stock of thought and sense
As might enable each to stand alone

And serve him for a fellow; with his own,
Joining the qualities that just before
Had graced some older favorite. Thus they wore
A fluctuating halo, yesterday
Set flicker and to-morrow filched away, —
Those upland objects each of separate name,
Each with an aspect never twice the same,
Waxing and waning as the new-born host
Of fancies, like a single night's hoar-frost,
Gave to familiar things a face grotesque;
Only, preserving through the mad burlesque
A grave regard. Conceive! the orpine patch
Blossoming earliest on the log-house-thatch
The day those archers wound along the vines —
Related to the Chief that left their lines
To climb with clinking step the northern stair
Up to the solitary chambers where
Sordello never came. Thus thrall reached thrall;
He o'er-festooning every interval,
As the adventurous spider, making light
Of distance, shoots her threads from depth to height,
From barbican to battlement: so flung
Fantasies forth and in their centre swung
Our architect, — the breezy morning fresh
Above, and merry, — all his waving mesh
Laughing with lucid dew-drops rainbow-edged.
   This world of ours by tacit pact is pledged
To laying such a spangled fabric low,
Whether by gradual brush or gallant blow.
But its abundant will was balked here: doubt
Rose tardily in one so fenced about
From most that nurtures judgment, care and pain:
Judgment, that dull expedient we are fain,
Less favored, to adopt betimes and force
Stead us, diverted from our natural course
Of joys — contrive some yet amid the dearth,
Vary and render them, it may be, worth
Most we forego. Suppose Sordello hence
Selfish enough, without a moral sense
However feeble; what informed the boy
Others desired a portion in his joy?
Or say a ruthful chance broke woof and warp —
A heron's nest beat down by March winds sharp,
A fawn breathless beneath the precipice,
A bird with unsoiled breast and unfilmed eyes
Warm in the brake — could these undo the trance

Lapping Sordello? Not a circumstance
That makes for you, friend Naddo! Eat fern-seed
And peer beside us and report indeed
If (your word) "genius" dawned with throes and stings
And the whole fiery catalogue, while springs,
Summers and winters quietly came and went.
  Time put at length that period to content,
By right the world should have imposed: bereft
Of its good offices, Sordello, left
To study his companions, managed rip
Their fringe off, learn the true relationship,
Core with its crust, their nature with his own:
Amid his wild-wood sights he lived alone.
As if the poppy felt with him! Though he
Partook the poppy's red effrontery
Till Autumn spoiled their fleering quite with rain,
And, turbanless, a coarse brown rattling crane
Lay bare. That's gone: yet why renounce, for that,
His disenchanted tributaries — flat
Perhaps, but scarce so utterly forlorn,
Their simple presence might not well be borne
Whose parley was a transport once: recall
The poppy's gifts, it flaunts you, after all,
A poppy: — why distrust the evidence
Of each soon satisfied and healthy sense?
The new-born judgment answered, " little boots
Beholding other creatures' attributes
And having none!" or, say that it sufficed,
" Yet, could one but possess, oneself," (enticed
Judgment) " some special office!" Nought beside
Serves you? " Well then, be somehow justified
For this ignoble wish to circumscribe
And concentrate, rather than swell, the tribe
Of actual pleasures: what, now, from without
Effects it? — proves, despite a lurking doubt,
Mere sympathy sufficient, trouble spared?
That, tasting joys by proxy thus, you fared
The better for them?" Thus much craved his soul.
Alas, from the beginning love is whole
And true; if sure of naught beside, most sure
Of its own truth at least: nor may endure
A crowd to see its face, that cannot know
How hot the pulses throb its heart below.
While its own helplessness and utter want
Of means to worthily be ministrant
To what it worships, do but fan the more

Its flame, exalt the idol far before
Itself as it would have it ever be.
Souls like Sordello, on the contrary,
Coerced and put to shame, retaining will,
Care little, take mysterious comfort still,
But look forth tremblingly to ascertain
If others judge their claims not urged in vain,
And say for them their stifled thoughts aloud.
So, they must ever live before a crowd:
— " Vanity," Naddo tells you.
       Whence contrive
A crowd, now? From these women just alive,
That archer-troop? Forth glided — not alone
Each painted warrior, every girl of stone,
Nor Adelaide (bent double o'er a scroll,
One maiden at her knees, that eve, his soul
Shook as he stumbled through the arras'd glooms
On them, for, 'mid quaint robes and weird perfumes,
Started the meagre Tuscan up, — her eyes,
The maiden's, also, bluer with surprise)
— But the entire out-world: whatever, scraps
And snatches, song and story, dreams perhaps,
Conceited the world's offices, and he
Had hitherto transferred to flower or tree,
Not counted a befitting heritage
Each, of its own right, singly to engage
Some man, no other, — such now dared to stand
Alone. Strength, wisdom, grace on every hand
Soon disengaged themselves, and he discerned
A sort of human life: at least, was turned
A stream of lifelike figures through his brain.
Lord, liegeman, valvassor and suzerain,
Ere he could choose, surrounded him; a stuff
To work his pleasure on; there, sure enough:
But as for gazing, what shall fix that gaze?
Are they to simply testify the ways
He who convoked them sends his soul along
With the cloud's thunder or a dove's brood-song?
— While they live each his life, boast each his own
Peculiar dower of bliss, stand each alone
In some one point where something dearest loved
Is easiest gained — far worthier to be proved
Than aught he envies in the forest-wights!
No simple and self-evident delights,
But mixed desires of unimagined range,
Contrasts or combinations, new and strange,

Irksome perhaps, yet plainly recognized
By this, the sudden company — loves prized
By those who are to prize his own amount
Of loves. Once care because such make account,
Allow that foreign recognitions stamp
The current value, and his crowd shall vamp
Him counterfeits enough ; and so their print
Be on the piece, 't is gold, attests the mint,
And " good," pronounce they whom his new appeal
Is made to : if their casual print conceal —
This arbitrary good of theirs o'ergloss
What he has lived without, nor felt the loss —
Qualities strange, ungainly, wearisome,
— What matter ? So must speech expand the dumb
Part-sigh, part-smile with which Sordello, late
Whom no poor woodland-sights could satiate,
Betakes himself to study hungrily
Just what the puppets his crude fantasy
Supposes notablest, popes, kings, priests, knights,
May please to promulgate for appetites ;
Accepting all their artificial joys
Not as he views them, but as he employs
Each shape to estimate the other's stock
Of attributes, whereon — a marshalled flock
Of authorized enjoyments — he may spend
Himself, be men, now, as he used to blend
With tree and flower — nay more entirely, else
'T were mockery : for instance, " how excels
My life that chieftain's ? " (who apprised the youth
Ecelin, here, becomes this month, in truth,
Imperial Vicar ?) " Turns he in his tent
Remissly ? Be it so — my head is bent
Deliciously amid my girls to sleep.
What if he stalks the Trentine-pass ? Yon steep
I climbed an hour ago with little toil :
We are alike there. But can I, too, foil
The Guelf's paid stabber, carelessly afford
Saint Mark's a spectacle, the sleight o' the sword
Baffling the treason in a moment ? " Here
No rescue ! Poppy he is none, but peer
To Ecelin, assuredly : his hand,
Fashioned no otherwise, should wield a brand
With Ecelin's success — try, now ! He soon
Was satisfied, returned as to the moon
From earth ; left each abortive boy's-attempt
For feats, from failure happily exempt,

In fancy at his beck. "One day I will
Accomplish it! Are they not older still
— Not grown up men and women? 'T is beside
Only a dream; and though I must abide
With dreams now, I may find a thorough vent
For all myself, acquire an instrument
For acting what these people act; my soul
Hunting a body out may gain its whole
Desire some day!" How else express chagrin
And resignation, show the hope steal in
With which he let sink from an aching wrist
The rough-hewn ash-bow? Straight, a gold shaft hissed
Into the Syrian air, struck Malek down
Superbly! "Crosses to the breach! God's Town
Is gained him back!" Why bend rough ash-bows more?
  Thus lives he: if not careless as before,
Comforted: for one may anticipate,
Rehearse the future, be prepared when fate
Shall have prepared in turn real men whose names
Startle, real places of enormous fames,
Este abroad and Ecelin at home
To worship him, — Mantua, Verona, Rome
To witness it. Who grudges time so spent?
Rather test qualities to heart's content —
Summon them, thrice selected, near and far —
Compress the starriest into one star,
And grasp the whole at once!
                                    The pageant thinned
Accordingly; from rank to rank, like wind
His spirit passed to winnow and divide;
Back fell the simpler phantasms; every side
The strong clave to the wise; with either classed
The beauteous; so, till two or three amassed
Mankind's beseemingnesses, and reduced
Themselves eventually, graces loosed,
Strengths lavished, all to heighten up One Shape
Whose potency no creature should escape.
Can it be Friedrich of the bowmen's talk?
Surely that grape-juice, bubbling at the stalk,
Is some gray scorching Saracenic wine
The Kaiser quaffs with the Miramoline —
Those swarthy hazel-clusters, seamed and chapped,
Or filberts russet-sheathed and velvet-capped,
Are dates plucked from the bough John Brienne sent,
To keep in mind his sluggish armament
Of Canaan: — Friedrich's, all the pomp and fierce

Demeanor! But harsh sounds and sights transpierce
So rarely the serene cloud where he dwells,
Whose looks enjoin, whose lightest words are spells
On the obdurate! That right arm indeed
Has thunder for its slave; but where's the need
Of thunder if the stricken multitude
Hearkens, arrested in its angriest mood,
While songs go up exulting, then dispread,
Dispart, disperse, lingering overhead
Like an escape of angels? 'T is the tune,
Nor much unlike the words his women croon
Smilingly, colorless and faint-designed
Each, as a worn-out queen's face some remind
Of her extreme youth's love-tales. "Eglamor
Made that!" Half minstrel and half emperor,
What but ill objects vexed him? Such he slew.
The kinder sort were easy to subdue
By those ambrosial glances, dulcet tones;
And these a gracious hand advanced to thrones
Beneath him. Wherefore twist and torture this,
Striving to name afresh the antique bliss,
Instead of saying, neither less nor more,
He had discovered, as our world before,
Apollo? That shall be the name; nor bid
Me rag by rag expose how patchwork hid
The youth — what thefts of every clime and day
Contributed to purfle the array
He climbed with (June at deep) some close ravine
'Mid clatter of its million pebbles sheen,
Over which, singing soft, the runnel slipped
Elate with rains: into whose streamlet dipped
He foot, yet trod, you thought, with unwet sock —
Though really on the stubs of living rock
Ages ago it crenelled; vines for roof,
Lindens for wall; before him, aye aloof,
Flittered in the cool some azure damsel-fly,
Born of the simmering quiet, there to die.
Emerging whence, Apollo still, he spied
Mighty descents of forest; multiplied
Tuft on tuft, here, the frolic myrtle-trees,
There gendered the grave maple stocks at ease,
And, proud of its observer, straight the wood
Tried old surprises on him; black it stood
A sudden barrier ('t was a cloud passed o'er)
So dead and dense, the tiniest brute no more
Must pass; yet presently (the cloud dispatched)

Each clump, behold, was glistering detached
A shrub, oak-boles shrunk into ilex-stems!
Yet could not he denounce the stratagems
He saw thro', till, hours thence, aloft would hang
White summer-lightnings; as it sank and sprang
To measure, that whole palpitating breast
Of heaven, 't was Apollo, nature prest
At eve to worship.
     Time stole: by degrees
The Pythons perish off; his votaries
Sink to respectful distance; songs redeem
Their pains, but briefer; their dismissals seem
Emphatic; only girls are very slow
To disappear — his Delians! Some that glow
O' the instant, more with earlier loves to wrench
Away, reserves to quell, disdains to quench;
Alike in one material circumstance —
All soon or late adore Apollo! Glance
The bevy through, divine Apollo's choice,
His Daphne! "We secure Count Richard's voice
In Este's counsels, good for Este's ends
As our Taurello," say his faded friends,
" By granting him our Palma!" — the sole child,
They mean, of Agnes Este who beguiled
Ecelin, years before this Adelaide
Wedded and turned him wicked: "but the maid
Rejects his suit," those sleepy women boast.
She, scorning all beside, deserves the most
Sordello: so, conspicuous in his world
Of dreams sat Palma. How the tresses curled
Into a sumptuous swell of gold and wound
About her like a glory! even the ground
Was bright as with spilt sunbeams; breathe not, breathe
Not! — poised, see, one leg doubled underneath,
Its small foot buried in the dimpling snow,
Rests, but the other, listlessly below,
O'er the couch-side swings feeling for cool air,
The vein-streaks swollen a richer violet where
The languid blood lies heavily; yet calm
On her slight prop, each flat and outspread palm,
As but suspended in the act to rise
By consciousness of beauty, whence her eyes
Turn with so frank a triumph, for she meets
Apollo's gaze in the pine glooms.
        Time fleets:
That's worst! Because the pre-appointed age

Approaches. Fate is tardy with the stage
And crowd she promised. Lean he grows and pale,
Though restlessly at rest. Hardly avail
Fancies to soothe him. Time steals, yet alone
He tarries here! The earnest smile is gone.
How long this might continue matters not;
— Forever, possibly; since to the spot
None come: our lingering Taurello quits
Mantua at last, and light our lady flits
Back to her place disburdened of a care.
Strange — to be constant here if he is there!
Is it distrust? Oh, never! for they both
Goad Ecelin alike, Romano's growth
Is daily manifest, with Azzo dumb
And Richard wavering: let but Friedrich come,
Find matter for the minstrelsy's report!
— Lured from the Isle and its young Kaiser's court
To sing us a Messina morning up,
And, double rillet of a drinking cup,
Sparkle along to ease the land of drouth,
Northward to Provence that, and thus far south
The other. What a method to apprise
Neighbors of births, espousals, obsequies!
Which in their very tongue the Troubadour
Records; and his performance makes a tour,
For Trouveres bear the miracle about,
Explain its cunning to the vulgar rout,
Until the Formidable House is famed
Over the country — as Taurello aimed,
Who introduced, although the rest adopt,
The novelty. Such games, her absence stopped,
Begin afresh now Adelaide, recluse
No longer, in the light of day pursues
Her plans at Mantua: whence an accident
Which, breaking on Sordello's mixed content,
Opened, like any flash that cures the blind,
The veritable business of mankind.

BOOK THE SECOND.

The woods were long austere with snow: at last
Pink leaflets budded on the beech, and fast
Larches, scattered through pine-tree solitudes,
Brightened, "as in the slumbrous heart o' the woods
Our buried year, a witch, grew young again
To placid incantations, and that stain
About were from her caldron, green smoke blent
With those black pines" — so Eglamor gave vent
To a chance fancy. Whence a just rebuke
From his companion; brother Naddo shook
The solemnest of brows; "Beware," he said,
"Of setting up conceits in nature's stead!"
Forth wandered our Sordello. Nought so sure
As that to-day's adventure will secure
Palma, the visioned lady — only pass
O'er yon damp mound and its exhausted grass,
Under that brake where sundawn feeds the stalks
Of withered fern with gold, into those walks
Of pine and take her! Buoyantly he went.
Again his stooping forehead was besprent
With dew-drops from the skirting ferns. Then wide
Opened the great morass, shot every side
With flashing water through and through; a-shine,
Thick-steaming, all alive. Whose shape divine,
Quivered i' the farthest rainbow-vapor, glanced
Athwart the flying herons? He advanced,
But warily; though Mincio leaped no more,
Each footfall burst up in the marish-floor
A diamond jet: and if he stopped to pick
Rose-lichen, or molest the leeches quick,
And circling blood-worms, minnow, newt or loach,
A sudden pond would silently encroach
This way and that. On Palma passed. The verge
Of a new wood was gained. She will emerge
Flushed, now, and panting, — crowds to see, — will own
She loves him — Boniface to hear, to groan,
To leave his suit! One screen of pine-trees still
Opposes: but — the startling spectacle —
Mantua, this time! Under the walls — a crowd
Indeed, real men and women, gay and loud

Round a pavilion. How he stood!
                              In truth
No prophecy had come to pass: his youth
In its prime now — and where was homage poured
Upon Sordello? — born to be adored,
And suddenly discovered weak, scarce made
To cope with any, cast into the shade
By this and this. Yet something seemed to prick
And tingle in his blood; a sleight — a trick —
And much would be explained. It went for nought —
The best of their endowments were ill bought
With his identity: nay, the conceit,
That this day's roving led to Palma's feet
Was not so vain — list! The word, " Palma! " Steal
Aside, and die, Sordello; this is real,
And this — abjure!
                  What next? The curtains see
Dividing! She is there; and presently
He will be there — the proper You, at length —
In your own cherished dress of grace and strength:
Most like, the very Boniface!
                              Not so.
It was a showy man advanced; but though
A glad cry welcomed him, then every sound
Sank and the crowd disposed themselves around,
— " This is not he," Sordello felt; while, " Place
For the best Troubadour of Boniface! "
Hollaed the Jongleurs, — " Eglamor, whose lay
Concludes his patron's Court of Love to-day! "
Obsequious Naddo strung the master's lute
With the new lute-string, " Elys," named to suit
The song: he stealthily at watch, the while,
Biting his lip to keep down a great smile
Of pride: then up he struck. Sordello's brain
Swam; for he knew a sometime deed again;
So, could supply each foolish gap and chasm
The minstrel left in his enthusiasm,
Mistaking its true version — was the tale
Not of Apollo? Only, what avail
Luring her down, that Elys an he pleased,
If the man dared no further? Has he ceased?
And, lo, the people's frank applause half done,
Sordello was beside him, had begun
(Spite of indignant twitchings from his friend
The Trouvere) the true lay with the true end,
Taking the other's names and time and place

For his. On flew the song, a giddy race,
After the flying story; word made leap
Out word, rhyme — rhyme; the lay could barely keep
Pace with the action visibly rushing past:
Both ended. Back fell Naddo more aghast
Than some Egyptian from the harassed bull
That wheeled abrupt and, bellowing, fronted full
His plague, who spied a scarab 'neath the tongue,
And found 't was Apis' flank his hasty prong
Insulted. But the people — but the cries,
The crowding round, and proffering the prize!
— For he had gained some prize. He seemed to shrink
Into a sleepy cloud, just at whose brink
One sight withheld him. There sat Adelaide,
Silent; but at her knees the very maid
Of the North Chamber, her red lips as rich,
The same pure fleecy hair; one weft of which,
Golden and great, quite touched his cheek as o'er
She leant, speaking some six words and no more.
He answered something, anything; and she
Unbound a scarf and laid it heavily
Upon him, her neck's warmth and all. Again
Moved the arrested magic; in his brain
Noises grew, and a light that turned to glare,
And greater glare, until the intense flare
Engulfed him, shut the whole scene from his sense.
And when he woke 't was many a furlong thence,
At home; the sun shining his ruddy wont;
The customary birds'-chirp; but his front
Was crowned — was crowned! Her scented scarf around
His neck! Whose gorgeous vesture heaps the ground?
A prize? He turned, and peeringly on him
Brooded the women-faces, kind and dim,
Ready to talk — "The Jongleurs in a troop
Had brought him back, Naddo and Squarcialupe
And Tagliafer; how strange! a childhood spent
In taking, well for him, so brave a bent!
Since Eglamor," they heard, "was dead with spite,
And Palma chose him for her minstrel."
           Light
Sordello rose — to think, now; hitherto
He had perceived. Sure, a discovery grew
Out of it all! Best live from first to last
The transport o'er again. A week he passed,
Sucking the sweet out of each circumstance,
From the bard's outbreak to the luscious trance

Bounding his own achievement. Strange! A man
Recounted an adventure, but began
Imperfectly; his own task was to fill
The frame-work up, sing well what he sung ill,
Supply the necessary points, set loose
As many incidents of little use
— More imbecile the other, not to see
Their relative importance clear as he!
But, for a special pleasure in the act
Of singing — had he ever turned, in fact,
From Elys, to sing Elys? — from each fit
Of rapture to contrive a song of it?
True, this snatch or the other seemed to wind
Into a treasure, helped himself to find
A beauty in himself; for, see, he soared
By means of that mere snatch, to many a hoard
Of fancies; as some falling cone bears soft
The eye along the fir-tree-spire, aloft
To a dove's nest. Then, how divine the cause
Why such performance should exact applause
From men, if they had fancies too? Did fate
Decree they found a beauty separate
In the poor snatch itself? — "Take Elys, there,
— 'Her head that's sharp and perfect like a pear,
So close and smooth are laid the few fine locks
Colored like honey oozed from topmost rocks
Sun-blanched the livelong summer' — if they heard
Just those two rhymes, assented at my word,
And loved them as I love them who have run
These fingers through those pale locks, let the sun
Into the white cool skin — who first could clutch,
Then praise — I needs must be a god to such.
Or what if some, above themselves, and yet
Beneath me, like their Eglamor, have set
An impress on our gift? So, men believe
And worship what they know not, nor receive
Delight from. Have they fancies — slow, perchance,
Not at their beck, which indistinctly glance
Until, by song, each floating part be linked
To each, and all grow palpable, distinct?"
He pondered this.
     Meanwhile, sounds low and drear
Stole on him, and a noise of footsteps, near
And nearer, while the underwood was pushed
Aside, the larches grazed, the dead leaves crushed
At the approach of men. The wind seemed laid;

Only, the trees shrunk slightly and a shade
Came o'er the sky although 't was mid-day yet:
You saw each half-shut downcast floweret
Flutter — " a Roman bride, when they 'd dispart
Her unbound tresses with the Sabine dart,
Holding that famous rape in memory still,
Felt creep into her curls the iron chill,
And looked thus," Eglamor would say — indeed
'T is Eglamor, no other, these precede
Home hither in the woods. " 'T were surely sweet
Far from the scene of one's forlorn defeat
To sleep!" judged Naddo, who in person led
Jongleurs and Trouveres, chanting at their head,
A scanty company; for, sooth to say,
Our beaten Troubadour had seen his day.
Old worshippers were something shamed, old friends
Nigh weary; still the death proposed amends.
" Let us but get them safely through my song
And home again!" quoth Naddo.
                                    All along,
This man (they rest the bier upon the sand)
— This calm corpse with the loose flowers in his hand,
Eglamor, lived Sordello's opposite.
For him indeed was Naddo's notion right,
And verse a temple-worship vague and vast,
A ceremony that withdrew the last
Opposing bolt, looped back the lingering veil
Which hid the holy place: should one so frail
Stand there without such effort? or repine
If much was blank, uncertain at the shrine
He knelt before, till, soothed by many a rite,
The power responded, and some sound or sight
Grew up, his own forever, to be fixed,
In rhyme, the beautiful, forever! — mixed
With his own life, unloosed when he should please,
Having it safe at hand, ready to ease
All pain, remove all trouble; every time
He loosed that fancy from its bonds of rhyme,
(Like Perseus when he loosed his naked love)
Faltering; so distinct and far above
Himself, these fancies! He, no genius rare,
Transfiguring in fire or wave or air
At will, but a poor gnome that, cloistered up
In some rock-chamber with his agate cup,
His topaz rod, his seed-pearl, in these few
And their arrangement finds enough to do

For his best art. Then, how he loved that art!
The calling marking him a man apart
From men — one not to care, take counsel for
Cold hearts, comfortless faces — (Eglamor
Was neediest of his tribe) — since verse, the gift,
Was his, and men, the whole of them, must shift
Without it, e'en content themselves with wealth
And pomp and power, snatching a life by stealth.
So, Eglamor was not without his pride!
The sorriest bat which cowers throughout noontide
While other birds are jocund, has one time
When moon and stars are blinded, and the prime
Of earth is his to claim, nor find a peer;
And Eglamor was noblest poet here —
He well knew, 'mid those April woods, he cast
Conceits upon in plenty as he passed,
That Naddo might suppose him not to think
Entirely on the coming triumph: wink
At the one weakness! 'Twas a fervid child,
That song of his; no brother of the guild
Had e'er conceived its like. The rest you know,
The exaltation and the overthrow:
Our poet lost his purpose, lost his rank,
His life — to that it came. Yet envy sank
Within him, as he heard Sordello out,
And, for the first time, shouted — tried to shout
Like others, not from any zeal to show
Pleasure that way: the common sort did so.
What else was Eglamor? who, bending down
As they, placed his beneath Sordello's crown,
Printed a kiss on his successor's hand,
Left one great tear on it, then joined his band
— In time; for some were watching at the door:
Who knows what envy may effect? "Give o'er,
Nor charm his lips, nor craze him!" (here one spied
And disengaged the withered crown) — " Beside
His crown? How prompt and clear those verses rang
To answer yours! nay, sing them!" And he sang
Them calmly. Home he went; friends used to wait
His coming, zealous to congratulate;
But, to a man, so quickly runs report,
Could do no less than leave him, and escort
His rival. That eve, then, bred many a thought:
What must his future life be? was he brought
So low, who stood so lofty this Spring morn?
At length he said, "Best sleep now with my scorn,

And by to-morrow I devise some plain
Expedient!" So, he slept, nor woke again.
They found as much, those friends, when they returned
O'erflowing with the marvels they had learned
About Sordello's paradise, his roves
Among the hills and vales and plains and groves,
Wherein, no doubt, this lay was roughly cast,
Polished by slow degrees, completed last
To Eglamor's discomfiture and death.
   Such form the chanters now, and, out of breath,
They lay the beaten man in his abode,
Naddo reciting that same luckless ode,
Doleful to hear. Sordello could explore
By means of it, however, one step more
In joy; and, mastering the round at length,
Learnt how to live in weakness as in strength,
When from his covert forth he stood, addressed
Eglamor, bade the tender ferns invest,
Primæval pines o'ercanopy his couch,
And, most of all, his fame — (shall I avouch
Eglamor heard it, dead though he might look,
And laughed as from his brow Sordello took
The crown, and laid on the bard's breast, and said
It was a crown, now, fit for poet's head?)
— Continue. Nor the prayer quite fruitless fell.
A plant they have, yielding a three-leaved bell
Which whitens at the heart ere noon, and ails
Till evening; evening gives it to her gales
To clear away with such forgotten things
As are an eyesore to the morn: this brings
Him to their mind, and bears his very name.
   So much for Eglamor. My own month came;
'T was a sunrise of blossoming and May.
Beneath a flowering laurel thicket lay
Sordello; each new sprinkle of white stars
That smell fainter of wine than Massic jars
Dug up at Baiæ, when the south wind shed
The ripest, made him happier; filleted
And robed the same, only a lute beside
Lay on the turf. Before him far and wide
The country stretched: Goito slept behind
— The castle and its covert, which confined
Him with his hopes and fears; so fain of old
To leave the story of his birth untold.
At intervals, 'spite the fantastic glow
Of his Apollo-life, a certain low

And wretched whisper, winding through the bliss,
Admonished, no such fortune could be his,
All was quite false and sure to fade one day :
The closelier drew he round him his array
Of brilliance to expel the truth. But when
A reason for his difference from men
Surprised him at the grave, he took no rest
While aught of that old life, superbly dressed
Down to its meanest incident, remained
A mystery : alas, they soon explained
Away Apollo! and the tale amounts
To this : when at Vicenza both her counts
Banished the Vivaresi kith and kin,
Those Maltraversi hung on Ecelin,
Reviled him as he followed ; he for spite
Must fire their quarter, though that self-same night
Among the flames young Ecelin was born
Of Adelaide, there too, and barely torn
From the roused populace hard on the rear,
By a poor archer when his chieftain's fear
Grew high ; into the thick Elcorte leapt,
Saved her, and died ; no creature left except
His child to thank. And when the full escape
Was known — how men impaled from chine to nape
Unlucky Prata, all to pieces spurned
Bishop Pistore's concubines, and burned
Taurello's entire household, flesh and fell,
Missing the sweeter prey — such courage well
Might claim reward. The orphan, ever since,
Sordello, had been nurtured by his prince
Within a blind retreat where Adelaide —
(For, once this notable discovery made,
The past at every point was understood)
— Might harbor easily when times were rude,
When Azzo schemed for Palma, to retrieve
That pledge of Agnes Este — loth to leave
Mantua unguarded with a vigilant eye,
While there Taurello bode ambiguously —
He who could have no motive now to moil
For his own fortunes since their utter spoil —
As it were worth while yet (went the report)
To disengage himself from her. In short,
Apollo vanished ; a mean youth, just named
His lady's minstrel, was to be proclaimed
— How shall I phrase it ? — Monarch of the World!
For, on the day when that array was furled

Forever, and in place of one a slave
To longings, wild indeed, but longings save
In dreams as wild, suppressed — one daring not
Assume the mastery such dreams allot,
Until a magical equipment, strength,
Grace, wisdom, decked him too, — he chose at length,
Content with unproved wits and failing frame,
In virtue of his simple will, to claim
That mastery, no less — to do his best
With means so limited, and let the rest
Go by, — the seal was set: never again
Sordello could in his own sight remain
One of the many, one with hopes and cares
And interests nowise distinct from theirs,
Only peculiar in a thriveless store
Of fancies, which were fancies and no more;
Never again for him and for the crowd
A common law was challenged and allowed
If calmly reasoned of, howe'er denied
By a mad impulse nothing justified
Short of Apollo's presence. The divorce
Is clear: why needs Sordello square his course
By any known example? Men no more
Compete with him than tree and flower before.
Himself, inactive, yet is greater far
Than such as act, each stooping to his star,
Acquiring thence his function; he has gained
The same result with meaner mortals trained
To strength or beauty, moulded to express
Each the idea that rules him; since no less
He comprehends that function, but can still
Embrace the others, take of might his fill
With Richard as of grace with Palma, mix
Their qualities, or for a moment fix
On one; abiding free meantime, uncramped
By any partial organ, never stamped
Strong, and to strength turning all energies —
Wise, and restricted to becoming wise —
That is, he loves not, nor possesses One
Idea that, star-like over, lures him on
To its exclusive purpose. "Fortunate!
This flesh of mine ne'er strove to emulate
A soul so various — took no casual mould
Of the first fancy and, contracted, cold,
Clogged her forever — soul averse to change
As flesh: whereas flesh leaves soul free to range,

Remains itself a blank, cast into shade,
Encumbers little, if it cannot aid.
So, range, free soul! — who, by self-consciousness,
The last drop of all beauty dost express —
The grace of seeing grace, a quintessence
For thee: while for the world, that can dispense
Wonder on men who, themselves, wonder — make
A shift to love at second-hand, and take
For idols those who do but idolize,
Themselves, — the world that counts men strong or wise,
Who, themselves, court strength, wisdom, — it shall bow
Surely in unexampled worship now,
Discerning me!" —
                (Dear monarch, I beseech,
Notice how lamentably wide a breach
Is here: discovering this, discover too
What our poor world has possibly to do
With it! As pigmy natures as you please —
So much the better for you; take your ease,
Look on, and laugh; style yourself God alone;
Strangle some day with a cross olive-stone:
All that is right enough: but why want us
To know that you yourself know thus and thus?)
"The world shall bow to me conceiving all
Man's life, who see its blisses, great and small,
Afar — not tasting any; no machine
To exercise my utmost will is mine:
Be mine mere consciousness! Let men perceive
What I could do, a mastery believe,
Asserted and established to the throng
By their selected evidence of song
Which now shall prove, whate'er they are, or seek
To be, I am — whose words, not actions speak,
Who change no standards of perfection, vex
With no strange forms created to perplex,
But just perform their bidding and no more,
At their own satiating-point give o'er,
While each shall love in me the love that leads
His soul to power's perfection." Song, not deeds,
(For we get tired) was chosen. Fate would brook
Mankind no other organ; he would look
For not another channel to dispense
His own volition by, receive men's sense
Of its supremacy; would live content,
Obstructed else, with merely verse for vent.
Nor should, for instance, strength an outlet seek

And, striving, be admired; nor grace bespeak
Wonder, displayed in gracious attitudes;
Nor wisdom, poured forth, change unseemly moods:
But he would give and take on song's one point.
Like some huge throbbing stone that, poised a-joint,
Sounds, to affect on its basaltic bed,
Must sue in just one accent; tempests shed
Thunder, and raves the windstorm: only let
That key by any little noise be set —
The far benighted hunter's halloo pitch
On that, the hungry curlew chance to scritch
Or serpent hiss it, rustling through the rift,
However loud, however low — all lift
The groaning monster, stricken to the heart.
Lo ye, the world's concernment, for its part,
And this, for his, will hardly interfere!
Its businesses in blood and blaze this year
But while the hour away — a pastime slight
Till he shall step upon the platform: right!
And, now thus much is settled, cast in rough,
Proved feasible, be counselled! thought enough, —
Slumber, Sordello! any day will serve:
Were it a less digested plan! how swerve
To-morrow? Meanwhile eat these sun-dried grapes,
And watch the soaring hawk there! Life escapes
Merrily thus. He thoroughly read o'er
His truchman Naddo's missive six times more,
Praying him visit Mantua and supply
A famished world. The evening star was high
When he reached Mantua, but his fame arrived
Before him: friends applauded, foes connived,
And Naddo looked an angel, and the rest
Angels, and all these angels would be blest
Supremely by a song — the thrice-renowned
Goito manufacture. Then he found
(Casting about to satisfy the crowd)
That happy vehicle, so late allowed,
A sore annoyance; 't was the song's effect
He cared for, scarce the song itself: reflect!
In the past life, what might be singing's use?
Just to delight his Delians, whose profuse
Praise, not the toilsome process which procured
That praise, enticed Apollo: dreams abjured,
No overleaping means for ends — take both

For granted or take neither! I am loth
To say the rhymes at last were Eglamor's;
But Naddo, chuckling, bade competitors
Go pine; "the master certes meant to waste
No effort, cautiously had probed the taste
He'd please anon: true bard, in short, disturb
His title if they could; nor spur nor curb,
Fancy nor reason, wanting in him; whence
The staple of his verses, common sense:
He built on man's broad nature — gift of gifts,
That power to build! The world contented shifts
With counterfeits enough, a dreary sort
Of warriors, statesmen, ere it can extort
Its poet-soul — that's, after all, a freak
(The having eyes to see and tongue to speak)
With our herd's stupid sterling happiness
So plainly incompatible that — yes —
Yes — should a son of his improve the breed
And turn out poet, he were cursed indeed!"
"Well, there's Goito and its woods anon,
If the worst happen; best go stoutly on
Now!" thought Sordello.
      Ay, and goes on yet!
You pother with your glossaries to get
A notion of the Troubadour's intent
In rondel, tenzon, virlai or sirvent —
Much as you study arras how to twirl
His angelot, plaything of page and girl
Once; but you surely reach, at last, — or, no!
Never quite reach what struck the people so,
As from the welter of their time he drew
Its elements successively to view,
Followed all actions backward on their course,
And catching up, unmingled at the source,
Such a strength, such a weakness, added then
A touch or two, and turned them into men.
Virtue took form, nor vice refused a shape;
Here heaven opened, there was hell agape,
As Saint this simpered past in sanctity,
Sinner the other flared portentous by
A greedy people. Then why stop, surprised
At his success? The scheme was realized
Too suddenly in one respect: a crowd
Praising, eyes quick to see, and lips as loud
To speak, delicious homage to receive,
The woman's breath to feel upon his sleeve,

Who said, " But Anafest —why asks he less
Than Lucio, in your verses? how confess,
It seemed too much but yestereve!"—the youth,
Who bade him earnestly, " Avow the truth!
You love Bianca, surely, from your song;
I knew I was unworthy!"— soft or strong,
In poured such tributes ere he had arranged
Ethereal ways to take them, sorted, changed,
Digested. Courted thus at unawares,
In spite of his pretensions and his cares,
He caught himself shamefully hankering
After the obvious petty joys that spring
From true life, fain relinquish pedestal
And condescend with pleasures — one and all
To be renounced, no doubt; for, thus to chain
Himself to single joys and so refrain
From tasting their quintessence, frustrates, sure,
His prime design; each joy must he abjure
Even for love of it.
     He laughed: what sage
But perishes if from his magic page
He look because, at the first line, a proof
'T was heard salutes him from the cavern roof?
" On! Give yourself, excluding aught beside,
To the day's task; compel your slave provide
Its utmost at the soonest; turn the leaf
Thoroughly conned. These lays of yours, in brief —
Cannot men bear, now, something better ? — fly
A pitch beyond this unreal pageantry
Of essences ? the period sure has ceased
For such: present us with ourselves, at least,
Not portions of ourselves, mere loves and hates
Made flesh: wait not!"
     Awhile the poet waits
However. The first trial was enough:
He left imagining, to try the stuff
That held the imaged thing, and, let it writhe
Never so fiercely, scarce allowed a tithe
To reach the light — his Language. How he sought
The cause, conceived a cure, and slow re-wrought
That Language, — welding words into the crude
Mass from the new speech round him, till a rude
Armor was hammered out, in time to be
Approved beyond the Roman panoply
Melted to make it, — boots not. This obtained
With some ado, no obstacle remained

To using it; accordingly he took
An action with its actors, quite forsook
Himself to live in each, returned anon
With the result — a creature, and, by one
And one, proceeded leisurely to equip
Its limbs in harness of his workmanship.
" Accomplished! Listen, Mantuans!" Fond essay!
Piece after piece that armor broke away,
Because perceptions whole, like that he sought
To clothe, reject so pure a work of thought
As language: thought may take perception's place
But hardly co-exist in any case,
Being its mere presentiment — of the whole
By parts, the simultaneous and the sole
By the successive and the many. Lacks
The crowd perception? painfully it tacks
Thought to thought, which Sordello, needing such,
Has rent perception into: it's to clutch
And reconstruct — his office to diffuse,
Destroy: as hard, then, to obtain a Muse
As to become Apollo. " For the rest,
E'en if some wondrous vehicle expressed
The whole dream, what impertinence in me
So to express it, who myself can be
The dream! nor, on the other hand, are those
I sing to, over-likely to suppose
A higher than the highest I present
Now, which they praise already: be content
Both parties, rather — they with the old verse,
And I with the old praise — far go, fare worse!"
A few adhering rivets loosed, upsprings
The angel, sparkles off his mail, which rings
Whirled from each delicatest limb it warps,
So might Apollo from the sudden corpse
Of Hyacinth have cast his luckless quoits.
He set to celebrating the exploits
Of Montfort o'er the Mountaineers.
                              Then came
The world's revenge: their pleasure, now his aim
Merely, — what was it? "Not to play the fool
So much as learn our lesson in your school!"
Replied the world. He found that, every time
He gained applause by any ballad-rhyme,
His auditory recognized no jot
As he intended, and, mistaking not
Him for his meanest hero, ne'er was dunce

Sufficient to believe him — all, at once.
His will . . . conceive it caring for his will!
— Mantuans, the main of them, admiring still
How a mere singer, ugly, stunted, weak,
Had Montfort at completely (so to speak)
His fingers' ends; while past the praise-tide swept
To Montfort, either's share distinctly kept:
The true meed for true merit! — his abates
Into a sort he most repudiates,
And on them angrily he turns. Who were
The Mantuans, after all, that he should care
About their recognition, ay or no?
In spite of the convention months ago,
(Why blink the truth?) was not he forced to help
This same ungrateful audience, every whelp
Of Naddo's litter, make them pass for peers
With the bright band of old Goito years,
As erst he toiled for flower or tree? Why, there
Sat Palma! Adelaide's funereal hair
Ennobled the next corner. Ay, he strewed
A fairy dust upon that multitude,
Although he feigned to take them by themselves;
His giants dignified those puny elves,
Sublimed their faint applause. In short, he found
Himself still footing a delusive round,
Remote as ever from the self-display
He meant to compass, hampered every way
By what he hoped assistance. Wherefore then
Continue, make believe to find in men
A use he found not?
     Weeks, months, years went by,
And lo, Sordello vanished utterly,
Sundered in twain; each spectral part at strife
With each; one jarred against another life;
The Poet thwarting hopelessly the Man
Who, fooled no longer, free in fancy ran
Here, there; let slip no opportunities
As pitiful, forsooth, beside the prize
To drop on him some no-time and acquit
His constant faith (the Poet-half's to wit —
That waiving any compromise between
No joy and all joy kept the hunger keen
Beyond most methods) — of incurring scoff
From the Man-portion — not to be put off
With self-reflectings by the Poet's scheme,
Though ne'er so bright; — who sauntered forth in dream,

Dressed anyhow, nor waited mystic frames,
Immeasurable gifts, astounding claims,
But just his sorry self — who yet might be
Sorrier for aught he in reality
Achieved, so pinioned Man's the Poet-part,
Fondling, in turn of fancy, verse; the Art
Developing his soul a thousand ways —
Potent, by its assistance, to amaze
The multitude with majesties, convince
Each sort of nature, that the nature's prince
Accosted it. Language, the makeshift, grew
Into a bravest of expedients, too;
Apollo, seemed it now, perverse had thrown
Quiver and bow away, the lyre alone
Sufficed. While, out of dream, his day's work went
To tune a crazy tenzon or sirvent —
So hampered him the Man-part, thrust to judge
Between the bard and the bard's audience, grudge
A minute's toil that missed its due reward!
But the complete Sordello, Man and Bard,
John's cloud-girt angel, this foot on the land,
That on the sea, with, open in his hand,
A bitter-sweetling of a book — was gone.
  Then, if internal struggles to be one
Which frittered him incessantly piecemeal,
Referred, ne'er so obliquely, to the real
Intruding Mantuans! ever with some call
To action while he pondered, once for all,
Which looked the easier effort — to pursue
This course, still leap o'er paltry joys, yearn through
The present ill-appreciated stage
Of self-revealment, and compel the age
Know him; or else, forswearing bard-craft, wake
From out his lethargy and nobly shake
Off timid habits of denial, mix
With men, enjoy like men. Ere he could fix
On aught, in rushed the Mantuans; much they cared
For his perplexity! Thus unprepared,
The obvious if not only shelter lay
In deeds, the dull conventions of his day
Prescribed the like of him: why not be glad
'T is settled Palma's minstrel, good or bad,
Submits to this and that established rule?
Let Vidal change, or any other fool,
His murrey-colored robe for filamot,
And crop his hair; too skin-deep, is it not,

Such vigor? Then, a sorrow to the heart,
His talk! Whatever topics they might start
Had to be groped for in his consciousness
Straight, and as straight delivered them by guess.
Only obliged to ask himself, " What was,"
A speedy answer followed ; but, alas,
One of God's large ones, tardy to condense
Itself into a period ; answers whence
A tangle of conclusions must be stripped
At any risk ere, trim to pattern clipped,
They matched rare specimens the Mantuan flock
Regaled him with, each talker from his stock
Of sorted-o'er opinions, every stage,
Juicy in youth or desiccate with age,
Fruits like the fig-tree's, rathe-ripe, rotten-rich,
Sweet-sour, all tastes to take: a practice which
He too had not impossibly attained,
Once either of those fancy-flights restrained ;
(For, at conjecture how might words appear
To others, playing there what happened here,
And occupied abroad by what he spurned
At home, 't was slipped, the occasion he returned
To seize :) he 'd strike that lyre adroitly — speech,
Would but a twenty-cubit plectre reach ;
A clever hand, consummate instrument,
Were both brought close ; each excellency went
For nothing, else. The question Naddo asked,
Had just a lifetime moderately tasked
To answer, Naddo's fashion. More disgust
And more : why move his soul, since move it must
At minute's notice or as good it failed
To move at all ? The end was, he retailed
Some ready-made opinion, put to use
This quip, that maxim, ventured reproduce
Gestures and tones — at any folly caught
Serving to finish with, nor too much sought
If false or true 't was spoken ; praise and blame
Of what he said grew pretty nigh the same
— Meantime awards to meantime acts : his soul,
Unequal to the compassing a whole,
Saw, in a tenth part, less and less to strive
About. And as for men in turn . . . contrive
Who could to take eternal interest
In them, so hate the worst, so love the best !
Though, in pursuance of his passive plan,
He hailed, decried, the proper way.

                                        As Man
So figured he; and how as Poet? Verse
Came only not to a stand-still. The worse,
That his poor piece of daily work to do
Was, not sink under any rivals; who
Loudly and long enough, without these qualms,
Tuned, from Bocafoli's stark-naked psalms,
To Plara's sonnets spoilt by toying with,
" As knops that stud some almug to the pith
Prickèd for gum, wry thence, and crinklèd worse
Than pursèd eyelids of a river-horse
Sunning himself o' the slime when whirrs the breeze " —
Gad-fly, that is. He might compete with these!
But — but —
             " Observe a pompion-twine afloat;
Pluck me one cup from off the castle-moat!
Along with cup you raise leaf, stalk and root,
The entire surface of the pool to boot.
So could I pluck a cup, put in one song
A single sight, did not my hand, too strong,
Twitch in the least the root-strings of the whole.
How should externals satisfy my soul?"
" Why that's precise the error Squarcialupe "
(Hazarded Naddo) " finds; ' the man can't stoop
To sing us out,' quoth he, ' a mere romance;
He 'd fain do better than the best, enhance
The subjects' rarity, work problems out
Therewith:' now, you 're a bard, a bard past doubt,
And no philosopher; why introduce
Crotchets like these? fine, surely, but no use
In poetry — which still must be, to strike,
Based upon common sense; there's nothing like
Appealing to our nature! what beside
Was your first poetry? No tricks were tried
In that, no hollow thrills, affected throes!
' The man,' said we, ' tells his own joys and woes:
We 'll trust him.' Would you have your songs endure?
Build on the human heart! — why, to be sure
Yours is one sort of heart — but I mean theirs,
Ours, every one's, the healthy heart one cares
To build on! Central peace, mother of strength,
That's father of . . . nay, go yourself that length,
Ask those calm-hearted doers what they do
When they have got their calm! And is it true,
Fire rankles at the heart of every globe?
Perhaps. But these are matters one may probe

Too deeply for poetic purposes:
Rather select a theory that . . . yes,
Laugh! what does that prove? — stations you midway
And saves some little o'er-refining. Nay,
That's rank injustice done me! I restrict
The poet? Don't I hold the poet picked
Out of a host of warriors, statesmen . . . did
I tell you? Very like! As well you hid
That sense of power, you have! True bards believe
All able to achieve what they achieve —
That is, just nothing — in one point abide
Profounder simpletons than all beside.
Oh, ay! The knowledge that you are a bard
Must constitute your prime, nay sole, reward!"
So prattled Naddo, busiest of the tribe
Of genius-haunters — how shall I describe
What grubs or nips or rubs or rips — your louse
For love, your flea for hate, magnanimous,
Malignant, Pappacoda, Tagliafer,
Picking a sustenance from wear and tear
By implements it sedulous employs
To undertake, lay down, mete out, o'er-toise
Sordello? Fifty creepers to elude
At once! They settled stanchly; shame ensued:
Behold the monarch of mankind succumb
To the last fool who turned him round his thumb,
As Naddo styled it! 'T was not worth oppose
The matter of a moment, gainsay those
He aimed at getting rid of; better think
Their thoughts and speak their speech, secure to slink
Back expeditiously to his safe place,
And chew the cud — what he and what his race
Were really, each of them. Yet even this
Conformity was partial. He would miss
Some point, brought into contact with them ere
Assured in what small segment of the sphere
Of his existence they attended him;
Whence blunders, falsehoods rectified — a grim
List — slur it over! How? If dreams were tried,
His will swayed sicklily from side to side,
Nor merely neutralized his waking act
But tended e'en in fancy to distract
The intermediate will, the choice of means.
He lost the art of dreaming: Mantuan scenes
Supplied a baron, say, he sang before,
Handsomely reckless, full to running o'er

Of gallantries; "abjure the soul, content
With body, therefore!" Scarcely had he bent
Himself in dream thus low, when matter fast
Cried out, he found, for spirit to contrast
And task it duly; by advances slight,
The simple stuff becoming composite,
Count Lori grew Apollo — best recall
His fancy! Then would some rough peasant-Paul,
Like those old Ecelin confers with, glance
His gay apparel o'er; that countenance
Gathered his shattered fancies into one,
And, body clean abolished, soul alone
Sufficed the gray Paulician: by and by,
To balance the ethereality,
Passions were needed; foiled he sank again.
 Meanwhile the world rejoiced ('t is time explain)
Because a sudden sickness set it free
From Adelaide. Missing the mother-bee,
Her mountain-hive Romano swarmed; at once
A rustle-forth of daughters and of sons
Blackened the valley. "I am sick too, old,
Half crazed I think; what good's the Kaiser's gold
To such an one? God help me! for I catch
My children's greedy sparkling eyes at watch —
'He bears that double breastplate on,' they say,
'So many minutes less than yesterday!'
Beside, Monk Hilary is on his knees
Now, sworn to kneel and pray till God shall please
Exact a punishment for many things
You know, and some you never knew; which brings
To memory, Azzo's sister Beatrix
And Richard's Giglia are my Alberic's
And Ecelin's betrothed; the Count himself
Must get my Palma: Ghibellin and Guelf
Mean to embrace each other." So began
Romano's missive to his fighting man
Taurello — on the Tuscan's death, away
With Friedrich sworn to sail from Naples' bay
Next month for Syria. Never thunder-clap
Out of Vesuvius' throat, like this mishap
Startled him. "That accursed Vicenza! I
Absent, and she selects this time to die!
Ho, fellows, for Vicenza!" Half a score
Of horses ridden dead, he stood before
Romano in his reeking spurs: too late —
"Boniface urged me, Este could not wait,"

The chieftain stammered ; " let me die in peace —
Forget me! Was it I who craved increase
Of rule? Do you and Friedrich plot your worst
Against the Father: as you found me first
So leave me now. Forgive me! Palma, sure,
Is at Goito still. Retain that lure —
Only be pacified!"
                    The country rung
With such a piece of news : on every tongue,
How Ecelin's great servant, congeed off,
Had done a long day's service, so, might doff
The green and yellow, and recover breath
At Mantua, whither, — since Retrude's death,
(The girlish slip of a Sicilian bride
From Otho's house, he carried to reside
At Mantua till the Ferrarese should pile
A structure worthy her imperial style,
The gardens raise, the statues there enshrine,
She never lived to see) — although his line
Was ancient in her archives and she took
A pride in him, that city, nor forsook
Her child when he forsook himself and spent
A prowess on Romano surely meant
For his own growth — whither he ne'er resorts
If wholly satisfied (to trust reports)
With Ecelin. So, forward in a trice
Were shows to greet him. " Take a friend's advice,"
Quoth Naddo to Sordello, " nor be rash
Because your rivals (nothing can abash
Some folks) demur that we pronounced you best
To sound the great man's welcome ; 't is a test,
Remember! Strojavacca looks asquint,
The rough fat sloven ; and there's plenty hint
Your pinions have received of late a shock —
Outsoar them, cobswan of the silver flock!
Sing well!" A signal wonder, song 's no whit
Facilitated.
              Fast the minutes flit ;
Another day, Sordello finds, will bring
The soldier, and he cannot choose but sing ;
So, a last shift, quits Mantua — slow, alone :
Out of that aching brain, a very stone,
Song must be struck. What occupies that front?
Just how he was more awkward than his wont
The night before, when Naddo, who had seen
Taurello on his progress, praised the mien

For dignity no crosses could affect—
Such was a joy, and might not he detect
A satisfaction if established joys
Were proved imposture? Poetry annoys
Its utmost: wherefore fret? Verses may come
Or keep away! And thus he wandered, dumb
Till evening, when he paused, thoroughly spent,
On a blind hill-top: down the gorge he went,
Yielding himself up as to an embrace.
The moon came out; like features of a face,
A querulous fraternity of pines,
Sad blackthorn clumps, leafless and grovelling vines
Also came out, made gradually up
The picture; 't was Goito's mountain-cup
And castle. He had dropped through one defile
He never dared explore, the Chief erewhile
Had vanished by. Back rushed the dream, enwrapped
Him wholly. 'T was Apollo now they lapped,
Those mountains, not a pettish minstrel meant
To wear his soul away in discontent,
Brooding on fortune's malice. Heart and brain
Swelled; he expanded to himself again,
As some thin seedling spice-tree starved and frail,
Pushing between cat's head and ibis' tail
Crusted into the porphyry pavement smooth,
— Suffered remain just as it sprung, to soothe
The Soldan's pining daughter, never yet
Well in her chilly green-glazed minaret, —
When rooted up, the sunny day she died,
And flung into the common court beside
Its parent tree. Come home, Sordello! Soon
Was he low muttering, beneath the moon,
Of sorrow saved, of quiet evermore, —
Since from the purpose, he maintained before,
Only resulted wailing and hot tears.
Ah, the slim castle! dwindled of late years,
But more mysterious; gone to ruin — trails
Of vine through every loop-hole. Nought avails
The night as, torch in hand, he must explore
The maple chamber: did I say, its floor
Was made of intersecting cedar beams?
Worn now with gaps so large, there blew cold streams
Of air quite from the dungeon; lay your ear
Close and 't is like, one after one, you hear
In the blind darkness water drop. The nests
And nooks retain their long ranged vesture-chests

Empty and smelling of the iris root
The Tuscan grated o'er them to recruit
Her wasted wits. Palma was gone that day,
Said the remaining women. Last, he lay
Beside the Carian group reserved and still.
 The Body, the Machine for Acting Will,
Had been at the commencement proved unfit;
That for Demonstrating, Reflecting it,
Mankind — no fitter: was the Will Itself
In fault?
 His forehead pressed the moonlit shelf
Beside the youngest marble maid awhile;
Then, raising it, he thought, with a long smile,
"I shall be king again!" as he withdrew
The envied scarf; into the font he threw
His crown.
 Next day, no poet! "Wherefore?" asked
Taurello, when the dance of Jongleurs, masked
As devils, ended; " don't a song come next?"
The master of the pageant looked perplexed
Till Naddo's whisper came to his relief.
" His Highness knew what poets were: in brief,
Had not the tetchy race prescriptive right
To peevishness, caprice? or, call it spite,
One must receive their nature in its length
And breadth, expect the weakness with the strength!"
— So phrasing, till, his stock of phrases spent,
The easy-natured soldier smiled assent,
Settled his portly person, smoothed his chin,
And nodded that the bull-bait might begin.

BOOK THE THIRD.

AND the font took them: let our laurels lie!
Braid moonfern now with mystic trifoly
Because once more Goito gets, once more,
Sordello to itself! A dream is o'er,
And the suspended life begins anew;
Quiet those throbbing temples, then, subdue
That cheek's distortion! Nature's strict embrace,
Putting aside the past, shall soon efface
Its print as well — factitious humors grown

Over the true — loves, hatreds not his own —
And turn him pure as some forgotten vest
Woven of painted byssus, silkiest
Tufting the Tyrrhene whelk's pearl-sheeted lip,
Left welter where a trireme let it slip
I' the sea, and vexed a satrap; so the stain
O' the world forsakes Sordello, with its pain,
Its pleasure: how the tinct loosening escapes,
Cloud after cloud! Mantua's familiar shapes
Die, fair and foul die, fading as they flit,
Men, women, and the pathos and the wit,
Wise speech and foolish, deeds to smile or sigh
For, good, bad, seemly or ignoble, die.
The last face glances through the eglantines,
The last voice murmurs 'twixt the blossomed vines
Of Men, of that machine supplied by thought
To compass self-perception with, he sought
By forcing half himself — an insane pulse
Of a god's blood, on clay it could convulse,
Never transmute — on human sights and sounds,
To watch the other half with; irksome bounds
It ebbs from to its source, a fountain sealed
Forever. Better sure be unrevealed
Than part revealed: Sordello well or ill
Is finished: then what further use of Will,
Point in the prime idea not realized,
An oversight? inordinately prized,
No less, and pampered with enough of each
Delight to prove the whole above its reach.
"To need become all natures, yet retain
The law of my own nature — to remain
Myself, yet yearn . . . as if that chestnut, think,
Should yearn for this first larch-bloom crisp and pink,
Or those pale fragrant tears where zephyrs stanch
March wounds along the fretted pine-tree branch!
Will and the means to show will, great and small,
Material, spiritual, — abjure them all
Save any so distinct, they may be left
To amuse, not tempt become! and, thus bereft,
Just as I first was fashioned would I be!
Nor, moon, is it Apollo now, but me
Thou visitest to comfort and befriend!
Swim thou into my heart, and there an end,
Since I possess thee! — nay, thus shut mine eyes
And know, quite know, by this heart's fall and rise,
When thou dost bury thee in clouds, and when

Out-standest : wherefore practise upon men
To make that plainer to myself ? "
                            Slide here
Over a sweet and solitary year
Wasted ; or simply notice change in him —
How eyes, once with exploring bright, grew dim
And satiate with receiving. Some distress
Was caused, too, by a sort of consciousness
Under the imbecility, — nought kept
That down ; he slept, but was aware he slept,
So, frustrated : as who brainsick made pact
Erst with the overhanging cataract
To deafen him, yet still distinguished plain
His own blood's measured clicking at his brain.
  To finish. One declining Autumn day —
Few birds about the heaven chill and gray,
No wind that cared trouble the tacit woods —
He sauntered home complacently, their moods
According, his and nature's. Every spark
Of Mantua life was trodden out; so dark
The embers, that the Troubadour, who sung
Hundreds of songs, forgot, its trick his tongue,
Its craft his brain, how either brought to pass
Singing at all ; that faculty might class
With any of Apollo's now. The year
Began to find its early promise sere
As well. Thus beauty vanishes ; thus stone
Outlingers flesh : nature's and his youth gone,
They left the world to you, and wished you joy,
When, stopping his benevolent employ,
A presage shuddered through the welkin ; harsh
The earth's remonstrance followed. 'T was the marsh
Gone of a sudden. Mincio, in its place,
Laughed, a broad water, in next morning's face,
And, where the mists broke up immense and white
I' the steady wind, burned like a spilth of light
Out of the crashing of a myriad stars.
And here was nature, bound by the same bars
Of fate with him !
                  " No ! youth once gone is gone :
Deeds let escape are never to be done.
Leaf-fall and grass-spring for the year ; for us —
Oh forfeit I unalterably thus
My chance ? nor two lives wait me, this to spend
Learning save that ? Nature has time, may mend
Mistake, she knows occasion will recur ;

Landslip or seabreach, how affects it her
With her magnificent resources? — I
Must perish once and perish utterly.
Not any strollings now at even-close
Down the field-path, Sordello! by thorn-rows
Alive with lamp-flies, swimming spots of fire
And dew, outlining the black cypress' spire
She waits you at, Elys, who heard you first
Woo her, the snow-month through, but ere she durst
Answer 't was April. Linden-flower-time-long
Her eyes were on the ground; 't is July, strong
Now; and because white dust-clouds overwhelm
The woodside, here or by the village elm
That holds the moon, she meets you, somewhat pale,
But letting you lift up her coarse flax veil
And whisper (the damp little hand in yours)
Of love, heart's love, your heart's love that endures
Till death. Tush! No mad mixing with the rout
Of haggard ribalds wandering about
The hot torchlit wine-scented island-house
Where Friedrich holds his wickedest carouse,
Parading, — to the gay Palermitans,
Soft Messinese, dusk Saracenic clans
Nuocera holds, — those tall grave dazzling Norse,
High-cheeked, lank-haired, toothed whiter than the morse,
Queens of the caves of jet stalactites,
He sent his barks to fetch through icy seas,
The blind night seas without a saving star,
And here in snowy birdskin robes they are,
Sordello! — here, mollitious alcoves gilt
Superb as Byzant domes that devils built!
— Ah, Byzant, there again! no chance to go
Ever like august cheery Dandolo,
Worshipping hearts about him for a wall,
Conducted, blind eyes, hundred years and all,
Through vanquished Byzant where friends note for him
What pillar, marble massive, sardius slim,
'T were fittest he transport to Venice' Square —
Flattered and promised life to touch them there
Soon, by those fervid sons of senators!
No more lives, deaths, loves, hatreds, peaces, wars!
Ah, fragments of a whole ordained to be,
Points in the life I waited! what are ye
But roundels of a ladder which appeared
Awhile the very platform it was reared
To lift me on? — that happiness I find

Proofs of my faith in, even in the blind
Instinct which bade forego you all unless
Ye led me past yourselves. Ay, happiness
Awaited me ; the way life should be used
Was to acquire, and deeds like you conduced
To teach it by a self-revealment, deemed
Life's very use, so long ! Whatever seemed
Progress to that, was pleasure ; aught that stayed
My reaching it — no pleasure. I have laid
The ladder down ; I climb not; still, aloft
The platform stretches ! Blisses strong and soft,
I dared not entertain, elude me ; yet
Never of what they promised could I get
A glimpse till now ! The common sort, the crowd,
Exist, perceive ; with Being are endowed,
However slight, distinct from what they See,
However bounded ; Happiness must be,
To feed the first by gleanings from the last,
Attain its qualities, and slow or fast
Become what they behold ; such peace-in-strife
By transmutation, is the Use of Life,
The Alien turning Native to the soul
Or body — which instructs me ; I am whole
There and demand a Palma ; had the world
Been from my soul to a like distance hurled,
'T were Happiness to make it one with me :
Whereas I must, ere I begin to Be,
Include a world, in flesh, I comprehend
In spirit now ; and this done, what's to blend
With ? Nought is Alien in the world — my Will
Owns all already ; yet can turn it still
Less Native, since my Means to correspond
With Will are so unworthy, 't was my bond
To tread the very joys that tantalize
Most now, into a grave, never to rise.
I die then ! Will the rest agree to die ?
Next Age or no ? Shall its Sordello try
Clue after clue, and catch at last the clue
I miss ? — that's underneath my finger too,
Twice, thrice a day, perhaps, — some yearning traced
Deeper, some petty consequence embraced
Closer ! Why fled I Mantua, then ? — complained
So much my Will was fettered, yet remained
Content within a tether half the range
I could assign it ? — able to exchange
My ignorance (I felt) for knowledge, and

Idle because I could thus understand —
Could e'en have penetrated to its core
Our mortal mystery, yet — fool — forbore,
Preferred elaborating in the dark
My casual stuff, by any wretched spark
Born of my predecessors, though one stroke
Of mine had brought the flame forth! Mantua's yoke,
My minstrel's-trade, was to behold mankind, —
My own concern was just to bring my mind
Behold, just extricate, for my acquist,
Each object suffered stifle in the mist
Which hazard, custom, blindness interpose
Betwixt things and myself."
                            Whereat he rose.
The level wind carried above the firs
Clouds, the irrevocable travellers,
Onward.
       " Pushed thus into a drowsy copse,
Arms twine about my neck, each eyelid drops
Under a humid finger; while there fleets,
Outside the screen, a pageant time repeats
Never again! To be deposed, immured
Clandestinely — still petted, still assured
To govern were fatiguing work — the Sight
Fleeting meanwhile! 'T is noontide: wreak ere night
Somehow my will upon it, rather! Slake
This thirst somehow, the poorest impress take
That serves! A blasted bud displays you, torn,
Faint rudiments of the full flower unborn;
But who divines what glory coats o'erclasp
Of the bulb dormant in the mummy's grasp
Taurello sent?" . . .
                 " Taurello? Palma sent
Your Trouvere," (Naddo interposing leant
Over the lost bard's shoulder) — " and, believe,
You cannot more reluctantly receive
Than I pronounce her message: we depart
Together. What avail a poet's heart
Verona's pomps and gauds? five blades of grass
Suffice him. News? Why, where your marish was,
On its mud-banks smoke rises after smoke
I' the valley, like a spout of hell new-broke.
Oh, the world's tidings! small your thanks, I guess,
For them. The father of our Patroness
Has played Taurello an astounding trick,
Parts between Ecelin and Alberic

His wealth and goes into a convent: both
Wed Guelfs: the Count and Palma plighted troth
A week since at Verona: and they want
You doubtless to contrive the marriage-chant
Ere Richard storms Ferrara." Then was told
The tale from the beginning — how, made bold
By Salinguerra's absence, Guelfs had burned
And pillaged till he unawares returned
To take revenge: how Azzo and his friend
Were doing their endeavor, how the end
O' the siege was nigh, and how the Count, released
From further care, would with his marriage-feast
Inaugurate a new and better rule,
Absorbing thus Romano.
                          " Shall I school
My master," added Naddo, " and suggest
How you may clothe in a poetic vest
These doings, at Verona? Your response
To Palma! Wherefore jest? ' Depart at once?'
A good resolve! In truth, I hardly hoped
So prompt an acquiescence. Have you groped
Out wisdom in the wilds here? — Thoughts may be
Over-poetical for poetry.
Pearl-white, you poets liken Palma's neck;
And yet what spoils an orient like some speck
Of genuine white, turning its own white gray?
You take me? Curse the cicala!"
                                One more day,
One eve — appears Verona! Many a group,
(You mind) instructed of the osprey's swoop
On lnyx and ounce, was gathering — Christendom
Sure to receive, whate'er the end was, from
The evening's purpose cheer or detriment,
Since Friedrich only waited some event
Like this, of Ghibellins establishing
Themselves within Ferrara, ere, as King
Of Lombardy, he'd glad descend there, wage
Old warfare with the Pontiff, disengage
His barons from the burghers, and restore
The rule of Charlemagne, broken of yore
By Hildebrand.
                I' the palace, each by each,
Sordello sat and Palma: little speech
At first in that dim closet, face with face
(Despite the tumult in the market-place)
Exchanging quick low laughters: now would rush

Word upon word to meet a sudden flush,
A look left off, a shifting lips' surmise —
But for the most part their two histories
Ran best through the locked fingers and linked arms.
And so the night flew on with its alarms
Till in burst one of Palma's retinue;
"Now, Lady!" gasped he. Then arose the two
And leaned into Verona's air, dead-still.
A balcony lay black beneath until
Out, 'mid a gush of torchfire, gray-haired men
Came on it and harangued the people: then
Sea-like that people surging to and fro
Shouted, "Hale forth the carroch — trumpets, ho,
A flourish! Run it in the ancient grooves!
Back from the bell! Hammer — that whom behooves
May hear the League is up! Peal — learn who list,
Verona means not first of towns break tryst
To-morrow with the League!"
       Enough. Now turn —
Over the eastern cypresses: discern!
Is any beacon set a-glimmer?
       Rang
The air with shouts that overpowered the clang
Of the incessant carroch, even: "Haste —
The candle's at the gateway! ere it waste,
Each soldier stand beside it, armed to march
With Tiso Sampier through the eastern arch!"
Ferrara's succored, Palma!
       Once again
They sat together; some strange thing in train
To say, so difficult was Palma's place
In taking, with a coy fastidious grace
Like the bird's flutter ere it fix and feed.
But when she felt she held her friend indeed
Safe, she threw back her curls, began implant
Her lessons; telling of another want
Goito's quiet nourished than his own;
Palma — to serve him — to be served, alone
Importing; Agnes' milk so neutralized
The blood of Ecelin. Nor be surprised
If, while Sordello fain had captive led
Nature, in dream was Palma subjected
To some out-soul, which dawned not though she pined
Delaying till its advent, heart and mind,
Their life. "How dared I let expand the force
Within me, till some out-soul, whose resource

It grew for, should direct it? Every law
Of life, its every fitness, every flaw,
Must One determine whose corporeal shape
Would be no other than the prime escape
And revelation to me of a Will
Orb-like o'ershrouded and inscrutable
Above, save at the point which, I should know,
Shone that myself, my powers, might overflow
So far, so much; as now it signified
Which earthly shape it henceforth chose my guide,
Whose mortal lip selected to declare
Its oracles, what fleshly garb would wear
— The first of intimations, whom to love;
The next, how love him. Seemed that orb, above
The castle-covert and the mountain-close,
Slow in appearing, — if beneath it rose
Cravings, aversions, — did our green precinct
Take pride in me, at unawares distinct
With this or that endowment, — how, repressed
At once, such jetting power shrank to the rest!
Was I to have a chance touch spoil me, leave
My spirit thence unfitted to receive
The consummating spell? — that spell so near
Moreover! 'Waits he not the waking year?
His almond-blossoms must be honey-ripe
By this; to welcome him, fresh runnels stripe
The thawed ravines; because of him, the wind
Walks like a herald. I shall surely find
Him now!'
    "And chief, that earnest April morn
Of Richard's Love-court, was it time, so worn
And white my cheek, so idly my blood beat,
Sitting that morn beside the Lady's feet
And saying as she prompted; till outburst
One face from all the faces — not then first
I knew it; where in maple chamber glooms,
Crowned with what sanguine-heart pomegranate blooms
Advanced it ever? Men's acknowledgment
Sanctioned my own: 't was taken, Palma's bent, —
Sordello, — recognized, accepted.
        "Dumb
She still sat scheming. Ecelin would come
Gaunt, scared, 'Cesano baffles me,' he 'd say:
'Better I fought it out, my father's way!
Strangle Ferrara in its drowning flats,
And you and your Taurello yonder — what 's

Romano's business there?' An hour's concern
To cure the froward Chief! — induced return
As heartened from those overmeaning eyes,
Wound up to persevere, — his enterprise
Marked out anew, its exigent of wit
Apportioned, — she at liberty to sit
And scheme against the next emergence, I —
To covet her Taurello-sprite, made fly
Or fold the wing — to con your horoscope
For leave command those steely shafts shoot ope,
Or straight assuage their blinding eagerness
In blank smooth snow. What semblance of success
To any of my plans for making you
Mine and Romano's? Break the first wall through,
Tread o'er the ruins of the Chief, supplant
His sons beside, still, vainest were the vaunt:
There, Salinguerra would obstruct me sheer,
And the insuperable Tuscan, here,
Stay me! But one wild eve that Lady died
In her lone chamber: only I beside:
Taurello far at Naples, and my sire
At Padua, Ecelin away in ire
With Alberic. She held me thus — a clutch
To make our spirits as our bodies touch —
And so began flinging the past up, heaps
Of uncouth treasure from their sunless sleeps
Within her soul; deeds rose along with dreams,
Fragments of many miserable schemes,
Secrets, more secrets, then — no, not the last —
'Mongst others, like a casual trick o' the past,
How . . . ay, she told me, gathering up her face,
All left of it, into one arch-grimace
To die with . . .
"Friend, 't is gone! but not the fear
Of that fell laughing, heard as now I hear.
Nor faltered voice, nor seemed her heart grow weak
When i' the midst abrupt she ceased to speak
— Dead, as to serve a purpose, mark! — for in
Rushed o' the very instant Ecelin
(How summoned, who divines?) — looking as if
He understood why Adelaide lay stiff
Already in my arms; for, 'Girl, how must
I manage Este in the matter thrust
Upon me, how unravel your bad coil? —
Since' (he declared) "'t is on your brow — a soil
Like hers, there!' then in the same breath, 'he lacked

No counsel after all, had signed no pact
With devils, nor was treason here or there,
Goito or Vicenza, his affair:
He buried it in Adelaide's deep grave,
Would begin life afresh, now, — would not slave
For any Friedrich's nor Taurello's sake!
What booted him to meddle or to make
In Lombardy?' And afterward I knew
The meaning of his promise to undo
All she had done — why marriages were made,
New friendships entered on, old followers paid
With curses for their pains, — new friends' amaze
At height, when, passing out by Gate St. Blaise,
He stopped short in Vicenza, bent his head
Over a friar's neck, — 'had vowed,' he said,
' Long since, nigh thirty years, because his wife
And child were saved there, to bestow his life
On God, his gettings on the Church.'
         " Exiled
Within Goito, still one dream beguiled
My days and nights; 't was found, the orb I sought
To serve, those glimpses came of Fomalhaut,
No other: but how serve it? — authorize
You and Romano mingle destinies?
And straight Romano's angel stood beside
Me who had else been Boniface's bride,
For Salinguerra 't was, with neck low bent,
And voice lightened to music, (as he meant
To learn not teach me,) who withdrew the pall
From the dead past and straight revived it all,
Making me see how first Romano waxed,
Wherefore he waned now, why, if I relaxed
My grasp (even I!) would drop a thing effete,
Frayed by itself, unequal to complete
Its course, and counting every step astray
A gain so much. Romano, every way
Stable, a Lombard House now — why start back
Into the very outset of its track?
This patching principle which late allied
Our House with other Houses — what beside
Concerned the apparition, the first Knight
Who followed Conrad hither in such plight
His utmost wealth was summed in his one steed?
For Ecelo, that prowler, was decreed
A task, in the beginning hazardous
To him as ever task can be to us;

As Life, the somewhat, hangs 'twixt nought and nought:
'T is Venice, and 't is Life — as good you sought
To spare me the Piazza's slippery stone
Or keep me to the unchoked canals alone,
As hinder Life the evil with the good
Which make up Living, rightly understood.
Only, do finish something ! Peasants, queens,
Take them, made happy by whatever means,
Parade them for the common credit, vouch
That a luckless residue, we send to crouch
In corners out of sight, was just as framed
For happiness, its portion might have claimed
As well, and so, obtaining joy, had stalked
Fastuous as any ! — such my project, balked
Already ; I hardly venture to adjust
The first rags, when you find me. To mistrust
Me ! — nor unreasonably. You, no doubt,
Have the true knack of tiring suitors out
With those thin lips on tremble, lashless eyes
Inveterately tear-shot — there, be wise,
Mistress of mine, there, there, as if I meant
You insult ! — shall your friend (not slave) be shent
For speaking home ? Beside, care-bit erased
Broken-up beauties ever took my taste
Supremely ; and I love you more, far more
Than her I looked should foot Life's temple-floor.
Years ago, leagues at distance, when and where
A whisper came, " Let others seek ! — thy care
Is found, thy life's provision ; if thy race
Should be thy mistress, and into one face
The many faces crowd ? " Ah, had I, judge,
Or no, your secret ? Rough apparel — grudge
All ornaments save tag or tassel worn
To hint we are not thoroughly forlorn —
Slouch bonnet, unloop mantle, careless go
Alone (that 's saddest, but it must be so)
Through Venice, sing now and now glance aside,
Aught desultory or undignified, —
Then, ravishingest lady, will you pass
Or not each formidable group, the mass
Before the Basilic (that feast gone by,
God's great day of the Corpus Domini)
And, wistfully foregoing proper men,
Come timid up to me for alms ? And then
The luxury to hesitate, feign do
Some unexampled grace ! — when, whom but you

Dare I bestow your own upon? And hear
Further before you say, it is to sneer
I call you ravishing; for I regret
Little that she, whose early foot was set
Forth as she 'd plant it on a pedestal,
Now, i' the silent city, seems to fall
Toward me — no wreath, only a lip's unrest
To quiet, surcharged eyelids to be pressed
Dry of their tears upon my bosom. Strange
Such sad chance should produce in thee such change,
My love! Warped souls and bodies! yet God spoke
Of right-hand, foot and eye — selects our yoke,
Sordello, as your poetship may find!
So, sleep upon my shoulder, child, nor mind
Their foolish talk; we 'll manage reinstate
Your old worth; ask moreover, when they prate
Of evil men past hope, " Don't each contrive,
Despite the evil you abuse, to live? —
Keeping, each losel, through a maze of lies,
His own conceit of truth? to which he hies
By obscure windings, tortuous, if you will,
But to himself not inaccessible;
He sees truth, and his lies are for the crowd
Who cannot see; some fancied right allowed
His vilest wrong, empowered the losel clutch
One pleasure from a multitude of such
Denied him." Then assert, " All men appear
To think all better than themselves, by here
Trusting a crowd they wrong; but really," say,
" All men think all men stupider than they,
Since, save themselves, no other comprehends
The complicated scheme to make amends
— Evil, the scheme by which, through Ignorance,
Good labors to exist." A slight advance, —
Merely to find the sickness you die through, —
And nought beside! but if one can't eschew
One's portion in the common lot, at least
One can avoid an ignorance increased
Tenfold by dealing out hint after hint
How nought were like dispensing without stint
The water of life — so easy to dispense
Beside, when one has probed the centre whence
Commotion 's born — could tell you of it all!
" — Meantime, just meditate my madrigal
O' the mugwort that conceals a dewdrop safe!"
What, dullard? we and you in smothery chafe,

Babes, baldheads, stumbled thus far into Zin
The Horrid, getting neither out nor in,
A hungry sun above us, sands that bung
Our throats, — each dromedary lolls a tongue,
Each camel churns a sick and frothy chap,
And you, 'twixt tales of Potiphar's mishap,
And sonnets on the earliest ass that spoke,
— Remark, you wonder any one needs choke
With founts about! Potsherd him, Gibeonites!
While awkwardly enough your Moses smites
The rock, though he forego his Promised Land
Thereby, have Satan claim his carcass, and
Figure as Metaphysic Poet . . . ah,
Mark ye the dim first oozings? Meribah!
Then, quaffing at the fount my courage gained,
Recall — not that I prompt ye — who explained . . .
"Presumptuous!" interrupts one. You, not I
'T is, brother, marvel at and magnify
Such office : " office," quotha? can we get
To the beginning of the office yet?
What do we here? simply experiment
Each on the other's power and its intent
When elsewhere tasked, — if this of mine were trucked
For yours to either's good, — we watch construct,
In short, an engine : with a finished one,
What it can do, is all, — nought, how 't is done.
But this of ours yet in probation, dusk
A kernel of strange wheelwork through its husk
Grows into shape by quarters and by halves ;
Remark this tooth's spring, wonder what that valve's
Fall bodes, presume each faculty's device,
Make out each other more or less precise —
The scope of the whole engine 's to be proved ;
We die : which means to say, the whole 's removed,
Dismounted wheel by wheel, this complex gin, —
To be set up anew elsewhere, begin
A task indeed, but with a clearer clime
Than the murk lodgment of our building-time.
And then, I grant you, it behoves forget
How 't is done — all that must amuse us yet
So long : and, while you turn upon your heel,
Pray that I be not busy slitting steel
Or shredding brass, camped on some virgin shore
Under a cluster of fresh stars, before
I name a tithe o' the wheels I trust to do!
So occupied, then, are we : hitherto,

At present, and a weary while to come,
The office of ourselves, — nor blind nor dumb,
And seeing somewhat of man's state, — has been,
For the worst of us, to say they so have seen;
For the better, what it was they saw; the best
Impart the gift of seeing to the rest:
"So that I glance," says such an one, "around,
And there's no face but I can read profound
Disclosures in; this stands for hope, that — fear,
And for a speech, a deed in proof, look here!
'Stoop, else the strings of blossom, where the nuts
O'erarch, will blind thee! Said I not? She shuts
Both eyes this time, so close the hazels meet!
Thus, prisoned in the Piombi, I repeat
Events one rove occasioned, o'er and o'er,
Putting 'twixt me and madness evermore
Thy sweet shape, Zanze! Therefore stoop!'
           'That's truth!'
(Adjudge you) 'the incarcerated youth
Would say that!'
    Youth? Plara the bard? Set down
That Plara spent his youth in a grim town
Whose cramped ill-featured streets huddled about
The minster for protection, never out
Of its black belfry's shade and its bells' roar.
The brighter shone the suburb, — all the more
Ugly and absolute that shade's reproof
Of any chance escape of joy, — some roof,
Taller than they, allowed the rest detect, —
Before the sole permitted laugh (suspect
Who could, 't was meant for laughter, that ploughed cheek's
Repulsive gleam!) when the sun stopped both peaks
Of the cleft belfry like a fiery wedge,
Then sank, a huge flame on its socket edge,
With leavings on the gray glass oriel-pane
Ghastly some minutes more. No fear of rain —
The minster minded that! in heaps the dust
Lay everywhere. This town, the minster's trust,
Held Plara; who, its denizen, bade hail
In twice twelve sonnets, Tempe's dewy vale."
"'Exact the town, the minster and the street!'"
"As all mirth triumphs, sadness means defeat:
Lust triumphs and is gay, Love's triumphed o'er
And sad: but Lucio's sad. I said before,
Love's sad, not Lucio; one who loves may be
As gay his love has leave to hope, as he

ONE OUGHT NOT BLAME BUT PRAISE THIS

Downcast that lusts' desire escapes the springe:
'T is of the mood itself I speak, what tinge
Determines it, else colorless, — or mirth,
Or melancholy, as from heaven or earth."
"'Ay, that's the variation's gist!' Indeed?
Thus far advanced in safety then, proceed!
And having seen too what I saw, be bold
And next encounter what I do behold
(That's sure) but bid you take on trust!"

Attack

The use and purpose of such sights? Alack,
Not so unwisely does the crowd dispense
On Salinguerras praise in preference
To the Sordellos: men of action, these!
Who, seeing just as little as you please,
Yet turn that little to account, — engage
With, do not gaze at, — carry on, a stage,
The work o' the world, not merely make report
The work existed ere their day! In short,
When at some future no-time a brave band
Sees, using what it sees, then shake my hand
In heaven, my brother! Meanwhile where's the hurt
Of keeping the Makers-see on the alert,
At whose defection mortals stare aghast
As though heaven's bounteous windows were slammed fast
Incontinent? Whereas all you, beneath,
Should scowl at, bruise their lips and break their teeth
Who ply the pullies, for neglecting you:
And therefore have I moulded, made anew
A Man, and give him to be turned and tried,
Be angry with or pleased at. On your side,
Have ye times, places, actors of your own?
Try them upon Sordello when full-grown,
And then — ah then! If Hercules first parched
His foot in Egypt only to be marched
A sacrifice for Jove with pomp to suit,
What chance have I? The demigod was mute
Till, at the altar, where time out of mind
Such guests became oblations, chaplets twined
His forehead long enough, and he began
Slaying the slayers, nor escaped a man.
Take not affront, my gentle audience! whom
No Hercules shall make his hecatomb,
Believe, nor from his brows your chaplet rend —
That's your kind suffrage, yours, my patron-friend,
Whose great verse blares unintermittent on

Like your own trumpeter at Marathon, —
You who, Platæa and Salamis being scant,
Put up with Ætna for a stimulant —
And did well, I acknowledged, as he loomed
Over the midland sea last month, presumed
Long, lay demolished in the blazing West
At eve, while towards him tilting cloudlets pressed
Like Persian ships at Salamis. Friend, wear
A crest proud as desert while I declare
Had I a flawless ruby fit to wring
Tears of its color from that painted king
Who lost it, I would, for that smile which went
To my heart, fling it in the sea, content,
Wearing your verse in place, an amulet
Sovereign against all passion, wear and fret!
My English Eyebright, if you are not glad
That, as I stopped my task awhile, the sad
Dishevelled form, wherein I put mankind
To come at times and keep my pact in mind,
Renewed me, — hear no crickets in the hedge,
Nor let a glowworm spot the river's edge
At home, and may the summer showers gush
Without a warning from the missel thrush!
So, to our business, now — the fate of such
As find our common nature — overmuch
Despised because restricted and unfit
To bear the burden they impose on it —
Cling when they would discard it; craving strength
To leap from the allotted world, at length
They do leap, — flounder on without a term,
Each a god's germ, doomed to remain a germ
In unexpanded infancy, unless . . .
But that's the story — dull enough, confess!
There might be fitter subjects to allure;
Still, neither misconceive my portraiture
Nor undervalue its adornments quaint:
What seems a fiend perchance may prove a saint.
Ponder a story ancient pens transmit,
Then say if you condemn me or acquit.
  John the Beloved, banished Antioch
For Patmos, bade collectively his flock
Farewell, but set apart the closing eve
To comfort those his exile most would grieve,
He knew: a touching spectacle, that house
In motion to receive him! Xanthus' spouse

You missed, made panther's meat a month since; but
Xanthus himself (his nephew 't was, they shut
'Twixt boards and sawed asunder), Polycarp,
Soft Charicle, next year no wheel could warp
To swear by Cæsar's fortune, with the rest
Were ranged; through whom the gray disciple pressed,
Busily blessing right and left, just stopped
To pat one infant's curls, the hangman cropped
Soon after, reached the portal. On its hinge
The door turns and he enters : what quick twinge
Ruins the smiling mouth, those wide eyes fix
Whereon, why like some spectral candlestick's
Branch the disciple's arms? Dead swooned he, woke
Anon, heaved sigh, made shift to gasp, heart-broke,
" Get thee behind me, Satan! Have I toiled
To no more purpose? Is the gospel foiled
Here too, and o'er my son's, my Xanthus' hearth,
Portrayed with sooty garb and features swarth —
Ah Xanthus, am I to thy roof beguiled
To see the — the — the Devil domiciled?"
Whereto sobbed Xanthus, " Father, 't is yourself
Installed, a limning which our utmost pelf
Went to procure against to-morrow's loss ;
And that 's no twy-prong, but a pastoral cross,
You 're painted with!"
                      His puckered brows unfold —
And you shall hear Sordello's story told.

BOOK THE FOURTH.

MEANTIME Ferrara lay in rueful case;
The lady-city, for whose sole embrace
Her pair of suitors struggled, felt their arms
A brawny mischief to the fragile charms
They tugged for — one discovering that to twist
Her tresses twice or thrice about his wrist
Secured a point of vantage — one, how best
He 'd parry that by planting in her breast
His elbow spike — each party too intent
For noticing, howe'er the battle went,
The conqueror would but have a corpse to kiss.
" May Boniface be duly damned for this!"
— Howled some old Ghibellin, as up he turned,

From the wet heap of rubbish where they burned
His house, a little skull with dazzling teeth :
" A boon, sweet Christ — let Salinguerra seethe
In hell forever, Christ, and let myself
Be there to laugh at him ! " — moaned some young Guelf
Stumbling upon a shrivelled hand nailed fast
To the charred lintel of the doorway, last
His father stood within to bid him speed.
The thoroughfares were overrun with weed
— Docks, quitchgrass, loathy mallows no man plants.
  The stranger, none of its inhabitants
Crept out of doors to taste fresh air again,
And ask the purpose of a splendid train
Admitted on a morning ; every town
Of the East League was come by envoy down
To treat for Richard's ransom : here you saw
The Vicentine, here snowy oxen draw
The Paduan carroch, its vermilion cross
On its white field. A-tiptoe o'er the fosse
Looked Legate Montelungo wistfully
After the flock of steeples he might spy
In Este's time, gone (doubts he) long ago
To mend the ramparts : sure the laggards know
The Pope 's as good as here ! They paced the streets
More soberly. At last, " Taurello greets
The League," announced a pursuivant, — " will match
Its courtesy, and labors to dispatch
At earliest Tito, Friedrich's Pretor, sent
On pressing matters from his post at Trent,
With Mainard Count of Tyrol, — simply waits
Their going to receive the delegates."
  " Tito ! " Our delegates exchanged a glance,
And, keeping the main way, admired askance
The lazy engines of outlandish birth,
Couched like a king each on its bank of earth —
Arbalist, manganel and catapult ;
While stationed by, as waiting a result,
Lean silent gangs of mercenaries ceased
Working to watch the strangers. " This, at least,
Were better spared ; he scarce presumes gainsay
The League's decision ! Get our friend away
And profit for the future : how else teach
Fools 't is not safe to stray within claw's reach
Ere Salinguerra's final gasp be blown ?
Those mere convulsive scratches find the bone.
Who bade him bloody the spent osprey's nare ? "

The carrochs halted in the public square.
Pennons of every blazon once a-flaunt,
Men prattled, freelier that the crested gaunt
White ostrich with a horse-shoe in her beak
Was missing, and whoever chose might speak
" Ecelin " boldly out : so, — " Ecelin
Needed his wife to swallow half the sin
And sickens by himself : the devil's whelp,
He styles his son, dwindles away, no help
From conserves, your fine triple-curded froth
Of virgin's blood, your Venice viper-broth —
Eh? Jubilate ! " — " Peace ! no little word
You utter here that 's not distinctly heard
Up at Oliero : he was absent sick
When we besieged Bassano — who, i' the thick
O' the work, perceived the progress Azzo made,
Like Ecelin, through his witch Adelaide ?
She managed it so well that, night by night,
At their bed-foot stood up a soldier-sprite,
First fresh, pale by-and-by without a wound,
And, when it came with eyes filmed as in swound,
They knew the place was taken." — " Ominous
That Ghibellins should get what cautelous
Old Redbeard sought from Azzo's sire to wrench
Vainly ; Saint George contrived his town a trench
O' the marshes, an impermeable bar."
* — Young Ecelin is meant the tutelar
Of Padua, rather ; veins embrace upon
His hand like Brenta and Bacchiglion."
What now ? — " The founts ! God's bread, touch not a plank !
A crawling hell of carrion — every tank
Choke full ! — found out just now to Cino's cost —
The same who gave Taurello up for lost,
And, making no account of fortune's freaks,
Refused to budge from Padua then, but sneaks
Back now with Concorezzi — 'faith ! they drag
Their carroch to San Vitale, plant the flag
On his own palace, so adroitly razed
He knew it not ; a sort of Guelf folk gazed
And laughed apart ; Cino disliked their air —
Must pluck up spirit, show he does not care —
Seats himself on the tank's edge — will begin
To hum, *za, za, Cavaler Ecelin* —
A silence ; he gets warmer, clinks to chime,
Now both feet plough the ground, deeper each time,
At last, *za, za,* and up with a fierce kick

Comes his own mother's face caught by the thick
Gray hair about his spur!"
                    Which means, they lift
The covering, Salinguerra made a shift
To stretch upon the truth; as well avoid
Further disclosures; leave them thus employed.
Our dropping Autumn morning clears apace,
And poor Ferrara puts a softened face
On her misfortunes. Let us scale this tall
Huge foursquare line of red brick garden-wall
Bastioned within by trees of every sort
On three sides, slender, spreading, long and short;
Each grew as it contrived, the poplar ramped,
The fig-tree reared itself, — but stark and cramped,
Made fools of, like tamed lions: whence, on the edge,
Running 'twixt trunk and trunk to smooth one ledge
Of shade, were shrubs inserted, warp and woof,
Which smothered up that variance. Scale the roof
Of solid tops, and o'er the slope you slide
Down to a grassy space level and wide,
Here and there dotted with a tree, but trees
Of rarer leaf, each foreigner at ease,
Set by itself: and in the centre spreads,
Borne upon three uneasy leopards' heads,
A laver, broad and shallow, one bright spirt
Of water bubbles in. The walls begirt
With trees leave off on either hand; pursue
Your path along a wondrous avenue
Those walls abut on, heaped of gleamy stone,
With aloes leering everywhere, gray-grown
From many a Moorish summer: how they wind
Out of the fissures! likelier to bind
The building than those rusted cramps which drop
Already in the eating sunshine. Stop,
You fleeting shapes above there! Ah, the pride
Or else despair of the whole country-side!
A range of statues, swarming o'er with wasps,
God, goddess, woman, man, the Greek rough-rasps
In crumbling Naples marble — meant to look
Like those Messina marbles Constance took
Delight in, or Taurello's self conveyed
To Mantua for his mistress, Adelaide,
A certain font with caryatides
Since cloistered at Goito; only, these
Are up and doing, not abashed, a troop
Able to right themselves — who see you, stoop

Their arms o' the instant after you ! Unplucked
By this or that, you pass ; for they conduct
To terrace raised on terrace, and, between,
Creatures of brighter mould and braver mien
Than any yet, the choicest of the Isle
No doubt. Here, left a sullen breathing-while,
Up-gathered on himself the Fighter stood
For his last fight, and, wiping treacherous blood
Out of the eyelids just held ope beneath
Those shading fingers in their iron sheath,
Steadied his strengths amid the buzz and stir
Of the dusk hideous amphitheatre
At the announcement of his over-match
To wind the day's diversion up, dispatch
The pertinacious Gaul : while, limbs one heap,
The Slave, no breath in her round mouth, watched leap
Dart after dart forth, as her hero's car
Clove dizzily the solid of the war
— Let coil about his knees for pride in him.
We reach the farthest terrace, and the grim
San Pietro Palace stops us.
      Such the state
Of Salinguerra's plan to emulate
Sicilian marvels, that his girlish wife
Retrude still might lead her ancient life
In her new home : whereat enlarged so much
Neighbors upon the novel princely touch
He took, — who here imprisons Boniface.
Here must the Envoys come to sue for grace ;
And here, emerging from the labyrinth
Below, Sordello paused beside the plinth
Of the door-pillar.
     He had really left
Verona for the cornfields (a poor theft
From the morass) where Este's camp was made.
The Envoys' march, the Legate's cavalcade —
All had been seen by him, but scarce as when, —
Eager for cause to stand aloof from men
At every point save the fantastic tie
Acknowledged in his boyish sophistry, —
He made account of such. A crowd, — he meant
To task the whole of it ; each part's intent
Concerned him therefore : and, the more he pried,
The less became Sordello satisfied
With his own figure at the moment. Sought
He respite from his task ? Descried he aught

Novel in the anticipated sight
Of all these livers upon all delight?
This phalanx, as of myriad points combined,
Whereby he still had imaged the mankind
His youth was passed in dreams of rivalling,
His age — in plans to prove at least such thing
Had been so dreamed, — which now he must impress
With his own will, effect a happiness
By theirs, — supply a body to his soul
Thence, and become eventually whole
With them as he had hoped to be without —
Made these the mankind he once raved about?
Because a few of them were notable,
Should all be figured worthy note? As well
Expect to find Taurello's triple line
Of trees a single and prodigious pine.
Real pines rose here and there; but, close among,
Thrust into and mixed up with pines, a throng
Of shrubs, he saw, — a nameless common sort
O'erpast in dreams, left out of the report
And hurried into corners, or at best
Admitted to be fancied like the rest.
Reckon that morning's proper chiefs — how few!
And yet the people grew, the people grew,
Grew ever, as if the many there indeed,
More left behind and most who should succeed, —
Simply in virtue of their mouths and eyes,
Petty enjoyments and huge miseries, —
Mingled with, and made veritably great
Those chiefs: he overlooked not Mainard's state
Nor Concorezzi's station, but instead
Of stopping there, each dwindled to be head
Of infinite and absent Tyrolese
Or Paduans; startling all the more, that these
Seemed passive and disposed of, uncared for,
Yet doubtless on the whole (like Eglamor)
Smiling; for if a wealthy man decays
And out of store of robes must wear, all days,
One tattered suit, alike in sun and shade,
'T is commonly some tarnished gay brocade
Fit for a feast-night's flourish and no more:
Nor otherwise poor Misery from her store
Of looks is fain upgather, keep unfurled
For common wear as she goes through the world,
The faint remainder of some worn-out smile
Meant for a feast-night's service merely. While

MEN NOT MACHINES BUT LIVING THINGS

Crowd upon crowd rose on Sordello thus, —
(Crowds no way interfering to discuss,
Much less dispute, life's joys with one employed
In envying them, — or, if they aught enjoyed,
Where lingered something indefinable
In every look and tone, the mirth as well
As woe, that fixed at once his estimate
Of the result, their good or bad estate) —
Old memories returned with new effect:
And the new body, ere he could suspect,
Cohered, mankind and he were really fused,
The new self seemed impatient to be used
By him, but utterly another way
Than that anticipated : strange to say,
They were too much below him, more in thrall
Than he, the adjunct than the principal.
What booted scattered units ? — here a mind
And there, which might repay his own to find,
And stamp, and use ? — a few, howe'er august,
If all the rest were grovelling in the dust?
No : first a mighty equilibrium, sure,
Should he establish, privilege procure
For all, the few had long possessed ! He felt
An error, an exceeding error melt —
While he was occupied with Mantuan chants,
Behoved him think of men, and take their wants,
Such as he now distinguished every side,
As his own want which might be satisfied, —
And, after that, think of rare qualities
Of his own soul demanding exercise.
It followed naturally, through no claim
On their part, which made virtue of the aim
At serving them, on his, — that, past retrieve,
He felt now in their toils, theirs, — nor could leave
Wonder how, in the eagerness to rule,
Impress his will on mankind, he (the fool !)
Had never even entertained the thought
That this his last arrangement might be fraught
With incidental good to them as well,
And that mankind's delight would help to swell
His own. So, if he sighed, as formerly
Because the merry time of life must fleet,
'T was deeplier now, — for could the crowds repeat
Their poor experiences ? His hand that shook
Was twice to be deplored. " The Legate, look !
With eyes, like fresh-blown thrush-eggs on a thread,

Faint-blue and loosely floating in his head,
Large tongue, moist open mouth; and this long while
That owner of the idiotic smile
Serves them!"
    He fortunately saw in time
His fault however, and since the office prime
Includes the secondary — best accept
Both offices; Taurello, its adept,
Could teach him the preparatory one,
And how to do what he had fancied done
Long previously, ere take the greater task.
How render first these people happy? Ask
The people's friends: for there must be one good,
One way to it — the Cause! — he understood
The meaning now of Palma; why the jar
Else, the ado, the trouble wide and far
Of Guelfs and Ghibellins, the Lombard hope
And Rome's despair? — 'twixt Emperor and Pope
The confused shifting sort of Eden tale —
Hardihood still recurring, still to fail —
That foreign interloping fiend, this free
And native overbrooding deity —
Yet a dire fascination o'er the palms
The Kaiser ruined, troubling even the calms
Of paradise — or, on the other hand,
The Pontiff, as the Kaisers understand,
One snake-like cursed of God to love the ground,
Whose heavy length breaks in the noon profound
Some saving tree — which needs the Kaiser, dressed
As the dislodging angel of that pest:
Yet flames that pest bedropped, flat head, full fold,
With coruscating dower of dyes. "Behold
The secret, so to speak, and master-spring
O' the contest! — which of the two Powers shall bring
Men good — perchance the most good — ay, it may
Be that! — the question, which best knows the way."
  And hereupon Count Mainard strutted past
Out of San Pietro; never seemed the last
Of archers, slingers: and our friend began
To recollect strange modes of serving man,
Arbalist, catapult, brake, manganel,
And more. "This way of theirs may, — who can tell? —
Need perfecting," said he: "let all be solved
At once! Taurello 't is, the task devolved
On late — confront Taurello!"
      And at last

He did confront him. Scarce an hour had past
When forth Sordello came, older by years
Than at his entry. Unexampled fears
Oppressed him, and he staggered off, blind, mute
And deaf, like some fresh-mutilated brute,
Into Ferrara — not the empty town
That morning witnessed : he went up and down
Streets whence the veil had been stripped shred by shred,
So that, in place of huddling with their dead
Indoors, to answer Salinguerra's ends,
Townsfolk make shift to crawl forth, sit like friends
With any one. A woman gave him choice
Of her two daughters, the infantile voice
Or the dimpled knee, for half a chain, his throat
Was clasped with ; but an archer knew the coat —
Its blue cross and eight lilies, — bade beware
One dogging him in concert with the pair
Though thrumming on the sleeve that hid his knife.
Night set in early, autumn dews were rife,
They kindled great fires while the Leaguers' mass
Began at every carroch — he must pass
Between the kneeling people. Presently
The carroch of Verona caught his eye
With purple trappings ; silently he bent
Over its fire, when voices violent
Began, " Affirm not whom the youth was like
That struck me from the porch, I did not strike
Again : I too have chestnut hair ; my kin
Hate Azzo and stand up for Ecelin.
Here, minstrel, drive bad thoughts away ! Sing ! Take
My glove for guerdon ! " And for that man's sake
He turned : " A song of Eglamor's ! " — scarce named,
When, " Our Sordello's rather ! " — all exclaimed ;
" Is not Sordello famousest for rhyme ? "
He had been happy to deny, this time, —
Profess as heretofore the aching head
And failing heart, — suspect that in his stead
Some true Apollo had the charge of them,
Was champion to reward or to condemn,
So his intolerable risk might shift
Or share itself ; but Naddo's precious gift
Of gifts, he owned, be certain ! At the close —
" I made that," said he to a youth who rose
As if to hear : 't was Palma through the band
Conducted him in silence by her hand.
    Back now for Salinguerra. Tito of Trent

Gave place to Palma and her friend; who went
In turn at Montelungo's visit — one
After the other were they come and gone, —
These spokesmen for the Kaiser and the Pope,
This incarnation of the People's hope,
Sordello, — all the say of each was said
And Salinguerra sat, himself instead
Of these to talk with, lingered musing yet.
'T was a drear vast presence-chamber roughly set
In order for the morning's use; full face,
The Kaiser's ominous sign-mark had first place,
The crowned grim twy-necked eagle, coarsely-blacked
With ochre on the naked wall; nor lacked
Romano's green and yellow either side;
But the new token Tito brought had tried
The Legate's patience — nay, if Palma knew
What Salinguerra almost meant to do
Until the sight of her restored his lip
A certain half-smile, three months' chieftainship
Had banished! Afterward, the Legate found
No change in him, nor asked what badge he wound
And unwound carelessly. Now sat the Chief
Silent as when our couple left, whose brief
Encounter wrought so opportune effect
In thoughts he summoned not, nor would reject.
Though time 't was now if ever, to pause — fix
On any sort of ending: wiles and tricks
Exhausted, judge! his charge, the crazy town,
Just managed to be hindered crashing down —
His last sound troops ranged — care observed to post
His best of the maimed soldiers innermost —
So much was plain enough, but somehow struck
Him not before. And now with this strange luck
Of Tito's news, rewarding his address
So well, what thought he of? — how the success
With Friedrich's rescript there, would either hush
Old Ecelin's scruples, bring the manly flush
To his young son's white cheek, or, last, exempt
Himself from telling what there was to tempt?
No: that this minstrel was Romano's last
Servant — himself the first! Could he contrast
The whole! — that minstrel's thirty years just spent
In doing nought, their notablest event
This morning's journey hither, as I told —
Who yet was lean, outworn and really old,
A stammering awkward man that scarce dared raise

His eye before the magisterial gaze —
And Salinguerra with his fears and hopes
Of sixty years, his Emperors and Popes,
Cares and contrivances, yet, you would say,
'T was a youth nonchalantly looked away
Through the embrasure northward o'er the sick
Expostulating trees — so agile, quick
And graceful turned the head on the broad chest
Encased in pliant steel, his constant vest,
Whence split the sun off in a spray of fire
Across the room; and, loosened of its tire
Of steel, that head let breathe the comely brown
Large massive locks discolored as if a crown
Encircled them, so frayed the basnet where
A sharp white line divided clean the hair;
Glossy above, glossy below, it swept
Curling and fine about a brow thus kept
Calm, laid coat upon coat, marble and sound :
This was the mystic mark the Tuscan found,
Mused of, turned over books about. Square-faced,
No lion more; two vivid eyes, enchased
In hollows filled with many a shade and streak
Settling from the bold nose and bearded cheek.
Nor might the half-smile reach them that deformed
A lip supremely perfect else — unwarmed,
Unwidened, less or more; indifferent
Whether on trees or men his thoughts were bent,
Thoughts rarely, after all, in trim and train
As now a period was fulfilled again :
Of such, a series made his life, compressed
In each, one story serving for the rest —
How his life-streams rolling arrived at last
At the barrier, whence, were it once overpast,
They would emerge, a river to the end, —
Gathered themselves up, paused, bade fate befriend,
Took the leap, hung a minute at the height,
Then fell back to oblivion infinite :
Therefore he smiled. Beyond stretched garden-grounds
Where late the adversary, breaking bounds,
Had gained him an occasion, That above,
That eagle, testified he could improve
Effectually. The Kaiser's symbol lay
Beside his rescript, a new badge by way
Of baldric; while, — another thing that marred
Alike emprise, achievement and reward, —
Ecelin's missive was conspicuous too.

What past life did those flying thoughts pursue?
As his, few names in Mantua half so old;
But at Ferrara, where his sires enrolled
It latterly, the Adelardi spared
No pains to rival them: both factions shared
Ferrara, so that, counted out, 't would yield
A product very like the city's shield,
Half black and white, or Ghibellin and Guelf
As after Salinguerra styled himself,
And Este who, till Marchesalla died,
(Last of the Adelardi) — never tried
His fortune there: with Marchesalla's child
Would pass, — could Blacks and Whites be reconciled,
And young Taurello wed Linguetta, — wealth
And sway to a sole grasp. Each treats by stealth
Already: when the Guelfs, the Ravennese
Arrive, assault the Pietro quarter, seize
Linguetta, and are gone! Men's first dismay
Abated somewhat, hurries down, to lay
The after indignation, Boniface,
This Richard's father. "Learn the full disgrace
Averted, ere you blame us Guelfs, who rate
Your Salinguerra, your sole potentate
That might have been, 'mongst Este's valvassors —
Ay, Azzo's — who, not privy to, abhors
Our step; but we were zealous." Azzo's then
To do with! Straight a meeting of old men:
" Old Salinguerra dead, his heir a boy,
What if we change our ruler and decoy
The Lombard Eagle of the azure sphere
With Italy to build in, fix him here,
Settle the city's troubles in a trice?
For private wrong, let public good suffice!"
In fine, young Salinguerra's stanchest friends
Talked of the townsmen making him amends,
Gave him a goshawk, and affirmed there was
Rare sport, one morning, over the green grass
A mile or so. He sauntered through the plain,
Was restless, fell to thinking, turned again
In time for Azzo's entry with the bride;
Count Boniface rode smirking at their side;
" She brings him half Ferrara," whispers flew,
" And all Ancona! If the stripling knew!"
   Anon the stripling was in Sicily
Where Heinrich ruled in right of Constance; he
Was gracious nor his guest incapable;

Each understood the other. So it fell,
One Spring, when Azzo, thoroughly at ease,
Had near forgotten by what precise degrees
He crept at first to such a downy seat,
The Count trudged over in a special heat
To bid him of God's love dislodge from each
Of Salinguerra's palaces, — a breach
Might yawn else, not so readily to shut,
For who was just arrived at Mantua but
The youngster, sword on thigh and tuft on chin,
With tokens for Celano, Ecelin,
Pistore, and the like! Next news, — no whit
Do any of Ferrara's domes befit
His wife of Heinrich's very blood: a band
Of foreigners assemble, understand
Garden-constructing, level and surround,
Build up and bury in. A last news crowned
The consternation: since his infant's birth,
He only waits they end his wondrous girth
Of trees that link San Pietro with Tomà,
To visit Mantua. When the Podestà
Ecelin, at Vicenza, called his friend
Taurello thither, what could be their end
But to restore the Ghibellins' late Head,
The Kaiser helping? He with most to dread
From vengeance and reprisal, Azzo, there
With Boniface beforehand, as aware
Of plots in progress, gave alarm, expelled
Both plotters: but the Guelfs in triumph yelled
Too hastily. The burning and the flight,
And how Taurello, occupied that night
With Ecelin, lost wife and son, I told:
— Not how he bore the blow, retained his hold,
Got friends safe through, left enemies the worst
O' the fray, and hardly seemed to care at first —
But afterward men heard not constantly
Of Salinguerra's House so sure to be!
Though Azzo simply gained by the event
A shifting of his plagues — the first, content
To fall behind the second and estrange
So far his nature, suffer such a change
That in Romano sought he wife and child
And for Romano's sake seemed reconciled
To losing individual life, which shrunk
As the other prospered — mortised in his trunk ;
Like a dwarf palm which wanton Arabs foil

Of bearing its own proper wine and oil,
By grafting into it the stranger-vine,
Which sucks its heart out, sly and serpentine,
Till forth one vine-palm feathers to the root,
And red drops moisten the insipid fruit.
Once Adelaide set on, — the subtle mate
Of the weak soldier, urged to emulate
The Church's valiant women deed for deed,
And paragon her namesake, win the meed
O' the great Matilda, — soon they overbore
The rest of Lombardy, — not as before
By an instinctive truculence, but patched
The Kaiser's strategy until it matched
The Pontiff's, sought old ends by novel means.
* Only, why is it Salinguerra screens
Himself behind Romano ? — him we bade
Enjoy our shine i' the front, not seek the shade ! "
— Asked Heinrich, somewhat of the tardiest
To comprehend. Nor Philip acquiesced
At once in the arrangement ; reasoned, plied
His friend with offers of another bride,
A statelier function — fruitlessly : 't was plain
Taurello through some weakness must remain
Obscure. And Otho, free to judge of both,
— Ecelin the unready, harsh and loth,
And this more plausible and facile wight
With every point a-sparkle — chose the right,
Admiring how his predecessors harped
On the wrong man : " thus," quoth he, " wits are warped
By outsides ! " Carelessly, meanwhile, his life
Suffered its many turns of peace and strife
In many lands — you hardly could surprise
The man ; who shamed Sordello (recognize !)
In this as much beside, that, unconcerned
What qualities were natural or earned,
With no ideal of graces, as they came
He took them, singularly well the same —
Speaking the Greek's own language, just because
Your Greek eludes you, leave the least of flaws
In contracts with him ; while, since Arab lore
Holds the stars' secret — take one trouble more
And master it ! 'T is done, and now deter
Who may the Tuscan, once Jove trined for her,
From Friedrich's path ! — Friedrich, whose pilgrimage
The same man puts aside, whom he 'll engage
To leave next year John Brienne in the lurch,

Come to Bassano, see Saint Francis' church
And judge of Guido the Bolognian's piece
Which, lend Taurello credit, rivals Greece —
Angels, with aureoles like golden quoits
Pitched home, applauding Ecelin's exploits.
For elegance, he strung the angelot,
Made rhymes thereto; for prowess, clove he not
Tiso, last siege, from crest to crupper? Why
Detail you thus a varied mastery
But to show how Taurello, on the watch
For men, to read their hearts and thereby catch
Their capabilities and purposes,
Displayed himself so far as displayed these:
While our Sordello only cared to know
About men as a means whereby he'd show
Himself, and men had much or little worth
According as they kept in or drew forth
That self; the other's choicest instruments
Surmised him shallow.
                     Meantime, malcontents
Dropped off, town after town grew wiser. "How
Change the world's face?" asked people; "as 't is now
It has been, will be ever: very fine
Subjecting things profane to things divine,
In talk! This contumacy will fatigue
The vigilance of Este and the League!
The Ghibellins gain on us!"— as it happed.
Old Azzo and old Boniface, entrapped
By Ponte Alto, both in one month's space
Slept at Verona: either left a brace
Of sons — but, three years after, either's pair
Lost Guglielm and Aldobrand its heir:
Azzo remained and Richard — all the stay
Of Este and Saint Boniface, at bay
As 't were. Then, either Ecelin grew old
Or his brain altered — not o' the proper mould
For new appliances — his old palm-stock
Endured no influx of strange strengths. He'd rock
As in a drunkenness, or chuckle low
As proud of the completeness of his woe,
Then weep real tears; — now make some mad onslaught
On Este, heedless of the lesson taught
So painfully, — now cringe for peace, sue peace
At price of past gain, bar of fresh increase
To the fortunes of Romano. Up at last
Rose Este, down Romano sank as fast.

And men remarked these freaks of peace and war
Happened while Salinguerra was afar:
Whence every friend besought him, all in vain,
To use his old adherent's wits again.
Not he! — " who had advisers in his sons,
Could plot himself, nor needed any one's
Advice." 'T was Adelaide's remaining stanch
Prevented his destruction root and branch
Forthwith; but when she died, doom fell, for gay
He made alliances, gave lands away
To whom it pleased accept them, and withdrew
Forever from the world. Taurello, who
Was summoned to the convent, then refused
A word at the wicket, patience thus abused,
Promptly threw off alike his imbecile
Ally's yoke, and his own frank, foolish smile.
Soon a few movements of the happier sort
Changed matters, put himself in men's report
As heretofore; he had to fight, beside,
And that became him ever. So, in pride
And flushing of this kind of second youth,
He dealt a good-will blow. Este in truth
Lay prone — and men remembered, somewhat late,
A laughing old outrageous stifled hate
He bore to Este — how it would outbreak
At times spite of disguise, like an earthquake
In sunny weather — as that noted day
When with his hundred friends he tried to slay
Azzo before the Kaiser's face: and how,
On Azzo's calm refusal to allow
A liegeman's challenge, straight he too was calmed:
As if his hate could bear to lie embalmed,
Bricked up, the moody Pharaoh, and survive
All intermediate crumblings, to arrive
At earth's catastrophe — 't was Este's crash
Not Azzo's he demanded, so, no rash
Procedure! Este's true antagonist
Rose out of Ecelin: all voices whist,
All eyes were sharpened, wits predicted. He
'T was, leaned in the embrasure absently,
Amused with his own efforts, now, to trace
With his steel-sheathed forefinger Friedrich's face
I' the dust: but as the trees waved sere, his smile
Deepened, and words expressed its thought erewhile.
" Ay, fairly housed at last, my old compeer?
That we should stick together, all the year

SALINGUERRA SOLILOQUIZES

I kept Vicenza! — How old Boniface,
Old Azzo caught us in its market-place,
He by that pillar, I at this, — caught each
In mid swing, more than fury of his speech,
Egging the rabble on to disavow
Allegiance to their Marquis — Bacchus, how
They boasted! Ecelin must turn their drudge,
Nor, if released, will Salinguerra grudge
Paying arrears of tribute due long since —
Bacchus! My man could promise then, nor wince,
The bones-and-muscles! Sound of wind and limb,
Spoke he the set excuse I framed for him:
And now he sits me, slavering and mute,
Intent on chafing each starved purple foot
Benumbed past aching with the altar slab —
Will no vein throb there when some monk shall blab
Spitefully to the circle of bald scalps,
'Friedrich's affirmed to be our side the Alps'
— Eh, brother Lactance, brother Anaclet?
Sworn to abjure the world, its fume and fret,
God's own now? Drop the dormitory bar,
Enfold the scanty gray serge scapular
Twice o'er the cowl to muffle memories out!
So! But the midnight whisper turns a shout,
Eyes wink, mouths open, pulses circulate
In the stone walls: the past, the world you hate
Is with you, ambush, open field — or see
The surging flame — we fire Vicenza — glee!
Follow, let Pilio and Bernardo chafe!
Bring up the Mantuans — through San Biagio — safe!
Ah, the mad people waken? Ah, they writhe
And reach us? If they block the gate? No tithe
Can pass — keep back, you Bassanese! The edge,
Use the edge — shear, thrust, hew, melt down the wedge,
Let out the black of those black upturned eyes!
Hell — are they sprinkling fire too? The blood fries
And hisses on your brass gloves as they tear
Those upturned faces choking with despair.
Brave! Slidder through the reeking gate! 'How now?
You six had charge of her?' And then the vow
Comes, and the foam spirts, hair's plucked, till one shriek
(I hear it) and you fling — you cannot speak —
Your gold-flowered basnet to a man who haled
The Adelaide he dared scarce view unveiled
This morn, naked across the fire: how crown
The archer that exhausted lays you down

Your infant, smiling at the flame, and dies?
While one, while mine . . .
         Bacchus! I think there lies
More than one corpse there " (and he paced the room)
" — Another cinder somewhere: 'twas my doom
Beside, my doom! If Adelaide is dead,
I live the same, this Azzo lives instead
Of that to me, and we pull, any how,
Este into a heap: the matter's now
At the true juncture slipping us so oft.
Ay, Heinrich died and Otho, please you, doffed
His crown at such a juncture! Still, if hold
Our Friedrich's purpose, if this chain enfold
The neck of . . . who but this same Ecelin
That must recoil when the best days begin!
Recoil? that's nought; if the recoiler leaves
His name for me to fight with, no one grieves:
But he must interfere, forsooth, unlock
His cloister to become my stumbling-block
Just as of old! Ay, ay, there 't is again —
The land's inevitable Head — explain
The reverences that subject us! Count
These Ecelins now! Not to say as fount,
Originating power of thought, — from twelve
That drop i' the trenches they joined hands to delve,
Six shall surpass him, but . . . why, men must twine
Somehow with something! Ecelin's a fine
Clear name! 'T were simpler, doubtless, twine with me
At once: our cloistered friend's capacity
Was of a sort! I had to share myself
In fifty portions, like an o'ertasked elf
That's forced illume in fifty points the vast
Rare vapor he's environed by. At last
My strengths, though sorely frittered, e'en converge
And crown . . . no, Bacchus, they have yet to urge
The man be crowned!
         That aloe, an he durst,
Would climb! Just such a bloated sprawler first
I noted in Messina's castle-court
The day I came, when Heinrich asked in sport
If I would pledge my faith to win him back
His right in Lombardy: 'for, once bid pack
Marauders,' he continued, 'in my stead
You rule, Taurello!' and upon this head
Laid the silk glove of Constance — I see her

Too, mantled head to foot in miniver,
Retrude following!
              I am absolved
From further toil: the empery devolved
On me, 't was Tito's word: I have to lay
For once my plan, pursue my plan my way,
Prompt nobody, and render an account
Taurello to Taurello! Nay, I mount
To Friedrich: he conceives the post I kept,
— Who did true service, able or inept,
Who's worthy guerdon, Ecelin or I.
Me guerdoned, counsel follows: would he vie
With the Pope really? Azzo, Boniface
Compose a right-arm Hohenstauffen's race
Must break ere govern Lombardy. I point
How easy 't were to twist, once out of joint,
The socket from the bone: my Azzo's stare
Meanwhile! for I, this idle strap to wear,
Shall — fret myself abundantly, what end
To serve? There's left me twenty years to spend
— How better than my old way? Had I one
Who labored to o'erthrow my work — a son
Hatching with Azzo superb treachery,
To root my pines up and then poison me,
Suppose — 't were worth while frustrate that! Beside,
Another life's ordained me: the world's tide
Rolls, and what hope of parting from the press
Of waves, a single wave through weariness
Gently lifted aside, laid upon shore?
My life must be lived out in foam and roar,
No question. Fifty years the province held
Taurello; troubles raised, and troubles quelled,
He in the midst — who leaves this quaint stone place,
These trees a year or two, then not a trace
Of him! How obtain hold, fetter men's tongues
Like this poor minstrel with the foolish songs —
To which, despite our bustle, he is linked?
— Flowers one may tease, that never grow extinct.
Ay, that patch, surely, green as ever, where
I set Her Moorish lentisk, by the stair,
To overawe the aloes; and we trod
Those flowers, how call you such? — into the sod;
A stately foreigner — a world of pain
To make it thrive, arrest rough winds — all vain!
It would decline; these would not be destroyed:

And now, where is it? where can you avoid
The flowers? I frighten children twenty years
Longer!— which way, too, Ecelin appears
To thwart me, for his son's besotted youth
Gives promise of the proper tiger-tooth:
They feel it at Vicenza! Fate, fate, fate,
My fine Taurello! Go you, promulgate
Friedrich's decree, and here's shall aggrandize
Young Ecelin — your Prefect's badge! a prize
Too precious, certainly.
      How now? Compete
With my old comrade? shuffle from their seat
His children? Paltry dealing! Don't I know
Ecelin? now, I think, and years ago!
What's changed — the weakness? did not I compound
For that, and undertake to keep him sound
Despite it? Here's Taurello hankering
After a boy's preferment — this plaything
To carry, Bacchus!" And he laughed.
           Remark
Why schemes wherein cold-blooded men embark
Prosper, when your enthusiastic sort
Fail: while these last are ever stopping short —
(So much they should — so little they can do!)
The careless tribe see nothing to pursue
If they desist; meantime their scheme succeeds.
 Thoughts were caprices in the course of deeds
Methodic with Taurello; so, he turned,
Enough amused by fancies fairly earned
Of Este's horror-struck submitted neck,
And Richard, the cowed braggart, at his beck,
To his own petty but immediate doubt
If he could pacify the League without
Conceding Richard; just to this was brought
That interval of vain discursive thought!
As, shall I say, some Ethiop, past pursuit
Of all enslavers, dips a shackled foot
Burnt to the blood, into the drowsy black
Enormous watercourse which guides him back
To his own tribe again, where he is king;
And laughs because he guesses, numbering
The yellower poison-wattles on the pouch
Of the first lizard wrested from its couch
Under the slime (whose skin, the while he strips
To cure his nostril with, and festered lips,
And eyeballs bloodshot through the desert-blast)

That he has reached its boundary, at last
May breathe; — thinks o'er enchantments of the South
Sovereign to plague his enemies, their mouth,
Eyes, nails, and hair; but, these enchantments tried
In fancy, puts them soberly aside
For truth, projects a cool return with friends,
The likelihood of winning mere amends
Ere long; thinks that, takes comfort silently,
Then, from the river's brink, his wrongs and he,
Hugging revenge close to their hearts, are soon
Off-striding for the Mountains of the Moon.

 Midnight: the watcher nodded on his spear,
Since clouds dispersing left a passage clear
For any meagre and discolored moon
To venture forth; and such was peering soon
Above the harassed city — her close lanes
Closer, not half so tapering her fanes,
As though she shrunk into herself to keep
What little life was saved, more safely. Heap
By heap the watch-fires mouldered, and beside
The blackest spoke Sordello and replied
Palma with none to listen. "T is your cause:
What makes a Ghibellin? There should be laws —
(Remember how my youth escaped! I trust
To you for manhood, Palma? tell me just
As any child) — there must be laws at work
Explaining this. Assure me, good may lurk
Under the bad, — my multitude has part
In your designs, their welfare is at heart
With Salinguerra, to their interest
Refer the deeds he dwelt on, — so divest
Our conference of much that scared me. Why
Affect that heartless tone to Tito? I
Esteemed myself, yes, in my inmost mind
This morn, a recreant to my race — mankind
O'erlooked till now: why boasts my spirit's force,
— Such force denied its object? why divorce
These, then admire my spirit's flight the same
As though it bore up, helped some half-orbed flame
Else quenched in the dead void, to living space?
That orb cast off to chaos and disgrace,
Why vaunt so much my unencumbered dance,
Making a feat's facilities enhance
Its marvel? But I front Taurello, one
Of happier fate, and all I should have done,
He does; the people's good being paramount

With him, their progress may perhaps account
For his abiding still; whereas you heard
The talk with Tito — the excuse preferred
For burning those five hostages, — and broached
By way of blind, as you and I approached,
I do believe."
     She spoke: then he, " My thought
Plainlier expressed! All to your profit — nought
Meantime of these, of conquests to achieve
For them, of wretchedness he might relieve
While profiting your party. Azzo, too,
Supports a cause : what cause? Do Guelfs pursue
Their ends by means like yours, or better?"
          When
The Guelfs were proved alike, men weighed with men,
And deed with deed, blaze, blood, with blood and blaze,
Morn broke : " Once more, Sordello, meet its gaze
Proudly — the people's charge against thee fails
In every point, while either party quails!
These are the busy ones: be silent thou!
Two parties take the world up, and allow
No third, yet have one principle, subsist
By the same injustice; whoso shall enlist
With either, ranks with man's inveterate foes.
So there is one less quarrel to compose :
The Guelf, the Ghibellin may be to curse —
I have done nothing, but both sides do worse
Than nothing. Nay, to me, forgotten, reft
Of insight, lapped by trees and flowers, was left
The notion of a service — ha? What lured
Me here, what mighty aim was I assured
Must move Taurello? What if there remained
A cause, intact, distinct from these, ordained
For me, its true discoverer?"
         Some one pressed
Before them here, a watcher, to suggest
The subject for a ballad : " They must know
The tale of the dead worthy, long ago
Consul of Rome — that's long ago for us,
Minstrels and bowmen, idly squabbling thus
In the world's corner — but too late no doubt,
For the brave time he sought to bring about.
— Not know Crescentius Nomentanus?" Then
He cast about for terms to tell him, when
Sordello disavowed it, how they used
Whenever their Superior introduced

A novice to the Brotherhood — ("for I
Was just a brown-sleeve brother, merrily
Appointed too," quoth he, "till Innocent
Bade me relinquish, to my small content,
My wife or my brown sleeves ") — some brother spoke
Ere nocturns of Crescentius, to revoke
The edict issued, after his demise,
Which blotted fame alike and effigies,
All out except a floating power, a name
Including, tending to produce the same
Great act. Rome, dead, forgotten, lived at least
Within that brain, though to a vulgar priest
And a vile stranger, — two not worth a slave
Of Rome's, Pope John, King Otho, — fortune gave
The rule there: so, Crescentius, haply dressed
In white, called Roman Consul for a jest,
Taking the people at their word, forth stepped
As upon Brutus' heel, nor ever kept
Rome waiting, — stood erect, and from his brain
Gave Rome out on its ancient place again,
Ay, bade proceed with Brutus' Rome, Kings styled
Themselves mere citizens of, and, beguiled
Into great thoughts thereby, would choose the gem
Out of a lapfull, spoil their diadem
— The Senate's cypher was so hard to scratch!
He flashes like a phanal, all men catch
The flame, Rome's just accomplished! when returned
Otho, with John, the Consul's step had spurned,
And Hugo Lord of Este, to redress
The wrongs of each. Crescentius in the stress
Of adverse fortune bent. "They crucified
Their Consul in the Forum; and abide
E'er since such slaves at Rome, that I — (for I
Was once a brown-sleeve brother, merrily
Appointed) — I had option to keep wife
Or keep brown sleeves, and managed in the strife
Lose both. A song of Rome!"
                                          And Rome, indeed,
Robed at Goito in fantastic weed,
The Mother-City of his Mantuan days,
Looked an established point of light whence rays
Traversed the world; for, all the clustered homes
Beside of men, seemed bent on being Romes
In their degree; the question was, how each
Should most resemble Rome, clean out of reach.
Nor, of the Two, did either principle

Struggle to change — but to possess — Rome, still,
Guelf Rome or Ghibellin Rome.
       Let Rome advance!
Rome, as she struck Sordello's ignorance —
How could he doubt one moment? Rome's the Cause!
Rome of the Pandects, all the world's new laws —
Of the Capitol, of Castle Angelo;
New structures, that inordinately glow,
Subdued, brought back to harmony, made ripe
By many a relic of the archetype
Extant for wonder; every upstart church
That hoped to leave old temples in the lurch,
Corrected by the Theatre forlorn
That, — as a mundane shell, its world late born, —
Lay and o'ershadowed it. These hints combined,
Rome typifies the scheme to put mankind
Once more in full possession of their rights.
" Let us have Rome again! On me it lights
To build up Rome — on me, the first and last:
For such a future was endured the past!"
And thus, in the gray twilight, forth he sprung
To give his thought consistency among
The very People — let their facts avail
Finish the dream grown from the archer's tale.

BOOK THE FIFTH.

Is it the same Sordello in the dusk
As at the dawn? — merely a perished husk
Now, that arose a power fit to build
Up Rome again? The proud conception chilled
So soon? Ay, watch that latest dream of thine
— A Rome indebted to no Palatine —
Drop arch by arch, Sordello! Art possessed
Of thy wish now, rewarded for thy quest
To-day among Ferrara's squalid sons?
Are this and this and this the shining ones
Meet for the Shining City? Sooth to say,
Your favored tenantry pursue their way
After a fashion! This companion slips
On the smooth causey, t' other blinkard trips
At his mooned sandal. "Leave to lead the brawls
Here i' the atria?" No, friend! He that sprawls
On aught but a stibadium . . . what his dues

Who puts the lustral vase to such an use?
Oh, huddle up the day's disasters! March,
Ye runagates, and drop thou, arch by arch,
Rome!
    Yet before they quite disband — a whim —
Study mere shelter, now, for him, and him,
Nay, even the worst, — just house them! Any cave
Suffices: throw out earth! A loophole? Brave!
They ask to feel the sun shine, see the grass
Grow, hear the larks sing? Dead art thou, alas,
And I am dead! But here's our son excels
At hurdle-weaving any Scythian, fells
Oak and devises rafters, dreams and shapes
His dream into a door-post, just escapes
The mystery of hinges. Lie we both
Perdue another age. The goodly growth
Of brick and stone! Our building-pelt was rough,
But that descendant's garb suits well enough
A portico-contriver. Speed the years —
What's time to us? At last, a city rears
Itself! nay, enter — what's the grave to us?
Lo, our forlorn acquaintance carry thus
The head! Successively sewer, forum, cirque —
Last age, an aqueduct was counted work,
But now they tire the artificer upon
Blank alabaster, black obsidion,
— Careful, Jove's face be duly fulgurant,
And mother Venus' kiss-creased nipples pant
Back into pristine pulpiness, ere fixed
Above the baths. What difference betwixt
This Rome and ours — resemblance what, between
That scurvy dumb-show and this pageant sheen —
These Romans and our rabble? Use thy wit!
The work marched: step by step, — a workman fit
Took each, nor too fit, — to one task, one time, —
No leaping o'er the petty to the prime,
When just the substituting osier lithe
For brittle bulrush, sound wood for soft withe,
To further loam-and-roughcast-work a stage, —
Exacts an architect, exacts an age:
No tables of the Mauritanian tree
For men whose maple log's their luxury!
That way was Rome built. "Better" (say you) "merge
At once all workmen in the demiurge,
All epochs in a lifetime, every task
In one!" So should the sudden city bask

I' the day — while those we 'd feast there, want the knack
Of keeping fresh-chalked gowns from speck and brack,
Distinguish not rare peacock from vile swan,
Nor Mareotic juice from Cæcuban.
" Enough of Rome ! 'T was happy to conceive
Rome on a sudden, nor shall fate bereave
Me of that credit : for the rest, her spite
Is an old story — serves my folly right
By adding yet another to the dull
List of abortions — things proved beautiful
Could they be done, Sordello cannot do."
  He sat upon the terrace, plucked and threw
The powdery aloe-cusps away, saw shift
Rome's walls, and drop arch after arch, and drift
Mist-like afar those pillars of all stripe,
Mounds of all majesty. " Thou archetype,
Last of my dreams and loveliest, depart ! "
  And then a low voice wound into his heart:
" Sordello ! " (low as some old Pythoness
Conceding to a Lydian King's distress
The cause of his long error — one mistake
Of her past oracle) " Sordello, wake !
God has conceded two sights to a man —
One, of men's whole work, time's completed plan,
The other, of the minute's work, man's first
Step to the plan's completeness : what 's dispersed
Save hope of that supreme step which, descried
Earliest, was meant still to remain untried
Only to give you heart to take your own
Step, and there stay — leaving the rest alone ?
Where is the vanity ? Why count as one
The first step, with the last step ? What is gone
Except Rome's aëry magnificence,
That last step you 'd take first ? — an evidence
You were God : be man now ! Let those glances fall !
The basis, the beginning step of all,
Which proves you just a man — is that gone too ?
Pity to disconcert one versed as you
In fate's ill-nature ! but its full extent
Eludes Sordello, even : the veil rent,
Read the black writing — that collective man
Outstrips the individual ! Who began
The acknowledged greatnesses ? Ay, your own art
Shall serve us : put the poet's mimes apart —
Close with the poet's self, and lo, a dim
Yet too plain form divides itself from him !

Alcamo's song enmeshes the lulled Isle,
Woven into the echoes left erewhile
By Nina, one soft web of song : no more
Turning his name, then, flower-like o'er and o'er !
An elder poet in the younger's place ;
Nina's the strength, but Alcamo's the grace :
Each neutralizes each then ! Search your fill ;
You get no whole and perfect Poet — still
New Ninas, Alcamos, till time's mid-night
Shrouds all — or better say, the shutting light
Of a forgotten yesterday.   Dissect
Every ideal workman — (to reject
In favor of your fearful ignorance
The thousand phantasms eager to advance,
And point you but to those within your reach) —
Were you the first who brought — (in modern speech)
The Multitude to be materialized ?
That loose eternal unrest — who devised
An apparition i' the midst ? The rout
Was checked, a breathless ring was formed about
That sudden flower : get round at any risk
The gold-rough pointel, silver-blazing disk
O' the lily ! Swords across it ! Reign thy reign
And serve thy frolic service, Charlemagne !
— The very child of over-joyousness,
Unfeeling thence, strong therefore :   Strength by stress
Of Strength comes of that forehead confident,
Those widened eyes expecting heart's content,
A calm as out of just-quelled noise ; nor swerves
For doubt, the ample cheek in gracious curves
Abutting on the upthrust nether lip :
He wills, how should he doubt then ?   Ages slip :
Was it Sordello pried into the work
So far accomplished, and discovered lurk
A company amid the other clans,
Only distinct in priests for castellans
And popes for suzerains (their rule confessed
Its rule, their interest its interest,
Living for sake of living — there an end, —
Wrapt in itself, no energy to spend
In making adversaries or allies), —
Dived you into its capabilities
And dared create, out of that sect, a soul
Should turn a multitude, already whole,
Into its body ? Speak plainer ! Is 't so sure
God's church lives by a King's investiture ?

288   SORDELLO

Look to last step! A staggering — a shock —
What's mere sand is demolished, while the rock
Endures : a column of black fiery dust
Blots heaven — that help was prematurely thrust
Aside, perchance! — but air clears, nought's erased
Of the true outline! Thus much being firm based,
The other was a scaffold. See him stand
Buttressed upon his mattock, Hildebrand
Of the huge brain-mask welded ply o'er ply
As in a forge; it buries either eye
White and extinct, that stupid brow; teeth clenched,
The neck tight-corded, too, the chin deep-trenched,
As if a cloud enveloped him while fought
Under its shade, grim prizers, thought with thought
At dead-lock, agonizing he, until
The victor thought leap radiant up, and Will,
The slave with folded arms and drooping lids
They fought for, lean forth flame-like as it bids.
Call him no flower — a mandrake of the earth,
Thwarted and dwarfed and blasted in its birth,
Rather, — a fruit of suffering's excess,
Thence feeling, therefore stronger : still by stress
Of Strength, work Knowledge! Full three hundred years
Have men to wear away in smiles and tears
Between the two that nearly seemed to touch,
Observe you! quit one workman and you clutch
Another, letting both their trains go by —
The actors-out of either's policy,
Heinrich, on this hand, Otho, Barbaross,
Carry the three Imperial crowns across,
Aix' Iron, Milan's Silver, and Rome's Gold —
While Alexander, Innocent uphold
On that, each Papal key — but, link on link,
Why is it neither chain betrays a chink ?
How coalesce the small and great ? Alack,
For one thrust forward, fifty such fall back !
Do the popes coupled there help Gregory
Alone ? Hark — from the hermit Peter's cry
At Claremont, down to the first serf that says
Friedrich's no liege of his while he delays
Getting the Pope's curse off him! The Crusade —
Or trick of breeding Strength by other aid
Than Strength, is safe. Hark — from the wild harangue
Of Vimmercato, to the carroch's clang
Yonder! The League — or trick of turning Strength
Against Pernicious Strength, is safe at length.

Yet hark — from Mantuan Albert making cease
The fierce ones, to Saint Francis preaching peace
Yonder! God's Truce — or trick to supersede
The very Use of Strength, is safe. Indeed
We trench upon the future. Who is found
To take next step, next age — trail o'er the ground —
Shall I say, gourd-like? — not the flower's display
Nor the root's prowess, but the plenteous way
O' the plant — produced by joy and sorrow, whence
Unfeeling and yet feeling, strongest thence?
Knowledge by stress of merely Knowledge? No —
E'en were Sordello ready to forego
His life for this, 't were overleaping work
Some one has first to do, howe'er it irk,
Nor stray a foot's breadth from the beaten road.
Who means to help must still support the load
Hildebrand lifted — ' why hast Thou,' he groaned,
' Imposed on me a burden, Paul had moaned,
And Moses dropped beneath?' Much done — and yet
Doubtless that grandest task God ever set
On man, left much to do: at his arm's wrench,
Charlemagne's scaffold fell; but pillars blench
Merely, start back again — perchance have been
Taken for buttresses: crash every screen,
Hammer the tenons better, and engage
A gang about your work, for the next age
Or two, of Knowledge, part by Strength and part
By Knowledge! Then, indeed, perchance may start
Sordello on his race — would time divulge
Such secrets! If one step's awry, one bulge
Calls for correction by a step we thought
Got over long since, why, till that is wrought,
No progress! And the scaffold in its turn
Becomes, its service o'er, a thing to spurn.
Meanwhile, if your half-dozen years of life
In store, dispose you to forego the strife,
Who takes exception? Only bear in mind,
Ferrara's reached, Goito's left behind:
As you then were, as half yourself, desist!
— The warrior-part of you may, an it list,
Finding real faulchions difficult to poise,
Fling them afar and taste the cream of joys
By wielding such in fancy, — what is bard
Of you may spurn the vehicle that marred
Elys so much, and in free fancy glut
His sense, yet write no verses — you have but

To please yourself for law, and once could please
What once appeared yourself, by dreaming these
Rather than doing these, in days gone by.
But all is changed the moment you descry
Mankind as half yourself, — then, fancy's trade
Ends once and always: how may half evade
The other half? men are found half of you.
Out of a thousand helps, just one or two
Can be accomplished presently: but flinch
From these (as from the faulchion, raised an inch,
Elys, described a couplet) and make proof
Of fancy, — then, while one half lolls aloof
I' the vines, completing Rome to the tip-top —
See if, for that, your other half will stop
A tear, begin a smile! The rabble's woes,
Ludicrous in their patience as they chose
To sit about their town and quietly
Be slaughtered, — the poor reckless soldiery,
With their ignoble rhymes on Richard, how
' Polt-foot,' sang they, ' was in a pitfall now,'
Cheering each other from the engine-mounts, —
That crippled sprawling idiot who recounts
How, lopped of limbs, he lay, stupid as stone,
Till the pains crept from out him one by one,
And wriggles round the archers on his head
To earn a morsel of their chestnut bread, —
And Cino, always in the self-same place
Weeping; beside that other wretch's case,
Eyepits to ear, one gangrene since he plied
The engine in his coat of raw sheep's hide
A double watch in the noon sun; and see
Lucchino, beauty, with the favors free,
Trim hacqueton, spruce beard and scented hair,
Campaigning it for the first time — cut there
In two already, boy enough to crawl
For latter orpine round the southern wall,
Tomà, where Richard's kept, because that whore
Marfisa, the fool never saw before,
Sickened for flowers this wearisomest siege:
And Tiso's wife — men liked their pretty liege,
Cared for her least of whims once, — Berta, wed
A twelvemonth gone, and, now poor Tiso's dead,
Delivering herself of his first child
On that chance heap of wet filth, reconciled
To fifty gazers!" — (Here a wind below
Made moody music augural of woe

From the pine barrier) — " What if, now the scene
Draws to a close, yourself have really been
— You, plucking purples in Goito's moss
Like edges of a trabea (not to cross
Your consul-humor) or dry aloe-shafts
For fasces, at Ferrara — he, fate wafts,
This very age, her whole inheritance
Of opportunities ? Yet you advance
Upon the last ! Since talking is your trade,
There 's Salinguerra left you to persuade :
Fail ! then " —
    " No — no — which latest chance secure ! "
Leaped up and cried Sordello : " this made sure,
The past were yet redeemable ; its work
Was — help the Guelfs, whom I, howe'er it irk,
Thus help ! " He shook the foolish aloe-haulm
Out of his doublet, paused, proceeded calm
To the appointed presence. The large head
Turned on its socket ; " And your spokesman," said
The large voice, " is Elcorte's happy sprout?
Few such " — (so finishing a speech no doubt
Addressed to Palma, silent at his side)
" — My sober councils have diversified.
Elcorte's son ! good : forward as you may,
Our lady's minstrel with so much to say ! "
The hesitating sunset floated back,
Rosily traversed in the wonted track
The chamber, from the lattice o'er the girth
Of pines, to the huge eagle blacked in earth
Opposite, — outlined sudden, spur to crest,
That solid Salinguerra, and caressed
Palma's contour ; 't was day looped back night's pall ;
Sordello had a chance left spite of all.
 And much he made of the convincing speech
Meant to compensate for the past and reach
Through his youth's daybreak of unprofit, quite
To his noon's labor, so proceed till night
Leisurely ! The great argument to bind
Taurello with the Guelf Cause, body and mind,
— Came the consummate rhetoric to that?
Yet most Sordello's argument dropped flat
Through his accustomed fault of breaking yoke,
Disjoining him who felt from him who spoke.
Was 't not a touching incident — so prompt
A rendering the world its just accompt,
Once proved its debtor ? Who 'd suppose, before

This proof, that he, Goito's god of yore,
At duty's instance could demean himself
So memorably, dwindle to a Guelf?
Be sure, in such delicious flattery steeped,
His inmost self at the out-portion peeped,
Thus occupied; then stole a glance at those
Appealed to, curious if her color rose
Or his lip moved, while he discreetly urged
The need of Lombardy becoming purged
At soonest of her barons; the poor part
Abandoned thus, missing the blood at heart
And spirit in brain, unseasonably off
Elsewhere! But, though his speech was worthy scoff,
Good-humored Salinguerra, famed for tact
And tongue, who, careless of his phrase, ne'er lacked
The right phrase, and harangued Honorius dumb
At his accession, — looked as all fell plumb
To purpose and himself found interest
In every point his new instructor pressed
— Left playing with the rescript's white wax seal
To scrutinize Sordello head and heel.
He means to yield assent sure? No, alas!
All he replied was, " What, it comes to pass
That poesy, sooner than politics,
Makes fade young hair?" To think such speech could fix
Taurello!
    Then a flash of bitter truth:
So fantasies could break and fritter youth
That he had long ago lost earnestness,
Lost will to work, lost power to even express
The need of working! Earth was turned a grave:
No more occasions now, though he should crave
Just one, in right of superhuman toil,
To do what was undone, repair such spoil,
Alter the past — nothing would give the chance!
Not that he was to die; he saw askance
Protract the ignominious years beyond
To dream in — time to hope and time despond,
Remember and forget, be sad, rejoice
As saved a trouble; he might, at his choice,
One way or other, idle life out, drop
No few smooth verses by the way — for prop,
A thyrsus, these sad people, all the same,
Should pick up, and set store by, — far from blame,
Plant o'er his hearse, convinced his better part
Survived him. " Rather tear men out the heart

O' the truth!'"— Sordello muttered, and renewed
His propositions for the Multitude.
  But Salinguerra, who at this attack
Had thrown great breast and ruffling corslet back
To hear the better, smilingly resumed
His task; beneath, the carroch's warning boomed;
He must decide with Tito; courteously
He turned then, even seeming to agree
With his admonisher — " Assist the Pope,
Extend Guelf domination, fill the scope
O' the Church, thus based on All, by All, for All —
Change Secular to Evangelical " —
Echoing his very sentence : all seemed lost,
When suddenly he looked up, laughingly almost,
To Palma: " This opinion of your friend's —
For instance, would it answer Palma's ends?
Best, were it not, turn Guelf, submit our Strength " —
(Here he drew out his baldric to its length)
— " To the Pope's Knowledge — let our captive slip,
Wide to the walls throw ope our gates, equip
Azzo with . . . what I hold here! Who 'll subscribe
To a trite censure of the minstrel tribe
Henceforward? or pronounce, as Heinrich used,
'Spear-heads for battle, burr-heads for the joust!'
— When Constance, for his couplets, would promote
Alcamo, from a parti-colored coat,
To holding her lord's stirrup in the wars.
Not that I see where couplet-making jars
With common sense : at Mantua I had borne
This chanted, better than their most forlorn
Of bull-baits, — that 's indisputable!"
                                      Brave!
Whom vanity nigh slew, contempt shall save!
All 's at an end : a Troubadour suppose
Mankind will class him with their friends or foes?
A puny uncouth ailing vassal think
The world and him bound in some special link?
Abrupt the visionary tether burst.
What were rewarded here, or what amerced
If a poor drudge, solicitous to dream
Deservingly, got tangled by his theme
So far as to conceit the knack or gift
Or whatsoe'er it be, of verse, might lift
The globe, a lever like the hand and head
Of — " Men of Action," as the Jongleurs said,
— " The Great Men," in the people's dialect?

And not a moment did this scorn affect
Sordello: scorn the poet? They, for once,
Asking " what was," obtained a full response.
Bid Naddo think at Mantua, he had but
To look into his promptuary, put
Finger on a set thought in a set speech:
But was Sordello fitted thus for each
Conjecture? Nowise; since within his soul,
Perception brooded unexpressed and whole.
A healthy spirit like a healthy frame
Craves aliment in plenty — all the same,
Changes, assimilates its aliment.
Perceived Sordello, on a truth intent?
Next day no formularies more you saw
Than figs or olives in a sated maw.
'T is Knowledge, whither such perceptions tend;
They lose themselves in that, means to an end,
The many old producing some one new,
A last unlike the first. If lies are true,
The Caliph's wheel-work man of brass receives
A meal, munched millet grains and lettuce leaves
Together in his stomach rattle loose;
You find them perfect next day to produce:
But ne'er expect the man, on strength of that,
Can roll an iron camel-collar flat
Like Haroun's self! I tell you, what was stored
Bit by bit through Sordello's life, outpoured
That eve, was, for that age, a novel thing:
And round those three the People formed a ring,
Of visionary judges whose award
He recognized in full — faces that barred
Henceforth return to the old careless life,
In whose great presence, therefore, his first strife
For their sake must not be ignobly fought;
All these, for once, approved of him, he thought,
Suspended their own vengeance, chose await
The issue of this strife to reinstate
Them in the right of taking it — in fact
He must be proved king ere they could exact
Vengeance for such king's defalcation. Last,
A reason why the phrases flowed so fast
Was in his quite forgetting for a time
Himself in his amazement that the rhyme
Disguised the royalty so much: he there —
And Salinguerra yet all unaware
Who was the lord, who liegeman!

"Thus I lay
On thine my spirit and compel obey
His lord, — my liegeman, — impotent to build
Another Rome, but hardly so unskilled
In what such builder should have been, as brook
One shame beyond the charge that I forsook
His function! Free me from that shame, I bend
A brow before, suppose new years to spend, —
Allow each chance, nor fruitlessly, recur —
Measure thee with the Minstrel, then, demur
At any crowd he claims! That I must cede
Shamed now, my right to my especial meed —
Confess thee fitter help the world than I
Ordained its champion from eternity,
Is much: but to behold thee scorn the post
I quit in thy behalf — to hear thee boast
What makes my own despair!" And while he rung
The changes on this theme, the roof up-sprung,
The sad walls of the presence-chamber died
Into the distance, or embowering vied
With far-away Goito's vine-frontier;
And crowds of faces — (only keeping clear
The rose-light in the midst, his vantage-ground
To fight their battle from) — deep clustered round
Sordello, with good wishes no mere breath,
Kind prayers for him no vapor, since, come death,
Come life, he was fresh sinewed every joint,
Each bone new-marrowed as whom gods anoint
Though mortal to their rescue. Now let sprawl
The snaky volumes hither! Is Typhon all
For Hercules to trample — good report
From Salinguerra only to extort?
"So was I" (closed he his inculcating,
A poet must be earth's essential king)
"So was I, royal so, and if I fail,
'T is not the royalty, ye witness quail,
But one deposed who, caring not exert
Its proper essence, trifled malapert
With accidents instead — good things assigned
As heralds of a better thing behind —
And, worthy through display of these, put forth
Never the inmost all-surpassing worth
That constitutes him king precisely since
As yet no other spirit may evince
Its like: the power he took most pride to test,
Whereby all forms of life had been professed

At pleasure, forms already on the earth,
Was but a means to power beyond, whose birth
Should, in its novelty, be kingship's proof.
Now, whether he came near or kept aloof
The several forms he longed to imitate,
Not there the kingship lay, he sees too late.
Those forms, unalterable first as last,
Proved him her copier, not the protoplast
Of nature: what would come of being free,
By action to exhibit tree for tree,
Bird, beast, for beast and bird, or prove earth bore
One veritable man or woman more?
Means to an end, such proofs are: what the end?
Let essence, whatsoe'er it be, extend—
Never contract. Already you include
The multitude; then let the multitude
Include yourself; and the result were new:
Themselves before, the multitude turn you.
This were to live and move and have, in them,
Your being, and secure a diadem
You should transmit (because no cycle yearns
Beyond itself, but on itself returns)
When, the full sphere in wane, the world o'erlaid
Long since with you, shall have in turn obeyed
Some orb still prouder, some displayer, still
More potent than the last, of human will,
And some new king depose the old. Of such
Am I — whom pride of this elates too much?
Safe, rather say, 'mid troops of peers again;
I, with my words, hailed brother of the train
Deeds once sufficed: for, let the world roll back,
Who fails, through deeds howe'er diverse, re-track
My purpose still, my task? A teeming crust —
Air, flame, earth, wave at conflict! Then, needs must
Emerge some Calm embodied, these refer
The brawl to;— yellow-bearded Jupiter?
No! Saturn; some existence like a pact
And protest against Chaos, some first fact
I' the faint of time. My deep of life, I know,
Is unavailing e'en to poorly show " . . .
(For here the Chief immeasurably yawned)
. . . " Deeds in their due gradation till Song dawned —
The fullest effluence of the finest mind,
All in degree, no way diverse in kind
From minds about it, minds which, more or less,
Lofty or low, move seeking to impress

Themselves on somewhat; but one mind has climbed
Step after step, by just ascent sublimed.
Thought is the soul of act, and, stage by stage,
Soul is from body still to disengage
As tending to a freedom which rejects
Such help and incorporeally affects
The world, producing deeds but not by deeds,
Swaying, in others, frames itself exceeds,
Assigning them the simpler tasks it used
To patiently perform till Song produced
Acts, by thoughts only, for the mind : divest
Mind of e'en Thought, and, lo, God's unexpressed
Will draws above us! All then is to win
Save that. How much for me, then? where begin
My work? About me, faces! and they flock,
The earnest faces. What shall I unlock
By song? behold me prompt, whate'er it be,
To minister : how much can mortals see
Of Life? No more than so? I take the task
And marshal you Life's elemental masque,
Show Men, on evil or on good lay stress,
This light, this shade make prominent, suppress
All ordinary hues that softening blend
Such natures with the level. Apprehend
Which sinner is, which saint, if I allot
Hell, Purgatory, Heaven, a blaze or blot,
To those you doubt concerning! I enwomb
Some wretched Friedrich with his red-hot tomb;
Some dubious spirit, Lombard Agilulph
With the black chastening river I engulf!
Some unapproached Matilda I enshrine
With languors of the planet of decline —
These, fail to recognize, to arbitrate
Between henceforth, to rightly estimate
Thus marshalled in the masque! Myself, the while,
As one of you, am witness, shrink or smile
At my own showing! Next age — what's to do?
The men and women stationed hitherto
Will I unstation, good and bad, conduct
Each nature to its farthest, or obstruct
At soonest, in the world : light, thwarted, breaks
A limpid purity to rainbow flakes,
Or shadow, massed, freezes to gloom : behold
How such, with fit assistance to unfold,
Or obstacles to crush them, disengage
Their forms, love, hate, hope, fear, peace make, **war wage**,

In presence of you all! Myself, implied
Superior now, as, by the platform's side,
I bade them do and suffer, — would last content
The world . . . no — that's too far! I circumvent
A few, my masque contented, and to these
Offer unveil the last of mysteries —
Man's inmost life shall have yet freer play:
Once more I cast external things away,
And natures composite, so decompose
That " . . . Why, he writes *Sordello!*
                                    " How I rose,
And how have you advanced! since evermore
Yourselves effect what I was fain before
Effect, what I supplied yourselves suggest,
What I leave bare yourselves can now invest.
How we attain to talk as brothers talk,
In half-words, call things by half-names, no balk
From discontinuing old aids. To-day
Takes in account the work of Yesterday:
Has not the world a Past now, its adept
Consults ere he dispense with or accept
New aids? a single touch more may enhance,
A touch less turn to insignificance
Those structures' symmetry the past has strewed
The world with, once so bare. Leave the mere rude
Explicit details! 't is but brother's speech
We need, speech where an accent's change gives each
The other's soul — no speech to understand
By former audience: need was then to expand,
Expatiate — hardly were we brothers! true —
Nor I lament my small remove from you,
Nor reconstruct what stands already. Ends
Accomplished turn to means: my art intends
New structure from the ancient: as they changed
The spoils of every clime at Venice, ranged
The horned and snouted Libyan god, upright
As in his desert, by some simple bright
Clay cinerary pitcher — Thebes as Rome,
Athens as Byzant rifled, till their Dome
From earth's reputed consummations razed
A seal, the all-transmuting Triad blazed
Above. Ah, whose that fortune? Ne'ertheless
E'en he must stoop contented to express
No tithe of what's to say — the vehicle
Never sufficient: but his work is still
For faces like the faces that select

The single service I am bound effect, —
That bid me cast aside such fancies, bow
Taurello to the Guelf cause, disallow
The Kaiser's coming — which with heart, soul, strength,
I labor for, this eve, who feel at length
My past career's outrageous vanity,
And would, as its amends, die, even die
Now I first estimate the boon of life,
If death might win compliance — sure, this strife
Is right for once — the People my support."
    My poor Sordello! what may we extort
By this, I wonder? Palma's lighted eyes
Turned to Taurello who, long past surprise,
Began, "You love him — what you'd say at large
Let me say briefly. First, your father's charge
To me, his friend, peruse: I guessed indeed
You were no stranger to the course decreed.
He bids me leave his children to the saints:
As for a certain project, he acquaints
The Pope with that, and offers him the best
Of your possessions to permit the rest
Go peaceably — to Ecelin, a stripe
Of soil the cursed Vicentines will gripe,
— To Alberic, a patch the Trevisan
Clutches already; extricate, who can,
Treville, Villarazzi, Puissolo,
Loria and Cartiglione! — all must go,
And with them go my hopes. 'T is lost, then!   Lost
This eve, our crisis, and some pains it cost
Procuring; thirty years — as good I'd spent
Like our admonisher! But each his bent
Pursues: no question, one might live absurd
Oneself this while, by deed as he by word
Persisting to obtrude an influence where
'T is made account of, much as . . . nay, you fare
With twice the fortune, youngster! — I submit,
Happy to parallel my waste of wit
With the renowned Sordello's: you decide
A course for me. Romano may abide
Romano, — Bacchus! After all, what dearth
Of Ecelins and Alberics on earth?
Say there's a prize in prospect, must disgrace
Betide competitors, unless they style
Themselves Romano? Were it worth my while
To try my own luck! But an obscure place
Suits me — there wants a youth to bustle, stalk

And attitudinize — some fight, more talk,
Most flaunting badges — how, I might make clear
Since Friedrich's very purposes lie here
— Here, pity they are like to lie! For me,
With station fixed unceremoniously
Long since, small use contesting; I am but
The liegeman — you are born the lieges — shut
That gentle mouth now! or resume your kin
In your sweet self; were Palma Ecelin
For me to work with! Could that neck endure
This bauble for a cumbrous garniture,
She should . . . or might one bear it for her? Stay —
I have not been so flattered many a day
As by your pale friend — Bacchus! The least help
Would lick the hind's fawn to a lion's whelp —
His neck is broad enough — a ready tongue
Beside — too writhled — but, the main thing, young —
I could . . . why, look ye!"
      And the badge was thrown
Across Sordello's neck: "This badge alone
Makes you Romano's Head — becomes superb
On your bare neck, which would, on mine, disturb
The pauldron," said Taurello. A mad act,
Nor even dreamed about before — in fact,
Not when his sportive arm rose for the nonce —
But he had dallied overmuch, this once,
With power: the thing was done, and he, aware
The thing was done, proceeded to declare —
(So like a nature made to serve, excel
In serving, only feel by service well!)
— That he would make Sordello that and more.
"As good a scheme as any. What's to pore
At in my face?" he asked — " ponder instead
This piece of news; you are Romano's Head!
One cannot slacken pace so near the goal,
Suffer my Azzo to escape heart-whole
This time! For you there's Palma to espouse —
For me, one crowning trouble ere I house
Like my compeer."
     On which ensued a strange
And solemn visitation; there came change
O'er every one of them; each looked on each:
Up in the midst a truth grew, without speech.
And when the giddiness sank and the haze
Subsided, they were sitting, no amaze,
Sordello with the baldric on, his sire

Silent, though his proportions seemed aspire
Momently ; and, interpreting the thrill
Right at its ebb, Palma was found there still
Relating somewhat Adelaide confessed
A year ago, while dying on her breast, —
Of a contrivance that Vicenza night,
When Ecelin had birth. "Their convoy's flight,
Cut off a moment, coiled inside the flame
That wallowed like a dragon at his game
The toppling city through — San Biagio rocks!
And wounded lies in her delicious locks
Retrude, the frail mother, on her face,
None of her wasted, just in one embrace
Covering her child : when, as they lifted her,
Cleaving the tumult, mighty, mightier
And mightiest Taurello's cry outbroke,
Leapt like a tongue of fire that cleaves the smoke,
Midmost to cheer his Mantuans onward — drown
His colleague Ecelin's clamor, up and down
The disarray : failed Adelaide see then
Who was the natural chief, the man of men ?
Outstripping time, her infant there burst swathe,
Stood up with eyes haggard beyond the scathe
From wandering after his heritage
Lost once and lost for aye — and why that rage,
That deprecating glance ? A new shape leant
On a familiar shape — gloatingly bent
O'er his discomfiture ; 'mid wreaths it wore,
Still one outflamed the rest — her child's before
'T was Salinguerra's for his child : scorn, hate,
Rage now might startle her when all too late !
Then was the moment ! — rival's foot had spurned
Never that House to earth else ! Sense returned —
The act conceived, adventured and complete,
They bore away to an obscure retreat
Mother and child — Retrude's self not slain "
(Nor even here Taurello moved) "though pain
Was fled ; and what assured them most 't was fled,
All pain, was, if they raised the pale hushed head
'T would turn this way and that, waver awhile,
And only settle into its old smile —
(Graceful as the disquieted water-flag
Steadying itself, remarked they, in the quag
On either side their path) — when suffered look
Down on her child. They marched : no sign once shook
The company's close litter of crossed spears

Till, as they reached Goito, a few tears
Slipped in the sunset from her long black lash,
And she was gone. So far the action rash;
No crime. They laid Retrude in the font,
Taurello's very gift, her child was wont
To sit beneath — constant as eve he came
To sit by its attendant girls the same
As one of them. For Palma, she would blend
With this magnific spirit to the end,
That ruled her first; but scarcely had she dared
To disobey the Adelaide who scared
Her into vowing never to disclose
A secret to her husband, which so froze
His blood at half-recital, she contrived
To hide from him Taurello's infant lived,
Lest, by revealing that, himself should mar
Romano's fortunes. And, a crime so far,
Palma received that action: she was told
Of Salinguerra's nature, of his cold
Calm acquiescence in his lot! But free
To impart the secret to Romano, she
Engaged to repossess Sordello of
His heritage, and hers, and that way doff
The mask, but after years, long years: while now,
Was not Romano's sign-mark on that brow?"
　　Across Taurello's heart his arms were locked:
And when he did speak 't was as if he mocked
The minstrel, " who had not to move," he said,
" Nor stir — should fate defraud him of a shred
Of his son's infancy? much less his youth!"
(Laughingly all this) — " which to aid, in truth,
Himself, reserved on purpose, had not grown
Old, not too old — 't was best they kept alone
Till now, and never idly met till now;"
— Then, in the same breath, told Sordello how
All intimations of this eve's event
Were lies, for Friedrich must advance to Trent,
Thence to Verona, then to Rome, there stop,
Tumble the Church down, institute a-top
The Alps a Prefecture of Lombardy:
— "That's now! — no prophesying what may be
Anon, with a new monarch of the clime,
Native of Gesi, passing his youth's prime
At Naples. Tito bids my choice decide
On whom" . . .
　　　　　" Embrace him, madman!" Palma cried,

Who through the laugh saw sweat-drops burst apace,
And his lips blanching : he did not embrace
Sordello, but he laid Sordello's hand
On his own eyes, mouth, forehead.
                               Understand,
This while Sordello was becoming flushed
Out of his whiteness ; thoughts rushed, fancies rushed ;
He pressed his hand upon his head and signed
Both should forbear him. " Nay, the best's behind ! "
Taurello laughed — not quite with the same laugh :
" The truth is, thus we scatter, ay, like chaff
These Guelfs, a despicable monk recoils
From : nor expect a fickle Kaiser spoils
Our triumph ! — Friedrich ? Think you, I intend
Friedrich shall reap the fruits of blood I spend
And brain I waste ? Think you, the people clap
Their hands at my out-hewing this wild gap
For any Friedrich to fill up ? 'T is mine —
That's yours : I tell you, towards some such design
Have I worked blindly, yes, and idly, yes,
And for another, yes — but worked no less
With instinct at my heart ; I else had swerved,
While now — look round ! My cunning has preserved
Samminiato — that's a central place
Secures us Florence, boy, — in Pisa's case,
By land as she by sea ; with Pisa ours,
And Florence, and Pistoia, one devours
The land at leisure ! Gloriously dispersed —
Brescia, observe, Milan, Piacenza first
That flanked us (ah, you know not !) in the March ;
On these we pile, as keystone of our arch,
Romagna and Bologna, whose first span
Covered the Trentine and the Valsugan ;
Sofia's Egna by Bolgiano's sure ! " . .
So he proceeded : half of all this, pure
Delusion, doubtless, nor the rest too true,
But what was undone he felt sure to do,
As ring by ring he wrung off, flung away
The pauldron-rings to give his sword-arm play —
Need of the sword now ! That would soon adjust
Aught wrong at present ; to the sword intrust
Sordello's whiteness, undersize : 't was plain
He hardly rendered right to his own brain —
Like a brave hound, men educate to pride
Himself on speed or scent nor aught beside,
As though he could not, gift by gift, match men !

Palma had listened patiently: but when
'T was time expostulate, attempt withdraw
Taurello from his child, she, without awe
Took off his iron arms from, one by one,
Sordello's shrinking shoulders, and, that done,
Made him avert his visage and relieve
Sordello (you might see his corslet heave
The while) who, loose, rose — tried to speak, then sank:
They left him in the chamber. All was blank.
  And even reeling down the narrow stair
Taurello kept up, as though unaware
Palma was by to guide him, the old device
 — Something of Milan — " how we muster thrice
The Torriani's strength there; all along
Our own Visconti cowed them " — thus the song
Continued even while she bade him stoop,
Thrid somehow, by some glimpse of arrow-loop,
The turnings to the gallery below,
Where he stopped short as Palma let him go.
When he had sat in silence long enough
Splintering the stone bench, braving a rebuff
She stopped the truncheon; only to commence
One of Sordello's poems, a pretence
For speaking, some poor rhyme of " Elys' hair
And head that's sharp and perfect like a pear,
So smooth and close are laid the few fine locks
Stained like pale honey oozed from topmost rocks
Sun-blanched the livelong summer " — from his worst
Performance, the Goito, as his first:
And that at end, conceiving from the brow
And open mouth no silence would serve now,
Went on to say the whole world loved that man
And, for that matter, thought his face, though wan,
Eclipsed the Count's — he sucking in each phrase
As if an angel spoke. The foolish praise
Ended, he drew her on his mailed knees, made
Her face a framework with his hands, a shade,
A crown, an aureole: there must she remain
(Her little mouth compressed with smiling pain
As in his gloves she felt her tresses twitch)
To get the best look at, in fittest niche
Dispose his saint. That done, he kissed her brow,
— " Lauded her father for his treason now,"
He told her, " only, how could one suspect
The wit in him? — whose clansman, recollect,
Was ever Salinguerra — she, the same,

Romano and his lady — so, might claim
To know all, as she should " — and thus begun
Schemes with a vengeance, schemes on schemes, " not one
Fit to be told that foolish boy," he said,
" But only let Sordello Palma wed,
— Then ! "
    'T was a dim long narrow place at best :
Midway a sole grate showed the fiery West,
As shows its corpse the world's end some split tomb —
A gloom, a rift of fire, another gloom,
Faced Palma — but at length Taurello set
Her free ; the grating held one ragged jet
Of fierce gold fire : he lifted her within
The hollow underneath — how else begin
Fate's second marvellous cycle, else renew
The ages than with Palma plain in view ?
Then paced the passage, hands clenched, head erect,
Pursuing his discourse ; a grand unchecked
Monotony made out from his quick talk
And the recurring noises of his walk ;
— Somewhat too much like the o'ercharged assent
Of two resolved friends in one danger blent,
Who hearten each the other against heart ;
Boasting there's nought to care for, when, apart
The boaster, all's to care for. He, beside
Some shape not visible, in power and pride
Approached, out of the dark, ginglingly near,
Nearer, passed close in the broad light, his ear
Crimson, eyeballs suffused, temples full-fraught,
Just a snatch of the rapid speech you caught,
And on he strode into the opposite dark,
Till presently the harsh heel's turn, a spark
I' the stone, and whirl of some loose embossed throng
That crashed against the angle aye so long
After the last, punctual to an amount
Of mailed great paces you could not but count, —
Prepared you for the pacing back again.
And by the snatches you might ascertain
That, Friedrich's Prefecture surmounted, left
By this alone in Italy, they cleft
Asunder, crushed together, at command
Of none, were free to break up Hildebrand,
Rebuild, he and Sordello, Charlemagne —
But garnished, Strength with Knowledge, " if we deign
Accept that compromise and stoop to give
Rome law, the Cæsar's Representative."

Enough, that the illimitable flood
Of triumphs after triumphs, understood
In its faint reflux (you shall hear) sufficed
Young Ecelin for appanage, enticed
Him on till, these long quiet in their graves,
He found 't was looked for that a whole life's braves
Should somehow be made good ; so, weak and worn,
Must stagger up at Milan, one gray morn
Of the to-come, and fight his latest fight.
But, Salinguerra's prophecy at height —
He voluble with a raised arm and stiff,
A blaring voice, a blazing eye, as if
He had our very Italy to keep
Or cast away, or gather in a heap
To garrison the better — ay, his word
Was, " run the cucumber into a gourd,
Drive Trent upon Apulia " — at their pitch
Who spied the continents and islands which
Grew mulberry-leaves and sickles, in the map —
(Strange that three such confessions so should hap
To Palma, Dante spoke with in the clear
Amorous silence of the Swooning-sphere, —
Cunizza, as he called her ! Never ask
Of Palma more ! She sat, knowing her task
Was done, the labor of it, — for, success
Concerned not Palma, passion's votaress)
Triumph at height, and thus Sordello crowned —
Above the passage suddenly a sound
Stops speech, stops walk : back shrinks Taurello, bids
With large involuntary asking lids,
Palma interpret. " 'T is his own foot-stamp —
Your hand ! His summons ! Nay, this idle damp
Befits not ! " Out they two reeled dizzily.
" Visconti 's strong at Milan," resumed he,
In the old, somewhat insignificant way —
(Was Palma wont, years afterward, to say)
As though the spirit's flight, sustained thus far,
Dropped at that very instant. Gone they are —
Palma, Taurello ; Eglamor anon,
Ecelin, — only Naddo 's never gone !
— Labors, this moonrise, what the Master meant —
" Is Squarcialupo speckled ? — purulent,
I 'd say, but when was Providence put out ?
He carries somehow handily about
His spite nor fouls himself ! " Goito's vines
Stand like a cheat detected — stark rough lines,

The moon breaks through, a gray mean scale against
The vault where, this eve's Maiden, thou remain'st
Like some fresh martyr, eyes fixed — who can tell?
As Heaven, now all 's at end, did not so well,
Spite of the faith and victory, to leave
Its virgin quite to death in the lone eve.
While the persisting hermit-bee . . . ha! wait
No longer: these in compass, forward fate!

BOOK THE SIXTH.

THE thought of Eglamor's least like a thought,
And yet a false one, was, "Man shrinks to nought
If matched with symbols of immensity;
Must quail, forsooth, before a quiet sky
Or sea, too little for their quietude:"
And, truly, somewhat in Sordello's mood
Confirmed its speciousness, while eve slow sank
Down the near terrace to the farther bank,
And only one spot left from out the night
Glimmered upon the river opposite —
A breadth of watery heaven like a bay,
A sky-like space of water, ray for ray,
And star for star, one richness where they mixed
As this and that wing of an angel, fixed,
Tumultuary splendors folded in
To die. Nor turned he till Ferrara's din
(Say, the monotonous speech from a man's lip
Who lets some first and eager purpose slip
In a new fancy's birth; the speech keeps on
Though elsewhere its informing soul be gone)
— Aroused him, surely offered succor. Fate
Paused with this eve; ere she precipitate
Herself, — best put off new strange thoughts awhile,
That voice, those large hands, that portentous smile, —
What help to pierce the future as the past,
Lay in the plaining city?
                        And at last
The main discovery and prime concern,
All that just now imported him to learn,
Truth's self, like yonder slow moon to complete
Heaven, rose again, and, naked at his feet,
Lighted his old life's every shift and change,

Effort with counter-effort ; nor the range
Of each looked wrong except wherein it checked
Some other — which of these could he suspect,
Prying into them by the sudden blaze ?
The real way seemed made up of all the ways —
Mood after mood of the one mind in him ;
Tokens of the existence, bright or dim,
Of a transcendent all-embracing sense
Demanding only outward influence,
A soul, in Palma's phrase, above his soul,
Power to uplift his power, — such moon's control
Over such sea-depths, — and their mass had swept
Onward from the beginning and still kept
Its course : but years and years the sky above
Held none, and so, untasked of any love,
His sensitiveness idled, now amort,
Alive now, and, to sullenness or sport
Given wholly up, disposed itself anew
At every passing instigation, grew
And dwindled at caprice, in foam-showers spilt,
Wedge-like insisting, quivered now a gilt
Shield in the sunshine, now a blinding race
Of whitest ripples o'er the reef — found place
For much display ; not gathered up and, hurled
Right from its heart, encompassing the world.
So had Sordello been, by consequence,
Without a function : others made pretence
To strength not half his own, yet had some core
Within, submitted to some moon, before
Them still, superior still whate'er their force, —
Were able therefore to fulfil a course,
Nor missed life's crown, authentic attribute.
To each who lives must be a certain fruit
Of having lived in his degree, — a stage,
Earlier or later in men's pilgrimage,
To stop at ; and to this the spirits tend
Who, still discovering beauty without end,
Amass the scintillations, make one star
— Something unlike them, self-sustained, afar, —
And meanwhile nurse the dream of being blest
By winning it to notice and invest
Their souls with alien glory, some one day
Whene'er the nucleus, gathering shape alway,
Round to the perfect circle — soon or late,
According as themselves are formed to wait ;

Whether mere human beauty will suffice
— The yellow hair and the luxurious eyes,
Or human intellect seem best, or each
Combine in some ideal form past reach
On earth, or else some shade of these, some aim,
Some love, hate even, take their place, the same,
So to be served — all this they do not lose,
Waiting for death to live, nor idly choose
What must be Hell — a progress thus pursued
Through all existence, still above the food
That's offered them, still fain to reach beyond
The widened range, in virtue of their bond
Of sovereignty. Not that a Palma's Love,
A Salinguerra's Hate, would equal prove
To swaying all Sordello: but why doubt
Some love meet for such strength, some moon without
Would match his sea? — or fear, Good manifest,
Only the Best breaks faith? — Ah but the Best
Somehow eludes us ever, still might be
And is not! Crave we gems? No penury
Of their material round us! Pliant earth
And plastic flame — what balks the mage his birth
— Jacinth in balls or lodestone by the block?
Flinders enrich the strand, veins swell the rock;
Nought more! Seek creatures? Life's i' the tempest, thought,
Clothes the keen hill-top, mid-day woods are fraught
With fervors: human forms are well enough!
But we had hoped, encouraged by the stuff
Profuse at nature's pleasure, men beyond
These actual men! — and thus are over-fond
In arguing, from Good the Best, from force
Divided — force combined, an ocean's course
From this our sea whose mere intestine pants
Might seem at times sufficient to our wants.
— External power? If none be adequate
And he stand forth ordained (a prouder fate)
Himself a law to his own sphere? — remove
All incompleteness, for that law, that love?
Nay, if all other laws be feints, — truth veiled
Helpfully to weak vision that had failed
To grasp aught but its special want, — for lure,
Embodied? Stronger vision could endure
The unbodied want: no part — the whole of **truth!**
The People were himself; nor, by the ruth
At their condition, was he less impelled

To alter the discrepancy beheld,
Than if, from the sound Whole, a sickly Part
Subtracted were transformed, decked out with art,
Then palmed on him as alien woe — the Guelf
To succor, proud that he forsook himself?
All is himself; all service, therefore, rates
Alike, nor serving one part, immolates
The rest: but all in time! "That lance of yours
Makes havoc soon with Malek and his Moors,
That buckler's lined with many a giant's beard,
Ere long, our champion, be the lance upreared,
The buckler wielded handsomely as now!
But view your escort, bear in mind your vow,
Count the pale tracts of sand to pass ere that,
And, if you hope we struggle through the flat,
Put lance and buckler by! Next half-month lacks
Mere sturdy exercise of mace and axe
To cleave this dismal brake of prickly-pear
Which bristling holds Cydippe by the hair,
Lames barefoot Agathon: this felled, we'll try
The picturesque achievements by and by —
Next life!"
     Ay, rally, mock, O People, urge
Your claims! — for thus he ventured, to the verge,
Push a vain mummery which perchance distrust
Of his fast-slipping resolution thrust
Likewise: accordingly the Crowd — (as yet
He had unconsciously contrived forget,
I' the whole, to dwell o' the points . . . one might assuage
The signal horrors easier than engage
With a dim vulgar vast unobvious grief
Not to be fancied off, nor gained relief
In brilliant fits, cured by a happy quirk,
But by dim vulgar vast unobvious work
To correspond . . .) — this Crowd then, forth they stood.
" And now content thy stronger vision, brood
On thy bare want; uncovered, turf by turf,
Study the corpse-face through the taint-worms' scurf!"
  Down sank the People's Then; uprose their Now
These sad ones render service to! And how
Piteously little must that service prove
— Had surely proved in any case! for, move
Each other obstacle away, let youth
Become aware it had surprised a truth
'T were service to impart — can truth be seized,
Settled forthwith, and, of the captive eased,

Its captor find fresh prey, since this alit
So happily, no gesture luring it,
The earnest of a flock to follow? Vain,
Most vain! a life to spend ere this he chain
To the poor crowd's complacence: ere the crowd
Pronounce it captured, he descries a cloud
Its kin of twice the plume; which he, in turn,
If he shall live as many lives, may learn
How to secure: not else. Then Mantua called
Back to his mind how certain bards were thralled
— Buds blasted, but of breath more like perfume
Than Naddo's staring nosegay's carrion bloom;
Some insane rose that burnt heart out in sweets,
A spendthrift in the spring, no summer greets;
Some Dularete, drunk with truths and wine,
Grown bestial, dreaming how become divine.
Yet to surmount this obstacle, commence
With the commencement, merits crowning! Hence
Must truth be casual truth, elicited
In sparks so mean, at intervals dispread
So rarely, that 't is like at no one time
Of the world's story has not truth, the prime
Of truth, the very truth which, loosed, had hurled
The world's course right, been really in the world
— Content the while with some mean spark by dint
Of some chance-blow, the solitary hint
Of buried fire, which, rip earth's breast, would stream
Sky-ward!
   Sordello's miserable gleam
Was looked for at the moment: he would dash
This badge, and all it brought, to earth, — abash
Taurello thus, perhaps persuade him wrest
The Kaiser from his purpose, — would attest
His own belief, in any case. Before
He dashes it however, think once more!
For, were that little, truly service? "Ay,
I' the end, no doubt; but meantime? Plain you spy
Its ultimate effect, but many flaws
Of vision blur each intervening cause.
Were the day's fraction clear as the life's sum
Of service, Now as filled as teems To-come
With evidence of good — nor too minute
A share to vie with evil! No dispute,
'T were fitliest maintain the Guelfs in rule:
That makes your life's work: but you have to school
Your day's work on these natures circumstanced

Thus variously, which yet, as each advanced
Or might impede the Guelf rule, must be moved
Now, for the Then's sake, — hating what you loved,
Loving old hatreds! Nor if one man bore
Brand upon temples while his fellow wore
The aureole, would it task you to decide:
But, portioned duly out, the future vied
Never with the unparcelled present! Smite
Or spare so much on warrant all so slight?
The present's complete sympathies to break,
Aversions bear with, for a future's sake
So feeble? Tito ruined through one speck,
The Legate saved by his sole lightish fleck?
This were work, true, but work performed at cost
Of other work; aught gained here, elsewhere lost.
For a new segment spoil an orb half-done?
Rise with the People one step, and sink — one?
Were it but one step, less than the whole face
Of things, your novel duty bids erase!
Harms to abolish! What, the prophet saith,
The minstrel singeth vainly then? Old faith,
Old courage, only borne because of harms,
Were not, from highest to the lowest, charms?
Flame may persist; but is not glare as stanch?
Where the salt marshes stagnate, crystals branch;
Blood dries to crimson; Evil's beautified
In every shape. Thrust Beauty then aside
And banish Evil! Wherefore? After all,
Is Evil a result less natural
Than Good? For overlook the seasons' strife
With tree and flower, — the hideous animal life,
(Of which who seeks shall find a grinning taunt
For his solution, and endure the vaunt
Of nature's angel, as a child that knows
Himself befooled, unable to propose
Aught better than the fooling) — and but care
For men, for the mere People then and there, —
In these, could you but see that Good and Ill
Claimed you alike! Whence rose their claim but still
From Ill, as fruit of Ill? What else could knit
You theirs but Sorrow? Any free from it
Were also free from you! Whose happiness
Could be distinguished in this morning's press
Of miseries? — the fool's who passed a gibe
'On thee,' jeered he, 'so wedded to thy tribe,
Thou carriest green and yellow tokens in

Thy very face that thou art Ghibellin!'
Much hold on you that fool obtained! Nay mount
Yet higher — and upon men's own account
Must Evil stay: for, what is joy? — to heave
Up one obstruction more, and common leave
What was peculiar, by such act destroy
Itself; a partial death is every joy;
The sensible escape, enfranchisement
Of a sphere's essence: once the vexed — content,
The cramped — at large, the growing circle — round,
All 's to begin again — some novel bound
To break, some new enlargement to entreat;
The sphere though larger is not more complete.
Now for Mankind's experience: who alone
Might style the unobstructed world his own?
Whom palled Goito with its perfect things?
Sordello's self: whereas for Mankind springs
Salvation by each hindrance interposed.
They climb; life's view is not at once disclosed
To creatures caught up, on the summit left,
Heaven plain above them, yet of wings bereft:
But lower laid, as at the mountain's foot.
So, range on range, the girdling forests shoot
'Twixt your plain prospect and the throngs who scale
Height after height, and pierce mists, veil by veil,
Heartened with each discovery; in their soul,
The Whole they seek by Parts — but, found that Whole,
Could they revert, enjoy past gains? The space
Of time you judge so meagre to embrace
The Parts were more than plenty, once attained
The Whole, to quite exhaust it: nought were gained
But leave to look — not leave to do: Beneath
Soon sates the looker — look Above, and Death
Tempts ere a tithe of Life be tasted. Live
First, and die soon enough, Sordello! Give
Body and spirit the first right they claim,
And pasture soul on a voluptuous shame
That you, a pageant-city's denizen,
Are neither vilely lodged 'midst Lombard men —
Can force joy out of sorrow, seem to truck
Bright attributes away for sordid muck,
Yet manage from that very muck educe
Gold; then subject nor scruple, to your cruce
The world's discardings! Though real ingots pay
Your pains, the clods that yielded them are clay
To all beside, — would clay remain, though quenched

Your purging-fire; who's robbed then? Had you wrenched
An ampler treasure forth! — As 't is, they crave
A share that ruins you and will not save
Them. Why should sympathy command you quit
The course that makes your joy, nor will remit
Their woe? Would all arrive at joy? Reverse
The order (time instructs you) nor coerce
Each unit till, some predetermined mode,
The total be emancipate; men's road
Is one, men's times of travel many; thwart
No enterprising soul's precocious start
Before the general march! If slow or fast
All straggle up to the same point at last,
Why grudge your having gained, a month ago,
The brakes at balm-shed, asphodels in blow,
While they were landlocked? Speed their Then, but how
This badge would suffer you improve your Now!"
 His time of action for, against, or with
Our world (I labor to extract the pith
Of this his problem) grew, that even-tide,
Gigantic with its power of joy, beside
The world's eternity of impotence
To profit though at his whole joy's expense.
"Make nothing of my day because so brief?
Rather make more: instead of joy, use grief
Before its novelty have time subside!
Wait not for the late savor, leave untried
Virtue, the creaming honey-wine, quick squeeze
Vice like a biting spirit from the lees
Of life! Together let wrath, hatred, lust, .
All tyrannies in every shape, be thrust
Upon this Now, which time may reason out
As mischiefs, far from benefits, no doubt;
But long ere then Sordello will have slipped
Away; you teach him at Goito's crypt,
There's a blank issue to that fiery thrill.
Stirring, the few cope with the many, still:
So much of sand as, quiet, makes a mass
Unable to produce three tufts of grass,
Shall, troubled by the whirlwind, render void
The whole calm glebe's endeavor: be employed!
And e'en though somewhat smart the Crowd for this,
Contribute each his pang to make your bliss,
'T is but one pang — one blood-drop to the bowl
Which brimful tempts the sluggish asp uncowl
At last, stains ruddily the dull red cape,

And, kindling orbs gray as the unripe grape
Before, avails forthwith to disentrance
The portent, soon to lead a mystic dance
Among you! For, who sits alone in Rome?
Have those great hands indeed hewn out a home,
And set me there to live? Oh life, life-breath,
Life-blood, — ere sleep, come travail, life ere death!
This life stream on my soul, direct, oblique,
But always streaming! Hindrances? They pique:
Helps? such . . . but why repeat, my soul o'ertops
Each height, then every depth profoundlier drops?
Enough that I can live, and would live! Wait
For some transcendent life reserved by Fate
To follow this? Oh, never! Fate, I trust
The same, my soul to; for, as who flings dust,
Perchance (so facile was the deed) she checked
The void with these materials to affect
My soul diversely: these consigned anew
To nought by death, what marvel if she threw
A second and superber spectacle
Before me? What may serve for sun, what still
Wander a moon above me? What else wind
About me like the pleasures left behind,
And how shall some new flesh that is not flesh
Cling to me? What's new laughter? Soothes the fresh
Sleep like sleep? Fate's exhaustless for my sake
In brave resource: but whether bids she slake
My thirst at this first rivulet, or count
No draught worth lip save from some rocky fount
Above i' the clouds, while here she's provident
Of pure loquacious pearl, the soft tree-tent
Guards, with its face of reate and sedge, nor fail
The silver globules and gold-sparkling grail
At bottom? Oh, 't were too absurd to slight
For the hereafter the to-day's delight!
Quench thirst at this, then seek next well-spring: wear
Home-lilies ere strange lotus in my hair!
Here is the Crowd, whom I with freest heart
Offer to serve, contented for my part
To give life up in service, — only grant
That I do serve; if otherwise, why want
Aught further of me? If men cannot choose
But set aside life, why should I refuse
The gift? I take it — I, for one, engage
Never to falter through my pilgrimage —
Nor end it howling that the stock or stone

Were enviable, truly: I, for one,
Will praise the world, you style mere anteroom
To palace — be it so! shall I assume
— My foot the courtly gait, my tongue the trope,
My mouth the smirk, before the doors fly ope
One moment? What? with guarders row on row,
Gay swarms of varletry that come and go,
Pages to dice with, waiting-girls unlace
The plackets of, pert claimants help displace,
Heart-heavy suitors get a rank for, — laugh
At yon sleek parasite, break his own staff
'Cross Beetle-brows the Usher's shoulder, — why,
Admitted to the presence by and by,
Should thought of having lost these make me grieve
Among new joys I reach, for joys I leave?
Cool citrine-crystals, fierce pyropus-stone,
Are floor-work there! But do I let alone
That black-eyed peasant in the vestibule
Once and forever? — Floor-work? No such fool!
Rather, were heaven to forestall earth, I 'd say
I, is it, must be blessed? Then, my own way
Bless me! Giver firmer arm and fleeter foot,
I 'll thank you: but to no mad wings transmute
These limbs of mine — our greensward was so soft!
Nor camp I on the thunder-cloud aloft:
We feel the bliss distinctlier, having thus
Engines subservient, not mixed up with us.
Better move palpably through heaven: nor, freed
Of flesh, forsooth, from space to space proceed
'Mid flying synods of worlds! No: in heaven's marge
Show Titan still, recumbent o'er his targe
Solid with stars — the Centaur at his game,
Made tremulously out in hoary flame!
  Life! Yet the very cup whose extreme dull
Dregs, even, I would quaff, was dashed, at full,
Aside so oft; the death I fly, revealed
So oft a better life this life concealed,
And which sage, champion, martyr, through each path
Have hunted fearlessly — the horrid bath,
The crippling-irons and the fiery chair.
'T was well for them; let me become aware
As they, and I relinquish life, too! Let
What masters life disclose itself! Forget
Vain ordinances, I have one appeal —
I feel, am what I feel, know what I feel;
So much is truth to me. What Is, then? Since

One object, viewed diversely, may evince
Beauty and ugliness — this way attract,
That way repel, — why gloze upon the fact?
Why must a single of the sides be right?
What bids choose this and leave the opposite?
Where's abstract Right for me? — in youth endued
With Right still present, still to be pursued,
Through all the interchange of circles, rife
Each with its proper law and mode of life,
Each to be dwelt at ease in: where, to sway
Absolute with the Kaiser, or obey
Implicit with his serf of fluttering heart,
Or, like a sudden thought of God's, to start
Up, Brutus in the presence, then go shout
That some should pick the unstrung jewels out —
Each, well!"
      And, as in moments when the past
Gave partially enfranchisement, he cast
Himself quite through mere secondary states
Of his soul's essence, little loves and hates,
Into the mid deep yearnings overlaid
By these; as who should pierce hill, plain, grove, glade,
And on into the very nucleus probe
That first determined there exist a globe.
As that were easiest, half the globe dissolved,
So seemed Sordello's closing-truth evolved
By his flesh-half's break up; the sudden swell
Of his expanding soul showed Ill and Well,
Sorrow and Joy, Beauty and Ugliness,
Virtue and Vice, the Larger and the Less,
All qualities, in fine, recorded here,
Might be but modes of Time and this one sphere,
Urgent on these, but not of force to bind
Eternity, as Time — as Matter — Mind,
If Mind, Eternity, should choose assert
Their attributes within a Life: thus girt
With circumstance, next change beholds them cinct
Quite otherwise — with Good and Ill distinct,
Joys, sorrows, tending to a like result —
Contrived to render easy, difficult,
This or the other course of . . . what new bond
In place of flesh may stop their flight beyond
Its new sphere, as that course does harm or good
To its arrangements. Once this understood,
As suddenly he felt himself alone,
Quite out of Time and this world: all was known.

What made the secret of his past despair?
— Most imminent when he seemed most aware
Of his own self-sufficiency; made mad
By craving to expand the power he had,
And not new power to be expanded? — just
This made it; Soul on Matter being thrust,
Joy comes when so much Soul is wreaked in Time
On Matter, — let the Soul's attempt sublime
Matter beyond the scheme and so prevent
By more or less that deed's accomplishment,
And Sorrow follows: Sorrow how avoid?
Let the employer match the thing employed,
Fit to the finite his infinity,
And thus proceed forever, in degree
Changed but in kind the same, still limited
To the appointed circumstance and dead
To all beyond. A sphere is but a sphere;
Small, Great, are merely terms we bandy here;
Since to the spirit's absoluteness all
Are like. Now, of the present sphere we call
Life, are conditions; take but this among
Many; the body was to be so long
Youthful, no longer: but, since no control
Tied to that body's purposes his soul,
She chose to understand the body's trade
More than the body's self — had fain conveyed
Her boundless, to the body's bounded lot.
Hence, the soul permanent, the body not, —
Scarcely its minute for enjoying here, —
The soul must needs instruct her weak compeer,
Run o'er its capabilities and wring
A joy thence, she held worth experiencing:
Which, far from half discovered even, — lo,
The minute gone, the body's power let go
Apportioned to that joy's acquirement! Broke
Morning o'er earth, he yearned for all it woke —
From the volcano's vapor-flag, winds hoist
Black o'er the spread of sea, — down to the moist
Dale's silken barley-spikes sullied with rain,
Swayed earthwards, heavily to rise again —
The Small, a sphere as perfect as the Great
To the soul's absoluteness. Meditate
Too long on such a morning's cluster-chord
And the whole music it was framed afford, —
The chord's might half discovered, what should pluck
One string, his finger, was found palsy-struck.

And then no marvel if the spirit, shown
A saddest sight — the body lost alone
Through her officious proffered help, deprived
Of this and that enjoyment Fate contrived, —
Virtue, Good, Beauty, each allowed slip hence, —
Vaingloriously were fain, for recompense,
To stem the ruin even yet, protract
The body's term, supply the power it lacked
From her infinity, compel it learn
These qualities were only Time's concern,
And body may, with spirit helping, barred —
Advance the same, vanquished — obtain reward,
Reap joy where sorrow was intended grow,
Of Wrong make Right, and turn Ill Good below.
And the result is, the poor body soon
Sinks under what was meant a wondrous boon,
Leaving its bright accomplice all aghast.
  So much was plain then, proper in the past;
To be complete for, satisfy the whole
Series of spheres — Eternity, his soul
Needs must exceed, prove incomplete for, each
Single sphere — Time. But does our knowledge reach
No farther? Is the cloud of hindrance broke
But by the failing of the fleshly yoke,
Its loves and hates, as now when death lets soar
Sordello, self-sufficient as before,
Though during the mere space that shall elapse
'Twixt his enthrallment in new bonds, perhaps?
Must life be ever just escaped, which should
Have been enjoyed? — nay, might have been and would,
Each purpose ordered right — the soul's no whit
Beyond the body's purpose under it —
Like yonder breadth of watery heaven, a bay,
And that sky-space of water, ray for ray
And star for star, one richness where they mixed
As this and that wing of an angel, fixed,
Tumultuary splendors folded in
To die — would soul, proportioned thus, begin
Exciting discontent, or surelier quell
The body if, aspiring, it rebel?
But how so order life? Still brutalize
The soul, the sad world's way, with muffled eyes
To all that was before, all that shall be
After this sphere — all and each quality
Save some sole and immutable Great Good
And Beauteous whither fate has loosed its hood

To follow? Never may some soul see All
— The Great Before and After, and the Small
Now, yet be saved by this the simplest lore,
And take the single course prescribed before,
As the king-bird with ages on his plumes
Travels to die in his ancestral glooms?
But where descry the Love that shall select
That course? Here is a soul whom, to affect,
Nature has plied with all her means, from trees
And flowers e'en to the Multitude!— and these,
Decides he save or no? One word to end!
  Ah my Sordello, I this once befriend
And speak for you. Of a Power above you still
Which, utterly incomprehensible,
Is out of rivalry, which thus you can
Love, though unloving all conceived by man—
What need! And of— none the minutest duct
To that out-nature, nought that would instruct
And so let rivalry begin to live —
But of a power its representative
Who, being for authority the same,
Communication different, should claim
A course, the first chose but this last revealed —
This Human clear, as that Divine concealed —
What utter need!   What has Sordello found?
Or can his spirit go the mighty round,
End where poor Eglamor begun? — So, says
Old fable, the two eagles went two ways
About the world : where, in the midst, they met,
Though on a shifting waste of sand, men set
Jove's temple. Quick, what has Sordello found?
For they approach — approach — that foot's rebound
Palma? No, Salinguerra though in mail;
They mount, have reached the threshold, dash the veil
Aside — and you divine who sat there dead,
Under his foot the badge: still, Palma said,
A triumph lingering in the wide eyes,
Wider than some spent swimmer's if he spies
Help from above in his extreme despair,
And, head far back on shoulder thrust, turns there
With short quick passionate cry : as Palma pressed
In one great kiss, her lips upon his breast,
It beat.   By this, the hermit-bee has stopped
His day's toil at Goito: the new-cropped

Dead vine-leaf answers, now 't is eve, he bit,
Twirled so, and filed all day : the mansion's fit,
God counselled for. As easy guess the word
That passed betwixt them, and become the third
To the soft small unfrighted bee, as tax
Him with one fault — so, no remembrance racks
Of the stone maidens and the font of stone
He, creeping through the crevice, leaves alone.
Alas, my friend, alas Sordello, whom
Anon they laid within that old font-tomb,
And, yet again, alas !
      And now is 't worth
Our while bring back to mind, much less set forth
How Salinguerra extricates himself
Without Sordello? Ghibellin and Guelf
May fight their fiercest out? If Richard sulked
In durance or the Marquis paid his mulct,
Who cares, Sordello gone ? The upshot, sure,
Was peace ; our chief made some frank overture
That prospered ; compliment fell thick and fast
On its disposer, and Taurello passed
With foe and friend for an outstripping soul,
Nine days at least. Then, — fairly reached the goal, —
He, by one effort, blotted the great hope
Out of his mind, nor further tried to cope
With Este, that mad evening's style, but sent
Away the Legate and the League, content
No blame at least the brothers had incurred,
— Dispatched a message to the Monk, he heard
Patiently first to last, scarce shivered at,
Then curled his limbs up on his wolfskin mat
And ne'er spoke more, — informed the Ferrarese
He but retained their rule so long as these
Lingered in pupilage, — and last, no mode
Apparent else of keeping safe the road
From Germany direct to Lombardy
For Friedrich, — none, that is, to guarantee
The faith and promptitude of who should next
Obtain Sofia's dowry, — sore perplexed —
(Sofia being youngest of the tribe
Of daughters, Ecelin was wont to bribe
The envious magnates with — nor, since he sent
Henry of Egna this fair child, had Trent
Once failed the Kaiser's purposes — " we lost
Egna last year, and who takes Egna's post —
Opens the Lombard gate if Friedrich knock ? ")

Himself espoused the Lady of the Rock
In pure necessity, and, so destroyed
His slender last of chances, quite made void
Old prophecy, and spite of all the schemes
Overt and covert, youth's deeds, age's dreams,
Was sucked into Romano. And so hushed
He up this evening's work, that, when 't was brushed
Somehow against by a blind chronicle
Which, chronicling whatever woe befell
Ferrara, noted this the obscure woe
Of " Salinguerra's sole son Giacomo
Deceased, fatuous and doting, ere his sire,"
The townsfolk rubbed their eyes, could but admire
Which of Sofia's five was meant.
       The chaps
Of earth's dead hope were tardy to collapse,
Obliterated not the beautiful
Distinctive features at a crash : but dull
And duller these, next year, as Guelfs withdrew
Each to his stronghold. Then (securely too
Ecelin at Campese slept ; close by,
Who likes may see him in Solagna lie,
With cushioned head and gloved hand to denote
The cavalier he was) — then his heart smote
Young Ecelin at last ; long since adult.
And, save Vicenza's business, what result
In blood and blaze ? (So hard to intercept
Sordello till his plain withdrawal !) Stepped
Then its new lord on Lombardy. I' the nick
Of time when Ecelin and Alberic
Closed with Taurello, come precisely news
That in Verona half the souls refuse
Allegiance to the Marquis and the Count —
Have cast them from a throne they bid him mount,
Their Podestà, through his ancestral worth.
Ecelin flew there, and the town henceforth
Was wholly his — Taurello sinking back
From temporary station to a track
That suited. News received of this acquist,
Friedrich did come to Lombardy : who missed
Taurello then ? Another year : they took
Vicenza, left the Marquis scarce a nook
For refuge, and, when hundreds two or three
Of Guelfs conspired to call themselves " The Free,"
Opposing Alberic, — vile Bassanese, —
(Without Sordello !) — Ecelin at ease

Slaughtered them so observably, that oft
A little Salinguerra looked with soft
Blue eyes up, asked his sire the proper age
To get appointed his proud uncle's page.
More years passed, and that sire had dwindled down
To a mere showy turbulent soldier, grown
Better through age, his parts still in repute,
Subtle — how else ? — but hardly so astute
As his contemporaneous friends professed ;
Undoubtedly a brawler : for the rest,
Known by each neighbor, and allowed for, let
Keep his incorrigible ways, nor fret
Men who would miss their boyhood's bugbear : " trap
The ostrich, suffer our bald osprey flap
A battered pinion ! " — was the word. In fine,
One flap too much and Venice's marine
Was meddled with ; no overlooking that !
She captured him in his Ferrara, fat
And florid at a banquet, more by fraud
Than force, to speak the truth ; there 's slender laud
Ascribed you for assisting eighty years
To pull his death on such a man ; fate shears
The life-cord prompt enough whose last fine thread
You fritter : so, presiding his board-head,
The old smile, your assurance all went well
With Friedrich (as if he were like to tell !)
In rushed (a plan contrived before) our friends,
Made some pretence at fighting, some amends
For the shame done his eighty years — (apart
The principle, none found it in his heart
To be much angry with Taurello) — gained
Their galleys with the prize, and what remained
But carry him to Venice for a show ?
— Set him, as 't were, down gently — free to go
His gait, inspect our square, pretend observe
The swallows soaring their eternal curve
'Twixt Theodore and Mark, if citizens
Gathered importunately, fives and tens,
To point their children the Magnifico,
All but a monarch once in firm-land, go
His gait among them now — " it took, indeed,
Fully this Ecelin to supersede
That man," remarked the seniors. Singular !
Sordello's inability to bar
Rivals the stage, that evening, mainly brought
About by his strange disbelief that aught

Was ever to be done, — this thrust the Twain
Under Taurello's tutelage, — whom, brain
And heart and hand, he forthwith in one rod
Indissolubly bound to baffle God
Who loves the world — and thus allowed the thin
Gray wizened dwarfish devil Ecelin,
And massy-muscled big-boned Alberic
(Mere man, alas!) to put his problem quick
To demonstration — prove wherever 's will
To do, there 's plenty to be done, or ill
Or good. Anointed, then, to rend and rip —
Kings of the gag and flesh-hook, screw and whip,
They plagued the world : a touch of Hildebrand
(So far from obsolete!) made Lombards band
Together, cross their coats as for Christ's cause,
And saving Milan win the world's applause.
Ecelin perished : and I think grass grew
Never so pleasant as in Valley Rù
By San Zenon where Alberic in turn
Saw his exasperated captors burn
Seven children and their mother ; then, regaled
So far, tied on to a wild horse, was trailed
To death through raunce and bramble-bush. I take
God's part and testify that 'mid the brake
Wild o'er his castle on the pleasant knoll,
You hear its one tower left, a belfry, toll —
The earthquake spared it last year, laying flat
The modern church beneath, — no harm in that!
Chirrups the contumacious grasshopper,
Rustles the lizard and the cushats chirre
Above the ravage : there, at deep of day
A week since, heard I the old Canon say
He saw with his own eyes a barrow burst
And Alberic's huge skeleton unhearsed
Only five years ago. He added, "June's
The month for carding off our first cocoons
The silkworms fabricate" — a double news,
Nor he nor I could tell the worthier. Choose!

And Naddo gone, all 's gone ; not Eglamor!
Believe, I knew the face I waited for,
A guest my spirit of the golden courts!
Oh strange to see how, despite ill-reports,
Disuse, some wear of years, that face retained
Its joyous look of love! Suns waxed and waned,
And still my spirit held an upward flight,
Spiral on spiral, gyres of life and light

More and more gorgeous — ever that face there
The last admitted! crossed, too, with some care
As perfect triumph were not sure for all,
But, on a few, enduring damp must fall,
— A transient struggle, haply a painful sense
Of the inferior nature's clinging — whence
Slight starting tears easily wiped away,
Fine jealousies soon stifled in the play
Of irrepressible admiration — not
Aspiring, all considered, to their lot
Who ever, just as they prepare ascend
Spiral on spiral, wish thee well, impend
Thy frank delight at their exclusive track,
That upturned fervid face and hair put back!
  Is there no more to say? He of the rhymes —
Many a tale, of this retreat betimes,
Was born: Sordello die at once for men?
The Chroniclers of Mantua tired their pen
Telling how *Sordello Prince Visconti* saved
Mantua, and elsewhere notably behaved —
Who thus, by fortune ordering events,
Passed with posterity, to all intents,
For just the god he never could become.
As Knight, Bard, Gallant, men were never dumb
In praise of him: while what he should have been,
Could be, and was not — the one step too mean
For him to take, — we suffer at this day
Because of: Ecelin had pushed away
Its chance ere Dante could arrive and take
That step Sordello spurned, for the world's sake:
He did much — but Sordello's chance was gone.
Thus, had Sordello dared that step alone,
Apollo had been compassed — 'twas a fit
He wished should go to him, not he to it
— As one content to merely be supposed
Singing or fighting elsewhere, while he dozed
Really at home — one who was chiefly glad
To have achieved the few real deeds he had,
Because that way assured they were not worth
Doing, so spared from doing them henceforth —
A tree that covets fruitage and yet tastes
Never itself, itself. Had he embraced
Their cause then, men had plucked Hesperian fruit
And, praising that, just thrown him in to boot
All he was anxious to appear, but scarce
Solicitous to be. A sorry farce

Such life is, after all! Cannot I say
He lived for some one better thing? this way. —
Lo, on a heathy brown and nameless hill
By sparkling Asolo, in mist and chill,
Morning just up, higher and higher runs
A child barefoot and rosy. See! the sun's
On the square castle's inner-court's low wall
Like the chine of some extinct animal
Half turned to earth and flowers; and through the haze
(Save where some slender patches of gray maize
Are to be overleaped) that boy has crossed
The whole hill-side of dew and powder-frost
Matting the balm and mountain camomile.
Up and up goes he, singing all the while
Some unintelligible words to beat
The lark, God's poet, swooning at his feet,
So worsted is he at "the few fine locks
Stained like pale honey oozed from topmost rocks
Sunblanched the livelong summer," — all that's left
Of the Goito lay! And thus bereft,
Sleep and forget, Sordello! In effect
He sleeps, the feverish poet — I suspect
Not utterly companionless; but, friends,
Wake up! The ghost's gone, and the story ends
I'd fain hope, sweetly; seeing, peri or ghoul,
That spirits are conjectured fair or foul,
Evil or good, judicious authors think,
According as they vanish in a stink
Or in a perfume. Friends, be frank! ye snuff
Civet, I warrant. Really? Like enough!
Merely the savor's rareness; any nose
May ravage with impunity a rose:
Rifle a musk-pod and 't will ache like yours!
I'd tell you that same pungency ensures
An after-gust, but that were overbold.
Who would has heard Sordello's story told.

PIPPA PASSES

A DRAMA

I DEDICATE MY BEST INTENTIONS, IN THIS POEM,
ADMIRINGLY TO THE AUTHOR OF "ION,"
AFFECTIONATELY TO MR. SERGEANT TALFOURD.

LONDON, 1841.

R. B.

NEW YEAR'S DAY AT ASOLO IN THE TREVISAN. *A large mean airy chamber. A girl,* PIPPA, *from the silk-mills, springing out of bed.*

DAY!
Faster and more fast,
O'er night's brim, day boils at last;
Boils, pure gold, o'er the cloud-cup's brim
Where spurting and suppressed it lay;
For not a froth-flake touched the rim
Of yonder gap in the solid gray
Of the eastern cloud, an hour away;
But forth one wavelet, then another, curled,
Till the whole sunrise, not to be suppressed,
Rose, reddened, and its seething breast
Flickered in bounds, grew gold, then overflowed the world.

Oh, Day, if I squander a wavelet of thee,
A mite of my twelve-hours' treasure,
The least of thy gazes or glances,
(Be they grants thou art bound to or gifts above measure)
One of thy choices or one of thy chances,
(Be they tasks God imposed thee or freaks at thy pleasure)
— My Day, if I squander such labor or leisure,
Then shame fall on Asolo, mischief on me!

Thy long blue solemn hours serenely flowing,
Whence earth, we feel, gets steady help and good —
Thy fitful sunshine-minutes, coming, going,
As if earth turned from work in gamesome mood —
All shall be mine! But thou must treat me not
As prosperous ones are treated, those who live

At hand here, and enjoy the higher lot,
In readiness to take what thou wilt give,
And free to let alone what thou refusest;
For, Day, my holiday, if thou ill-usest
Me, who am only Pippa, — old-year's sorrow,
Cast off last night, will come again to-morrow:
Whereas, if thou prove gentle, I shall borrow
Sufficient strength of thee for new-year's sorrow.
All other men and women that this earth
Belongs to, who all days alike possess,
Make general plenty cure particular dearth,
Get more joy one way, if another, less:
Thou art my single day, God lends to leaven
What were all earth else, with a feel of heaven, —
Sole light that helps me through the year, thy sun's!
Try now! Take Asolo's Four Happiest Ones —
And let thy morning rain on that superb
Great haughty Ottima; can rain disturb
Her Sebald's homage? All the while thy rain
Beats fiercest on her shrub-house window-pane,
He will but press the closer, breathe more warm
Against her cheek; how should she mind the storm?
And, morning past, if mid-day shed a gloom
O'er Jules and Phene, — what care bride and groom
Save for their dear selves? 'T is their marriage-day;
And while they leave church and go home their way,
Hand clasping hand, within each breast would be
Sunbeams and pleasant weather spite of thee.
Then, for another trial, obscure thy eve
With mist, — will Luigi and his mother grieve —
The lady and her child, unmatched, forsooth,
She in her age, as Luigi in his youth,
For true content? The cheerful town, warm, close
And safe, the sooner that thou art morose,
Receives them. And yet once again, outbreak
In storm at night on Monsignor, they make
Such stir about, — whom they expect from Rome
To visit Asolo, his brothers' home,
And say here masses proper to release
A soul from pain, — what storm dares hurt his peace?
Calm would he pray, with his own thoughts to ward
Thy thunder off, nor want the angels' guard.
But Pippa — just one such mischance would spoil
Her day that lightens the next twelvemonth's toil
At wearisome silk-winding, coil on coil!
And here I let time slip for nought!

Aha, you foolhardy sunbeam, caught
With a single splash from my ewer!
You that would mock the best pursuer,
Was my basin over-deep?
One splash of water ruins you asleep,
And up, up, fleet your brilliant bits
Wheeling and counterwheeling,
Reeling, broken beyond healing:
Now grow together on the ceiling!
That will task your wits.
Whoever it was quenched fire first, hoped to see
Morsel after morsel flee
As merrily, as giddily . . .
Meantime, what lights my sunbeam on,
Where settles by degrees the radiant cripple?
Oh, is it surely blown, my martagon?
New-blown and ruddy as St. Agnes' nipple,
Plump as the flesh-bunch on some Turk bird's poll!
Be sure if corals, branching 'neath the ripple
Of ocean, bud there, — fairies watch unroll
Such turban-flowers; I say, such lamps disperse
Thick red flame through that dusk green universe!
I am queen of thee, floweret!
And each fleshy blossom
Preserve I not — (safer
Than leaves that embower it,
Or shells that embosom)
— From weevil and chafer?
Laugh through my pane then; solicit the bee;
Gibe him, be sure; and, in midst of thy glee,
Love thy queen, worship me!

— Worship whom else? For am I not, this day,
Whate'er I please? What shall I please to-day?
My morn, noon, eve and night — how spend my day?
To-morrow I must be Pippa who winds silk,
The whole year round, to earn just bread and milk:
But, this one day, I have leave to go,
And play out my fancy's fullest games;
I may fancy all day — and it shall be so —
That I taste of the pleasures, am called by the names
Of the Happiest Four in our Asolo!

See! Up the hillside yonder, through the morning,
Some one shall love me, as the world calls love:
I am no less than Ottima, take warning!

The gardens, and the great stone house above,
And other house for shrubs, all glass in front,
Are mine; where Sebald steals, as he is wont,
To court me, while old Luca yet reposes :
And therefore, till the shrub-house door uncloses,
I . . . what now ? — give abundant cause for prate
About me — Ottima, I mean — of late,
Too bold, too confident she 'll still face down
The spitefullest of talkers in our town.
How we talk in the little town below!
    But love, love, love — there 's better love, I know!
This foolish love was only day's first offer;
I choose my next love to defy the scoffer:
For do not our Bride and Bridegroom sally
Out of Possagno church at noon?
Their house looks over Orcana valley :
Why should not I be the bride as soon
As Ottima? For I saw, beside,
Arrive last night that little bride —
Saw, if you call it seeing her, one flash
Of the pale snow-pure cheek and black bright tresses,
Blacker than all except the black eyelash ;
I wonder she contrives those lids no dresses!
— So strict was she, the veil
Should cover close her pale
Pure cheeks — a bride to look at and scarce touch,
Scarce touch, remember, Jules! For are not such
Used to be tended, flower-like, every feature,
As if one's breath would fray the lily of a creature?
A soft and easy life these ladies lead :
Whiteness in us were wonderful indeed.
Oh, save that brow its virgin dimness,
Keep that foot its lady primness,
Let those ankles never swerve
From their exquisite reserve,
Yet have to trip along the streets like me,
All but naked to the knee !
How will she ever grant her Jules a bliss
So startling as her real first infant kiss?
Oh, no — not envy, this !

    — Not envy, sure !— for if you gave me
Leave to take or to refuse,
In earnest, do you think I 'd choose
That sort of new love to enslave me?
Mine should have lapped me round from the beginning;

As little fear of losing it as winning:
Lovers grow cold, men learn to hate their wives,
And only parents' love can last our lives.
At eve the Son and Mother, gentle pair,
Commune inside our turret: what prevents
My being Luigi? While that mossy lair
Of lizards through the winter-time is stirred
With each to each imparting sweet intents
For this new-year, as brooding bird to bird —
(For I observe of late, the evening walk
Of Luigi and his mother, always ends
Inside our ruined turret, where they talk,
Calmer than lovers, yet more kind than friends)
— Let me be cared about, kept out of harm,
And schemed for, safe in love as with a charm;
Let me be Luigi! If I only knew
What was my mother's face — my father, too!
   Nay, if you come to that, best love of all
Is God's; then why not have God's love befall
Myself as, in the palace by the Dome,
Monsignor? — who to-night will bless the home
Of his dead brother; and God bless in turn
That heart which beats, those eyes which mildly burn
With love for all men! I, to-night at least,
Would be that holy and beloved priest.

Now wait! — even I already seem to share
In God's love: what does New-year's hymn declare?
What other meaning do these verses bear?

> *All service ranks the same with God:*
> *If now, as formerly he trod*
> *Paradise, his presence fills*
> *Our earth, each only as God wills*
> *Can work — God's puppets, best and worst,*
> *Are we; there is no last nor first.*

> *Say not " a small event!" Why " small"?*
> *Costs it more pain that this, ye call*
> *A " great event," should come to pass,*
> *Than that? Untwine me from the mass*
> *Of deeds which make up life, one deed*
> *Power shall fall short in or exceed!*

And more of it, and more of it! — oh yes —
I will pass each, and see their happiness,

And envy none — being just as great, no doubt,
Useful to men, and dear to God, as they!
A pretty thing to care about
So mightily, this single holiday!
But let the sun shine! Wherefore repine?
— With thee to lead me, O Day of mine,
Down the grass path gray with dew,
Under the pine-wood, blind with boughs,
Where the swallow never flew
Nor yet cicala dared carouse —
No, dared carouse! [*She enters the street.*

I. MORNING. *Up the Hillside, inside the Shrub-house.* LUCA'S *Wife,* OTTIMA, *and her Paramour, the German* SEBALD.

Seb. [*sings.*] *Let the watching lids wink!*
 Day's ablaze with eyes, think!
 Deep into the night, drink!
Otti. Night? Such may be your Rhine-land nights, perhaps!
But this blood-red beam through the shutter's chink
— We call such light, the morning: let us see!
Mind how you grope your way, though! How these tall
Naked geraniums straggle! Push the lattice
Behind that frame! — Nay, do I bid you? — Sebald,
It shakes the dust down on me! Why, of course
The slide-bolt catches. Well, are you content,
Or must I find you something else to spoil?
Kiss and be friends, my Sebald! Is 't full morning?
Oh, don't speak then!
 Seb. Ay, thus it used to be!
Ever your house was, I remember, shut
Till mid-day; I observed that, as I strolled
On mornings through the vale here; country girls
Were noisy, washing garments in the brook,
Hinds drove the slow white oxen up the hills:
But no, your house was mute, would ope no eye!
And wisely: you were plotting one thing there,
Nature, another outside. I looked up —
Rough white wood shutters, rusty iron bars,
Silent as death, blind in a flood of light.
Oh, I remember! — and the peasants laughed
And said, "The old man sleeps with the young wife."
This house was his, this chair, this window — his.
 Otti. Ah, the clear morning! I can see St. Mark's;
That black streak is the belfry. Stop: Vicenza

Should lie . . . there's Padua, plain enough, that blue!
Look o'er my shoulder, follow my finger!
    Seb.   Morning?
It seems to me a night with a sun added.
Where's dew, where's freshness? That bruised plant, I bruised
In getting through the lattice yestereve,
Droops as it did. See, here's my elbow's mark
I' the dust o' the sill.
    Otti.   Oh, shut the lattice, pray!
    Seb. Let me lean out. I cannot scent blood here,
Foul as the morn may be.
                        There, shut the world out!
How do you feel now, Ottima? There, curse
The world and all outside! Let us throw off
This mask: how do you bear yourself? Let's out
With all of it!
    Otti.   Best never speak of it.
    Seb. Best speak again and yet again of it,
Till words cease to be more than words. "His blood,"
For instance — let those two words mean, "His blood"
And nothing more. Notice, I'll say them now,
"His blood."
    Otti.   Assuredly if I repented
The deed —
    Seb.   Repent? Who should repent, or why?
What puts that in your head? Did I once say
That I repented?
    Otti.   No; I said the deed . . .
    Seb. "The deed" and "the event" — just now it was
"Our passion's fruit" — the devil take such cant!
Say, once and always, Luca was a wittol,
I am his cut-throat, you are . . .
    Otti.   Here's the wine;
I brought it when we left the house above,
And glasses too — wine of both sorts. Black? White then?
    Seb. But am not I his cut-throat? What are you?
    Otti. There trudges on his business from the Duomo
Benet the Capuchin, with his brown hood
And bare feet; always in one place at church,
Close under the stone wall by the south entry.
I used to take him for a brown cold piece
Of the wall's self, as out of it he rose
To let me pass — at first, I say, I used:
Now, so has that dumb figure fastened on me,
I rather should account the plastered wall
A piece of him, so chilly does it strike.
This, Sebald?

Seb.   No, the white wine — the white wine!
Well, Ottima, I promised no new year
Should rise on us the ancient shameful way;
Nor does it rise. Pour on! To your black eyes!
Do you remember last damned New Year's day?
     Otti. You brought those foreign prints. We looked at them
Over the wine and fruit. I had to scheme
To get him from the fire. Nothing but saying
His own set wants the proof-mark, roused him up
To hunt them out.
     Seb.   'Faith, he is not alive
To fondle you before my face.
     Otti.   Do you
Fondle me then! Who means to take your life
For that, my Sebald?
     Seb.   Hark you, Ottima!
One thing to guard against. We'll not make much
One of the other — that is, not make more
Parade of warmth, childish officious coil,
Than yesterday: as if, sweet, I supposed
Proof upon proof were needed now, now first,
To show I love you — yes, still love you — love you
In spite of Luca and what's come to him
— Sure sign we had him ever in our thoughts,
White sneering old reproachful face and all!
We'll even quarrel, love, at times, as if
We still could lose each other, were not tied
By this: conceive you?
     Otti.   Love!
     Seb.   Not tied so sure!
Because though I was wrought upon, have struck
His insolence back into him — am I
So surely yours? — therefore forever yours?
     Otti. Love, to be wise, (one counsel pays another,)
Should we have — months ago, when first we loved,
For instance that May morning we two stole
Under the green ascent of sycamores —
If we had come upon a thing like that
Suddenly . . .
     Seb.   "A thing" — there again — "a thing!"
     Otti. Then, Venus' body, had we come upon
My husband Luca Gaddi's murdered corpse
Within there, at his couch-foot, covered close —
Would you have pored upon it? Why persist
In poring now upon it? For 't is here
As much as there in the deserted house:
You cannot rid your eyes of it. For me,

Now he is dead I hate him worse: I hate . . .
Dare you stay here? I would go back and hold
His two dead hands, and say, " I hate you worse,
Luca, than " . . .
 Seb.   Off, off — take your hands off mine,
'T is the hot evening — off! oh, morning is it?
 Otti. There's one thing must be done; you know what thing.
Come in and help to carry. We may sleep
Anywhere in the whole wide house to-night.
 Seb. What would come, think you, if we let him lie
Just as he is? Let him lie there until
The angels take him! He is turned by this
Off from his face beside, as you will see.
 Otti. This dusty pane might serve for looking-glass.
Three, four — four gray hairs! Is it so you said
A plait of hair should wave across my neck?
No — this way.
 Seb.   Ottima, I would give your neck,
Each splendid shoulder, both those breasts of yours,
That this were undone! Killing! Kill the world,
So Luca lives again! — ay, lives to sputter
His fulsome dotage on you — yes, and feign
Surprise that I return at eve to sup,
When all the morning I was loitering here —
Bid me dispatch my business and begone.
I would . . .
 Otti. See!
 Seb.   No, I 'll finish. Do you think
I fear to speak the bare truth once for all?
All we have talked of, is, at bottom, fine
To suffer; there's a recompense in guilt;
One must be venturous and fortunate:
What is one young for, else? In age we 'll sigh
O'er the wild reckless wicked days flown over;
Still, we have lived: the vice was in its place.
But to have eaten Luca's bread, have worn
His clothes, have felt his money swell my purse —
Do lovers in romances sin that way?
Why, I was starving when I used to call
And teach you music, starving while you plucked me
These flowers to smell!
 Otti.   My poor lost friend!
 Seb.   He gave me
Life, nothing less: what if he did reproach
My perfidy, and threaten, and do more —
Had he no right? What was to wonder at?

He sat by us at table quietly:
Why must you lean across till our cheeks touched?
Could he do less than make pretence to strike?
'T is not the crime's sake — I'd commit ten crimes
Greater, to have this crime wiped out, undone!
And you — O how feel you? Feel you for me?
   Otti. Well then, I love you better now than ever,
And best (look at me while I speak to you) —
Best for the crime; nor do I grieve, in truth,
This mask, this simulated ignorance,
This affectation of simplicity,
Falls off our crime; this naked crime of ours
May not now be looked over: look it down!
Great? let it be great; but the joys it brought,
Pay they or no its price? Come: they or it!
Speak not! The past, would you give up the past
Such as it is, pleasure and crime together?
Give up that noon I owned my love for you?
The garden's silence: even the single bee
Persisting in his toil, suddenly stopped,
And where he hid you only could surmise
By some campanula chalice set a-swing.
Who stammered — "Yes, I love you?"
   Seb.   And I drew
Back; put far back your face with both my hands
Lest you should grow too full of me — your face
So seemed athirst for my whole soul and body!
   Otti. And when I ventured to receive you here,
Made you steal hither in the mornings —
   Seb.   When
I used to look up 'neath the shrub-house here,
Till the red fire on its glazed windows spread
To a yellow haze?
   Otti.   Ah — my sign was, the sun
Inflamed the sere side of yon chestnut-tree
Nipped by the first frost.
   Seb.   You would always laugh
At my wet boots: I had to stride through grass
Over my ankles.
   Otti.   Then our crowning night!
   Seb. The July night?
   Otti.   The day of it too, Sebald!
When heaven's pillars seemed o'erbowed with heat,
Its black-blue canopy suffered descend
Close on us both, to weigh down each to each,
And smother up all life except our life.
So lay we till the storm came.

Seb. How it came!
Otti. Buried in woods we lay, you recollect;
Swift ran the searching tempest overhead;
And ever and anon some bright white shaft
Burned through the pine-tree roof, here burned and there,
As if God's messenger through the close wood screen
Plunged and replunged his weapon at a venture,
Feeling for guilty thee and me: then broke
The thunder like a whole sea overhead —
Seb. Yes!
Otti. — While I stretched myself upon you, hands
To hands, my mouth to your hot mouth, and shook
All my locks loose, and covered you with them —
You, Sebald, the same you!
Seb. Slower, Ottima!
Otti. And as we lay —
Seb. Less vehemently! Love me!
Forgive me! Take not words, mere words, to heart!
Your breath is worse than wine. Breathe slow, speak slow!
Do not lean on me!
Otti. Sebald, as we lay,
Rising and falling only with our pants,
Who said, "Let death come now! 'T is right to die!
Right to be punished! Nought completes such bliss
But woe!" Who said that?
Seb. How did we ever rise?
Was 't that we slept? Why did it end?
Otti. I felt you
Taper into a point the ruffled ends
Of my loose locks 'twixt both your humid lips.
My hair is fallen now: knot it again!
Seb. I kiss you now, dear Ottima, now and now!
This way? Will you forgive me — be once more
My great queen?
Otti. Bind it thrice about my brow;
Crown me your queen, your spirit's arbitress,
Magnificent in sin. Say that!
Seb. I crown you
My great white queen, my spirit's arbitress,
Magnificent . . .

> [*From without is heard the voice of* PIPPA *singing* —
>
> *The year's at the spring*
> *And day 's at the morn;*
> *Morning 's at seven;*
> *The hillside 's dew-pearled;*

The lark's on the wing;
The snail's on the thorn:
God's in his heaven —
All's right with the world!

[PIPPA *passes.*

Seb. God's in his heaven! Do you hear that? Who spoke? You, you spoke!
    Otti. Oh— that little ragged girl!
She must have rested on the step: we give them
But this one holiday the whole year round.
Did you ever see our silk-mills — their inside?
There are ten silk-mills now belong to you.
She stoops to pick my double heartsease . . . Sh!
She does not hear: call you out louder!
    Seb. Leave me!
Go, get your clothes on — dress those shoulders!
    Otti. Sebald?
Seb. Wipe off that paint! I hate you.
    Otti. Miserable!
    Seb. My God, and she is emptied of it now!
Outright now! — how miraculously gone
All of the grace — had she not strange grace once?
Why, the blank cheek hangs listless as it likes,
No purpose holds the features up together,
Only the cloven brow and puckered chin
Stay in their places: and the very hair,
That seemed to have a sort of life in it,
Drops, a dead web!
    Otti. Speak to me — not of me!
    Seb. — That round great full-orbed face, where not an angle
Broke the delicious indolence — all broken!
    Otti. To me — not of me! Ungrateful, perjured cheat!
A coward too: but ingrate's worse than all!
Beggar — my slave — a fawning, cringing lie!
Leave me! Betray me! I can see your drift!
A lie that walks and eats and drinks!
    Seb. My God!
Those morbid olive faultless shoulder-blades —
I should have known there was no blood beneath!
    Otti. You hate me then? You hate me then?
    Seb. To think
She would succeed in her absurd attempt,
And fascinate by sinning, show herself
Superior — guilt from its excess superior
To innocence! That little peasant's voice

Has righted all again. Though I be lost,
I know which is the better, never fear,
Of vice or virtue, purity or lust,
Nature or trick! I see what I have done,
Entirely now! Oh I am proud to feel
Such torments — let the world take credit thence —
I, having done my deed, pay too its price!
I hate, hate — curse you! God's in his heaven!
 Otti.   — Me!
Me! no, no, Sebald, not yourself — kill me!
Mine is the whole crime. Do but kill me — then
Yourself — then — presently — first hear me speak!
I always meant to kill myself — wait, you!
Lean on my breast — not as a breast; don't love me
The more because you lean on me, my own
Heart's Sebald! There, there, both deaths presently!
 Seb. My brain is drowned now — quite drowned: all I feel
Is . . . is, at swift-recurring intervals,
A hurry-down within me, as of waters
Loosened to smother up some ghastly pit:
There they go — whirls from a black fiery sea!
 Otti. Not me — to him, O God, be merciful!

Talk by the way, while PIPPA *is passing from the hillside to Orcana. Foreign Students of Painting and Sculpture, from Venice, assembled opposite the house of* JULES, *a young French Statuary, at Possagno.*

 1*st Student.* Attention! My own post is beneath this window, but the pomegranate clump yonder will hide three or four of you with a little squeezing, and Schramm and his pipe must lie flat in the balcony. Four, five — who's a defaulter? We want everybody, for Jules must not be suffered to hurt his bride when the jest's found out.

 2*d Stud.* All here! Only our poet's away — never having much meant to be present, moonstrike him! The airs of that fellow, that Giovacchino! He was in violent love with himself, and had a fair prospect of thriving in his suit, so unmolested was it, — when suddenly a woman falls in love with him, too; and out of pure jealousy he takes himself off to Trieste, immortal poem and all : whereto is this prophetical epitaph appended already, as Bluphocks assures me, — " *Here a mammoth-poem lies, Fouled to death by butterflies.*" His own fault, the simpleton! Instead of cramp couplets, each like a knife in your entrails, he should write, says Bluphocks, both classically and intelligibly. — *Æsculapius, an Epic. Catalogue of the drugs:*

Hebe's plaister — One strip Cools your lip. Phœbus' emulsion — One bottle Clears your throttle. Mercury's bolus — One box Cures . . .

3d Stud. Subside, my fine fellow! If the marriage was over by ten o'clock, Jules will certainly be here in a minute with his bride.

2d Stud. Good! — only, so should the poet's muse have been universally acceptable, says Bluphocks, *et canibus nostris* . . . and Delia not better known to our literary dogs than the boy Giovacchino!

1st Stud. To the point, now. Where's Gottlieb, the newcomer? Oh, — listen, Gottlieb, to what has called down this piece of friendly vengeance on Jules, of which we now assemble to witness the winding-up. We are all agreed, all in a tale, observe, when Jules shall burst out on us in a fury by and by: I am spokesman — the verses that are to undeceive Jules bear my name of Lutwyche — but each professes himself alike insulted by this strutting stone-squarer, who came alone from Paris to Munich, and thence with a crowd of us to Venice and Possagno here, but proceeds in a day or two alone again — oh, alone indubitably! — to Rome and Florence. He, forsooth, take up his portion with these dissolute, brutalized, heartless bunglers! — so he was heard to call us all. Now, is Schramm brutalized, I should like to know? Am I heartless?

Gott. Why, somewhat heartless; for, suppose Jules a coxcomb as much as you choose, still, for this mere coxcombry, you will have brushed off — what do folks style it? — the bloom of his life. Is it too late to alter? These love-letters now, you call his — I can't laugh at them.

4th Stud. Because you never read the sham letters of our inditing which drew forth these.

Gott. His discovery of the truth will be frightful.

4th Stud. That's the joke. But you should have joined us at the beginning: there's no doubt he loves the girl — loves a model he might hire by the hour!

Gott. See here! "He has been accustomed," he writes, "to have Canova's women about him, in stone, and the world's women beside him, in flesh; these being as much below, as those above, his soul's aspiration: but now he is to have the reality." There you laugh again! I say, you wipe off the very dew of his youth.

1st Stud. Schramm! (Take the pipe out of his mouth, somebody!) Will Jules lose the bloom of his youth?

Schramm. Nothing worth keeping is ever lost in this world: look at a blossom — it drops presently, having done its service and lasted its time; but fruits succeed, and where would be the blossom's place could it continue? As well affirm that your eye is no longer in your body, because its earliest favorite, whatever it may have first loved to look on, is dead and done with — as that any affection is lost to the soul when its first object, whatever happened first to satisfy it, is superseded in due course. Keep but ever looking, whether with the body's eye or the mind's, and you will soon find something to look on! Has a man done wondering at women? — there follow men, dead and alive, to wonder at. Has he done wondering at men? — there 's God to wonder at: and the faculty of wonder may be, at the same time, old and tired enough with respect to its first object, and yet young and fresh sufficiently, so far as concerns its novel one. Thus . . .

1*st Stud.* Put Schramm's pipe into his mouth again! There, you see! Well, this Jules . . . a wretched fribble — oh, I watched his disportings at Possagno, the other day! Canova's gallery — you know: there he marches first resolvedly past great works by the dozen without vouchsafing an eye: all at once he stops full at the *Psiche-fanciulla* — cannot pass that old acquaintance without a nod of encouragement — " In your new place, beauty? Then behave yourself as well here as at Munich — I see you!" Next he posts himself deliberately before the unfinished *Pietà* for half an hour without moving, till up he starts of a sudden, and thrusts his very nose into — I say, into — the group; by which gesture you are informed that precisely the sole point he had not fully mastered in Canova's practice was a certain method of using the drill in the articulation of the knee-joint — and that, likewise, has he mastered at length! Good-bye therefore, to poor Canova — whose gallery no longer needs detain his successor Jules, the predestinated novel thinker in marble!

5*th Stud.* Tell him about the women : go on to the women!

1*st Stud.* Why, on that matter he could never be supercilious enough. How should we be other (he said) than the poor devils you see, with those debasing habits we cherish? He was not to wallow in that mire, at least: he would wait, and love only at the proper time, and meanwhile put up with the *Psiche-fanciulla*. Now, I happened to hear of a young Greek — real Greek girl at Malamocco; a true Islander, do you see, with Alciphron's "hair like sea-moss" — Schramm knows! — white and quiet as an apparition, and fourteen years old at farthest, — a daughter of Natalia, so she swears — that hag Natalia, who helps us to models at three *lire* an hour. We selected this girl for the heroine of our jest. So first, Jules received a scented letter — somebody had seen his Tydeus at the Academy, and my picture was nothing to it: a profound admirer bade him persevere —

would make herself known to him ere long. (Paolina, my little friend of the *Fenice*, transcribes divinely.) And in due time, the mysterious correspondent gave certain hints of her peculiar charms — the pale cheeks, the black hair — whatever, in short, had struck us in our Malamocco model: we retained her name, too — Phene, which is, by interpretation, sea-eagle. Now, think of Jules finding himself distinguished from the herd of us by such a creature! In his very first answer he proposed marrying his monitress: and fancy us over these letters, two, three times a day, to receive and dispatch! I concocted the main of it: relations were in the way — secrecy must be observed — in fine, would he wed her on trust, and only speak to her when they were indissolubly united? St — st — Here they come!

6th Stud. Both of them! Heaven's love, speak softly, speak within yourselves!

5th Stud. Look at the bridegroom! Half his hair in storm and half in calm, — patted down over the left temple, — like a frothy cup one blows on to cool it: and the same old blouse that he murders the marble in.

2d Stud. Not a rich vest like yours, Hannibal Scratchy! — rich, that your face may the better set it off.

6th Stud. And the bride! Yes, sure enough, our Phene! Should you have known her in her clothes? How magnificently pale!

Gott. She does not also take it for earnest, I hope?

1st Stud. Oh, Natalia's concern, that is! We settle with Natalia.

6th Stud. She does not speak — has evidently let out no word. The only thing is, will she equally remember the rest of her lesson, and repeat correctly all those verses which are to break the secret to Jules?

Gott. How he gazes on her! Pity — pity!

1st Stud. They go in: now, silence! You three, — not nearer the window, mind, than that pomegranate: just where the little girl, who a few minutes ago passed us singing, is seated!

II. NOON. *Over Orcana. The house of* JULES, *who crosses its threshold with* PHENE : *she is silent, on which* JULES *begins* —

Do not die, Phene! I am yours now, you
Are mine now; let fate reach me how she likes,
If you'll not die: so, never die! Sit here —
My work-room's single seat. I over-lean
This length of hair and lustrous front; they turn

Like an entire flower upward: eyes, lips, last
Your chin — no, last your throat turns: 't is their scent
Pulls down my face upon you. Nay, look ever
This one way till I change, grow you — I could
Change into you, beloved!
     You by me,
And I by you; this is your hand in mine,
And side by side we sit: all 's true. Thank God!
I have spoken: speak you!
      O my life to come!
My Tydeus must be carved that 's there in clay;
Yet how be carved, with you about the room?
Where must I place you? When I think that once
This room-full of rough block-work seemed my heaven
Without you! Shall I ever work again,
Get fairly into my old ways again,
Bid each conception stand while, trait by trait,
My hand transfers its lineaments to stone?
Will my mere fancies live near you, their truth —
The live truth, passing and repassing me,
Sitting beside me?
    Now speak!
       Only first,
See, all your letters! Was 't not well contrived?
Their hiding-place is Psyche's robe; she keeps
Your letters next her skin: which drops out foremost?
Ah, — this that swam down like a first moonbeam
Into my world!
    Again those eyes complete
Their melancholy survey, sweet and slow,
Of all my room holds; to return and rest
On me, with pity, yet some wonder too:
As if God bade some spirit plague a world,
And this were the one moment of surprise
And sorrow while she took her station, pausing
O'er what she sees, finds good, and must destroy!
What gaze you at? Those? Books, I told you of;
Let your first word to me rejoice them, too:
This minion, a Coluthus, writ in red,
Bistre and azure by Bessarion's scribe —
Read this line . . . no, shame — Homer's be the Greek
First breathed me from the lips of my Greek girl!
This Odyssey in coarse black vivid type
With faded yellow blossoms 'twixt page and page,
To mark great places with due gratitude;
 " *He said, and on Antinous directed*

A bitter shaft" . . . a flower blots out the rest!
Again upon your search? My statues, then!
— Ah, do not mind that — better that will look
When cast in bronze — an Almaign Kaiser, that,
Swart-green and gold, with truncheon based on hip.
This, rather, turn to! What, unrecognized?
I thought you would have seen that here you sit
As I imagined you, — Hippolyta,
Naked upon her bright Numidian horse.
Recall you this then? " Carve in bold relief " —
So you commanded — " carve, against I come,
A Greek, in Athens, as our fashion was,
Feasting, bay-filleted and thunder-free,
Who rises 'neath the lifted myrtle-branch.
' Praise those who slew Hipparchus!' cry the guests,
' While o'er thy head the singer's myrtle waves
As erst above our champion: stand up, all!' "
See, I have labored to express your thought.
Quite round, a cluster of mere hands and arms
(Thrust in all senses, all ways, from all sides,
Only consenting at the branch's end
They strain toward) serves for frame to a sole face,
The Praiser's, in the centre: who with eyes
Sightless, so bend they back to light inside
His brain where visionary forms throng up,
Sings, minding not that palpitating arch
Of hands and arms, nor the quick drip of wine
From the drenched leaves o'erhead, nor crowns cast off,
Violet and parsley crowns to trample on —
Sings, pausing as the patron-ghosts approve,
Devoutly their unconquerable hymn.
But you must say a " well " to that — say " well "!
Because you gaze — am I fantastic, sweet?
Gaze like my very life's-stuff, marble — marbly
Even to the silence! Why, before I found
The real flesh Phene, I inured myself
To see, throughout all nature, varied stuff
For better nature's birth by means of art:
With me, each substance tended to one form
Of beauty — to the human archetype.
On every side occurred suggestive germs
Of that — the tree, the flower — or take the fruit, —
Some rosy shape, continuing the peach,
Curved beewise o'er its bough; as rosy limbs,
Depending, nestled in the leaves; and just
From a cleft rose-peach the whole Dryad sprang.

But of the stuffs one can be master of,
How I divined their capabilities!
From the soft-rinded smoothening facile chalk
That yields your outline to the air's embrace,
Half-softened by a halo's pearly gloom;
Down to the crisp imperious steel, so sure
To cut its one confided thought clean out
Of all the world. But marble! — 'neath my tools
More pliable than jelly — as it were
Some clear primordial creature dug from depths
In the earth's heart, where itself breeds itself,
And whence all baser substance may be worked;
Refine it off to air, you may, — condense it
Down to the diamond; — is not metal there,
When o'er the sudden speck my chisel trips?
— Not flesh, as flake off flake I scale, approach,
Lay bare those bluish veins of blood asleep?
Lurks flame in no strange windings where, surprised
By the swift implement sent home at once,
Flushes and glowings radiate and hover
About its track?
    Phene? what — why is this?
That whitening cheek, those still dilating eyes!
Ah, you will die — I knew that you would die!

  PHENE *begins, on his having long remained silent.*

Now the end's coming; to be sure, it must
Have ended sometime! Tush, why need I speak
Their foolish speech? I cannot bring to mind
One half of it, beside; and do not care
For old Natalia now, nor any of them.
Oh, you — what are you? — if I do not try
To say the words Natalia made me learn,
To please your friends, — it is to keep myself
Where your voice lifted me, by letting that
Proceed: but can it? Even you, perhaps,
Cannot take up, now you have once let fall,
The music's life, and me along with that —
No, or you would! We'll stay, then, as we are:
Above the world.
    You creature with the eyes!
If I could look forever up to them,
As now you let me, — I believe, all sin,
All memory of wrong done, suffering borne,
Would drop down, low and lower, to the earth
Whence all that's low comes, and there touch and stay

— Never to overtake the rest of me,
All that, unspotted, reaches up to you,
Drawn by those eyes! What rises is myself,
Not me the shame and suffering; but they sink,
Are left, I rise above them. Keep me so,
Above the world!
　　　　　　　But you sink, for your eyes
Are altering — altered! Stay — " I love you, love " . . .
I could prevent it if I understood:
More of your words to me: was 't in the tone
Or the words, your power?
　　　　　　　　　　Or stay — I will repeat
Their speech, if that contents you! Only change
No more, and I shall find it presently
Far back here, in the brain yourself filled up.
Natalia threatened me that harm should follow
Unless I spoke their lesson to the end,
But harm to me, I thought she meant, not you.
Your friends, — Natalia said they were your friends
And meant you well, — because, I doubted it,
Observing (what was very strange to see)
On every face, so different in all else,
The same smile girls like me are used to bear,
But never men, men cannot stoop so low;
Yet your friends, speaking of you, used that smile,
That hateful smirk of boundless self-conceit
Which seems to take possession of the world
And make of God a tame confederate,
Purveyor to their appetites . . . you know!
But still Natalia said they were your friends,
And they assented though they smiled the more,
And all came round me, — that thin Englishman
With light lank hair seemed leader of the rest;
He held a paper — " What we want," said he,
Ending some explanation to his friends —
" Is something slow, involved and mystical,
To hold Jules long in doubt, yet take his taste
And lure him on until, at innermost
Where he seeks sweetness' soul, he may find — this!
— As in the apple's core, the noisome fly:
For insects on the rind are seen at once,
And brushed aside as soon, but this is found
Only when on the lips or loathing tongue."
And so he read what I have got by heart:
I 'll speak it, — " Do not die, love! I am yours " . . .
No — is not that, or like that, part of words

Yourself began by speaking? Strange to lose
What cost such pains to learn! Is this more right?

> *I am a painter who cannot paint;*
> *In my life, a devil rather than saint;*
> *In my brain, as poor a creature too:*
> *No end to all I cannot do!*
> *Yet do one thing at least I can —*
> *Love a man or hate a man*
> *Supremely: thus my lore began.*
> *Through the Valley of Love I went,*
> *In the lovingest spot to abide,*
> *And just on the verge where I pitched my tent,*
> *I found Hate dwelling beside.*
> *(Let the Bridegroom ask what the painter meant,*
> *Of his Bride, of the peerless Bride!)*
> *And further, I traversed Hate's grove,*
> *In the hatefullest nook to dwell;*
> *But lo, where I flung myself prone, couched Love*
> *Where the shadow threefold fell.*
> *(The meaning — those black bride's eyes above,*
> *Not a painter's lip should tell!)*

" And here," said he, " Jules probably will ask,
' You have black eyes, Love, — you are, sure enough,
My peerless bride, — then do you tell indeed
What needs some explanation! What means this?' "
— And I am to go on, without a word —

> *So, I grew wise in Love and Hate,*
> *From simple that I was of late.*
> *Once, when I loved, I would enlace*
> *Breast, eyelids, hands, feet, form and face*
> *Of her I loved, in one embrace —*
> *As if by mere love I could love immensely!*
> *Once, when I hated, I would plunge*
> *My sword, and wipe with the first lunge*
> *My foe's whole life out like a sponge —*
> *As if by mere hate I could hate intensely!*
> *But now I am wiser, know better the fashion*
> *How passion seeks aid from its opposite passion:*
> *And if I see cause to love more, hate more*
> *Than ever man loved, ever hated before —*
> *And seek in the Valley of Love*
> *The nest, or the nook in Hate's Grove,*
> *Where my soul may surely reach*

> The essence, nought less, of each,
> The Hate of all Hates, the Love
> Of all Loves, in the Valley or Grove, —
> I find them the very warders
> Each of the other's borders.
> When I love most, Love is disguised
> In Hate; and when Hate is surprised
> In Love, then I hate most: ask
> How Love smiles through Hate's iron casque,
> Hate grins through Love's rose-braided mask, —
> And how, having hated thee,
> I sought long and painfully
> To reach thy heart, nor prick
> The skin but pierce to the quick —
> Ask this, my Jules, and be answered straight
> By thy bride — how the painter Lutwyche can hate!

JULES *interposes.*

Lutwyche! Who else? But all of them, no doubt,
Hated me: they at Venice — presently
Their turn, however! You I shall not meet:
If I dreamed, saying this would wake me.
           Keep
What's here, the gold — we cannot meet again,
Consider! and the money was but meant
For two years' travel, which is over now,
All chance or hope or care or need of it.
This — and what comes from selling these, my casts
And books and medals, except . . . let them go
Together, so the produce keeps you safe
Out of Natalia's clutches! If by chance
(For all's chance here) I should survive the gang
At Venice, root out all fifteen of them,
We might meet somewhere, since the world is wide.

    [*From without is heard the voice of* PIPPA, *singing* —
> Give her but a least excuse to love me!
> When — where —
> How — can this arm establish her above me,
> If fortune fixed her as my lady there,
> There already, to eternally reprove me?
> (" Hist!" — said Kate the Queen;
> But "Oh!" — cried the maiden, binding her tresses,
> "'T is only a page that carols unseen,
> Crumbling your hounds their messes!")

*Is she wronged? — To the rescue of her honor,
My heart!
Is she poor? — What costs it to be styled a donor?
Merely an earth to cleave, a sea to part.
But that fortune should have thrust all this upon her!*
("Nay, list!" — bade Kate the Queen;
*And still cried the maiden, binding her tresses,
"'T is only a page that carols unseen,
Fitting your hawks their jesses!"*)   [PIPPA *passes.*

JULES *resumes.*

What name was that the little girl sang forth?
Kate? The Cornaro, doubtless, who renounced
The crown of Cyprus to be lady here
At Asolo, where still her memory stays,
And peasants sing how once a certain page
Pined for the grace of her so far above
His power of doing good to, "Kate the Queen —
She never could be wronged, be poor," he sighed,
"Need him to help her!"
      Yes, a bitter thing
To see our lady above all need of us;
Yet so we look ere we will love; not I,
But the world looks so. If whoever loves
Must be, in some sort, god or worshipper,
The blessing or the blest one, queen or page,
Why should we always choose the page's part?
Here is a woman with utter need of me, —
I find myself queen here, it seems!
        How strange!
Look at the woman here with the new soul,
Like my own Psyche, — fresh upon her lips
Alit, the visionary butterfly,
Waiting my word to enter and make bright,
Or flutter off and leave all blank as first.
This body had no soul before, but slept
Or stirred, was beauteous or ungainly, free
From taint or foul with stain, as outward things
Fastened their image on its passiveness:
Now, it will wake, feel, live — or die again!
Shall to produce form out of unshaped stuff
Be Art — and further, to evoke a soul
From form be nothing? This new soul is mine!

Now, to kill Lutwyche, what would that do? — save
A wretched dauber, men will hoot to death

Without me, from their hooting. Oh, to hear
God's voice plain as I heard it first, before
They broke in with their laughter! I heard them
Henceforth, not God.
     To Ancona — Greece — some isle!
I wanted silence only; there is clay
Everywhere. One may do whate'er one likes
In Art: the only thing is, to make sure
That one does like it — which takes pains to know.
 Scatter all this, my Phene — this mad dream!
Who, what is Lutwyche, what Natalia's friends,
What the whole world except our love — my own,
Own Phene? But I told you, did I not,
Ere night we travel for your land — some isle
With the sea's silence on it? Stand aside —
I do but break these paltry models up
To begin Art afresh. Meet Lutwyche, I —
And save him from my statue meeting him?
Some unsuspected isle in the far seas!
Like a god going through his world, there stands
One mountain for a moment in the dusk,
Whole brotherhoods of cedars on its brow:
And you are ever by me while I gaze
— Are in my arms as now — as now — as now!
Some unsuspected isle in the far seas!
Some unsuspected isle in far-off seas!

Talk by the way, while PIPPA *is passing from Orcana to the Turret. Two or three of the Austrian Police loitering with* BLUPHOCKS, *an English vagabond, just in view of the Turret.*

*Bluphocks.** So, that is your Pippa, the little girl who passed us singing? Well, your Bishop's Intendant's money shall be honestly earned : — now, don't make me that sour face because I bring the Bishop's name into the business; we know he can have nothing to do with such horrors: we know that he is a saint and all that a bishop should be, who is a great man beside. *Oh were but every worm a maggot, Every fly a grig, Every bough a Christmas fagot, Every tune a jig!* In fact, I have abjured all religions; but the last I inclined to was the Arminian: for I have travelled, do you see, and at Koenigsberg, Prussia Improper (so styled because there's a sort of bleak hungry sun there), you might remark over a venerable house-porch, a certain Chaldee inscription ; and brief as it is, a mere glance at it used absolutely to change the mood of every bearded

---

* "He maketh his sun to rise on the evil and on the good, and sendeth rain on the just and on the unjust."

passenger. In they turned, one and all; the young and lightsome, with no irreverent pause, the aged and decrepit, with a sensible alacrity: 't was the Grand Rabbi's abode, in short. Struck with curiosity, I lost no time in learning Syriac — (these are vowels, you dogs, — follow my stick's end in the mud — *Celarent, Darii, Ferio!*) and one morning presented myself, spelling-book in hand, a, b, c, — I picked it out letter by letter, and what was the purport of this miraculous posy? Some cherished legend of the past, you'll say — "*How Moses hocuspocussed Egypt's land with fly and locust,*" — or, "*How to Jonah sounded harshish, Get thee up and go to Tarshish,*" — or, "*How the angel meeting Balaam, Straight his ass returned a salaam.*" In no wise! "*Shackabrack — Boach — somebody or other — Isaach, Re-cei-ver, Pur-cha-ser and Ex-chan-ger of — Stolen Goods!*" So, talk to me of the religion of a bishop! I have renounced all bishops save Bishop Beveridge! — mean to live so — and die — *As some Greek dog-sage, dead and merry, Hellward bound in Charon's wherry, With food for both worlds, under and upper, Lupine-seed and Hecate's supper, And never an obolus* . . . (Though thanks to you, or this Intendant through you, or this Bishop through his Intendant — I possess a burning pocket-full of *zwanzigers*) . . . *To pay the Stygian Ferry!*

1st Pol. There is the girl, then; go and deserve them the moment you have pointed out to us Signor Luigi and his mother. [*To the rest.*] I have been noticing a house yonder, this long while: not a shutter unclosed since morning!

2d Pol. Old Luca Gaddi's, that owns the silk-mills here: he dozes by the hour, wakes up, sighs deeply, says he should like to be Prince Metternich, and then dozes again, after having bidden young Sebald, the foreigner, set his wife to playing draughts. Never molest such a household, they mean well.

Blup. Only, cannot you tell me something of this little Pippa, I must have to do with? One could make something of that name. Pippa—that is, short for Felippa—rhyming to *Panurge consults Hertrippa* —*Believest thou, King Agrippa?* Something might be done with that name.

2d Pol. Put into rhyme that your head and a ripe muskmelon would not be dear at half a *zwanziger!* Leave this fooling, and look out; the afternoon's over or nearly so.

3d Pol. Where in this passport of Signor Luigi does our Principal instruct you to watch him so narrowly? There? What's there beside a simple signature? (That English fool's busy watching.)

2d Pol. Flourish all round — "Put all possible obstacles in his way;" oblong dot at the end — "Detain him till further advices reach you;" scratch at bottom — "Send him back on pretence of some informality in the above;" ink-spirt on right-hand side (which is the case here) — "Arrest him at once." Why and wherefore, I don't concern myself, but my instructions amount to this: if Signor Luigi leaves home to-night for Vienna — well and good, the passport deposed with us for our *visa* is really for his own use, they have misinformed the Office, and he means well; but let him stay over to-night — there has been the pretence we suspect, the accounts of his corresponding and holding intelligence with the Carbonari are correct, we arrest him at once, to-morrow comes Venice, and presently Spielberg. Bluphocks makes the signal, sure enough! That is he, entering the turret with his mother, no doubt.

III. EVENING. *Inside the Turret on the Hill above Asolo.* LUIGI *and his* MOTHER *entering.*

Mother. If there blew wind, you'd hear a long sigh, easing
The utmost heaviness of music's heart.
 Luigi. Here in the archway?
 Mother.   Oh no, no — in farther,
Where the echo is made, on the ridge.
 Luigi.   Here surely, then.
How plain the tap of my heel as I leaped up!
Hark — "Lucius Junius!" The very ghost of a voice
Whose body is caught and kept by . . . what are those?
Mere withered wallflowers, waving overhead?
They seem an elvish group with thin bleached hair
That lean out of their topmost fortress — look
And listen, mountain men, to what we say,
Hand under chin of each grave earthy face.
Up and show faces all of you! — "All of you!"
That's the king dwarf with the scarlet comb; old Franz,
Come down and meet your fate? Hark — "Meet your fate!"
 Mother. Let him not meet it, my Luigi — do not
Go to his City! Putting crime aside,
Half of these ills of Italy are feigned:
Your Pellicos and writers for effect,
Write for effect.
 Luigi.   Hush! Say A writes, and B.
 Mother. These A's and B's write for effect, I say.
Then, evil is in its nature loud, while good
Is silent; you hear each petty injury,
None of his virtues; he is old beside,
Quiet and kind, and densely stupid. Why
Do A and B not kill him themselves?

Luigi. They teach
Others to kill him — me — and, if I fail,
Others to succeed; now, if A tried and failed,
I could not teach that: mine's the lesser task.
Mother, they visit night by night . . .
    Mother. — You, Luigi?
Ah, will you let me tell you what you are?
    Luigi. Why not? Oh, the one thing you fear to hint,
You may assure yourself I say and say
Ever to myself! At times — nay, even as now
We sit — I think my mind is touched, suspect
All is not sound: but is not knowing that,
What constitutes one sane or otherwise?
I know I am thus — so, all is right again.
I laugh at myself as through the town I walk,
And see men merry as if no Italy
Were suffering; then I ponder — "I am rich,
Young, healthy; why should this fact trouble me,
More than it troubles these?" But it does trouble.
No, trouble's a bad word: for as I walk
There's springing and melody and giddiness,
And old quaint turns and passages of my youth,
Dreams long forgotten, little in themselves,
Return to me — whatever may amuse me:
And earth seems in a truce with me, and heaven
Accords with me, all things suspend their strife,
The very cicala laughs "There goes he, and there!
Feast him, the time is short; he is on his way
For the world's sake: feast him this once, our friend!"
And in return for all this, I can trip
Cheerfully up the scaffold-steps. I go
This evening, mother!
    Mother. But mistrust yourself —
Mistrust the judgment you pronounce on him!
    Luigi. Oh, there I feel — am sure that I am right!
    Mother. Mistrust your judgment then, of the mere means
To this wild enterprise: say, you are right, —
How should one in your state e'er bring to pass
What would require a cool head, a cold heart,
And a calm hand? You never will escape.
    Luigi. Escape? To even wish that, would spoil all.
The dying is best part of it. Too much
Have I enjoyed these fifteen years of mine,
To leave myself excuse for longer life:
Was not life pressed down, running o'er with joy,
That I might finish with it ere my fellows

Who, sparelier feasted, make a longer stay?
I was put at the board-head, helped to all
At first; I rise up happy and content.
God must be glad one loves his world so much.
I can give news of earth to all the dead
Who ask me: — last year's sunsets, and great stars
Which had a right to come first and see ebb
The crimson wave that drifts the sun away —
Those crescent moons with notched and burning rims
That strengthened into sharp fire, and there stood,
Impatient of the azure — and that day
In March, a double rainbow stopped the storm —
May's warm slow yellow moonlit summer nights —
Gone are they, but I have them in my soul!
    Mother. (He will not go!)
    Luigi.   You smile at me? 'Tis true,
Voluptuousness, grotesqueness, ghastliness,
Environ my devotedness as quaintly
As round about some antique altar wreathe
The rose festoons, goats' horns, and oxen's skulls.
    Mother. See now: you reach the city, you must cross
His threshold — how?
    Luigi.   Oh, that's if we conspired!
Then would come pains in plenty, as you guess —
But guess not how the qualities most fit
For such an office, qualities I have,
Would little stead me, otherwise employed,
Yet prove of rarest merit only here.
Every one knows for what his excellence
Will serve, but no one ever will consider
For what his worst defect might serve: and yet
Have you not seen me range our coppice yonder
In search of a distorted ash? — I find
The wry spoilt branch a natural perfect bow.
Fancy the thrice-sage, thrice-precautioned man
Arriving at the palace on my errand!
No, no! I have a handsome dress packed up —
White satin here, to set off my black hair;
In I shall march — for you may watch your life out
Behind thick walls, make friends there to betray you;
More than one man spoils everything. March straight —
Only, no clumsy knife to fumble for,
Take the great gate, and walk (not saunter) on
Through guards and guards — I have rehearsed it all
Inside the turret here a hundred times.
Don't ask the way of whom you meet, observe!

But where they cluster thickliest is the door
Of doors; they 'll let you pass — they 'll never blab
Each to the other, he knows not the favorite,
Whence he is bound and what 's his business now.
Walk in — straight up to him; you have no knife:
Be prompt, how should he scream? Then, out with you!
Italy, Italy, my Italy!
You 're free, you 're free! Oh mother, I could dream
They got about me — Andrea from his exile,
Pier from his dungeon, Gualtier from his grave!
 Mother. Well, you shall go. Yet seems this patriotism
The easiest virtue for a selfish man
To acquire: he loves himself — and next, the world —
If he must love beyond, — but nought between:
As a short-sighted man sees nought midway
His body and the sun above. But you
Are my adored Luigi, ever obedient
To my least wish, and running o'er with love:
I could not call you cruel or unkind.
Once more, your ground for killing him! — then go!
 Luigi. Now do you try me, or make sport of me?
How first the Austrians got these provinces . . .
(If that is all, I 'll satisfy you soon)
— Never by conquest but by cunning, for
That treaty whereby . . .
 Mother.   Well?
 Luigi.   (Sure, he 's arrived,
The tell-tale cuckoo: spring 's his confidant,
And he lets out her April purposes!)
Or . . . better go at once to modern time.
He has . . . they have . . . in fact, I understand
But can't restate the matter; that 's my boast:
Others could reason it out to you, and prove
Things they have made me feel.
 Mother.   Why go to-night?
Morn 's for adventure. Jupiter is now
A morning-star. I cannot hear you, Luigi!
 Luigi. "I am the bright and morning-star," saith God —
And, "to such an one I give the morning-star."
The gift of the morning-star! Have I God's gift
Of the morning-star?
 Mother.   Chiara will love to see
That Jupiter an evening-star next June.
 Luigi. True, mother. Well for those who live through June!
Great noontides, thunder-storms, all glaring pomps
That triumph at the heels of June the god

Leading his revel through our leafy world.
Yes, Chiara will be here.
 Mother.   In June : remember,
Yourself appointed that month for her coming.
 Luigi. Was that low noise the echo?
 Mother.   The night-wind.
She must be grown — with her blue eyes upturned
As if life were one long and sweet surprise:
In June she comes.
 Luigi.   We were to see together
The Titian at Treviso. There, again!

    [*From without is heard the voice of* PIPPA, *singing —*
A king lived long ago,
In the morning of the world,
When earth was nigher heaven than now ;
And the king's locks curled,
Disparting o'er a forehead full
As the milk-white space 'twixt horn and horn
Of some sacrificial bull —
Only calm as a babe new-born:
For he was got to a sleepy mood,
So safe from all decrepitude,
Age with its bane, so sure gone by,
(The gods so loved him while he dreamed)
That, having lived thus long, there seemed
No need the king should ever die.
 Luigi. No need that sort of king should ever die!
Among the rocks his city was:
Before his palace, in the sun,
He sat to see his people pass,
And judge them every one
From its threshold of smooth stone.
They haled him many a valley-thief
Caught in the sheep-pens, robber-chief
Swarthy and shameless, beggar-cheat,
Spy-prowler, or rough pirate found
On the sea-sand left aground ;
And sometimes clung about his feet,
With bleeding lip and burning cheek,
A woman, bitterest wrong to speak
Of one with sullen thickset brows:
And sometimes from the prison-house
The angry priests a pale wretch brought,
Who through some chink had pushed and pressed
On knees and elbows, belly and breast,

Worm-like into the temple, — caught
He was by the very god,
Who ever in the darkness strode
Backward and forward, keeping watch
O'er his brazen bowls, such rogues to catch!
These, all and every one,
The king judged, sitting in the sun.
Luigi. That king should still judge sitting in the sun!
His councillors, on left and right,
Looked anxious up, — but no surprise
Disturbed the king's old smiling eyes
Where the very blue had turned to white.
'T is said, a Python scared one day
The breathless city, till he came,
With forky tongue and eyes on flame,
Where the old king sat to judge alway;
But when he saw the sweepy hair
Girt with a crown of berries rare
Which the god will hardly give to wear
To the maiden who singeth, dancing bare
In the altar-smoke by the pine-torch lights,
At his wondrous forest rites, —
Seeing this, he did not dare
Approach that threshold in the sun,
Assault the old king smiling there.
Such grace had kings when the world begun!
[PIPPA *passes.*
Luigi. And such grace have they, now that the world ends!
The Python at the city, on the throne,
And brave men, God would crown for slaying him,
Lurk in by-corners lest they fall his prey.
Are crowns yet to be won in this late time,
Which weakness makes me hesitate to reach?
'T is God's voice calls: how could I stay?   Farewell!

Talk by the way, while PIPPA *is passing from the Turret to the Bishop's Brother's House, close to the Duomo S. Maria.   Poor Girls sitting on the steps.*

1st *Girl.* There goes a swallow to Venice — the stout seafarer!
Seeing those birds fly, makes one wish for wings.
Let us all wish; you, wish first!
   2d *Girl.*   I? This sunset
To finish.
   3d *Girl.*, That old — somebody I know,
Grayer and older than my grandfather,

To give me the same treat he gave last week —
Feeding me on his knee with fig-peckers,
Lampreys and red Breganze-wine, and mumbling
The while some folly about how well I fare,
Let sit and eat my supper quietly :
Since had he not himself been late this morning
Detained at — never mind where, — had he not . . .
" Eh, baggage, had I not ! " —
  2d Girl.   How she can lie !
  3d Girl. Look there — by the nails !
  2d Girl.   What makes your fingers red ?
  3d Girl. Dipping them into wine to write bad words with
On the bright table : how he laughed !
  1st Girl.   My turn.
Spring 's come and summer 's coming. I would wear
A long loose gown, down to the feet and hands,
With plaits here, close about the throat, all day ;
And all night lie, the cool long nights, in bed ;
And have new milk to drink, apples to eat,
Deuzans and junetings, leather-coats . . . ah, I should say,
This is away in the fields — miles !
  3d Girl.   Say at once
You 'd be at home : she 'd always be at home !
Now comes the story of the farm among
The cherry orchards, and how April snowed
White blossoms on her as she ran. Why, fool,
They 've rubbed the chalk-mark out, how tall you were,
Twisted your starling's neck, broken his cage,
Made a dung-hill of your garden !
  1st Girl.   They destroy
My garden since I left them ? well — perhaps
I would have done so : so I hope they have !
A fig-tree curled out of our cottage wall ;
They called it mine, I have forgotten why,
It must have been there long ere I was born :
Cric — cric — I think I hear the wasps o'erhead
Pricking the papers strung to flutter there
And keep off birds in fruit-time — coarse long papers,
And the wasps eat them, prick them through and through.
  3d Girl. How her mouth twitches ! Where was I ? — before
She broke in with her wishes and long gowns
And wasps — would I be such a fool ! — Oh, here !
This is my way : I answer every one
Who asks me why I make so much of him —
  (If you say, " you love him " — straight " he 'll not be
    gulled ! ")

" He that seduced me when I was a girl
Thus high — had eyes like yours, or hair like yours,
Brown, red, white," — as the case may be : that pleases!
See how that beetle burnishes in the path!
There sparkles he along the dust: and, there —
Your journey to that maize-tuft spoiled at least!
    1*st Girl.* When I was young, they said if you killed one
Of those sunshiny beetles, that his friend
Up there, would shine no more that day nor next.
    2*d Girl.* When you were young? Nor are you young, that's true.
How your plump arms, that were, have dropped away!
Why, I can span them. Cecco beats you still?
No matter, so you keep your curious hair.
I wish they'd find a way to dye our hair
Your color — any lighter tint, indeed,
Than black: the men say they are sick of black,
Black eyes, black hair!
    4*th Girl.*   Sick of yours, like enough.
Do you pretend you ever tasted lampreys
And ortolans? Giovita, of the palace,
Engaged (but there's no trusting him) to slice me .
Polenta with a knife that had cut up
An ortolan.
    2*d Girl.* Why, there! Is not that Pippa
We are to talk to, under the window, — quick! —
Where the lights are?
    1*st Girl.*   That she? No, or she would sing,
For the Intendant said . . .
    3*d Girl.*   Oh, you sing first!
Then, if she listens and comes close . . . I'll tell you, —
Sing that song the young English noble made,
Who took you for the purest of the pure,
And meant to leave the world for you — what fun!
    2*d Girl.* [*sings.*]

> *You'll love me yet! — and I can tarry*
>   *Your love's protracted growing :*
> *June reared that bunch of flowers you carry,*
>   *From seeds of April's sowing.*

> *I plant a heartfull now : some seed*
>   *At least is sure to strike,*
> *And yield — what you'll not pluck indeed,*
>   *Not love, but, may be, like.*

You'll look at least on love's remains,
A grave's one violet:
Your look? — that pays a thousand pains.
What's death? You'll love me yet!

3d *Girl*. [*to* PIPPA *who approaches.*] Oh you may come closer — we shall not eat you! Why, you seem the very person that the great rich handsome Englishman has fallen so violently in love with. I'll tell you all about it.

IV. NIGHT. *Inside the Palace by the Duomo.* MONSIGNOR, *dismissing his* Attendants.

Mon. Thanks, friends, many thanks! I chiefly desire life now, that I may recompense every one of you. Most I know something of already. What, a repast prepared? *Benedicto benedicatur* . . . ugh, ugh! Where was I? Oh, as you were remarking, Ugo, the weather is mild, very unlike winter-weather: but I am a Sicilian, you know, and shiver in your Julys here. To be sure, when 't was full summer at Messina, as we priests used to cross in procession the great square on Assumption Day, you might see our thickest yellow tapers twist suddenly in two, each like a falling star, or sink down on themselves in a gore of wax. But go, my friends, but go! [*To the* Intendant.] Not you, Ugo! [*The others leave the apartment.*] I have long wanted to converse with you, Ugo.

Inten. Uguccio —

Mon. . . . 'guccio Stefani, man! of Ascoli, Fermo and Fossombruno; — what I do need instructing about, are these accounts of your administration of my poor brother's affairs. Ugh! I shall never get through a third part of your accounts: take some of these dainties before we attempt it, however. Are you bashful to that degree? For me, a crust and water suffice.

Inten. Do you choose this especial night to question me?

Mon. This night, Ugo. You have managed my late brother's affairs since the death of our elder brother: fourteen years and a month, all but three days. On the Third of December, I find him . . .

Inten. If you have so intimate an acquaintance with your brother's affairs, you will be tender of turning so far back: they will hardly bear looking into, so far back.

Mon. Ay, ay, ugh, ugh, — nothing but disappointments here below! I remark a considerable payment made to yourself on this Third of December. Talk of disappointments! There was a young fellow here, Jules, a foreign sculptor I did my utmost to advance, that the Church might be a gainer by us both: he was going on hopefully enough, and of a sudden he notifies to me some marvellous change that has happened in his notions of Art. Here's his letter, — " He never had a clearly conceived Ideal within his brain till to-day. Yet since his hand could manage a chisel, he has practised expressing other men's Ideals; and, in the very perfection he has attained to, he foresees an ultimate failure: his unconscious hand will pursue its prescribed course of old years, and will reproduce with a fatal expertness the ancient types, let the novel one appear never so palpably to his spirit. There is but one method of escape: confiding the virgin type to as chaste a hand, he will turn painter instead of sculptor, and paint, not carve, its characteristics," — strike out, I dare say, a school like Correggio: how think you, Ugo?

Inten. Is Correggio a painter?

Mon. Foolish Jules! and yet, after all, why foolish? He may — probably will, fail egregiously; but if there should arise a new painter, will it not be in some such way, by a poet now, or a musician, (spirits who have conceived and perfected an Ideal through some other channel) transferring it to this, and escaping our conventional roads by pure ignorance of them; eh, Ugo? If you have no appetite, talk at least, Ugo!

Inten. Sir, I can submit no longer to this course of yours. First, you select the group of which I formed one, — next you thin it gradually, — always retaining me with your smile, — and so do you proceed till you have fairly got me alone with you between four stone walls. And now then? Let this farce, this chatter end now: what is it you want with me?

Mon. Ugo!

Inten. From the instant you arrived, I felt your smile on me as you questioned me about this and the other article in those papers — why your brother should have given me this villa, that *podere*, — and your nod at the end meant, — what?

Mon. Possibly that I wished for no loud talk here. If once you set me coughing, Ugo! —

Inten. I have your brother's hand and seal to all I possess: now ask me what for! what service I did him — ask me!

Mon. I would better not: I should rip up old disgraces, let out my poor brother's weaknesses. By the way, Maffeo of Forli, (which, I forgot to observe, is your true name,) was the interdict ever taken off you for robbing that church at Cesena?

Inten. No, nor needs be: for when I murdered your brother's friend, Pasquale, for him . . .

Mon. Ah, he employed you in that business, did he? Well, I must let you keep, as you say, this villa and that *podere*, for fear the world should find out my relations were of so indifferent a stamp? Maffeo, my family is the oldest in Messina, and century after century have my progenitors gone on polluting themselves with every wickedness under heaven: my own father . . . rest his soul! — I have, I know, a chapel to support that it may rest: my dear two dead brothers were, — what you know tolerably well; I, the youngest, might have rivalled them in vice, if not in wealth: but from my boyhood I came out from among them, and so am not partaker of their plagues. My glory springs from another source; or if from this, by contrast only, — for I, the bishop, am the brother of your employers, Ugo. I hope to repair some of their wrong, however; so far as my brother's ill-gotten treasure reverts to me, I can stop the consequences of his crime: and not one *soldo* shall escape me. Maffeo, the sword we quiet men spurn away, you shrewd knaves pick up and commit murders with; what opportunities the virtuous forego, the villanous seize. Because, to pleasure myself apart from other considerations, my food would be millet-cake, my dress sackcloth, and my couch straw, — am I therefore to let you, the off-scouring of the earth, seduce the poor and ignorant by appropriating a pomp these will be sure to think lessens the abominations so unaccountably and exclusively associated with it? Must I let villas and *poderi* go to you, a murderer and thief, that you may beget by means of them other murderers and thieves? No — if my cough would but allow me to speak!

Inten. What am I to expect? You are going to punish me?

Mon. — Must punish you, Maffeo. I cannot afford to cast away a chance. I have whole centuries of sin to redeem, and only a month or two of life to do it in. How should I dare to say . . .

Inten. " Forgive us our trespasses "?

Mon. My friend, it is because I avow myself a very worm, sinful beyond measure, that I reject a line of conduct you would applaud perhaps. Shall I proceed, as it were, a-pardoning? — I? — who have no symptom of reason to assume that aught less than my strenuousest efforts will keep myself out of mortal sin, much less keep others out. No: I do trespass, but will not double that by allowing you to trespass.

Inten. And suppose the villas are not your brother's to give, nor yours to take? Oh, you are hasty enough just now!

Mon. 1, 2 — N° 3! — ay, can you read the substance of a letter, N° 3, I have received from Rome? It is precisely on the ground there mentioned, of the suspicion I have that a certain child of my late elder brother, who would have succeeded to his estates, was murdered in infancy by you, Maffeo, at the instigation of my late younger brother — that the Pontiff enjoins on me not merely the bringing that Maffeo to condign punishment, but the taking all pains, as guardian of the infant's heritage for the Church, to recover it parcel by parcel, howsoever, whensoever, and wheresoever. While you are now gnawing those fingers, the police are engaged in sealing up your papers, Maffeo, and the mere raising my voice brings my people from the next room to dispose of yourself. But I want you to confess quietly, and save me raising my voice. Why, man, do I not know the old story? The heir between the succeeding heir, and this heir's ruffianly instrument, and their complot's effect, and the life of fear and bribes and ominous smiling silence? Did you throttle or stab my brother's infant? Come now!

Inten. So old a story, and tell it no better? When did such an instrument ever produce such an effect? Either the child smiles in his face; or, most likely, he is not fool enough to put himself in the employer's power so thoroughly: the child is always ready to produce — as you say — howsoever, wheresoever and whensoever.

Mon. Liar!

Inten. Strike me? Ah, so might a father chastise! I shall sleep soundly to-night at least, though the gallows await me tomorrow; for what a life did I lead! Carlo of Cesena reminds me of his connivance, every time I pay his annuity; which happens commonly thrice a year. If I remonstrate, he will confess all to the good bishop — you!

Mon. I see through the trick, caitiff! I would you spoke truth for once. All shall be sifted, however—seven times sifted.

Inten. And how my absurd riches encumbered me! I dared not lay claim to above half my possessions. Let me but once unbosom myself, glorify Heaven, and die!

Sir, you are no brutal dastardly idiot like your brother I frightened to death: let us understand one another. Sir, I will make away with her for you — the girl — here close at hand; not the stupid obvious kind of killing; do not speak — know nothing of her nor of me! I see her every day — saw her this morning: of course there is to be no killing; but at Rome the courtesans perish off every three years, and I can entice her thither — have indeed begun operations already. There's a certain lusty blue-eyed florid-complexioned English knave, I and the Police employ occasionally. You assent, I perceive — no, that's not it — assent I do not say — but you will let me convert my present havings and holdings into cash, and give me time to cross the Alps? 'T is but a little black-eyed pretty singing Felippa, gay silk-winding girl. I have kept her out of harm's way up to this present; for I always intended to make your life a plague to you with her. 'T is as well settled once and forever. Some women I have procured will pass Bluphocks, my handsome scoundrel, off for somebody; and once Pippa entangled! — you conceive? Through her singing? Is it a bargain?

[*From without is heard the voice of* PIPPA, *singing* —
Overhead the tree-tops meet,
Flowers and grass spring 'neath one's feet;
There was nought above me, nought below,
My childhood had not learned to know :
For, what are the voices of birds
— Ay, and of beasts, — but words, our words,
Only so much more sweet?
The knowledge of that with my life begun.
But I had so near made out the sun,
And counted your stars, the seven and one,
Like the fingers of my hand :
Nay, I could all but understand
Wherefore through heaven the white moon ranges;
And just when out of her soft fifty changes
No unfamiliar face might overlook me —
Suddenly God took me.

[PIPPA *passes.*

Mon. [*springing up.*] My people — one and all — all — within there! Gag this villain — tie him hand and foot! He dares . . I know not half he dares — but remove him — quick! *Miserere mei, Domine!* Quick, I say!

PIPPA'S *Chamber again.* *She enters it.*

The bee with his comb,
The mouse at her dray,
The grub in his tomb,
While winter away;
But the fire-fly and hedge-shrew and lob-worm, I pray,
How fare they?
Ha, ha, thanks for your counsel, my Zanze!
" Feast upon lampreys, quaff Breganze " —
The summer of life so easy to spend,
And care for to-morrow so soon put away!
But winter hastens at summer's end,
And fire-fly, hedge-shrew, lob-worm, pray,
How fare they?
No bidding me then to . . . what did Zanze say?
" Pare your nails pearlwise, get your small feet shoes
More like " . . . (what said she?) — " and less like canoes!"
How pert that girl was! — would I be those pert

Impudent staring women! It had done me,
However, surely no such mighty hurt
To learn his name who passed that jest upon me:
No foreigner, that I can recollect,
Came, as she says, a month since, to inspect
Our silk-mills — none with blue eyes and thick rings
Of raw-silk-colored hair, at all events.
Well, if old Luca keep his good intents,
We shall do better, see what next year brings!
I may buy shoes, my Zanze, not appear
More destitute than you perhaps next year!
Bluph . . . something! I had caught the uncouth name
But for Monsignor's people's sudden clatter
Above us — bound to spoil such idle chatter
As ours: it were indeed a serious matter
If silly talk like ours should put to shame
The pious man, the man devoid of blame,
The . . . ah but — ah but, all the same,
No mere mortal has a right
To carry that exalted air;
Best people are not angels quite:
While — not the worst of people's doings scare
The devil; so there's that proud look to spare!
   Which is mere counsel to myself, mind! for
I have just been the holy Monsignor:
And I was you too, Luigi's gentle mother,
And you too, Luigi! — how that Luigi started
Out of the turret — doubtlessly departed
On some good errand or another,
For he passed just now in a traveller's trim,
And the sullen company that prowled
About his path, I noticed, scowled
As if they had lost a prey in him.
And I was Jules the sculptor's bride,
And I was Ottima beside,
And now what am I? — tired of fooling.
Day for folly, night for schooling!
New year's day is over and spent,
Ill or well, I must be content.
   Even my lily's asleep, I vow:
Wake up — here's a friend I've plucked you
Call this flower a heart's-ease now!
Something rare, let me instruct you,
Is this, with petals triply swollen,
Three times spotted, thrice the pollen;
While the leaves and parts that witness

Old proportions and their fitness,
Here remain unchanged, unmoved now;
Call this pampered thing improved now!
Suppose there's a king of the flowers
And a girl-show held in his bowers —
"Look ye, buds, this growth of ours,"
Says he, "Zanze from the Brenta,
I have made her gorge polenta
Till both cheeks are near as bouncing
As her . . . name there's no pronouncing!
See this heightened color too,
For she swilled Breganze wine
Till her nose turned deep carmine;
'T was but white when wild she grew.
And only by this Zanze's eyes
Of which we could not change the size,
The magnitude of all achieved
Otherwise, may be perceived."

Oh what a drear dark close to my poor day!
How could that red sun drop in that black cloud?
Ah Pippa, morning's rule is moved away,
Dispensed with, never more to be allowed!
Day's turn is over, now arrives the night's.
Oh lark, be day's apostle
To mavis, merle and throstle,
Bid them their betters jostle
From day and its delights!
But at night, brother howlet, over the woods,
Toll the world to thy chantry;
Sing to the bats' sleek sisterhoods
Full complines with gallantry:
Then, owls and bats,
Cowls and twats,
Monks and nuns, in a cloister's moods,
Adjourn to the oak-stump pantry!
        [*After she has begun to undress herself.*
Now, one thing I should like to really know:
How near I ever might approach all these
I only fancied being, this long day:
— Approach, I mean, so as to touch them, so
As to . . . in some way . . . move them — if you please,
Do good or evil to them some slight way.
For instance, if I wind
Silk to-morrow, my silk may bind
                [*Sitting on the bedside.*

And border Ottima's cloak's hem.
Ah me, and my important part with them,
This morning's hymn half promised when I rose!
True in some sense or other, I suppose.
                                    [*As she lies down.*
God bless me! I can pray no more to-night.
No doubt, some way or other, hymns say right.

*All service ranks the same with God —
With God, whose puppets, best and worst,
Are we; there is no last nor first.*
                                    [*She sleeps.*

KING VICTOR AND KING CHARLES

A TRAGEDY

So far as I know, this tragedy is the first artistic consequence of what Voltaire termed "a terrible event without consequences;" and although it professes to be historical, I have taken more pains to arrive at the history than most readers would thank me for particularizing: since acquainted, as I will hope them to be, with the chief circumstances of Victor's remarkable European career — nor quite ignorant of the sad and surprising facts I am about to reproduce (a tolerable account of which is to be found, for instance, in Abbé Roman's *Récit*, or even the fifth of Lord Orrery's Letters from Italy) — I cannot expect them to be versed, nor desirous of becoming so, in all the detail of the memoirs, correspondence, and relations of the time. From these only may be obtained a knowledge of the fiery and audacious temper, unscrupulous selfishness, profound dissimulation, and singular fertility in resources, of Victor — the extreme and painful sensibility, prolonged immaturity of powers, earnest good purpose and vacillating will of Charles — the noble and right woman's manliness of his wife — and the ill-considered rascality and subsequent better-advised rectitude of D'Ormea. When I say, therefore, that I cannot but believe my statement (combining as it does what appears correct in Voltaire and plausible in Condorcet) more true to person and thing than any it has hitherto been my fortune to meet with, no doubt my word will be taken, and my evidence spared as readily.

R. B.

LONDON, 1842.

PERSONS.

VICTOR AMADEUS, *First King of Sardinia.*
CHARLES EMMANUEL, *his Son, Prince of Piedmont.*
POLYXENA, *Wife of Charles.*
D'ORMEA, *Minister.*

SCENE. — *The Council Chamber of Rivoli Palace, near Turin, communicating with a Hall at the back, an Apartment to the left and another to the right of the stage.*

TIME, 1730–1.

FIRST YEAR, 1730. — KING VICTOR.

PART I.

CHARLES, POLYXENA.

Cha. You think so? Well, I do not.
Pol.   My beloved,
All must clear up; we shall be happy yet:
This cannot last forever — oh, may change
To-day or any day!

Cha. — May change? Ah yes — May change!
Pol. Endure it, then.
Cha. No doubt, a life
Like this drags on, now better and now worse.
My father may . . . may take to loving me;
And he may take D'Ormea closer yet
To counsel him; — may even cast off her
— That bad Sebastian; but he also may
. . . Or no, Polyxena, my only friend,
He may not force you from me?
Pol. Now, force me
From you! — me, close by you as if there gloomed
No Sebastians, no D'Ormeas on our path —
At Rivoli or Turin, still at hand,
Arch-counsellor, prime confidant . . . force me!
Cha. Because I felt as sure, as I feel sure
We clasp hands now, of being happy once.
Young was I, quite neglected, nor concerned
By the world's business that engrossed so much
My father and my brother: if I peered
From out my privacy, — amid the crash
And blaze of nations, domineered those two.
'T was war, peace — France our foe, now — England, friend —
In love with Spain — at feud with Austria! Well —
I wondered, laughed a moment's laugh for pride
In the chivalrous couple, then let drop
My curtain — " I am out of it," I said —
When . . .
Pol. You have told me, Charles.
Cha. Polyxena —
When suddenly, — a warm March day, just that!
Just so much sunshine as the cottage child
Basks in delighted, while the cottager
Takes off his bonnet, as he ceases work,
To catch the more of it — and it must fall
Heavily on my brother! Had you seen
Philip — the lion-featured! not like me!
Pol. I know —
Cha. And Philip's mouth yet fast to mine,
His dead cheek on my cheek, his arm still round
My neck, — they bade me rise, " for I was heir
To the Duke," they said, " the right hand of the Duke: "
Till then he was my father, not the Duke.
So . . . let me finish . . . the whole intricate
World's-business their dead boy was born to, I

Must conquer, — ay, the brilliant thing he was,
I, of a sudden must be: my faults, my follies,
— All bitter truths were told me, all at once,
To end the sooner. What I simply styled
Their overlooking me, had been contempt:
How should the Duke employ himself, forsooth,
With such an one, while lordly Philip rode
By him their Turin through? But he was punished,
And must put up with — me! 'T was sad enough
To learn my future portion and submit.
And then the wear and worry, blame on blame!
For, spring-sounds in my ears, spring-smells about,
How could I but grow dizzy in their pent
Dim palace-rooms at first? My mother's look
As they discussed my insignificance,
She and my father, and I sitting by, —
I bore; I knew how brave a son they missed;
Philip had gayly run state-papers through,
While Charles was spelling at them painfully!
But Victor was my father spite of that.
"Duke Victor's entire life has been," I said,
" Innumerable efforts to one end;
And on the point now of that end's success,
Our Ducal turning to a Kingly crown,
Where 's time to be reminded 't is his child
He spurns?" And so I suffered — scarcely suffered,
Since I had you at length!
   Pol.   To serve in place
Of monarch, minister and mistress, Charles!
   Cha. But, once that crown obtained, then was 't not like
Our lot would alter? " When he rests, takes breath,
Glances around, sees who there 's left to love —
Now that my mother 's dead, sees I am left —
Is it not like he 'll love me at the last?"
Well, Savoy turns Sardinia; the Duke 's King:
Could I — precisely then — could you expect
His harshness to redouble? These few months
Have been . . . have been . . . Polyxena, do you
And God conduct me, or I lose myself!
What would he have? What is 't they want with me?
Him with this mistress and this minister,
— You see me and you hear him; judge us both!
Pronounce what I should do, Polyxena!
   Pol. Endure, endure, beloved! Say you not
He is your father? All 's so incident
To novel sway! Beside, our life must change:

Or you 'll acquire his kingcraft, or he 'll find
Harshness a sorry way of teaching it.
I bear this — not that there 's so much to bear.
  Cha. You bear? Do not I know that you, though bound
To silence for my sake, are perishing
Piecemeal beside me? And how otherwise
When every creephole from the hideous Court
Is stopped ; the Minister to dog me, here —
The Mistress posted to entrap you, there!
And thus shall we grow old in such a life ;
Not careless, never estranged, — but old : to alter
Our life, there is so much to alter!
  Pol.   Come —
Is it agreed that we forego complaint
Even at Turin, yet complain we here
At Rivoli? 'T were wiser you announced
Our presence to the King. What's now afoot
I wonder? Not that any more 's to dread
Than every day's embarrassment : but guess
For me, why train so fast succeeded train
On the high-road, each gayer still than each!
I noticed your Archbishop's pursuivant,
The sable cloak and silver cross; such pomp
Bodes . . . what now, Charles? Can you conceive ?
  Cha.   **Not I.**
  Pol. A matter of some moment —
  Cha.   There 's our life!
Which of the group of loiterers that stare
From the lime-avenue, divines that I —
About to figure presently, he thinks,
In face of all assembled — am the one
Who knows precisely least about it?
  Pol.   Tush!
D'Ormea's contrivance!
  Cha.   Ay, how otherwise
Should the young Prince serve for the old King's foil?
— So that the simplest courtier may remark
'T were idle raising parties for a Prince
Content to linger the court's laughing-stock.
Something, 't is like, about that weary business
[*Pointing to papers he has laid down, and which* POLYXENA *examines*
— Not that I comprehend three words, of course,
After all last night's study.
  Pol.   The faint heart!
Why, as we rode and you rehearsed just now
Its substance . . . (that 's the folded speech I mean,

Concerning the Reduction of the Fiefs)
— What would you have? — I fancied while you spoke,
Some tones were just your father's.
  Cha.   Flattery!
 Pol. I fancied so: — and here lurks, sure enough,
My note upon the Spanish Claims! You've mastered
The fief-speech thoroughly: this other, mind,
Is an opinion you deliver, — stay,
Best read it slowly over once to me;
Read — there's bare time; you read it firmly — loud
— Rather loud, looking in his face, — don't sink
Your eye once — ay, thus! "If Spain claims" . . . begin
— Just as you look at me!
  Cha.   At you! Oh truly,
You have I seen, say, marshalling your troops,
Dismissing councils, or, through doors ajar,
Head sunk on hand, devoured by slow chagrins
— Then radiant, for a crown had all at once
Seemed possible again! I can behold
Him, whose least whisper ties my spirit fast,
In this sweet brow, nought could divert me from
Save objects like Sebastian's shameless lip,
Or worse, the clipped gray hair and dead white face
And dwindling eye as if it ached with guile,
D'Ormea wears . . .
   [*As he kisses her, enter from the* KING'S *apartment* D'ORMEA.
     I said he would divert
My kisses from your brow!
 D'O. [*Aside.*] Here! So, King Victor
Spoke truth for once: and who's ordained, but I
To make that memorable? Both in call,
As he declared! Were't better gnash the teeth,
Or laugh outright now?
  Cha. [*to* POL.] What's his visit for?
 D'O. [*Aside.*] I question if they even speak to me.
 Pol. [*to* CHA.] Face the man! He'll suppose you fear him
   else.
[*Aloud.*] The Marquis bears the King's command, no doubt?
 D'O. [*Aside.*] Precisely! — If I threatened him, perhaps?
Well, this at least is punishment enough!
Men used to promise punishment would come.
 Cha. Deliver the King's message, Marquis!
 D'O. [*Aside.*]   Ah —
So anxious for his fate? [*Aloud.*] A word, my Prince,
Before you see your father — just one word
Of counsel!

Cha.   Oh, your counsel certainly!
Polyxena, the Marquis counsels us!
Well, sir? Be brief, however!
    D'O.   What? You know
As much as I? — preceded me, most like,
In knowledge! So! ('T is in his eye, beside —
His voice: he knows it, and his heart's on flame
Already!) You surmise why you, myself,
Del Borgo, Spava, fifty nobles more,
Are summoned thus?
    Cha.   Is the Prince used to know,
At any time, the pleasure of the King,
Before his minister? — Polyxena,
Stay here till I conclude my task: I feel
Your presence (smile not) through the walls, and take
Fresh heart. The King's within that chamber?
    D'O. [*Passing the table whereon a paper lies, exclaims, as he glances
        at it,*   "Spain!"
    Pol. [*Aside to* CHA.] Tarry awhile: what ails the minister?
    D'O. Madam, I do not often trouble you.
The Prince loathes, and you scorn me — let that pass!
But since it touches him and you, not me,
Bid the Prince listen!
    Pol. [*to* CHA.]   Surely you will listen:
— Deceit? — Those fingers crumpling up his vest?
    Cha. Deceitful to the very fingers' ends!
    D'O. [*who has approached them, overlooks the other paper* CHARLES
        continues to hold.
My project for the Fiefs! As I supposed!
Sir, I must give you light upon those measures
— For this is mine, and that I spied of Spain,
Mine too!
    Cha.   Release me! Do you gloze on me
Who bear in the world's face (that is, the world
You make for me at Turin) your contempt?
— Your measures? — When was not a hateful task
D'Ormea's imposition? Leave my robe!
What post can I bestow, what grant concede?
Or do you take me for the King?
    D'O.   Not I!
Not yet for King, — not for, as yet, thank God,
One who in . . . shall I say a year, a month?
Ay! — shall be wretcheder than e'er was slave
In his Sardinia, — Europe's spectacle
And the world's by-word! What? The Prince aggrieved
That I excluded him our counsels? Here
        [*Touching the paper in* CHARLES's *hand.*

Accept a method of extorting gold
From Savoy's nobles, who must wring its worth
In silver first from tillers of the soil,
Whose hinds again have to contribute brass
To make up the amount: there's counsel, sir,
My counsel, one year old; and the fruit, this —
Savoy's become a mass of misery
And wrath, which one man has to meet — the King:
You're not the King! Another counsel, sir!
Spain entertains a project (here it lies)
Which, guessed, makes Austria offer that same King
Thus much to baffle Spain; he promises;
Then comes Spain, breathless lest she be forestalled,
Her offer follows; and he promises . . .
  Cha. — Promises, sir, when he has just agreed
To Austria's offer?
  D'O.   That's a counsel, Prince!
But past our foresight, Spain and Austria (choosing
To make their quarrel up between themselves
Without the intervention of a friend)
Produce both treaties, and both promises . . .
  Cha. How?
  D'O.   Prince, a counsel! And the fruit of that
Both parties covenant afresh, to fall
Together on their friend, blot out his name,
Abolish him from Europe. So, take note,
Here's Austria and here's Spain to fight against,
And what sustains the King but Savoy here,
A miserable people mad with wrongs?
You're not the King!
  Cha.   Polyxena, you said
All would clear up: all does clear up to me.
  D'O. Clear up! 'T is no such thing to envy, then?
You see the King's state in its length and breadth?
You blame me now for keeping you aloof
From counsels and the fruit of counsels? Wait
Till I explain this morning's business!
  Cha. [*Aside.*]   No —
Stoop to my father, yes, — D'Ormea, no;
— The King's son, not to the King's counsellor!
I will do something, but at least retain
The credit of my deed! [*Aloud.*] Then it is this
You now expressly come to tell me?
  D'O.   This
To tell! You apprehend me?
  Cha.   Perfectly.

Further, D'Ormea, you have shown yourself,
For the first time these many weeks and months,
Disposed to do my bidding?
  D'O.   From the heart!
 Cha. Acquaint my father, first, I wait his pleasure:
Next . . . or, I'll tell you at a fitter time.
Acquaint the King!
 D'O. [*Aside.*] If I 'scape Victor yet!
First, to prevent this stroke at me: if not, —
Then, to avenge it! [*To* CHA.] Gracious sir, I go. [*Goes.*
 Cha. God, I forbore! Which more offends, that man
Or that man's master? Is it come to this?
Have they supposed (the sharpest insult yet)
I needed e'en his intervention? No!
No — dull am I, conceded, — but so dull,
Scarcely! Their step decides me.
 Pol.   How decides?
 Cha. You would be freed D'Ormea's eye and hers?
— Could fly the court with me and live content?
So, this it is for which the knights assemble!
The whispers and the closeting of late,
The savageness and insolence of old,
— For this!
 Pol. What mean you?
 Cha.   How? You fail to catch
Their clever plot? I missed it, but could you?
These last two months of care to inculcate
How dull I am, — D'Ormea's present visit
To prove that, being dull, I might be worse
Were I a King — as wretched as now dull —
You recognize in it no winding up
Of a long plot?
 Pol. Why should there be a plot?
 Cha. The crown's secure now; I should shame the crown:
An old complaint; the point is, how to gain
My place for one, more fit in Victor's eyes,
His mistress the Sebastian's child.
 Pol.   In truth?
 Cha. They dare not quite dethrone Sardinia's Prince:
But they may descant on my dulness till
They sting me into even praying them
Grant leave to hide my head, resign my state,
And end the coil. Not see now? In a word,
They'd have me tender them myself my rights
As one incapable; — some cause for that,
Since I delayed thus long to see their drift!

I shall apprise the King he may resume
My rights this moment.
 Pol.   Pause! I dare not think
So ill of Victor.
 Cha.   Think no ill of him!
 Pol. — Nor think him, then, so shallow as to suffer
His purpose be divined thus easily.
And yet — you are the last of a great line;
There's a great heritage at stake; new days
Seemed to await this newest of the realms
Of Europe: — Charles, you must withstand this!
 Cha.   Ah —
You dare not then renounce the splendid court
For one whom all the world despises? Speak!
 Pol. My gentle husband, speak I will, and truth.
Were this as you believe, and I once sure
Your duty lay in so renouncing rule,
I could . . . could? Oh what happiness it were —
To live, my Charles, and die, alone with you!
 Cha. I grieve I asked you. To the presence, then!
By this, D'Ormea acquaints the King, no doubt,
He fears I am too simple for mere hints,
And that no less will serve than Victor's mouth
Demonstrating in council what I am.
I have not breathed, I think, these many years!
 Pol. Why, it may be! — if he desire to wed
That woman, call legitimate her child.
 Cha. You see as much? Oh, let his will have way!
You'll not repent confiding in me, love?
There's many a brighter spot in Piedmont, far,
Than Rivoli. I'll seek him: or, suppose
You hear first how I mean to speak my mind?
— Loudly and firmly both, this time, be sure!
I yet may see your Rhine-land, who can tell?
Once away, ever then away! I breathe.
 Pol. And I too breathe.
 Cha.   Come, my Polyxena!

KING VICTOR.

Part II.

Enter King Victor, *bearing the regalia on a cushion, from his apartment. He calls loudly* —

D'Ormea! — for patience fails me, treading thus
Among the obscure trains I have laid, — my knights
Safe in the hall here — in that anteroom,
My son, — D'Ormea, where? Of this, one touch —
                                 [*Laying down the crown.*
This fireball to these mute black cold trains — then
Outbreak enough!
[*Contemplating it.*] To lose all, after all!
This, glancing o'er my house for ages — shaped,
Brave meteor, like the crown of Cyprus now,
Jerusalem, Spain, England, every change
The braver, — and when I have clutched a prize
My ancestry died wan with watching for,
To lose it! — by a slip, a fault, a trick
Learnt to advantage once and not unlearned
When past the use, — " just this once more " (I thought)
" Use it with Spain and Austria happily,
And then away with trick! " An oversight
I'd have repaired thrice over, any time
These fifty years, must happen now! There's peace
At length; and I, to make the most of peace,
Ventured my project on our people here,
As needing not their help: which Europe knows,
And means, cold-blooded, to dispose herself
(Apart from plausibilities of war)
To crush the new-made King — who ne'er till now
Feared her. As Duke, I lost each foot of earth
And laughed at her: my name was left, my sword
Left, all was left! But she can take, she knows,
This crown, herself conceded . . .
                                 That's to try,
Kind Europe! My career's not closed as yet!
This boy was ever subject to my will,
Timid and tame — the fitter! D'Ormea, too —
What if the sovereign also rid himself
Of thee, his prime of parasites? — I delay!
D'Ormea!   [*As* D'Ormea *enters, the King seats himself.*
    My son, the Prince — attends he?

D'O.   Sir,
He does attend. The crown prepared! — it seems
That you persist in your resolve.
         Vic.   Who's come?
The chancellor and the chamberlain? My knights?
   D'O. The whole Annunziata.   If, my liege,
Your fortune had not tottered worse than now . . .
       Vic. Del Borgo has drawn up the schedules? mine —
My son's, too? Excellent! Only, beware
Of the least blunder, or we look but fools.
First, you read the Annulment of the Oaths;
Del Borgo follows . . . no, the Prince shall sign;
Then let Del Borgo read the Instrument:
On which, I enter.
   D'O.   Sir, this may be truth;
You, sir, may do as you affect — may break
Your engine, me, to pieces: try at least
If not a spring remain worth saving! Take
My counsel as I've counselled many times!
What if the Spaniard and the Austrian threat?
There's England, Holland, Venice — which ally
Select you?
      Vic.   Aha! Come, D'Ormea, — "truth"
Was on your lip a minute since. Allies?
I've broken faith with Venice, Holland, England
— As who knows if not you?
      D'O.   But why with me
Break faith — with one ally, your best, break faith?
     Vic. When first I stumbled on you, Marquis — 't was
At Mondovi — a little lawyer's clerk . . .
      D'O. Therefore your soul's ally! — who brought you through
Your quarrel with the Pope, at pains enough —
Who simply echoed you in these affairs —
On whom you cannot therefore visit these
Affairs' ill fortune — whom you trust to guide
You safe (yes, on my soul) through these affairs!
     Vic. I was about to notice, had you not
Prevented me, that since that great town kept
With its chicane D'Ormea's satchel stuffed
And D'Ormea's self sufficiently recluse,
He missed a sight, — my naval armament
When I burned Toulon. How the skiff exults
Upon the galliot's wave! — rises its height,
O'ertops it even; but the great wave bursts,
And hell-deep in the horrible profound
Buries itself the galliot: shall the skiff
Think to escape the sea's black trough in turn?

Apply this : you have been my minister
— Next me, above me possibly ; — sad post,
Huge care, abundant lack of peace of mind ;
Who would desiderate the eminence ?
You gave your soul to get it ; you 'd yet give
Your soul to keep it, as I mean you shall,
D'Ormea ! What if the wave ebbed with me ?
Whereas it cants you to another crest ;
I toss you to my son ; ride out your ride !
  D' O. Ah, you so much despise me ?
  Vic.   You, D'Ormea ?
Nowise : and I 'll inform you why. A king
Must in his time have many ministers,
And I 've been rash enough to part with mine
When I thought proper. Of the tribe, not one
(. . . Or wait, did Pianezze ? . . . ah, just the same !)
Not one of them, ere his remonstrance reached
The length of yours, but has assured me (commonly
Standing much as you stand, — or nearer, say,
The door to make his exit on his speech)
— I should repent of what I did. D'Ormea,
Be candid, you approached it when I bade you
Prepare the schedules ! But you stopped in time,
You have not so assured me : how should I
Despise you then ?
     Enter CHARLES.
  Vic. [*changing his tone.*] Are you instructed ? Do
My order, point by point ! About it, sir !
  D' O. You so despise me ! [*Aside.*] One last stay remains —
The boy's discretion there.
    [*To* CHARLES.] For your sake, Prince,
I pleaded, wholly in your interest,
To save you from this fate !
  Cha. [*Aside.*]   Must I be told
The Prince was supplicated for — by him ?
  Vic. [*to D' O.*] Apprise Del Borgo, Spava and the rest,
Our son attends them ; then return.
  D' O.   One word !
  Cha. [*Aside.*] A moment's pause and they would drive me hence,
I do believe !
  D' O. [*Aside.*] Let but the boy be firm !
  Vic. You disobey ?
  Cha. [*to D' O.*] You do not disobey
Me, at least ? Did you promise that or no ?
  D' O. Sir, I am yours : what would you ? Yours am I !

Cha. When I have said what I shall say, 't is like
Your face will ne'er again disgust me. Go!
Through you, as through a breast of glass, I see.
And for your conduct, from my youth till now,
Take my contempt! You might have spared me much,
Secured me somewhat, nor so harmed yourself:
That's over now. Go, ne'er to come again!
  D'O. As son, the father — father, as the son!
My wits! My wits! [*Goes.*
  Vic. [*Seated.*] And you, what meant you, pray,
Speaking thus to D'Ormea?
  Cha.   Let us not
Waste words upon D'Ormea! Those I spent
Have half unsettled what I came to say.
His presence vexes to my very soul.
  Vic. One called to manage a kingdom, Charles, needs heart
To bear up under worse annoyances
Than seems D'Ormea — to me, at least.
  Cha. [*Aside.*]   Ah, good!
He keeps me to the point! Then be it so.
[*Aloud.*] Last night, sir, brought me certain papers — these —
To be reported on, — your way of late.
Is it last night's result that you demand?
  Vic. For God's sake, what has night brought forth? Pronounce
The . . . what's your word? — result!
  Cha.   Sir, that had proved
Quite worthy of your sneer, no doubt: — a few
Lame thoughts, regard for you alone could wring,
Lame as they are, from brains like mine, believe!
As 't is, sir, I am spared both toil and sneer.
These are the papers.
  Vic.   Well, sir? I suppose
You hardly burned them. Now for your result!
  Cha. I never should have done great things of course,
But . . . oh my father, had you loved me more!
  Vic. Loved? [*Aside.*] Has D'Ormea played me false, I
    wonder?
[*Aloud.*] Why, Charles, a king's love is diffused — yourself
May overlook, perchance, your part in it.
Our monarchy is absolutest now
In Europe, or my trouble's thrown away.
I love, my mode, that subjects each and all
May have the power of loving, all and each,
Their mode: I doubt not, many have their sons
To trifle with, talk soft to, all day long:
I have that crown, this chair, D'Ormea, Charles!

Cha. 'T is well I am a subject then, not you.
Vic. [*Aside.*] D'Ormea has told him everything.
                                    [*Aloud.*] Aha,
I apprehend you: when all 's said, you take
Your private station to be prized beyond
My own, for instance?
    Cha.   — Do and ever did
So take it: 't is the method you pursue
That grieves . . .
    Vic.   These words! Let me express, my friend,
Your thoughts. You penetrate what I supposed
Secret. D'Ormea plies his trade betimes!
I purpose to resign my crown to you.
    Cha. To me?
    Vic.   Now, — in that chamber.
    Cha.   You resign
The crown to me?
    Vic.   And time enough, Charles, sure?
Confess with me, at four-and-sixty years
A crown 's a load. I covet quiet once
Before I die, and summoned you for that.
    Cha. 'T is I will speak: you ever hated me,
I bore it, — have insulted me, borne too —
Now you insult yourself; and I remember
What I believed you, what you really are,
And cannot bear it. What! My life has passed
Under your eye, tormented as you know, —
Your whole sagacities, one after one,
At leisure brought to play on me — to prove me
A fool, I thought and I submitted; now
You 'd prove . . . what would you prove me?
    Vic.   This to me?
I hardly know you!
    Cha.   Know me? Oh indeed
You do not! Wait till I complain next time
Of my simplicity! — for here 's a sage
Knows the world well, is not to be deceived,
And his experience and his Macchiavels,
D'Ormeas, teach him — what? — that I this while
Have envied him his crown! He has not smiled,
I warrant, — has not eaten, drunk, nor slept,
For I was plotting with my Princess yonder!
Who knows what we might do or might not do?
Go now, be politic, astound the world!
That sentry in the antechamber — nay,
The varlet who disposed this precious trap
                        [*Pointing to the crown.*

That was to take me — ask them if they think
Their own sons envy them their posts! — Know me!
   Vic. But you know me, it seems; so, learn, in brief,
My pleasure. This assembly is convened . . .
   Cha. Tell me, that woman put it in your head!
You were not sole contriver of the scheme,
My father!
   Vic.   Now observe me, sir! I jest
Seldom — on these points, never. Here, I say,
The knights assemble to see me concede,
And you accept, Sardinia's crown.
   Cha.   Farewell!
'T were vain to hope to change this: I can end it.
Not that I cease from being yours, when sunk
Into obscurity: I'll die for you,
But not annoy you with my presence. Sir,
Farewell! Farewell!   [*Enter* D'ORMEA.
   D'O. [*Aside.*] Ha, sure he's changed again —
Means not to fall into the cunning trap!
Then Victor, I shall yet escape you, Victor!
   Vic. [*suddenly placing the crown upon the head of* CHARLES.
D'Ormea, your King!
[*To* CHARLES.]   My son, obey me! Charles,
Your father, clearer-sighted than yourself,
Decides it must be so. 'Faith, this looks real!
My reasons after; reason upon reason
After: but now, obey me! Trust in me!
By this, you save Sardinia, you save me!
Why, the boy swoons! [*To D'O.*] Come this side!
   D'O. [*as* CHARLES *turns from him to* VICTOR.] You persist?
   Vic. Yes, I conceive the gesture's meaning. 'Faith,
He almost seems to hate you: how is that?
Be reassured, my Charles! Is't over now?
Then, Marquis, tell the new King what remains
To do! A moment's work. Del Borgo reads
The Act of Abdication out, you sign it,
Then I sign; after that, come back to me.
   D'O. Sir, for the last time, pause!
   Vic.   Five minutes longer
I am your sovereign, Marquis. Hesitate —
And I'll so turn those minutes to account
That . . . Ay, you recollect me! [*Aside.*] Could I bring
My foolish mind to undergo the reading
That Act of Abdication!
                [*As* CHARLES *motions* D'ORMEA *to precede him.*
                Thanks, dear Charles!
                      [CHARLES *and* D'ORMEA *retire.*

Vic. A novel feature in the boy, — indeed
Just what I feared he wanted most. Quite right,
This earnest tone : your truth, now for effect !
It answers every purpose : with that look,
That voice, — I hear him : " I began no treaty,"
(He speaks to Spain,) " nor ever dreamed of this
You show me ; this I from my soul regret ;
But if my father signed it, bid not me
Dishonor him — who gave me all, beside : "
And, " true," says Spain, " 't were harsh to visit that
Upon the Prince." Then come the nobles trooping :
" I grieve at these exactions — I had cut
This hand off ere impose them ; but shall I
Undo my father's deed ? " — and they confer :
" Doubtless he was no party, after all ;
Give the Prince time ! "
      Ay, give us time, but time !
Only, he must not, when the dark day comes,
Refer our friends to me and frustrate all.
We 'll have no child's play, no desponding fits,
No Charles at each cross turn entreating Victor
To take his crown again. Guard against that !
    Enter D'ORMEA.
Long live King Charles !
      No — Charles's counsellor !
Well, is it over, Marquis ? Did I jest ?
 D'O. " King Charles ! " What then may you be ?
 Vic.   Anything !
A country gentleman that, cured of bustle,
Now beats a quick retreat toward Chambery,
Would hunt and hawk and leave you noisy folk
To drive your trade without him. I 'm Count Remont —
Count Tende — any little place's Count !
 D'O. Then Victor, Captain against Catinat
At Staffarde, where the French beat you ; and Duke
At Turin, where you beat the French ; King late
Of Savoy, Piedmont, Montferrat, Sardinia,
— Now, " any little place's Count " —
 Vic.   Proceed !
 D'O. Breaker of vows to God, who crowned you first ;
Breaker of vows to man, who kept you since ;
Most profligate to me who outraged God
And man to serve you, and am made pay crimes
I was but privy to, by passing thus
To your imbecile son — who, well you know,
Must — (when the people here, and nations there,

Clamor for you the main delinquent, slipped
From King to — " Count of any little place ")
Must needs surrender me, all in his reach, —
I, sir, forgive you : for I see the end —
See you on your return — (you will return) —
To him you trust, a moment . . .
  Vic.   Trust him? How?
My poor man, merely a prime-minister,
Make me know where my trust errs!
  D'O.   In his fear,
His love, his — but discover for yourself
What you are weakest, trusting in!
  Vic.   Aha,
D'Ormea, not a shrewder scheme than this
In your repertory? You know old Victor —
Vain, choleric, inconstant, rash — (I 've heard
Talkers who little thought the King so close) —
Felicitous now, were 't not, to provoke him
To clean forget, one minute afterward,
His solemn act, and call the nobles back
And pray them give again the very power
He has abjured ? — for the dear sake of what?
Vengeance on you, D'Ormea ! No : such am I,
Count Tende or Count anything you please,
— Only, the same that did the things you say,
And, among other things you say not, used
Your finest fibre, meanest muscle, — you
I used, and now, since you will have it so,
Leave to your fate — mere lumber in the midst,
You and your works. Why, what on earth beside
Are you made for, you sort of ministers?
  D'O. Not left, though, to my fate ! Your witless son
Has more wit than to load himself with lumber :
He foils you that way, and I follow you.
  Vic. Stay with my son — protect the weaker side!
  D'O. Ay, to be tossed the people like a rag,
And flung by them for Spain and Austria's sport,
Abolishing the record of your part
In all this perfidy!
  Vic.   Prevent, beside,
My own return !
  D'O.   That 's half prevented now!
'T will go hard but you find a wondrous charm
In exile, to discredit me. The Alps,
Silk-mills to watch, vines asking vigilance —
Hounds open for the stag, your hawk 's a-wing —

Brave days that wait the Louis of the South,
Italy's Janus!
  Vic. So, the lawyer's clerk
Won't tell me that I shall repent!
  D'O.   You give me
Full leave to ask if you repent?
  Vic.   Whene'er
Sufficient time's elapsed for that, you judge!
      [*Shouts inside,* "KING CHARLES!"
  D'O. Do you repent?
  Vic. [*after a slight pause.*] . . . I've kept them waiting?
Yes!
Come in, complete the Abdication, sir! [*They go out.*
     Enter POLYXENA.
  Pol. A shout! The sycophants are free of Charles!
Oh is not this like Italy? No fruit
Of his or my distempered fancy, this,
But just an ordinary fact! Beside,
Here they've set forms for such proceedings; Victor
Imprisoned his own mother: he should know,
If any, how a son's to be deprived
Of a son's right. Our duty's palpable.
Ne'er was my husband for the wily king
And the unworthy subjects: be it so!
Come you safe out of them, my Charles! Our life
Grows not the broad and dazzling life, I dreamed
Might prove your lot; for strength was shut in you
None guessed but I — strength which, untrammelled once,
Had little shamed your vaunted ancestry —
Patience and self-devotion, fortitude,
Simplicity and utter truthfulness
— All which, they shout to lose!
        So, now my work
Begins — to save him from regret. Save Charles
Regret? — the noble nature! He's not made
Like these Italians: 't is a German soul.
     CHARLES *enters crowned.*
Oh, where's the King's heir? Gone: — the Crown-prince?
Gone: —
Where's Savoy? Gone! — Sardinia? Gone! But Charles
Is left! And when my Rhine-land bowers arrive,
If he looked almost handsome yester-twilight
As his gray eyes seemed widening into black
Because I praised him, then how will he look?
Farewell, you stripped and whited mulberry-trees
Bound each to each by lazy ropes of vine!

Now I'll teach you my language: I'm not forced
To speak Italian now, Charles?
[*She sees the crown.*] What is this?
Answer me — who has done this? Answer!
 Cha.   He!
I am King now.
 Pol.   Oh worst, worst, worst of all!
Tell me! What, Victor? He has made you King?
What's he then? What's to follow this? You, King?
 Cha. Have I done wrong? Yes, for you were not by!
 Pol. Tell me from first to last.
 Cha.   Hush — a new world
Brightens before me; he is moved away
— The dark form that eclipsed it, he subsides
Into a shape supporting me like you,
And I, alone, tend upward, more and more
Tend upward: I am grown Sardinia's King.
 Pol. Now stop: was not this Victor, Duke of Savoy
At ten years old?
 Cha.   He was.
 Pol.   And the Duke spent,
Since then, just four-and-fifty years in toil
To be — what?
 Cha.   King.
 Pol.   Then why unking himself?
 Cha. Those years are cause enough.
 Pol.   The only cause?
 Cha. Some new perplexities.
 Pol.   Which you can solve
Although he cannot?
 Cha.   He assures me so.
 Pol. And this he means shall last — how long?
 Cha.   How long?
Think you I fear the perils I confront?
He's praising me before the people's face —
My people!
 Pol.   Then he's changed — grown kind, the King?
Where can the trap be?
 Cha.   Heart and soul I pledge!
My father, could I guard the crown you gained,
Transmit as I received it, — all good else
Would I surrender!
 Pol.   Ah, it opens then
Before you, all you dreaded formerly?
You are rejoiced to be a king, my Charles?
 Cha. So much to dare? The better, — much to dread?

The better. I'll adventure though alone.
Triumph or die, there's Victor still to witness
Who dies or triumphs — either way, alone!
    Pol. Once I had found my share in triumph, Charles,
Or death.
    Cha.   But you are I! But you I call
To take, Heaven's proxy, vows I tendered Heaven
A moment since. I will deserve the crown!
    Pol. You will. [*Aside.*] No doubt it were a glorious thing
For any people, if a heart like his
Ruled over it. I would I saw the trap.
                  Enter VICTOR.
'T is he must show me.
    Vic.   So, the mask falls off
An old man's foolish love at last. Spare thanks!
I know you, and Polyxena I know.
Here's Charles — I am his guest now — does he bid me
Be seated? And my light-haired blue-eyed child
Must not forget the old man far away
At Chambery, who dozes while she reigns.
    Pol. Most grateful shall we now be, talking least
Of gratitude — indeed of anything
That hinders what yourself must need to say
To Charles.
    Cha.   Pray speak, sir!
    Vic.   'Faith, not much to say:
Only what shows itself, you once i' the point
Of sight. You're now the King: you'll comprehend
Much you may oft have wondered at — the shifts,
Dissimulation, wiliness I showed.
For what's our post? Here's Savoy and here's Piedmont,
Here's Montferrat — a breadth here, a space there —
To o'er-sweep all these, what's one weapon worth?
I often think of how they fought in Greece
(Or Rome, which was it? You're the scholar, Charles!)
You made a front-thrust? But if your shield too
Were not adroitly planted, some shrewd knave
Reached you behind; and him foiled, straight if thong
And handle of that shield were not cast loose,
And you enabled to outstrip the wind,
Fresh foes assailed you, either side; 'scape these,
And reach your place of refuge — e'en then, odds
If the gate opened unless breath enough
Were left in you to make its lord a speech.
Oh, you will see!
    Cha.   No: straight on shall I go,
Truth helping; win with it or die with it.

Vic. 'Faith, Charles, you 're not made Europe's fighting-man!
The barrier-guarder, if you please. You clutch
Hold and consolidate, with envious France
This side, with Austria that, the territory
I held — ay, and will hold . . . which *you* shall hold
Despite the couple! But I 've surely earned
Exemption from these weary politics,
— The privilege to prattle with my son
And daughter here, though Europe wait the while.
 Pol. Nay, sir, — at Chambery, away forever,
As soon you will be, 't is farewell we bid you:
Turn these few fleeting moments to account!
'T is just as though it were a death.
  Vic.   Indeed!
 Pol. [*Aside.*] Is the trap there?
 Cha.   Ay, call this parting — death!
The sacreder your memory becomes.
If I misrule Sardinia, how bring back
My father?
 Vic. I mean . . .
 Pol. [*who watches* VICTOR *narrowly this while.*]
        Your father does not mean
You should be ruling for your father's sake:
It is your people must concern you wholly
Instead of him. You mean this, sir? (He drops
My hand!)
 Cha. That people is now part of me.
 Vic. About the people! I took certain measures
Some short time since . . . Oh, I know well, you know
But little of my measures! These affect
The nobles; we 've resumed some grants, imposed
A tax or two: prepare yourself, in short,
For clamor on that score. Mark me: you yield
No jot of aught entrusted you!
 Pol.   No jot
You yield!
 Cha. My father, when I took the oath,
Although my eye might stray in search of yours,
I heard it, understood it, promised God
What you require. Till from this eminence
He move me, here I keep, nor shall concede
The meanest of my rights.
 Vic. [*Aside.*]   The boy 's a fool!
— Or rather, I 'm a fool: for, what 's wrong here?
To-day the sweets of reigning: let to-morrow
Be ready with its bitters.

Enter D'ORMEA.

                                  There's beside
Somewhat to press upon your notice first.
    Cha. Then why delay it for an instant, sir?
That Spanish claim perchance? And, now you speak,
— This morning, my opinion was mature,
Which, boy-like, I was bashful in producing
To one I ne'er am like to fear in future!
My thought is formed upon that Spanish claim.
    Vic. Betimes indeed. Not now, Charles! You require
A host of papers on it.
    D'O. [*coming forward.*] Here they are.
[*To* CHA.] I, sir, was minister and much beside
Of the late monarch; to say little, him
I served: on you I have, to say e'en less,
No claim. This case contains those papers: with them
I tender you my office.
    Vic. [*hastily.*]   Keep him, Charles!
There's reason for it — many reasons: you
Distrust him, nor are so far wrong there, — but
He's mixed up in this matter — he 'll desire
To quit you, for occasions known to me:
Do not accept those reasons: have him stay!
    Pol. [*Aside.*] His minister thrust on us!
    Cha. [*to* D'ORMEA.]   Sir, believe,
In justice to myself, you do not need
E'en this commending: howsoe'er might seem
My feelings toward you, as a private man,
They quit me in the vast and untried field
Of action. Though I shall myself (as late
In your own hearing I engaged to do)
Preside o'er my Sardinia, yet your help
Is necessary. Think the past forgotten
And serve me now!
    D'O.   I did not offer you
My service — would that I could serve you, sir!
As for the Spanish matter . . .
    Vic.   But dispatch
At least the dead, in my good daughter's phrase,
Before the living! Help to house me safe
Ere with D'Ormea you set the world agape!
Here is a paper — will you overlook
What I propose reserving for my needs?
I get as far from you as possible:
Here's what I reckon my expenditure.
    Cha. [*reading.*] A miserable fifty thousand crowns!

Vic. Oh, quite enough for country gentlemen!
Beside, the exchequer happens . . . but find out
All that, yourself!
    Cha. [*still reading.*] "Count Tende" — what means this?
    Vic. Me: you were but an infant when I burst
Through the defile of Tende upon France.
Had only my allies kept true to me!
No matter. Tende's, then, a name I take
Just as . . .
    D'O.   — The Marchioness Sebastian takes
The name of Spigno.
    Cha.   How, sir?
    Vic. [*to* D'ORMEA.]   Fool! All that
Was for my own detailing. [*To* CHARLES.] That anon!
    Cha. [*to* D'ORMEA.] Explain what you have said, sir!
    D'O.   I supposed
The marriage of the King to her I named,
Profoundly kept a secret these few weeks,
Was not to be one, now he's Count.
    Pol. [*Aside.*]   With us
The minister — with him the mistress!
    Cha. [*to* VICTOR.]   No —
Tell me you have not taken her — that woman —
To live with, past recall!
    Vic.   And where's the crime . . .
    Pol. [*to* CHARLES.] True, sir, this is a matter past recall
And past your cognizance. A day before,
And you had been compelled to note this — now
Why note it? The King saved his House from shame:
What the Count did, is no concern of yours.
    Cha. [*after a pause.*] The Spanish claim, D'Ormea!
    Vic.   Why, my son,
I took some ill-advised . . . one's age, in fact,
Spoils everything: though I was over-reached,
A younger brain, we'll trust, may extricate
Sardinia readily. To-morrow, D'Ormea,
Inform the King!
    D'O. [*without regarding* VICTOR, *and leisurely.*]
    Thus stands the case with Spain:
When first the Infant Carlos claimed his proper
Succession to the throne of Tuscany . . .
    Vic. I tell you, that stands over! Let that rest!
There is the policy!
    Cha. [*to* D'ORMEA.] Thus much I know,
And more — too much. The remedy?
    D'O.   Of course!
No glimpse of one.

Vic. No remedy at all!
It makes the remedy itself — time makes it.
D'O. [*to* CHARLES.] But if . . .
Vic. [*still more hastily.*] In fine, I shall take care of that:
And, with another project that I have . . .
D'O. [*turning on him.*] Oh, since Count Tende means to take again
King Victor's crown! —
Pol. [*throwing herself at* VICTOR's *feet.*] E'en now retake it, sir!
Oh, speak! We are your subjects both, once more!
Say it — a word effects it! You meant not,
Nor do mean now, to take it: but you must!
'T is in you — in your nature — and the shame 's
Not half the shame 't would grow to afterwards!
Cha. Polyxena!
Pol. A word recalls the knights —
Say it! — What 's promising and what 's the past?
Say you are still King Victor!
D'O. Better say
The Count repents, in brief! [VICTOR *rises.*
Cha. With such a crime
I have not charged you, sir!
Pol. Charles turns from me!

SECOND YEAR, 1731. — KING CHARLES.

PART I.

Enter QUEEN POLYXENA *and* D'ORMEA. — *A pause.*

Pol. And now, sir, what have you to say?
D'O. Count Tende . . .
Pol. Affirm not I betrayed you; you resolve
On uttering this strange intelligence
— Nay, post yourself to find me ere I reach
The capital, because you know King Charles
Tarries a day or two at Evian baths
Behind me: — but take warning, — here and thus
[*Seating herself in the royal seat*
I listen, if I listen — not your friend.
Explicitly the statement, if you still
Persist to urge it on me, must proceed:
I am not made for aught else.
D'O. Good! Count Tende . . .
Pol. I, who mistrust you, shall acquaint King Charles,
Who even more mistrusts you.

D'O.   Does he so?
Pol. Why should he not?
D'O.   Ay, why not?   Motives, seek
You virtuous people, motives! Say, I serve
God at the devil's bidding — will that do?
I 'm proud: our people have been pacified,
Really I know not how —
    Pol.   By truthfulness.
D'O. Exactly; that shows I had nought to do
With pacifying them. Our foreign perils
Also exceed my means to stay: but here
'T is otherwise, and my pride 's piqued. Count Tende
Completes a full year's absence: would you, madam,
Have the old monarch back, his mistress back,
His measures back? I pray you, act upon
My counsel, or they will be.
    Pol.   When?
    D'O.   Let 's think.
Home-matters settled — Victor 's coming now;
Let foreign matters settle — Victor 's here
Unless I stop him; as I will, this way.
    Pol. [*reading the papers he presents.*] If this should prove
         a plot 'twixt you and Victor?
You seek annoyances to give the pretext
For what you say you fear!
    D'O.   Oh, possibly!
I go for nothing. Only show King Charles
That thus Count Tende purposes return,
And style me his inviter, if you please!
    Pol. Half of your tale is true; most like, the Count
Seeks to return: but why stay you with us?
To aid in such emergencies.
    D'O.   Keep safe
Those papers: or, to serve me, leave no proof
I thus have counselled! when the Count returns,
And the King abdicates, 't will stead me little
To have thus counselled.
    Pol.   The King abdicate!
    D'O. He 's good, we knew long since — wise, we discover —
Firm, let us hope: — but I 'd have gone to work
With him away. Well!
    [CHARLES *without.*]   In the Council Chamber?
    D'O. All 's lost!
    Pol. Oh, surely not King Charles! He 's changed —
That 's not this year's care-burdened voice and step:
'T is last year's step, the Prince's voice!

D'O.					I know.
		Enter CHARLES — D'ORMEA *retiring a little.*
	Cha. Now wish me joy, Polyxena! Wish it me
The old way!					[*She embraces him.*
			There was too much cause for that!
But I have found myself again. What news
At Turin? Oh, if you but felt the load
I'm free of — free! I said this year would end
Or it, or me — but I am free, thank God!
	Pol. How, Charles?
	Cha.			You do not guess? The day I found
Sardinia's hideous coil, at home, abroad,
And how my father was involved in it, —
Of course, I vowed to rest and smile no more
Until I cleared his name from obloquy.
We did the people right — 't was much to gain
That point, redress our nobles' grievance, too —
But that took place here, was no crying shame:
All must be done abroad, — if I abroad
Appeased the justly-angered Powers, destroyed
The scandal, took down Victor's name at last
From a bad eminence, I then might breathe
And rest! No moment was to lose. Behold
The proud result — a Treaty, Austria, Spain
Agree to —
	D'O. [*Aside.*] I shall merely stipulate
For an experienced headsman.
	Cha.			Not a soul
Is compromised: the blotted past's a blank:
Even D'Ormea escapes unquestioned. See!
It reached me from Vienna; I remained
At Evian to dispatch the Count his news;
'T is gone to Chambery a week ago —
And here am I: do I deserve to feel
Your warm white arms around me?
	D'O. [*coming forward.*]		He knows that?
	Cha. What, in Heaven's name, means this?
	D'O.					He knows that matters
Are settled at Vienna? Not too late!
Plainly, unless you post this very hour
Some man you trust (say, me) to Chambery
And take precautions I acquaint you with,
Your father will return here.
	Cha.				Are you crazed,
D'Ormea? Here? For what? As well return
To take his crown!
	D'O.		He will return for that.

Cha. [*to* POLYXENA.] You have not listened to this man?
Pol. He spoke
About your safety — and I listened.
[*He disengages himself from her arms.*
Cha. [*to* D'ORMEA.] What
Apprised you of the Count's intentions?
D'O. Me?
His heart, sir; you may not be used to read
Such evidence however; therefore read
[*Pointing to* POLYXENA'S *papers.*
My evidence.
Cha. [*to* POLYXENA.] Oh, worthy this of you!
And of your speech I never have forgotten,
Though I professed forgetfulness; which haunts me
As if I did not know how false it was;
Which made me toil unconsciously thus long
That there might be no least occasion left
For aught of its prediction coming true!
And now, when there is left no least occasion
To instigate my father to such crime —
When I might venture to forget (I hoped)
That speech and recognize Polyxena —
Oh worthy, to revive, and tenfold worse,
That plague! D'Ormea at your ear, his slanders
Still in your hand! Silent?
Pol. As the wronged are.
Cha. And you, D'Ormea, since when have you presumed
To spy upon my father? I conceive
What that wise paper shows, and easily.
Since when?
D'O. The when and where and how belong
To me. 'T is sad work, but I deal in such.
You ofttimes serve yourself; I 'd serve you here:
Use makes me not so squeamish. In a word,
Since the first hour he went to Chambery,
Of his seven servants, five have I suborned.
Cha. You hate my father?
D'O. Oh, just as you will!
[*Looking at* POLYXENA.
A minute since, I loved him — hate him, now!
What matter? — if you ponder just one thing:
Has he that treaty? — he is setting forward
Already. Are your guards here?
Cha. Well for you
They are not! [*To* POL.] Him I knew of old, but you —
To hear that pickthank, further his designs! [*To* D'O.

Guards? — were they here, I'd bid them, for your trouble,
Arrest you.
 D'O. Guards you shall not want. I lived
The servant of your choice, not of your need.
You never greatly needed me till now
That you discard me. This is my arrest.
Again I tender you my charge — its duty
Would bid me press you read those documents.
Here, sir!   [*Offering his badge of office.*
 Cha. [*taking it.*] The papers also! Do you think
I dare not read them?
 Pol.   Read them, sir!
 Cha.   They prove,
My father, still a month within the year
Since he so solemnly consigned it me,
Means to resume his crown? They shall prove that,
Or my best dungeon . . .
 D'O.   Even say, Chambery!
'T is vacant, I surmise, by this.
 Cha.   You prove
Your words or pay their forfeit, sir. Go there!
Polyxena, one chance to rend the veil
Thickening and blackening 'twixt us two! Do say,
You'll see the falsehood of the charges proved!
Do say, at least, you wish to see them proved
False charges — my heart's love of other times!
 Pol. Ah, Charles!
 Cha. [*to* D'ORMEA.] Precede me, sir!
 D'O.   And I'm at length
A martyr for the truth! No end, they say,
Of miracles. My conscious innocence!
  [*As they go out, enter — by the middle door, at which he pauses —*
  VICTOR.
 Vic. Sure I heard voices? No. Well, I do best
To make at once for this, the heart o' the place.
The old room! Nothing changed! So near my seat,
D'Ormea? [*Pushing away the stool which is by the* KING'S
 chair.
    I want that meeting over first,
I know not why. Tush, he, D'Ormea, slow
To hearten me, the supple knave? That burst
Of spite so eased him! He'll inform me . . .
          What?
Why come I hither? All's in rough: let all
Remain rough. There's full time to draw back — nay,
There's nought to draw back from, as yet; whereas,
If reason should be, to arrest a course

Of error — reason good, to interpose
And save, as I have saved so many times,
Our House, admonish my son's giddy youth,
Relieve him of a weight that proves too much —
Now is the time, — or now, or never.
         'Faith,
This kind of step is pitiful, not due
To Charles, this stealing back — hither, because
He's from his capital! Oh Victor! Victor!
But thus it is. The age of crafty men
Is loathsome; youth contrives to carry off
Dissimulation; we may intersperse
Extenuating passages of strength,
Ardor, vivacity and wit — may turn
E'en guile into a voluntary grace:
But one's old age, when graces drop away
And leave guile the pure staple of our lives —
Ah, loathsome!
    Not so — or why pause I? Turin
Is mine to have, were I so minded, for
The asking; all the army's mine — I've witnessed
Each private fight beneath me; all the Court's
Mine too; and, best of all, D'Ormea's still
D'Ormea and mine. There's some grace clinging yet.
Had I decided on this step, ere midnight
I'd take the crown.
     No. Just this step to rise
Exhausts me. Here am I arrived: the rest
Must be done for me. Would I could sit here
And let things right themselves, the masque unmasque
Of the old King, crownless, gray hair and hot blood, —
The young King, crowned, but calm before his time,
They say, — the eager mistress with her taunts, —
And the sad earnest wife who motions me
Away — ay, there she knelt to me! E'en yet
I can return and sleep at Chambery
A dream out.
    Rather shake it off at Turin,
King Victor! Say: to Turin — yes, or no?
'T is this relentless noonday-lighted chamber,
Lighted like life but silent as the grave,
That disconcerts me. That's the change must strike.
No silence last year! Some one flung doors wide
(Those two great doors which scrutinize me now)
And out I went 'mid crowds of men — men talking,
Men watching if my lip fell or brow knit,
Men saw me safe forth, put me on my road:

That makes the misery of this return.
Oh had a battle done it! Had I dropped,
Haling some battle, three entire days old,
Hither and thither by the forehead — dropped
In Spain, in Austria, best of all, in France —
Spurned on its horns or underneath its hoofs,
When the spent monster went upon its knees
To pad and pash the prostrate wretch — I, Victor,
Sole to have stood up against France, beat down
By inches, brayed to pieces finally
In some vast unimaginable charge,
A flying hell of horse and foot and guns
Over me, and all's lost, forever lost,
There's no more Victor when the world wakes up!
Then silence, as of a raw battlefield,
Throughout the world. Then after (as whole days
After, you catch at intervals faint noise
Through the stiff crust of frozen blood) — there creeps
A rumor forth, so faint, no noise at all,
That a strange old man, with face outworn for wounds,
Is stumbling on from frontier town to town,
Begging a pittance that may help him find
His Turin out; what scorn and laughter follow
The coin you fling into his cap! And last,
Some bright morn, how men crowd about the midst
O' the market-place, where takes the old king breath
Ere with his crutch he strike the palace-gate
Wide ope!
   To Turin, yes or no — or no?
   Re-enter CHARLES *with papers.*
 Cha. Just as I thought! A miserable falsehood
Of hirelings discontented with their pay
And longing for enfranchisement! A few
Testy expressions of old age that thinks
To keep alive its dignity o'er slaves
By means that suit their natures!
  [*Tearing them.*] Thus they shake
My faith in Victor!
      [*Turning, he discovers* VICTOR.
 Vic. [*after a pause.*] Not at Evian, Charles?
What's this? Why do you run to close the doors?
No welcome for your father?
 Cha. [*Aside.*]   Not his voice!
What would I give for one imperious tone
Of the old sort! That's gone forever.
 Vic.   Must
I ask once more . . .

Cha.   No — I concede it, sir!
You are returned for . . . true, your health declines;
True, Chambery's a bleak unkindly spot;
You'd choose one fitter for your final lodge —
Veneria, or Moncaglier — ay, that's closed
And I concede it.
    Vic.   I received advices
Of the conclusion of the Spanish matter,
Dated from Evian Baths . . .
    Cha.   And you forbore
To visit me at Evian, satisfied
The work I had to do would fully task
The little wit I have, and that your presence
Would only disconcert me —
    Vic.   Charles?
    Cha.   — Me, set
Forever in a foreign course to yours,
And . . .
    Sir, this way of wile were good to catch,
But I have not the sleight of it. The truth!
Though I sink under it! What brings you here?
    Vic. Not hope of this reception, certainly,
From one who'd scarce assume a stranger mode
Of speech, did I return to bring about
Some awfullest calamity!
    Cha.   — You mean,
Did you require your crown again! Oh yes,
I should speak otherwise! But turn not that
To jesting! Sir, the truth! Your health declines?
Is aught deficient in your equipage?
Wisely you seek myself to make complaint,
And foil the malice of the world which laughs
At petty discontents; but I shall care
That not a soul knows of this visit. Speak!
    Vic. [*Aside.*] Here is the grateful much-professing son
Prepared to worship me, for whose sole sake
I think to waive my plans of public good!
[*Aloud.*] Nay, Charles, if I did seek to take once more
My crown, were so disposed to plague myself,
What would be warrant for this bitterness?
I gave it — grant I would resume it — well?
    Cha. I should say simply — leaving out the why
And how — you made me swear to keep that crown:
And as you then intended . . .
    Vic.   Fool! What way
Could I intend or not intend? As man,

With a man's will, when I say " I intend,"
I can intend up to a certain point,
No farther. I intended to preserve
The crown of Savoy and Sardinia whole :
And if events arise demonstrating
The way, I hoped should guard it, rather like
To lose it . . .
    Cha.   Keep within your sphere and mine!
It is God's province we usurp on, else.
Here, blindfold through the maze of things we walk
By a slight clue of false, true, right and wrong ;
All else is rambling and presumption. I
Have sworn to keep this kingdom : there's my truth.
    Vic. Truth, boy, is here, within my breast ; and in
Your recognition of it, truth is, too ;
And in the effect of all this tortuous dealing
With falsehood, used to carry out the truth,
— In its success, this falsehood turns, again,
Truth for the world! But you are right : these themes
Are over-subtle. I should rather say
In such a case, frankly, — it fails, my scheme :
I hoped to see you bring about, yourself,
What I must bring about. I interpose
On your behalf — with my son's good in sight —
To hold what he is nearly letting go,
Confirm his title, add a grace perhaps.
There's Sicily, for instance, — granted me
And taken back, some years since : till I give
That island with the rest, my work's half done.
For his sake, therefore, as of those he rules . . .
    Cha. Our sakes are one ; and that, you could not say,
Because my answer would present itself
Forthwith : — a year has wrought an age's change.
This people's not the people now, you once
Could benefit ; nor is my policy
Your policy.
    Vic. [*with an outburst.*] I know it! You undo
All I have done — my life of toil and care!
I left you this the absolutest rule
In Europe : do you think I sit and smile,
Bid you throw power to the populace —
See my Sardinia, that has kept apart,
Join in the mad and democratic whirl
Whereto I see all Europe haste full tide ?
England casts off her kings ; France mimics England :

This realm I hoped was safe! Yet here I talk,
When I can save it, not by force alone,
But bidding plagues, which follow sons like you,
Fasten upon my disobedient . . .
   [*Recollecting himself.*] Surely
I could say this — if minded so — my son ?
 Cha. You could not. Bitterer curses than **your curse**
Have I long since denounced upon myself
If I misused my power. In fear of these
I entered on those measures — will abide
By them : so, I should say, Count Tende . . .
 Vic.   **No!**
But no! But if, my Charles, your — more than old —
Half-foolish father urged these arguments,
And then confessed them futile, but said plainly
That he forgot his promise, found his strength
Fail him, had thought at savage Chambery
Too much of brilliant Turin, Rivoli here,
And Susa, and Veneria, and Superga —
Pined for the pleasant places he had built
When he was fortunate and young —
 Cha.   My father!
 Vic. Stay yet! — and if he said he could not die
Deprived of baubles he had put aside,
He deemed, forever — of the Crown that binds
Your brain up, whole, sound and impregnable,
Creating kingliness — the Sceptre too,
Whose mere wind, should you wave it, back would beat
Invaders — and the golden Ball which throbs
As if you grasped the palpitating heart
Indeed o' the realm, to mould as choose you may !
— If I must totter up and down the streets
My sires built, where myself have introduced
And fostered laws and letters, sciences,
The civil and the military arts !
Stay, Charles ! I see you letting me pretend
To live my former self once more — King Victor,
The venturous yet politic : they style me
Again, the Father of the Prince : friends wink
Good-humoredly at the delusion you
So sedulously guard from all rough truths
That else would break upon my dotage ! — You —
Whom now I see preventing my old shame —
I tell not, point by cruel point, my tale —
For is 't not in your breast my brow is hid ?
Is not your hand extended ? Say you not . . .

Enter D'ORMEA, *leading in* POLYXENA.

 Pol. [*advancing and withdrawing* CHARLES — *to* VICTOR.]
In this conjuncture even, he would say
(Though with a moistened eye and quivering lip)
The suppliant is my father. I must save
A great man from himself, nor see him fling
His well-earned fame away : there must not follow
Ruin so utter, a break-down of worth
So absolute : no enemy shall learn,
He thrust his child 'twixt danger and himself,
And, when that child somehow stood danger out,
Stole back with serpent wiles to ruin Charles
— Body, that's much, — and soul, that's more — and realm,
That's most of all ! No enemy shall say . . .
 D'O. Do you repent, sir ?
 Vic. [*resuming himself.*] D'Ormea ? This is well !
Worthily done, King Charles, craftily done !
Judiciously you post these, to o'erhear
The little your importunate father thrusts
Himself on you to say ! — Ah, they 'll correct
The amiable blind facility
You show in answering his peevish suit.
What can he need to sue for ? Thanks, D'Ormea !
You have fulfilled your office : but for you,
The old Count might have drawn some few more livres
To swell his income ! Had you, lady, missed
The moment, a permission might be granted
To buttress up my ruinous old pile !
But you remember properly the list
Of wise precautions I took when I gave
Nearly as much away — to reap the fruits
I should have looked for !
 Cha.   Thanks, sir : degrade me,
So you remain yourself ! Adieu !
 Vic.   I 'll not
Forget it for the future, nor presume
Next time to slight such mediators ! Nay —
Had I first moved them both to intercede,
I might secure a chamber in Moncaglier
— Who knows ?
 Cha.   Adieu !
 Vic.   You bid me this adieu
With the old spirit ?
 Cha.   Adieu !
 Vic.   Charles — Charles !
 Cha.   Adieu !
           [VICTOR *goes.*

Cha. You were mistaken, Marquis, as you hear!
'T was for another purpose the Count came.
The Count desires Moncaglier. Give the order!
   D'O. [*leisurely.*] Your minister has lost your confidence,
Asserting late, for his own purposes,
Count Tende would . . .
   Cha. [*flinging his badge back.*] Be still the minister!
And give a loose to your insulting joy ;
It irks me more thus stifled than expressed :
Loose it!
   D'O.   There 's none to loose, alas!   I see
I never am to die a martyr.
   Pol.   Charles!
   Cha. No praise, at least, Polyxena — no praise!

KING CHARLES.

PART II.

D'ORMEA seated, folding papers he has been examining.

This at the last effects it : now, King Charles
Or else King Victor — that 's a balance : but now,
D'Ormea the arch-culprit, either turn
O' the scale, — that 's sure enough. A point to solve,
My masters, moralists, whate'er your style !
When you discover why I push myself
Into a pitfall you 'd pass safely by,
Impart to me among the rest ! No matter.
Prompt are the righteous ever with their rede
To us the wrongful : lesson them this once !
For safe among the wicked are you set,
D'Ormea ! We lament life's brevity,
Yet quarter e'en the threescore years and ten,
Nor stick to call the quarter roundly " life."
D'Ormea was wicked, say, some twenty years ;
A tree so long was stunted ; afterward,
What if it grew, continued growing, till
No fellow of the forest equalled it ?
'T was a stump then ; a stump it still must be :
While forward saplings, at the outset checked,
In virtue of that first sprout keep their style
Amid the forest's green fraternity.
Thus I shoot up to surely get lopped down
And bound up for the burning. Now for it !
    Enter CHARLES *and* POLYXENA *with* Attendants.

D'O. [*rises.*] Sir, in the due discharge of this my office —
This enforced summons of yourself from Turin,
And the disclosure I am bound to make
To-night, — there must already be, I feel,
So much that wounds . . .
  Cha.   Well, sir?
  D'O.   — That I, perchance,
May utter also what, another time,
Would irk much, — it may prove less irksome now.
  Cha. What would you utter?
  D'O.   That I from my soul
Grieve at to-night's event: for you I grieve,
E'en grieve for . . .
  Cha.   Tush, another time for talk!
My kingdom is in imminent danger?
  D'O.   Let
The Count communicate with France — its King,
His grandson, will have Fleury's aid for this,
Though for no other war.
  Cha.   First for the levies:
What forces can I muster presently?
     [D'ORMEA *delivers papers which* CHARLES *inspects.*
  Cha. Good — very good. Montorio . . . how is this?
— Equips me double the old complement
Of soldiers?
  D'O. Since his land has been relieved
From double imposts, this he manages:
But under the late monarch . . .
  Cha.   Peace! I know.
Count Spava has omitted mentioning
What proxy is to head these troops of his.
  D'O. Count Spava means to head his troops himself.
Something to fight for now; " Whereas," says he,
" Under the sovereign's father " . . .
  Cha.   It would seem
That all my people love me.
  D'O.   Yes.
   [*To* POLYXENA *while* CHARLES *continues to inspect the papers.*
      A temper
Like Victor's may avail to keep a state;
He terrifies men and they fall not off;
Good to restrain: best, if restraint were all.
But, with the silent circle round him, ends
Such sway: our King's begins precisely there.
For to suggest, impel and set at work,
Is quite another function. Men may slight,

In time of peace, the King who brought them peace:
In war, — his voice, his eyes, help more than fear.
They love you, sir!
    Cha. [*to Attendants.*] Bring the regalia forth!
Quit the room! And now, Marquis, answer me!
Why should the King of France invade my realm?
    D'O. Why? Did I not acquaint your Majesty
An hour ago?
    Cha. I choose to hear again
What then I heard.
    D'O. Because, sir, as I said,
Your father is resolved to have his crown
At any risk; and, as I judge, calls in
The foreigner to aid him.
    Cha. And your reason
For saying this?
    D'O. [*Aside.*] Ay, just his father's way!
[*To* CH.] The Count wrote yesterday to your forces' Chief,
Rhebinder — made demand of help —
    Cha. To try
Rhebinder — he's of alien blood. Aught else?
    D'O. Receiving a refusal, — some hours after,
The Count called on Del Borgo to deliver
The Act of Abdication: he refusing,
Or hesitating, rather —
    Cha. What ensued?
    D'O. At midnight, only two hours since, at Turin,
He rode in person to the citadel
With one attendant, to Soccorso gate,
And bade the governor, San Remi, open —
Admit him.
    Cha. For a purpose I divine.
These three were faithful, then?
    D'O. They told it me:
And I —
    Cha. Most faithful —
    D'O. Tell it you — with this
Moreover of my own: if, an hour hence,
You have not interposed, the Count will be
O' the road to France for succor.
    Cha. Very good!
You do your duty now to me your monarch
Fully, I warrant! — have, that is, your project
For saving both of us disgrace, no doubt?
    D'O. I give my counsel, — and the only one.
A month since, I besought you to employ

Restraints which had prevented many a pang:
But now the harsher course must be pursued.
These papers, made for the emergency,
Will pain you to subscribe: this is a list
Of those suspected merely — men to watch;
This — of the few of the Count's very household
You must, however reluctantly, arrest;
While here's a method of remonstrance — sure
Not stronger than the case demands — to take
With the Count's self.
 Cha.   Deliver those three papers.
 Pol. [*while* CHARLES *inspects them — to* D'ORMEA.]
Your measures are not over-harsh, sir: France
Will hardly be deterred from her intents
By these.
 D'O. If who proposes might dispose,
I could soon satisfy you. Even these,
Hear what he'll say at my presenting!
 Cha. [*who has signed them.*] There!
About the warrants! You've my signature.
What turns you pale? I do my duty by you
In acting boldly thus on your advice.
 D'O. [*reading them separately.*] Arrest the people I sus-
  pected merely?
 Cha. Did you suspect them?
 D'O.   Doubtless: but — but — sir,
This Forquieri's governor of Turin,
And Rivarol and he have influence over
Half of the capital! Rabella, too?
Why, sir —
 Cha. Oh, leave the fear to me!
 D'O. [*still reading.*]   You bid me
Incarcerate the people on this list?
Sir —
 Cha. But you never bade arrest those men,
So close related to my father too,
On trifling grounds?
 D'O.   Oh, as for that, St. George,
President of Chambery's senators,
Is hatching treason! still —
   [*More troubled.*] Sir, Count Cumiane
Is brother to your father's wife! What's here?
Arrest the wife herself?
 Cha.   You seem to think
A venial crime this plot against me. Well?
 D'O. [*who has read the last paper.*] Wherefore am I thus
   ruined? Why not take

My life at once? This poor formality
Is, let me say, unworthy you! Prevent it
You, madam! I have served you, am prepared
For all disgraces: only, let disgrace
Be plain, be proper — proper for the world
To pass its judgment on 'twixt you and me!
Take back your warrant, I will none of it!
    Cha. Here is a man to talk of fickleness!
He stakes his life upon my father's falsehood;
I bid him . . .
    D'O.   Not you! Were he trebly false,
You do not bid me . . .
    Cha.   Is 't not written there?
I thought so: give — I 'll set it right.
    D'O.   Is it there?
Oh yes, and plain — arrest him now — drag here
Your father! And were all six times as plain,
Do you suppose I trust it?
    Cha.   Just one word!
You bring him, taken in the act of flight,
Or else your life is forfeit.
    D'O.   Ay, to Turin
I bring him, and to-morrow?
    Cha.   Here and now!
The whole thing is a lie, a hateful lie,
As I believed and as my father said.
I knew it from the first, but was compelled
To circumvent you; and the great D'Ormea,
That baffled Alberoni and tricked Coscia,
The miserable sower of such discord
'Twixt sire and son, is in the toils at last.
Oh I see! you arrive — this plan of yours,
Weak as it is, torments sufficiently
A sick old peevish man — wrings hasty speech,
An ill-considered threat from him; that 's noted;
Then out you ferret papers, his amusement
In lonely hours of lassitude — examine
The day-by-day report of your paid spies —
And back you come: all was not ripe, you find,
And, as you hope, may keep from ripening yet,
But you were in bare time! Only, 't were best
I never saw my father — these old men
Are potent in excuses: and meanwhile,
D'Ormea 's the man I cannot do without!
    Pol. Charles —
    Cha.   Ah, no question! You against me too!

You'd have me eat and drink and sleep, live, die,
With this lie coiled about me, choking me!
No, no, D'Ormea! You venture life, you say,
Upon my father's perfidy: and I
Have, on the whole, no right to disregard
The chains of testimony you thus wind
About me; though I do — do from my soul
Discredit them: still I must authorize
These measures, and I will. Perugia!
    [*Many* Officers *enter.*]   Count —
You and Solar, with all the force you have,
Stand at the Marquis' orders: what he bids,
Implicitly perform! You are to bring
A traitor here; the man that's likest one
At present, fronts me; you are at his beck
For a full hour! he undertakes to show
A fouler than himself, — but, failing that,
Return with him, and, as my father lives,
He dies this night! The clemency you blame
So oft, shall be revoked — rights exercised,
Too long abjured.
[*To* D'Ormea.]   Now, sir, about the work!
To save your king and country! Take the warrant!
    D'O. You hear the sovereign's mandate, Count Perugia?
Obey me! As your diligence, expect
Reward! All follow to Montcaglier!
    Cha. [*in great anguish.*] D'Ormea!   [D'Ormea *goes.*
He goes, lit up with that appalling smile!
                            [*To* Polyxena *after a pause.*
At least you understand all this?
    Pol.   These means
Of our defence — these measures of precaution?
    Cha. It must be the best way: I should have else
Withered beneath his scorn.
    Pol.   What would you say?
    Cha. Why, do you think I mean to keep the crown,
Polyxena?
    Pol.   You then believe the story
In spite of all — that Victor comes?
    Cha.   Believe it?
I know that he is coming — feel the strength
That has upheld me leave me at his coming!
'T was mine, and now he takes his own again.
Some kinds of strength are well enough to have;
But who's to have that strength? Let my crown go!
I meant to keep it; but I cannot — cannot!

Only, he shall not taunt me — he, the first . . .
See if he would not be the first to taunt me
With having left his kingdom at a word,
With letting it be conquered without stroke,
With . . . no — no — 't is no worse than when he left!
I 've just to bid him take it, and, that over,
We 'll fly away — fly, for I loathe this Turin,
This Rivoli, all titles loathe, all state.
We 'd best go to your country — unless God
Send I die now!
 Pol.   Charles, hear me!
 Cha.   And again
Shall you be my Polyxena — you 'll take me
Out of this woe! Yes, do speak, and keep speaking!
I would not let you speak just now, for fear
You 'd counsel me against him: but talk, now,
As we two used to talk in blessed times:
Bid me endure all his caprices; take me
From this mad post above him!
 Pol.   I believe
We are undone, but from a different cause.
All your resources, down to the least guard,
Are at D'Ormea's beck. What if, the while,
He act in concert with your father? We
Indeed were lost. This lonely Rivoli —
Where find a better place for them?
 Cha. [*pacing the room.*]   And why
Does Victor come? To undo all that 's done,
Restore the past, prevent the future! Seat
His mistress in your seat, and place in mine
. . . Oh, my own people, whom will you find there,
To ask of, to consult with, to care for,
To hold up with your hands? Whom? One that 's false —
False — from the head's crown to the foot's sole, false!
The best is, that I knew it in my heart
From the beginning, and expected this,
And hated you, Polyxena, because
You saw through him, though I too saw through him,
Saw that he meant this while he crowned me, while
He prayed for me, — nay, while he kissed my brow,
I saw —
 Pol. But if your measures take effect,
D'Ormea true to you?
 Cha.   Then worst of all!
I shall have loosed that callous wretch on him!
Well may the woman taunt him with his child —

I, eating here his bread, clothed in his clothes,
Seated upon his seat, let slip D'Ormea
To outrage him! We talk — perchance he tears
My father from his bed; the old hands feel
For one who is not, but who should be there:
He finds D'Ormea! D'Ormea too finds him!
The crowded chamber when the lights go out —
Closed doors — the horrid scuffle in the dark —
The accursed prompting of the minute! My guards!
To horse — and after, with me — and prevent!
    Pol. [*seizing his hand.*] King Charles! Pause here upon
        this strip of time
Allotted you out of eternity!
Crowns are from God: you in his name hold yours.
Your life's no least thing, were it fit your life
Should be abjured along with rule; but now,
Keep both! Your duty is to live and rule —
You, who would vulgarly look fine enough
In the world's eye, deserting your soul's charge, —
Ay, you would have men's praise, this Rivoli
Would be illumined! While, as 't is, no doubt,
Something of stain will ever rest on you;
No one will rightly know why you refused
To abdicate; they 'll talk of deeds you could
Have done, no doubt, — nor do I much expect
Future achievement will blot out the past,
Envelop it in haze — nor shall we two
Live happy any more. 'T will be, I feel,
Only in moments that the duty's seen
As palpably as now: the months, the years
Of painful indistinctness are to come,
While daily must we tread these palace-rooms
Pregnant with memories of the past: your eye
May turn to mine and find no comfort there,
Through fancies that beset me, as yourself,
Of other courses, with far other issues,
We might have taken this great night: such bear,
As I will bear! What matters happiness?
Duty! There's man's one moment: this is yours!
    [*Putting the crown on his head, and the sceptre in his hand, she places*
      him on his seat: a long pause and silence.
        Enter D'ORMEA *and* VICTOR, *with* Guards.
    Vic. At last I speak; but once — that once, to you!
'T is you I ask, not these your varletry,
Who's King of us?
    Cha. [*from his seat.*] Count Tende . . .

Vic.   What your spies
Assert I ponder in my soul, I say —
Here to your face, amid your guards! I choose
To take again the crown whose shadow I gave —
For still its potency surrounds the weak
White locks their felon hands have discomposed.
Or I'll not ask who's King, but simply, who
Withholds the crown I claim? Deliver it!
I have no friend in the wide world: nor France
Nor England cares for me: you see the sum
Of what I can avail. Deliver it!
    Cha. Take it, my father!
                            And now say in turn,
Was it done well, my father — sure not well,
To try me thus! I might have seen much cause
For keeping it — too easily seen cause!
But, from that moment, e'en more wofully
My life had pined away, than pine it will.
Already you have much to answer for.
My life to pine is nothing, — her sunk eyes
Were happy once! No doubt, my people think
I am their King still . . . but I cannot strive!
Take it!
    Vic. [*one hand on the crown* CHARLES *offers, the other on his
        neck.*] So few years give it quietly,
My son! It will drop from me. See you not?
A crown's unlike a sword to give away —
That, let a strong hand to a weak hand give!
But crowns should slip from palsied brows to heads
Young as this head: yet mine is weak enough,
E'en weaker than I knew. I seek for phrases
To vindicate my right. 'Tis of a piece!
All is alike gone by with me — who beat
Once D'Orleans in his lines — his very lines!
To have been Eugene's comrade, Louis's rival,
And now . . .
    Cha. [*putting the crown on him, to the rest.*] The King
        speaks, yet none kneels, I think!
    Vic. I am then King! As I became a King
Despite the nations, kept myself a King,
So I die King, with Kingship dying too
Around me! I have lasted Europe's time!
What wants my story of completion? Where
Must needs the damning break show? Who mistrusts
My children here — tell they of any break
'Twixt my day's sunrise and its fiery fall?

And who were by me when I died but they?
D'Ormea there!
  Cha.   What means he?
  Vic.   Ever there!
Charles — how to save your story! Mine must go!
Say — say that you refused the crown to me!
Charles, yours shall be my story! You immured
Me, say, at Rivoli. A single year
I spend without a sight of you, then die.
That will serve every purpose — tell that tale
The world!
  Cha.   Mistrust me? Help!
  Vic.   Past help, past reach!
'T is in the heart — you cannot reach the heart :
This broke mine, that I did believe, you, Charles,
Would have denied me and disgraced me.
  Pol.   Charles
Has never ceased to be your subject, sir!
He reigned at first through setting up yourself
As pattern : if he e'er seemed harsh to you,
'T was from a too intense appreciation
Of your own character : he acted you —
Ne'er for an instant did I think it real,
Nor look for any other than this end.
I hold him worlds the worse on that account;
But so it was.
  Cha. [*to* POLYX.] I love you now indeed!
[*To* VICTOR.] You never knew me!
  Vic.   Hardly till this moment,
When I seem learning many other things
Because the time for using them is past.
If 't were to do again! That's idly wished.
Truthfulness might prove policy as good
As guile. Is this my daughter's forehead? Yes:
I've made it fitter now to be a queen's
Than formerly : I've ploughed the deep lines there
Which keep too well a crown from slipping off.
No matter. Guile has made me King again.
Louis — 't was in King Victor's time : — long since,
When Louis reigned and, also, Victor reigned.
How the world talks already of us two!
God of eclipse and each discolored star,
Why do I linger then?
         Ha! Where lurks he?
D'Ormea! Nearer to your King! Now stand!
     [*Collecting his strength as* D'ORMEA *approaches.*
You lied, D'Ormea! I do not repent.   [*Dies.*

NOTES

The number of the page is given, followed immediately by the number of the line on the page. The word or passage which is interpreted is given in italics. All the passages on a page are put into one paragraph, but in case there is more than one the page number is not repeated and the number of the line is put in parenthesis.

PAULINE. 4:38, *his award;* (40) *his whom all honor;* 5:1, *poet;* (2) *sun-treader,* all refer to Shelley.

8:38, *A god wandering after beauty,* Apollo seeking Daphnis, Ovid, *Metamorphoses,* i. 554. (39) *A giant,* Atlas, as described by Ovid, *Metamorphoses,* iv. 744. (40) *an old hunter,* Peleus, at his wedding with Thetis. (41) *A high-crested chief,* Nestor, who sailed to Tenedos after Trojan war, *Odyssey,* iii. 200.

9:9, *Swift-footed,* Hermes, who carried messages of gods to Hades, whose wife was Proserpine.

10:36, *man preferred to a system* is said by Mrs. Orr to be Plato, but the editors of *Poet-Lore* think Shelley is referred to.

11:27, *Plato had the key to life* refers to his ideal state and idealistic philosophy.

12:27, *Arab birds,* pelicans, that fly all night far from land; but some think Birds of Paradise are meant.

13:30, *branch from the gold forest,* golden bough which Cumæan Sybil told Æneas he must bring to Proserpine to gain admittance to Hades, *Æneid,* vi. 136.

14:26, *that king treading the purple,* Agamemnon warned by Cassandra that Clytemnestra would take his life, in Browning's translation of Æschylus' *Agamemnon,* page 28, line 22. (31) *him sitting alone in blood,* Actæon torn to pieces by his dogs, Ovid, *Metamorphoses,* iii. (32) *the boy with white breast,* Orestes avenging the death of his father, Agamemnon, described in *Choephoræ* of Æschylus.

16:27, *Andromeda, and she is with me,* described in Ovid, *Metamorphoses,* iv. 792. Also that of a picture by Pondoro di Caravaggio, an engraving of which Browning had always before his eyes while he was writing this and his other earlier poem. Of this Sharp says in his *Life:* "It is strange that among all his father's collection of drawings and engravings nothing had such fascination for him as an engraving of a picture of Andromeda and Perseus by Caravaggio. The story of the innocent victim and the divine deliverer was one of which in his boyhood he never tired of hearing : and as he grew older the charm of its pictorial presentment had for him a deeper and more complex significance."

23:45, *the fair pale sister,* Antigone, who committed suicide to escape Creon's sentence of death by being buried alive for having interred her brother Polynices at night, Sophocles, *Antigone,* i. 760.

PARACELSUS. 32: 44, *Trithemius*, Johann, Abbot of St. Jacob, Wurzburg, 1461–1516, teacher of Paracelsus in astrology, alchemy, and magic, in which he was a special adept.

38: 14, *riveled*, wrinkled; *burgonet*, a form of helmet.

45: 18, *twine amaranth*, assertion of immortality, amaranth being with Greeks and Romans a sacred plant and emblem of immortal life, therefore worn at funerals.

46: 10, *Turk verse along a scimitar;* Turks, Arabs, and other Mohammedans adorn scimitars and other weapons with verses of *Koran*. (29) *genethliac*, calculator of horoscopes, or astrologer.

52: 15, *fire-labarum;* Constantine, founder of Constantinople, used cross as standard, called by him labarum, from *laver*, to command.

56: 24, *wyvern*, flying serpent, figured on coats of arms.

64: 17, *pansies*, Paracelsus' favorite flowers.

66: 14, *Rhasis*, Rhazes, an Arab physician of tenth century.

68: 7, *Castellanus*, Pierre Duchatel, French prelate, for whom Erasmus secured a place as corrector of press to Frobenius. (8) *Munsterus*, Thomas Münzer, taught Hebrew and theology at Basle, took part in peasants' war and was executed, 1490–1525; *Frobenius*, celebrated printer, publisher of Erasmus's works, cured by Paracelsus, 1460–1527.

70: 19, *rear-mice,* leather-winged bats. (22) *Lachen*, village on Lake Zurich.

71: 20, *sudary*, handkerchief or napkin on which face of Virgin Mary was impressed when she used it. (24) *suffumigation*, fumigation by smoke as a medical remedy, used by Hippocrates. (29) *cross-grained devil in my sword*, legend that Paracelsus had a devil or familiar spirit in his sword that he could call upon to do his bidding, described in *Hudibras*, ii. 3: —

> Bumbastus kept a devil's bird
> Shut in the pummel of his sword,
> That taught him all the cunning pranks
> Of past and future mountebanks.

Naudæus, in *History of Magic*, says of this familiar spirit, "that though the alchemists maintain that it was the secret of the philosopher's stone, yet it were more rational to believe that, if there was anything in it, it was certainly two or three doses of his laudanum, which he never went without, because he did strange things with it, and used it as a medicine to cure almost all diseases."

78: 10, *a sick wretch describes the ape*, vision seen in delirium.

79: 26, *Spain's cork-groves;* cork-oak grows in Catalonia and Valencia, provinces of eastern Spain.

81: 7, *Præclare, Optime*, Bravo! well done.

82: 40, *Aëtius*, famous Greek medical writer, died at Constantinople, 367; *Oribasius*, physician of Emperor Julian, 326–403. (41) *Serapion*, Syrian physician of Damascus, wrote two medical treatises, ninth century; *Avicenna*, Arab physician and philosopher of tenth century; *Averröes*, Moorish philosopher of thirteenth century, introduced Aristotle among Mohammedans.

83: 11, *Carolostadius*, reformer, one of Luther's earliest supporters, became Antinomian fanatic at Wittemberg and leader of iconoclasts, banished, died at Basle, 1541.

84:1, *gangs of peasants* refers to peasants' war led by Münzer.

85:26, *Johannes Oporinus*, Paracelsus' secretary for three years, chief of his followers, professor of Greek, also printer and bookseller. See page 126, Browning's note 5. *Sic itur ad astra*, such is the way to the stars, meaning that this is the way to immortality. (30) *Liechtenfels*, Canon Cornelius of Liechtenfels, who, when dying of gout, called in Paracelsus, received two small pills, and recovered, but refused to pay the bill. See Browning's note 6.

88:18, *Quid multa?* Why say more?

90:6, *cassia*, cinnamon; *sandal*, small tree that is very fragrant. (7) *labdanum*, fragrant exudation from the plants *Cystus creticus* and *Cystus ladaniferus; aloe*, fragrant resin of agalloch or lign-aloe. (8) *nard*, spikenard, fragrant oil of valerian.

92:41, *Fiat experientia corpore vili*, Let the experiment be made on a body of no value.

117:18, *Thus he dwells in all ;* Paracelsus sums up teachings of Kabbalah, which are stated in *Encyclopedia Britannica*, xiii. 812. The same ideas were entertained by the Neo-Platonists.

STRAFFORD. 130: 32, *training infant villanies ;* Wentworth used his authority in Ireland to manipulate justice to his own ends, that he might gain wealth.

137:28, *nibble at what you do*, inquiries made about the Court as to the conduct of Wentworth.

138:9, *your profit in the customs ;* in a letter to Laud, Wentworth wrote : " I have a share for a short time in these customs, which, while his majesty's revenue is then increased more than £20,000 by year, proves, nevertheless, a greater profit to me than ever I dreamed of."

139:8, *picked up the Queen's glove ;* Wentworth succeeded ill in his efforts to secure the good-will of the Queen. (12) *these insects refers* to Wentworth's dislike of the Court attendants and their gossip.

140:34, *you twice prayed so humbly ;* Wentworth asked Charles to make him an earl, and again proffered the same request in order that his enemies might be thereby refuted.

141:5, *I refused, the first ;* in fact he wrote the king asking that no other person be informed that his request had been refused.

153:19, *Squires are not the Giant's friends.* Wentworth wrote : "The army altogether unexercised, . . . the worst I ever saw. Our horse all cowardly, . . . a general disaffection to the King's service, none sensible of his dishonor. In one word, here alone to fight with all these evils without any one to help."

154:22, *you that told me first ;* here the poet draws on his imagination, making Lady Carlisle win Strafford to become the king's champion.

155:29, *showing the George*, St. George fighting the dragon, on badge of order of the Garter.

159:28, *Theobald's*, manor in Hertfordshire, built for Elizabeth.

166:11, *rufflers*, swaggerers.

183, scene ii, song of children, *O bell' andare;* this boat-song is from Ledi's "Bacco," and has been long naturalized in the joyous and delicate version of Leigh Hunt. "When the play was rehearsing,

416 NOTES

Mr. Browning gave Macready a lilt which he had composed for the children's song in Act V. His object was just to give the children a thing children would croon; but the two little professional singers, Master and Miss Walker, preferred something that should exhibit their powers more effectually, and a regular song was substituted, scarcely, it will be thought, to the improvement of the play." This lilt composed by Browning is given here: —

184: 20, *The ignoble Term . . . the Genius on his orb*, the Roman god Terminus, who presided over boundaries, Genius being the image that represented a guardian spirit. Browning wrote of these references: "Suppose the enemies of a man to have thrown down the image and replaced it by a mere Term, and you will have what I put in Strafford's head. Putting the Genius on the pedestal usurped, means — or tries to mean — substituting eventually the true notion of Strafford's endeavor and performance in the world, for what he conceives to be the ignoble and distorted conception of these by his contemporary judges."

185: 32, *his Sejanus, Richelieu and what not*, Eliot's denunciation of Buckingham, including Strafford, before Parliament, in 1629; the meaning here being that Strafford may have aimed to do for Charles what Richelieu had done for the kings of France.

SORDELLO. 193: 4, *friendless-people's friend*, Don Quixote, which work was intended by Cervantes to present the interests of the common people, and Browning undertakes the same cause. (6) *Pentapolin named o' the Naked Arm, Don Quixote*, I. iii. described by the knight when he sees two flocks of sheep: "Know, friend Sancho, that yonder army before us is commanded by the Emperor Alifanfaron, sovereign of the island of Trapoban; and the other is commanded by his enemy the king of the Garamanteans, known by the name of Pentapolin with the naked arm, because he always engages in battle with the right arm bare."

195:1, *stay — thou, spirit*, Shelley. (6) *the thunder-phrase of the Athenian*, Æschylus, who fought as a young man at Marathon, and whose powerful dramas kept alive the great Athenian traditions. (10) *Sidney*, Sir Philip Sidney. (19) the *Second Friedrich*, grandson of Barbarossa, crowned as emperor of the Holy Roman Empire, in 1220, by *Honorius*, third pope of that name. (26) *A single eye*, Sordello. (43) *Count Richard of Saint Boniface*, son of Richard of San Bonifaccio, ruler of Verona, a count of the Guelf party. (44) *Azzo, Este's Lord*, Azzo VII., Marquis of Este and Ancona, leader of Guelf party from 1215. (45) *Taurello Salinguerra*, leader of Ghibelline party in Ferrara, and its lieutenant in Italy under Ecelin, his name meaning *Bullock Sally-in-war*.

196:1, *Ecelin Romano*, Frederick's chief in northern Italy, a powerful noble, fierce, hard and oppressive, and who raised the house of the Romano to a position of grandeur and influence. (6) *Lombard League*, a union of the cities of Lombardy in opposition to the Emperor and in favor of the Pope, formed in 1175 against Barbarossa, and included Bologna, Milan, Verona, Mantua, Brescia, Turin, Padua, and other cities, to the number of fifteen. (11) *purple pavis*, a pavise or pavese, large shield covering the whole body, used when attacking a fortress; when prone its owner was helpless. That used by the Este party was purple in color. (14) *your pushing-by* refers to Este's venturesome spirit, and that he cannot accomplish what he promises; "your" meaning Este, though spoken to a third person. (17) *Duke o' the Rood ;* Azzo was a knight of the Order of the Holy Cross or Rood, and in being head of the Lombard League might become the Pope's chief supporter. (19) *the hill-cat*, Ecelin, who was little better than a pirate in his methods of warfare. (22) *the lion hunts*, Azzo, Lord of Este. (24) *like an osprey*, Salinguerra, whose mild and generous life was in strange contrast with that of his brother-in-law, the brutal and murderous Ecelin, whose life was devoted to constant outrages and plunderings. (27) *Kaiser*, Friedrich or Frederick II., one of the greatest rulers of the Middle Ages, liberal, broad-minded, a ripe scholar, a troubadour of no mean ability, and a man of great personal capacities, he ruled with a powerful hand, and though nearly all his life under the ban of the Church, held his Empire loyal to himself. (34) *Pontiff*, Honorius III., the opponent of Friedrich, and using every influence against him. (35) *Oliero*, the monastery entered by Ecelin when he became tired of the world. (41) *Cino Bocchimpane chanced to meet Buccio Virtu*, representatives of the Guelf and Ghibelline parties among the people. (42) *God's wafer*, the wafer used in the mass, an oath here, *Ostia di Dio*, the Host of God. (43) *Tutti Santi*, Italian for All Saints.

197:1, *To Padua;* Salinguerra, though head of the Ghibelline party, resided in Ferrara, and was a vassal of Azzo, head of the Guelf party. The Guelfs thought this not consistent, and forced Salinguerra and his adherents out of the city; but in a short time, by means of a treaty, they were permitted to return, only to force out the Guelfs the next year, a year being called by Browning a week; *Podestà*, mayor or chief of a city. (16) *Azzo, stunned awhile*, refers to the expulsion by Salinguerra from Ferrara of Azzo and his party, the effort of Azzo and Richard, called by Browning lynx and ounce, to reinstate themselves, and their encamping about the city with their armies. (22) *within their walls men fed on men;* probably this did not happen, but indicates the straits to which the besieged were reduced. (23) *Taurello calls a parley;* Salinguerra induces Richard to enter the city with a company of horsemen, under plea of treating for peace, and then imprisons him and his companions, upon which Azzo retires from the siege. (44) *dropped the mask;* Friedrich had been promising to lead a crusade in order to restore the confidence of the Pope, set sail in August, 1218, but returned in three days. (45) *John of Brienne*, King of Jerusalem, whose daughter the Emperor had married, and who charged the Emperor with failing in his promises, as well as neglecting his wife for Bianca, who gave birth to two sons by him.

198:2, *leisure to retrieve;* Friedrich did not wish to undertake a crusade because it would have given his opponents an opportunity during his absence to recover ground lost by them under Otho and Barbarossa. (4) *Alps less easy to recross*, that he might keep free communication between Germany and northern Italy, and thus prevent any advantage to the papal party. (6) *was excommunicate;* Gregory IX., Honorius' successor, excommunicated Friedrich Sept. 30, 1229, because of his friendship to the Moslem, his delay in undertaking a crusade, and his supposed insincerity. (7) *triple-bearded Teuton*, Barbarossa, who was said by legend to be asleep in Unsterberg, and would come to life when his beard had grown three times around his council-table of rock.

199:6, *Arpo or Yoland* refers to obscure and perhaps unknown origin of the house of Romano, that began with Germans who crossed the Alps with Conrad II., and who held the Trentine Pass into Italy. (9) *the Trevisan*, the province of Treviso, with its capital city of the same name. (10) *Conrad*, Conrad III., founder of house of Hohenstauffens, Emperors of Germany, in whose time Guelf and Ghibelline feud began. (11) *Ecelo*, first of the Ecelin family, grandfather of the Ecelin of this poem. (13) *Godego, Ramon, Loria*, etc., villages and cities in the hills between Venice and the Alps. (15) *Suabian's fief*, of these towns and cities the emperor was over-lord as head of the Suabian lords. (18) *Vale of Trent*, Trent or Tridentium in Tyrol; the valley affords a way of entrance into Italy from the north. (19) *Roncaglia*, town in same region as those just named, at which Frederick I. held a diet in 1154, and established himself Emperor over this region of northern Italy, proving it of immense value in holding the peninsula as a part of the Empire. (22) *sadness fills them all;* Ecelin was made ruler of the region in the Asolan hills and Julian Alps by Frederick I., and his fierce character made the people fear his rule. (36) *Otho*, third of that name, who was ambitious to establish the Empire in Italy.

200:13, *Rovigo's Polesine*, cities north of the Po, Rovigo being twenty-seven miles from Padua. (14) *Ancona's march*, the region governed, with Ancona, on Adriatic, as capital. (22) *Father Porphyry*, imaginary abbot, who destroys documents in order to favor the Este family. (26) *Twenty-four*, the magistrates of Verona, who discuss in his palace Richard's escape from the clutches of Salinguerra. (30) *cressets*, lamps borne on long poles as torch-lights. (33) *carroch*, or caroccio, a great cart drawn by oxen, which held a bell, the standard of the army and the Sacred Host, and carried soldiers in front and behind.

201:15, *Armenian bridegroom*, custom among Armenians of being buried in their wedding costume. (17) *gate-vein*, chief vein in passing blood from abdomen to heart, here used of Sordello as the first to write in the vernacular, and therefore to open the way for Dante; also called *forerunner* of the same Florentine. (36) *John's transcendent vision*, Apocalypse or Revelation of Saint John. (45) *half is slough;* the Mincio, in flowing from the lake of Garda to Po, makes a large swamp about the city of Mantua.

202:7, *Goito*, castle at foot of mountains overlooking Mantua. (23) *Arab's wisdom*, proverbs in Arabic letters engraved on walls of room. (38) *Caryatides*, figures of women supporting entablatures, so called from Caryatis, as Diana was named, from Carya, town in Arcadia.

203:39, *with all his wives;* Ecelin was four times married, to Agnes Este, Speronella Dalesmannini, Cecilia di Abano, and Adelaide di Mangone. Beside these he stole Maria di Camposanpietro, and had a daughter by her, who may be the Auria mentioned.

205:5, *a legend;* several primitive theories of creation run along the general lines stated by the poet.

206:19, *that Pisan pair*, Nicolo Pisano (Nicholas of Pisa) and his son Giovanni, sculptors and architects of Pisa, were among the leaders in restoring the calmness and freedom of the Greek style. (21) *Guidone*, Guido da Sienna, whose picture of 1221, now in Sienna, marks the very beginning of the Renaissance. (23) *Saint Eufemia's sacristy*, a brick church in Verona of the thirteenth century, containing a picture of the saint ; and also, it is said, her body reposes there. (35) *pyx*, sacred coffer, containing relics of saints, which in the Middle Ages were regarded as essential to a church. (37) *so they found at Babylon;* "It is said that after the city of Seleucia was burnt, the soldiers searching the temple of Apollo found a narrow hole, and when this was opened in the hope of finding something of value in it, there issued from some deep gulf, which the secret magic of the Chaldeans had closed up, a pestilence laden with the strength of incurable disease, which polluted the whole world with contagion, in the time of Verus and Marcus Antoninus, and from the borders of Persia to Gaul and the Rhine." — Ammianus Marcellinus, i. 607. (38) *mad Lucius and sage Antonine*, Lucius Verus and Marcus Aurelius Antoninus, joint Emperors, Verus being in command of Roman army in the East in 163-5.

207:4, *Loxian*, Apollo. (23) *foreign women-servants*, kept about him because they could not inform him of passing occurrences, owing to their inability to speak his tongue. (33) *palmer-worm*, a kind of caterpillar, so called from its travelling habits.

208:12, *orpine*, a yellow plant called popularly Livelong or Stonecrop, *Sedum Telephium*. (20) *adventurous spider*, species of Orbweaver, *Orbitelariæ*, popularly called garden, geometric or diadem spider, which swathes its prey round and round with its web, and makes with its web a long bridge from point to point, but cannot shoot it to great distances, as the poet says it can.

209: 2, *Naddo*, a typical critic of poets; *eat fern-seed*, supposed anciently to make one invisible. (17) *fleering*, from Icelandic *flyra*, to grin, and refers to appearance of laughter in the poppy when in full bloom. (18) *crane*, the seed-vessel of the ripe poppy.

210: 14, *Adelaide bent double o'er a scroll;* this last wife of Ecelin was accused of magic and astrology. (31) *valvassor and suzerain*, in feudal law a vassal holding rule under a great lord is a valvassor, while the lord himself is a suzerain.

211: 30, *Ecelin becomes Imperial Vicar*, so made by Otho IV., in 1209, as his representative in Italy. (33) *Guelf's paid stabber;* Professor Sonnenschein says: "In 1209 Otho IV. entered Italy, and held his court near Verona. All the chief lords of Venetia, but especially Eccelin II., da Romano, and Azzo VI., Marquis d'Este, were summoned to attend. Those two gentlemen had profited by the long interregnum which preceded Otho's reign. They had used the various discords between the towns to increase each his own faction; and the hatred between the two was more bitter than ever. A dramatic scene took place at the meeting before the Emperor. When Eccelin saw Azzo, he said, in the presence of the whole court, ' We were intimate in our youth, and I believed him to be my friend. One day we were in Venice together, walking together on the Place of St. Mark, when his assassins flung themselves upon me to stab me; and at the same moment the Marquis seized my arms, to prevent me from defending myself; and if I had not by a violent effort escaped, I should have been killed, as was one of my soldiers by my side. I denounce him, therefore, before this assembly as a traitor; and of you, Sire, I demand permission to prove by a single combat his treachery to me as well as to Salinguerra, and to the podesta of Vicenza.' Shortly afterwards, Salinguerra arrived, followed by a hundred men at arms, and throwing himself at the feet of the Emperor, he made a similar accusation against the Marquis, and also demanded the ordeal of battle. Azzo replied to him, that he had on his hands plenty of gentlemen more noble than Salinguerra ready to fight for him if he was so anxious for battle. Then Otho commanded all three to be silent, and declared that he should not accord to any of them the privilege of fighting for any of their past quarrels. From these two chiefs the Emperor expected greater service than from all other Italians; and he secured their allegiance by confirming the lordship of the Marches of Ancona upon the Marquis, and by declaring Eccelin to be imperial deputy and permanent podesta of Vicenza." (34) *the sleight o' the sword*, measured for Ecelin's escape, as just narrated above.

212: 13, *struck Malek down*, a supposititious Moor struck down by Sordello. (40) *the Miramoline*, a Saracen prince of North Africa, whose title was Emiral Maromenium, Prince of the Faithful, another reference to the friendship of Friedrich for the Mohammedans. (43) *dates plucked*, John of Brienne, king of Jerusalem, sent his son-in-law, Frederick II., a bunch of dates as a reminder of his promise to undertake a crusade, in order that the king might recover his kingdom.

213: 34, *crenelled*, grooved. (36) *damsel-fly*, dragon-fly.

214: 9, *the Pythons*, disappearance of pythons owing to attacks of

NOTES 421

Apollo, reference to destruction of Python which lived in caves of Parnassus. (13) *Delians*, priestesses of Apollo at temple of Delos, the statues of girls being so regarded by Sordello. (19) *Daphne ;* Sordello regards leader of these girls as the nymph who loved and was changed into a laurel-tree, Ovid, *Metamorphoses,* i. v.

215: 21, *Northward to Provence that, and thus far south the other,* refers to movements of troubadours or singers and makers of songs, and trouveres or story-tellers, between southern France, the chief seat of their art, and Sicily, where they were in high favor in the Emperor's court at Messina. (24) *in their very tongue ;* the troubadours sang in Provençal, the language of the common people.

217: 25, *Jongleurs,* singers of the songs of the troubadours. (26) *Court of Love,* poetical tournament held by troubadours, in charge of companies of ladies, one or more of whom acted as judge. (28) *Elys ;* Browning himself says this "is merely the ideal subject, with such a name, of Eglamour's poem, and referred to in other places as his (Sordello's) type of perfection, realized according to his faculty;" the word has meaning of lily, also of lute-string.

218: 8, *scarab 'neath the tongue,* a knot under the tongue of the sacred bull Apis, in shape like a scarabæus, that was one of the signs of his divinity, here applied by Naddo to Sordello as indicative of his poetical gifts. (35) *Squarcialupe and Tagliafer,* imaginary jongleurs.

220: 4, *a Roman bride ;* the early Roman bride had her hair parted on her wedding day with a spear, perhaps a remnant of marriage by capture, and said to be an emblem of her husband's authority over her. (42) *a poor gnome ;* the Rosicrucians made gnomes controllers of mines.

222: 26, *a plant yielding a three-leaved bell,* day-lily, St. Bruno's lily, *Hemerocallis liliastrum.* (32) *My own month,* May, Browning's birth-month. (36) *Massic jars dug up at Baiæ,* Baiæ, a health and fashion resort near Naples, where the famous Massic wine was much used ; jars here named after the wine contained in them.

223: 12, *Vicenza banished the Vivaresi kith and kin,* opening of the Guelf and Ghibelline conflict in 1194 ; Ecelin, being at head of Vivaresi or Ghibelline party, was exiled from Vicenza by the Counts of Vicenza, who headed the Guelf faction. (14) *Maltraversi,* a noble family of Padua, belonging to the Guelf party. (21) *Elcorte,* Sordello's father, who, according to some of the old chroniclers, was a song-writer attached to the Count of Saint Boniface, with whose wife he eloped; the incidents here described by the poet being of the same kind, more legend than fact.

226: 5, *huge throbbing stone ;* Ossian describes bards walking about a rocking stone, and making it move by their singing, as a battle oracle. (27) *truchman,* an interpreter.

227: 25, *rondel, tenzon, virlai or sirvent,* forms of verse used by the troubadours and jongleurs; rondel, from rotundus, a thirteen-verse song with repeat in third and fourth verses; tenzon, a musical contest or dialogue between two troubadours, each inventing music and song in reply to the other; virlai, short poem in two rhymes; sirvent, a war-song with which the troubadours cheered their soldiers, no special form of verse being used. (27) *angelot,* a mediaeval lute.

228: 1, *Anafest and Lucio,* imaginary persons. (5) *Bianca ;* the youth supposes Sordello in love with this woman; in Dean Milman's tragedy of *Fazio*, the wife of Fazio, who tried to save her husband's life, but failed and went mad. (39) *rewrought that language*, Sordello's attempt to combine dialects of Verona, Cremona, and Brescia into a true Tuscan popular speech, as described by Dante in his *De Vulgari Eloquio*.

229: 32, *sparkles off*, intransitive verb, meaning that the new language will sparkle as does bright mail. (34) *Apollo from the sudden corpse of Hyacinth*; in training Hyacinth Apollo accidentally killed him while they were playing quoits. (37) *Montfort*, Simon de Montfort, who led crusade against the Albigenses of Languedoc, an event that brought the troubadour movement to an end.

230: 2, "In this passage the word 'will' is used in a peculiar and somewhat undefinable sense, in which it reappears throughout the poem. It means the power in virtue of which we feel potentially an experience or quality; i. e., while one may not actually realize a thing, he feels that he has the spiritual capacity to realize it." — W. J. Alexander, *Introduction to the Poetry of Browning*. "In this, as in other places in this poem, Browning seems to use the word 'will' as equivalent to imagination and the capacity to realize in himself all his images." — Annie Wall, *Sordello's Story Retold in Prose*. (34) *the Poet thwarting hopelessly the Man who;* here "who" refers to Poet, the subject down to "bright" in line 45; the "who" that follows refers to Man.

231: 14, *Quiver and bow away, the lyre alone;* here quiver and bow symbolize the inner content or imaginative gift of the poet, while the lyre expresses his mastery of language. (21) *John's cloud-girt angel,* Revelation, x. 1–10. (44) *Vidal*, troubadour of Toulouse, one of wildest of these poets and most adventurous, disliked by Sordello, and referred to by Dante in *Purgatorio*, xxvi. 113. (45) *murrey-colored*, dark red or mulberry color; *filamot*, yellow-brown, from *feuille-morte*.

232: 15, *rathe-ripe*, Anglo-Saxon *hrathe*, quick, here used in sense of early ripe. (24) *plectre*, or plectrum, the ivory or horn staff with which a lyre is struck, a twenty-cubit one being very large.

233: 6, *Bocafoli's stark-naked psalms*, an imaginary poet of strong realism. (7) *Plara's sonnets*, imaginary poet of superfine style. (8) *knops that stud some almug*, knops means knobs, Anglo-Saxon *cnoep;* and almug is red sandal wood of China and India, mentioned in 2 Chronicles, ix. 10, 11. (13) *pompion*, pumpkin.

234: 19, *Pappacoda, Tagliafer*, typical jongleurs, Tagliafer or Taillefer being the famous minstrel of William of Normandy, who sang the magic song of Roland in front of the army at the battle of Senlac. (22) *o'er toise*, old French *toise*, long measure, here meaning overstretch.

235: 7, *Count Lori*, Loria of Naples, here a typical gallant. (8) *peasant-Paul*, belonging to Paulicians or Paterini, the sect to which Ecelin is said to have united himself. (21) *I am sick, too;* Ecelin, owing to his Paterini ideas, entered convent at Oliero in 1223, having divided his lands between the Pope and his two sons, and planned to unite them in marriage with Beatrix Este and Giglia Saint Boniface, also to marry his daughter Palma to Count Richard

236: 9, *congeed*, French *conger*, permitted to take leave, meaning ironical politeness. (11) *green and yellow;* a green mantle and gold circlet formed the livery of Ecelin, and also of the Emperor. (12) *Retrude,* wife of Taurello Salinguerra, daughter of Henry VI. (31) *Strojavacca,* typical troubadour acting as rival to Sordello. (34) *cob-swan,* head-swan, leader of flock, from Anglo-Saxon *cop,* head.

237:24, *cat's head and ibis' tail,* Egyptian symbols from sacred animals set in mosaic of the pavement. (27) *Soldan,* Sultan.

238:1, *iris root,* orris-root. (5) *Carian group,* sculpture of the Caryatides or Carian women at feast of Diana Caryatis. (30) *moonfern,* moonwort ; *hemionitis,* a healing plant; *trifoly,* clover, trifolium, supposed to have magical qualities.

239:3, *byssus,* silky fibres by which shell-fish fasten themselves to rocks, and of which silk has been spun. (4) *Tyrrhene whelk,* shellfish from which Tyrian purple was made, and exported from Tyre. (5) *trireme,* ancient ship or galley with three galleries of oars.

240:35, *spilth,* spilled or turned out, here meaning flash or sudden burst of light.

241:20, *island-house,* Emperor's country villa near Palermo, Sicily, called La Favara. (24) *Nuocera,* a colony of Saracens from Sicily, between Pompeii and Amalfi, settled there by Frederick II. (26) *mollitious,* soft and luxurious. (27) *Byzant domes,* those of Byzantium or Constantinople, considered as built by the devil because the enemies most hated by Christians erected them. (29) *Dandalo;* " Enrico Dandalo, one of the patrician family of that name in Venice, was chosen doge in 1192, although already blind and seventy-two years old. After naval successes against the Pisans, he was applied to at the time of the fourth crusade to furnish vessels for transport to Constantinople. After making terms most advantageous to the Republic, he himself led the enterprise to success, and shared with the French in pillage of the city, and very largely in booty and privileges accruing. The four horses of St. Mark's Church were brought over to Venice by him." — Professor Sonnenschein. (33) *sardius,* Carnelian stone. (34) *transport to Venice' Square ;* this square is adorned with beautiful columns brought from temples and buildings pillaged in many cities by the Venetians.

243:29, *bulb dormant ;* hyacinth bulbs were buried with the dead by the Egyptians as symbols of immortality.

244:11, *the end of the siege was nigh,* that of Ferrara. (28) *You mind* refers back to the opening of the poem. (38) *the rule of Charlemagne broken by Hildebrand ;* the Holy Roman Empire as established by Charlemagne was subverted by the methods of Hildebrand in making the Church its superior, and it was Frederick's ambition to restore it to its former prestige and power.

245 : 18, *Now turn;* Verona was on the side of Richard, but the adherents of the other party in the city were preparing to aid Ferrara, now undergoing a siege. (23) *the candle's at the gateway ;* candle burning at the gate is made a measure of time, as in laws of King Alfred and in other mediæval customs. (25) *Tiso Sampier;* Tissolin di Campo St. Pierre and Ecelin I. were intimate friends until the claims of a marriage portion divided them, Ecelin grasping for the whole, a lasting feud arose between them. (26) *Ferrara's succored, Palma,* the helping of Ferrara by the opposition party in Ve-

rona, this remark being from the Ghibelline side, while the words beginning above with "Now, Lady," are from the Guelf point of view. (36) *Agnes' milk;* Palma had the mildness of her mother, Agnes Este, as compared with the fierceness of her father, Ecelin.

246:41, *Cesano,* city of Emilia, between Bologna and Ancona, that often changed sides in the fierce struggles of the time, described by Dante, *Inferno,* xxvii. 47–52, as living midway between tyranny and freedom.

247:18, *insuperable Tuscan,* Ecelin's wife Adelaide.

248:20, *the orb I sought to serve;* Browning identifies his Palma with Dante's Cunizza, placed by him in third heaven of Venus, *Paradiso,* ix. 13–36, daughter of Ecelin the monk, and sister of Ecelin the cut-throat; but she was devoted to love. (21) *Fomalhaut;* this star in constellation of the Southern Fish is associated by the poet with Venus, in primitive form a fish-goddess, and made by Dante (*Purgatorio,* i. 19–21), and also by Browning, a love influence. (40) *first knight who followed Conrad;* Ecelo was an adventurous follower of Conrad II.

249:6, *Saponian strength;* Browning explained this as referring to the Saponi family, a branch of the Ecelin, which settled in Lombardy before time of Sordello. (13) *Podesta among the Vicentines;* Ecelin was at head of Vicenza, and afterwards held power in Padua. (21) *Alberic,* Palma's younger brother ; *lion's-crine,* lion's hair, Latin *crinis,* hair, meaning yellow or golden. (34) *Adelaide of Susa,* Marchioness of Piedmont, contemporary of Matilda, Countess of Tuscany, and who mediated between Pope and Emperor, both these women being effective rulers and of great influence in their time on Italian politics. (39) *Our Adelaide,* Adelaide of Tuscany, who kept Trentine Pass open for the Emperor, as Adelaide of Susa did that through the Alps into France for the Pope.

251:44, *Verona's Lady,* Palma. (45) *Brennus,* general of Gauls, who, in 385 B. C., marched on Rome, climbed the Tarpeian rock, and was about to enter the citadel, when the sacred geese gave the alarm, and the invaders were driven back by Manlius, and all killed.

252:7, *platan,* plane-tree. (8) *archimage,* a superior magician or head of the Magi. (20) *put aside entrance — thy synod,* not permit any fresh thought or new ideas to enter the synod.

253:23, *colibri,* humming-birds.

254:2, *Bassanese,* Bassano on the Brenta, an old home of the Ecelin. (14) *Giudecca,* Venetian canal.

255:14, *fastuous,* haughty. (22) *shent,* blamed, Anglo-Saxon, *scendan.* (41) *Basilic,* Basilica of St. Mark's in Venice. (42) *Corpus Domini,* Body of the Lord, the feast of Sacrament Day, Thursday after Trinity Sunday.

256:11, *God spoke of right-hand, foot and eye,* Matthew v. 29. (19) *losel,* lose-all, worthless fellow. (45) *mugwort,* herb of the genus Artemisia.

257:1, *Zin the horrid,* desert without water, Numbers xx. 1. (9) *Potsherd him, Gibeonites,* Joshua ix. and x. (14) *Meribah,* Numbers xx. 13.

258:14, *Piombi,* in Ducal palace at Venice terrible torture-cells immediately under the roof. (17) *Zanze,* imaginary object of beauty.

259:33, *Hercules first parched*, legend of journey of Hercules to Egypt in search of apples of Hesperides, captured by Busiris, the king, who was about to sacrifice him to Zeus when he broke bonds, and slew Busiris and his servants. (44) *my patron-friend*, Walter Savage Landor, one of the first admirers of Browning's poetry, and who praised it when others criticised.

260:1, *like your own trumpeter at Marathon* refers to poems of Landor treating of Æschylus and his service at battle of Marathon and his use of his experiences in his drama of *The Persians*, as well as his going to Sicily, where King Hiero was then building city of Ætna; likewise to Browning's visit to Landor, near Ætna. (10) *a flawless ruby;* Polycrates of Samos had a ruby he threw into the sea by advice of Amasis, King of Egypt, because the great luck it gave him might bring on him vengeance of the gods ; but a fish presented to him was found to contain it in its stomach. (14) *your verse*, Landor's poem of appreciation. (16) *my English Eyebright*, one of Browning's early friends, whose name Euphrasia means Eyebright, the flower of that name being *Euphrasia officinalis*. (45) *Xanthus*, a disciple of St. John in *A Death in the Desert*.

261:3, *Polycarp*, early Christian martyr, said to be disciple of St. John. (4) *Charicle*, imaginary disciple with Polycarp. (24) *twyprong, pastoral cross;* first is forked prong of hazel or almond used by magicians in raising the devil, contrasted with Y-shaped cross on priest's vestments.

262:10, *quitchgrass*, dog-grass, or couch-grass, which is very difficult of extermination. (20) *Montelungo*, Gregorio di Montemongo, pontifical legate of Gregory IX. (28) *Tito*, Friedrich's representative from Trent. (30) *Mainard*, Lord of Tyrol, capital at Görz. (36) *arbalist*, cross-bow; *manganel*, battering-ram ; *catapult*, engine for throwing stones into besieged city or camp.

263:3, *crested white ostrich with horse-shoe in beak*, crest of Ecelin. (23) *cautelous*, wary, old French *cautelle*, inability of Barbarossa to conquer Alexandria, built by Lombard League. (29) *Brenta and Bacchiglion;* the first, a river near Padua; the other, a river that runs by Vicenza and Padua. (36) *Concorezzi*, noble family in Padua. (37) *San Vitale*, village near Vicenza.

264:39, *Messina marbles Constance took delight in;* Constance, Norman heiress of Sicily, married Henry VI., and therefore Messina became seat of the Emperors, the marbles being statues in their palace.

265:7, *the Fighter*, and 16, *the Slave*, statues in Taurello's gardenterrace.

270:12, *twy-necked eagle*, the two-headed eagle that was symbol of the Empire. (16) *Palma knew what Salinguerra meant to do*, to assume for himself the chief place.

271:13, *basnet*, bascinet, light helmet of basin-shape.

272:1, *what past life;* there follows an account of the life and experiences of Taurello Salinguerra, who belonged to the Torelli family of Ferrara, and was a beneficent and noble ruler. (4) *Adelardi*, a noble family of Ferrara opposed to the Torelli. (13) *Blacks and Whites;* the Guelfs were called Neri or Blacks, and the Ghibellines the Bianchi or Whites (14) *Taurello wed Linguetta;* when

Taurello was a young man he proposed to wed Linguetta Marchesalla, heiress of her family; but the opposing or Guelf faction, led by the Adelardi, carried her off, and, on pretense of a hunt, got him out of the city, while Azzo entered it with Linguetta. Taurello went to court of Henry VI., married Retrude, and returned to Ferrara, built a palace, was soon after attacked, and his wife mortally wounded; at last he was successful and secured the city.

274: 10, *Matilda,* Countess of Tuscany, 1046-1114, friend and helper of Hildebrand, a powerful defender of the Church and a great ruler. (18) *Heinrich,* Henry VI., Emperor, 1190-1197. (19) *Philip,* rival to Otho as Emperor, 1197-1208. (24) *Otho,* Otho IV., papal contestant to Empire against Frederick II. (43) *Jove trined for her;* Adelaide's belief in astrology led her to think it an auspicious event when Jupiter, the earth, and a third planet made a triangle of 120 degrees or a third of the zodiac. (44) *from Friedrich's path;* the poet here assumes that Adelaide led Frederick II. to oppose the Pope and not undertake a crusade, using Taurello for this purpose, seeing in him certain astrologic signs favorable to his success.

275: 2, *Guido the Bolognian,* a little known painter of the twelfth century. (7) *clove he not Tiso, last siege;* the skill of Taurello as a leader is referred to, and not exact history, as W. M. Rossetti's translation of Muratori's account of this shows, who says : "Salinguerra, the old fox, fearing lest the populace should rise against him on account of the rigors of the siege, sent to the Marquis, conceding to him to enter Ferrara, where concord between the parties might be amicably treated of. The Marquis fell unsuspiciously into the net, and with one hundred noblemen of his party he entered the city. Thereupon Salinguerra, raising a rumor that the new-comers insolently seized upon provisions and committed other outrages, shouted To arms! to arms! Some of the visitors had the good fortune of escaping along with the Marquis; the others were slain, and among these Tisolino of Campo San Pietro, a most noble Paduan knight, was stopped while retiring by the peasants of a village named Girzola or Guzola, and killed." (27) *old Azzo and old Boniface,* heads of the Este and Boniface houses, whose sons Aldrovandio Este and Guglielm Boniface died in three years after the deaths of their fathers, and were succeeded by Azzo VII. and Richard Boniface, so often mentioned in the poem. (33) *at bay;* the power of Taurello in Ferrara became too strong for that of Azzo.

276: 45, *old compeer;* Taurello so describes Ecelin, and recalls their experiences together.

277: 22, *scapular,* a monk's garment worn over shoulder and breast in two strips, usually called scapulary. (23) *cowl,* monk's hood. (29) *Pilio and Bernardo,* imaginary persons of Guelf faction. (30) *San Biagio,* St. Biase, village near Lake of Garda.

279: 35, *poor minstrel,* Sordello. (39) *lentisk,* the mastich-tree of north Africa, *Pistacia lentiscus.*

280: 4, *his son's besotied youth,* Ecelin III., whose fiendish temper made him a cut-throat and son of the devil, as he was called, or, as Ariosto said : —

> Fierce Ecelin, that most unhuman lord,
> Who shall be deemed by men a child of hell.

NOTES

40, *poison-wattles*, the excrescence or lobe of flesh on a lizard's neck.

282: 40, *Crescentius Nomentanus;* in 998 "Rome made a bold attempt to shake off the Saxon yoke, and the consul Crescentius was the Brutus of the Republic. From the condition of the subject and an exile, he twice rose to the command of the city, oppressed, expelled, and created the popes, and formed a conspiracy for restoring the authority of the Greek emperors. In the fortress of St. Angelo, he maintained an obstinate siege, till the unfortunate consul was betrayed by a promise of safety; his body was suspended on a gibbet, and his head was exposed on the battlements of the castle."—Gibbon, chap. xlix.

283: 3, *Innocent*, third of that name, Pope in 1198, who put down the party that favored wives for monks and secular ways of living. (12) *vulgar priest and a vile stranger;* John XV. and Otho III. are meant. (26) *phanal*, beacon-light. (32) *Consul;* Crescentius was so put to death.

284: 5, *Rome of the Pandects;* Justinian's laws abridged and digested, made in sixth century, were called *Pandects*, and these furnished the common law of the Empire. (38) *mooned sandal;* crescent was worn on toe of shoes at this time. (40) *atria*, chief room, with court and fountain, in Roman house. (41) *stibadium*, reclining couch used by Romans at meals.

285: 26, *obsidian*, glassy product of volcanoes. (27) *fulgurant*, like flash of lightning. (41) *Mauritanian tree*, citrus-wood of North Africa, Mauritania being one of its countries. (44) *demiurge*, secondary creator or instrument through which God creates.

286: 4, *Mareotic juice from Cæcuban;* Lake Mareotis in Egypt was famous for its wine, which is here regarded as better than that of Cæcubum in Latium. (19) *Pythoness conceding to a Lydian King;* priestess of Apollo gave Crœsus of Lydia an oracle he interpreted in his own favor, but it led to the destruction of his kingdom by Cyrus, Herodotus i. 26.

287: 1, *Alcamo*, Sicilian poet of Palermo, 1112–1178. (3) *Nina*, poetess of Sicily, first woman who wrote in Italian. (4) *turning his name o'er and o'er;* Nina is spoken of as one "whose love of her art caused her to become enamored of a poet whom she had never seen. This fortunate bard (who returned her poetical passion) was called Dante; but we cannot plead in her excuse that he had anything else in common with the great poet of that name. She was so engrossed by her passion for her lover that she wished herself always to be called The Nina of Dante." (36) *priests for castellans and popes for suzerains*, the feudalization of the church, making priests like governors of castles and popes like great lords.

288: 8, *Hildebrand of the huge brain-mask*, the great feudal organizer of the Catholic Church, who made it superior in power to the Empire and became Pope Gregory in 1073; the brain-mask referring to his astuteness and ability to bring about the greatest ends through others, and when his own mighty intellectual force was hidden. (19) *mandrake thwarted and dwarfed*, old superstition that the forked root of the mandrake caused it to shriek with pain, as Hildebrand is supposed to have done with his great labor. (30) *the three Imperial crowns*, three crowns worn by Emperor in succession, that of the crowning at Aachen as King of Franks, that at Pavia or Milan as King of Sicily, and that at Rome as Emperor ; the first being of iron, the second of silver, and the third of gold. (32) *Alexander*, second pope of that name, who was put into office by Hildebrand, in 1061 ; *Innocent*, the third of the name, 1198, who became a great Papal ruler. (38) *Peter's cry*, Peter the Hermit preaching the crusades, the first begun at Claremont in 1095. (44) *wild harangue of Vimmercato*, place of formation of a league against Frederick I., likened to the effort being made to overcome the liberal policy of Frederick II., and his wish to check the authority of the Popes.

289:1, *Mantuan Albert*, Patriarch of Jerusalem, umpire between Emperor and Pope. (2) *Saint Francis*, of Assisi, founder of Order of St. Francis, 1182-1226, who preached peace, and regarded all creatures as his " brothers and sisters." (3) *God's Truce*, " Truce of God," or suspension of arms in 999.

290:33, *hacqueton*, quilted jacket worn under armor.

291:4, *trabea*, Roman toga worn as regal robe.

292:44, *thyrsus*, spear carried at feasts of Bacchus, wrapped about with ivy.

294:20, *the Caliph's wheel-work man of brass* refers to Haroun al Raschid, 756-809, the renowned Caliph, who had great love of mechanics, and who sent to Charlemagne a manikin such as the poet describes.

297:28, *Friedrich with his red-hot tomb*, as described by Dante, *Inferno*, x. 120, who placed the Emperor in a fiery tomb of his city of flame. (29) *Lombard Agiluph*, King of Lombardy, chosen by Theodolinda to succeed her husband, Authari, in 590. (31) *Matilda I enshrine*, Dante, in *Purgatorio*, xxviii. 53-64, meets the famous Tuscan Countess, and she becomes his guide in place of Virgil, shooting upon him glances of Venus, the planet that goes with the sun in rising and setting.

298:34, *the spoils of every clime at Venice ;* this city was in Middle Ages the great commercial centre of the West, and into St. Mark's Cathedral were gathered spoils from every clime. (35) *snouted god*, Set. (37) *cinerary pitcher*, great jar used for burial purposes. (39) *earth's reputed consummations ;* finest treasures of the world were brought to St. Mark's. (40) *all-transmuting Triad ;* St. Mark, St. Pantaleon, and St. Lawrence Justiniani were the patron saints of Venice, whose statues stood in St. Mark's, regarded as in their combined powers giving the city its prosperity.

300:17, *writhled*, wrinkled or shrunken. (22) *pauldron*, part of armor plate to defend shoulders.

301:12, *Retrude the frail mother* refers to death of Retrude at sack of Ferrara and loss of her child, the future Sordello. Line 8, " Cut off a moment," to line 26, " That deprecating glance ? " gives a sentence of which she is the subject. In line 21 Sordello is referred to as the natural chief, but now an infant. In line 26, " A new shape," Adelaide becomes the subject, who rejoices at the misery of Sordello. She finds Taurello is superior to her husband Ecelin, and steals his child to rear him in secret. Her object in this is to prevent Taurello's growing power from passing to his child and taking the place of her own as chief of the Emperor.

NOTES   429

302:43, *Native of Gesi*, city in province of Ancona, of which Frederick II. was a native.

303:23, *Samminiato secures us Florence, in Pisa's case;* the possession of the hill Samminiato will control Florence as the possession of Florence will control Pisa. (26) *Pistoia;* the command of Florence will control all the neighboring cities. (31) *whose first span;* the power of the Emperor would gradually pass, from its entrance into Italy at the Trentine pass in the Alps, to include the southern regions of Romagna and Bologna. (32) *Valsugan*, town on the Brenta, between Trent and Venice. (33) *Sofia's Egna by Bolgiano's sure;* the pass of Bolgiano was insured to the Ghibellins by the marriage of Sofia Ecelin and Henry of Egna.

304:14, *Torriani*, Lombard faction of Valsassina, fighting the Visconti, a Ghibellin family with Otho Visconti, archbishop of Milan, at its head, 1262. The first were democrats, the other family aristocrats.

305:43, *rebuild Charlemagne;* Taurello and Sordello were to destroy the papal strength and give new power to the Empire as represented by Charlemagne, its founder.

306:17, *Drive Trent upon Apulia*, push the interests of the Empire from the extreme north to the extreme south of Italy. (21) *To Palma, Dante spoke with in the clear amorous silence of the swooningsphere, — Cunizza, as he called her;* Cunizza was sister to Ecelin III., and is mentioned by Dante in *Paradiso*, ix. 32. She was married to Richard St. Boniface, but had an intrigue with Sordello, *Purgatorio*, vi. Then she lived with a soldier, married a nobleman of Braganza, and finally a gentleman of Verona. She was described as a lady who "lived lovingly in dress, song, and sport, but consented not to any impropriety or unlawful act." Browning changes Cunizza into Palma for some reason of his own, as he here admits. (42) *purulent*, diseased, maturated.

309:23, *jacinth*, hyacinth of mineralogy, several kinds of stone. 24, *flinders*, fragments of shining metal.

310:19, *Cydippe by the hair, lames barefoot Agathon*, imaginary persons who meet with difficulties, but probably drawn from Ovid, story of Cydippe and Acantius.

311:15, *Dularete*, imaginary person like Naddo, representing cultivated but sensuous artistic temperament.

314:15, *brakes at balm-shed*, brake-ferns at time of shedding their seeds. (45) *the sluggish asp;* as the asp drains the blood of its victim its cowl becomes stained with the blood and its eyes become bright.

315:32, *reate*, a water weed. (33) *gold-sparkling grail*, yellow gravel.

316:16, *citrine-crystals*, quartz of a yellow and pellucid kind; *pyropus-stone*, carbuncle of fiery redness. (31) *Titan*, constellation of Orion. (32) *Centaur*, constellation of that name in southern hemisphere.

317:14, *Brutus*, feigned madness of Lucius Brutus before Tarquin, but sane efforts to overthrow him when out of his presence.

320:5, *the king-bird*, Egyptian Phoenix, sacred to Osiris, is said by Herodotus, ii. 73, to travel to Heliopolis once in five hundred years to die, enters temple of Sun with gold and crimson plumes, and buries its father (or itself) in an egg of myrrh. (28) *old fable, the two eagles;* according to Pindar, fourth Pythian ode, Jove's golden eagles were placed near the sacred tripod, from which one flew east and the other west until they met at Delphi or Pytho.

321:18, *our chief* refers to efforts made in 1225 to secure the release of Richard from Taurello, which were successful.

322:6, *hushed up this evening's work,* a plain suggestion that the poet had made his own Sordello in the poem, using the chroniclers to give historic setting to his incidents. (20) *Campese,* on Brenta, near Bassano. (21) *Solagna,* village near Vicenza. (32) *in Verona half the souls refuse allegiance to the Marquis and the Count;* on his release Richard went to Verona, but in a few months many leading persons in the city joined with the Montecchi family, Ghibellins, and drove him out, led thereto, says Muratori, by Taurello's money. Ecelin di Romano went to the help of this movement, being a chief ally of Taurello.

323:18, *she captured him in his Ferrara;* Taurello was captured at siege of Ferrara by the papal party in 1240, being then eighty years of age. He was imprisoned at Venice, where, according to Milman, *History of Latin Christianity,* book x, chap. iv., he lived for five years.

324:7, *big-boned Alberic,* second son of Ecelin the Monk, Podesta of Vicenza in 1236, and though detested by the Lombards was not so fiendish as his older brother, called "the devil." (11) *anointed to rend and rip;* the older of the Ecelin brothers was called by himself the "scourge of God," and such he was at capture of Padua in 1237, when he committed the most atrocious barbarities; and these he carried into all northern Italy. (14) *Lombards band together,* league against Ecelin the devil; he gained the victory and seized Mantua and Brescia, but another uprising led to his defeat in 1259, when he was captured, refused to eat, tore bandages from his wounds, and died. (18) *Valley Rù by San Zenon,* Alberic's castle in eastern Alps, where he was besieged in 1260, betrayed by his followers, tied to tail of a horse, and dragged to death, his sons torn in pieces, his wife and two daughters burned at the stake. (23) *raunce,* broken stone or marble. (30) *cushats chirre,* wood-pigeon's or ring-dove's cooing note.

325:19, *Sordello Prince Visconti;* Aliprando, in his chronicle of Milan, makes Sordello a member of the Visconti family, and gives him a very flattering history. Miss Wall says: " The chronicles of Mantua tell how Sordello, Prince Visconti, saved that city and elsewhere distinguished himself greatly; that he was famous as a minstrel and fortunate as a lover; he was praised for the very things he never did and never could have done."

326:17, *the few fine locks;* a child of modern Asola is made by the poet to sing these lines, attributed to Sordello's first poem. (33) *rifle a musk-pod;* the aim of the poet has been to produce an enduring fragrance like that of musk, that at first causes an ache, but gradually becomes attractive.

PIPPA PASSES. 329:16, *martagon,* lily, *Lilium Martagon.* (17) *St. Agnes',* martyr of fourth century, who was beautiful and admired. (18) *Turk bird's poll,* turkey, because brought from Turkey.

NOTES 431

330:15, *Possagno church*, designed by Canova, native of the city, in form a circular temple.

334:9, *proof-mark*, indications of first or later impressions of a print.

335:11, *he is turned*, superstition that murdered man's face looks towards heaven for vengeance.

340:8, *et canibus nostris*, and to our dogs, Virgil, *Eclogues*, iii. 67. 14, *all in a tale*, compelled to tell the same story.

341:19, *Psiche-fanciulla*, one of Canova's finest works, representing Psyche as a girl with butterfly. (23) *unfinished Pieta*, in Possagno church a statue of Mary with dead Christ in her arms. (39) *Malamocco*, island near Venice with town ; *Alciphron*, Greek philosopher of time of Alexander the Great. (43) *lire*, Italian coin of value of twenty cents. (45) *Tydeus at the Academy*, one of heroes of Theban war, and Academy of Fine Arts, Venice.

342:2, *Fenice*, Phenix, leading theatre in Venice. (20) *Hannibal Scratchy*, burlesque spelling of Annibale Caracci, famous Italian painter.

343:34, *Coluthus*, Greek poet of sixth century, native of Lycopolis in Egypt, whose poem on the Rape of Helen was discovered by Bessarion, Greek cardinal of fifteenth century. (35) *bistre*, dark brown paint made of wood soot. (41) *Antinous*, *Odyssey*, xxii. 10.

344:13, *thunder-free;* protection from lightning was anciently thought to be secured by wearing the crown of bay or laurel. (15) *Hipparchus*, Athenian tyrant and patron of letters, who was slain in 514 B. C., at festival of Panathenaea by participants who concealed their daggers in the myrtle branches they bore. (29) *parsley crowns;* the kind of parsley known to us as celery was used by ancients for its fragrance, leaves being made into crowns for drinking bouts.

348:37, *Kate the Queen*, Caterina Cornaro, 1454–1510, Queen of Cyprus, but abdicated, and was given a palace at Asola by Venice, her native city.

349:9, *jesses*, strap about hawk's leg, to which is attached strap held by falconer.

350:29, *Bluphocks*, reported to mean "Blue Fox," a hit at *Edinburgh Review*, which was bound in blue and fox. (30) *Intendant,* superintendent of estates inherited by a bishop. (36) *grig*, cricket.

351:6, *Celarent, Darii, Ferio*, words used in logic, without other meaning. (8) *posy*, poesy. (22) *zwanzigers*, twenty-kreuzer, piece of Austrian money. (35) *Panurge consults Hertrippa ;* in Rabelais' *Gargantua and Pantagruel* Panurge consults Hertrippa as to his marriage.

352:6, *deposed*, obsolete form of deposited. (10) *Carbonari*, Italian secret society seeking liberation from Austria. (27) *Old Franz*, Francis I., Emperor of Austria.

355:9, *Andrea, Pier, Gualtier*, conspirators against Austrian rule in Italy. (35) *I am the bright and morning star*, Revelation ii. 28.

356:8, *Titian at Treviso*, altar-piece by Titian in chapel of Annunciata, cathedral of Treviso.

358:2, *fig-peckers*, bird that lives on figs. (17) *deuzans*, variety of apples; *junetings*, early kind of apples; *leather-coats*, golden russet apples.

432　　　　　　　　　　　NOTES

359: 19, *ortolans*, small singing-birds much esteemed by epicures for the table. (21) *polenta*, pudding made of corn-meal.

360: 11, *Benedicto benedicatur*, a specially strong form of benediction.

361: 32, *podere*, small farm.

362: 12, *soldo*, copper coin, of value of sou or penny. (21) *poderi*, plural of podere.

364: 13, *the seven and one*, Pleiades and Aldebaran. (23) *Miserere mei, Domine*, Be merciful to me, O Lord. (25) *dray*, nest. (28) *hedge-shrew*, field-mouse; *lob-worm*, larger than earth-worm, of same kind.

366: 25, *mavis*, English song-thrush ; *merle*, English black-bird ; *throstle*, a thrush. (33) *cowls and twats;* Browning said of the word twats: "The word struck me as a distinctive part of a nun's attire that might fitly pair off with the cowl appropriated to a monk," thus used to mean a hood.

KING VICTOR AND KING CHARLES. 371: 33, *Is it not like he'll love me at the last?* Victor had a brilliant son who died at seventeen, then he devoted himself ardently to the education of Charles, made him familiar with all state affairs, and did nothing without discussing it with his son; but otherwise treated him harshly, giving him no liberties.

375: 10, *Spain entertains a project*, that of return of Bourbons to Italy; both France and Austria made overtures to Victor for his aid if an attempt of this kind was made; he made promises to both, and when his double attitude was about being disclosed he abdicated in favor of Charles.

379: 5, *Annunziata*, chief order of knights of the Kingdom of Savoy. (7) *Del Borgo*, Minister of Foreign Affairs, an intriguer, but adroit. (18) *D'Ormea*, Minister of State, who had been raised to power by Victor, to whom he had rendered important services, but had been very poor and without family connections at first. (31) *galliot*, Dutch sailing vessel used for trade.

382: 11, *You resign the crown to me?* "He called his son to him, and declared to him his design. The young prince, astonished, troubled, fearing perhaps that this overture was only a trap in order to prove him, said to the King all that was proper to turn him from such a design. He prayed the King, if he really thought a time of repose was necessary to his health, to confer upon him the temporary exercise of authority, reserving the right to retake the crown when he thought proper. He ended by throwing himself at his father's feet and conjuring him to change his resolution."

383: 30, *Act of Abdication*, read September 3, 1730, by Marquis Del Borgo, in presence of ministers, knights, and the great of the nation, giving Victor's reasons, old age, and wish for rest before his death.

384: 30, *Captain against Catinat*, battle of Straffarde, when French gained victory over Savoy and ravaged the country; but at battle of Turin Victor severely beat the French.

386: 1, Louis of the South, as rival of Louis XIV. of France.

391: 8, *Marchioness Sebastian;* after death of his queen, Victor married Anna Teresa Canali, a lady in waiting to his queen and daughter, but did not make it known until his abdication. He made her Countess of Spigno, and was ruled by her to a large degree.

399:5, *Moncaglier*, town four miles south of Turin.

401:17, *Susa and Superga*, towns in neighborhood of Turin.

(31) *fostered laws and letters;* Victor was very public-spirited, did much for education and arts, founded a college at Turin, and prepared *Victorian Code* of four volumes for governing his kingdom.

404:13, *Fleury's aid*, Cardinal, supposed to be a helper of Victor, but probably intrigued against him.

405:14, *Rhebinder*, marshal of the army. (17) *Count called on Del Borgo to deliver the Act of Abdication;* after leaving the throne Victor took up his abode in the old castle of Chambéry, with his marchioness. Here *ennui* beset him, even the company of his lady not being sufficient to overcome it. He had an attack of apoplexy, which rendered his mental faculties feeble, and caused him to be irritable, and subject to violent fits of passion. The marchioness had set her heart on being a queen, no less than a king's consort, and she had no rest till she had stirred up Victor to seize again the crown he had voluntarily laid aside.

The king, his son, twice visited Victor in his retirement; and in the second interview, which took place in the summer of 1731, as Charles Emanuel accompanied his queen, Polyxena of Hesse, to the baths of Evian, he found his father querulous, captious, and dissatisfied with the policy pursued by the new government. Victor directed from Chambéry the councils of his son, and he, apparently, complained both that his instructions had not been literally followed, and that during and after his illness the communications of the ministers with him had suffered interruption.

Charles Emanuel quitted his father after three days, and proceeded to Evian; but he had scarcely arrived at this place when a young Savoyard priest, by name Michon, announced to him that, having been admitted to view the royal apartments at Chambéry, he had, by the sheerest chance, overheard a conversation between the old king and the marchioness, from which it was clear that they contemplated a journey to Turin, with a view to possess themselves of the royal authority.

Charles Emanuel lost no time in crossing the Alps, and followed the less frequented path of the little St. Bernard to avoid an encounter with his father on Mont Cenis. Through this latter mountain, in fact, the old king had travelled with his best speed, but he nevertheless only reached Rivoli in time to hear the cannon announcing his son's arrival at the royal palace in the capital. Charles did not fail to pay his respects to his father on the morrow. Victor pleaded, as a reason for his return, his desire to live in a more genial climate than that of Savoy; and the young king, who had in reality advised such a removal at the time of his stay in Chambéry, showed himself satisfied with his father's resolution, however sudden, and placed the castle of Moncalieri at Victor's disposal.

At Moncalieri the old king received the homage of his son's ministers, and gave vent in their presence to his ill-humor and dissatisfaction, and even allowed himself some harsh and threatening expressions against them. The marchioness, always by his side, gave herself queenly airs, and her demeanor to the young queen, both at Chambéry and at her new residence, gave Charles Emanuel the first hint of his father's intentions, while at the same time it obliged him, were it only out of regard to the royal lady who shared his throne, to frustrate them.

On the twenty-fifth of September, 1731, in the evening, Victor Amadeus sent for the Marquis del Borgo, and bade him deliver up the deed of abdication. The minister in the greatest perplexity gave some evasive answer, and hastened to convey to the king the unexpected demand. Charles Emanuel was a modest, submissive son; a man of upright, pious, generous nature. His first impulse was, it seems, compliance with his father's wishes. Awakened from his sleep by del Borgo, he summoned his ministers around him, and with them the Archbishop of Turin, Charles Arboreo of Gattinara, and other conspicuous personages. To these he communicated his father's desires, adding that he was ready for his own part to give his consent, but that he did not deem himself authorized to divest himself of the royal dignity without at least the knowledge of those in whose presence he had solemnly accepted it.

The king's lay advisers, not unmindful of Victor's threats, were terrified at the prospect of his return to power ; they dared not nevertheless too openly propose a son's rebellion against his father, and none of them ventured to break silence. The archbishop, Gattinara, strongly and at full length demonstrated the unreasonableness of Victor's pretensions ; when, at his persuasion, it was unanimously resolved that the tranquillity of the country did not admit of a repeal of the king's act of abdication.

407: 13, *arrest him now ;* whilst they were yet deliberating, a note was handed to the king, by which the baron of St. Remy, commander of the citadel of Turin, announced that at midnight Victor had come from Moncalieri, on horseback, followed by a single aid-de-camp, and asked for admittance into the fortress. The commander had firmly but respectfully answered that the gates of the citadel could not be opened without an order from the king, whereupon the old king, in a towering passion, had turned his horse's head back to Moncalieri. This last proof of Victor's readiness to resort to extreme measures determined the still wavering minds in the king's council. An order of arrest against Victor was drawn up, which Charles Emanuel signed with trembling hand, with tears in his eyes.

The marquis of Ormea, who had been raised to power by the father, who now conducted the affairs of the son, and was more than any other man implicated in these fatal differences between them, took the warrant from Charles's reluctant hands, and on the night of the twenty-seventh and twenty-eighth of September repaired to Moncalieri. He had encompassed the castle with troops summoned from the neighborhood of the capital, and charged four colonels with the conduct of the dangerous expedition. These walked, without resistance, into the old king's apartments, where he was found plunged in one of his fits of lethargic sleep. The marchioness awoke and bounded up with a scream, but she was hurried away, and conveyed first to a nunnery at Carignano, then to a state prison, at the castle of Ceva. Not a few of her relatives and partisans were arrested in the course of the same night.

The chevalier Solaro, one of the colonels, next proceeded to possess himself of the king's sword, which lay on a table by his bedside; and at length succeeded, not without great difficulty, in breaking the king's heavy slumbers. Victor sat up in his bed; he looked hard at the faces of his disturbers, and inquired on what errand they came; on hearing it he burst into a paroxysm of fury; he refused to accompany them, to dress, to rise from his bed. They had to wrap him in his bedclothes, and thus to force him from the chamber. The soldiers had been chosen for their character of reliable steadiness and discipline, but were not proof against the passionate appeals of the man who had so often led them to victory. Murmurs were heard from the midst of them, and a regiment of dragoons, addressed by Victor in the courtyard, gave signs of open mutiny. The colonel, count of Perosa, however, with great presence of mind, ordered silence, in the king's name, and under penalty of death, and drowned the old king's voice by a roll of the drums. They thus shut him up in one of the court carriages, into which he would admit no companion, and followed him on horseback, with a large escort, to the castle of Rivoli.

407:23, *Alberoni and Coscia*, cardinals who opposed D'Ormea in Victor's contentions with the Church.

411:12, *Take it, my father;* it appears probable that Charles did desire to give back the crown to his father. (31) *beat D'Orleans in his lines;* at battle of Turin this duke was wounded. (32) *Eugene*, governor-general of Turin, his comrade at battle of Turin.

412:8, *tell that tale the world;* Rivoli was for some time a very hard prison to Victor Amadeus, with bars at the windows, a strong guard at the doors, and unbroken silence and solitude within. His ungovernable rage made him like a maniac; and he cracked a marble table with his fist in a paroxysm of anguish and fury. Melancholy followed, the rigor of his prison was relaxed, books, papers, and friends were allowed him, and at last the companionship of the marchioness. At his own request he was returned to Moncalieri; and he there began to prepare for approaching death. Through his confessor he begged for a last interview with his son. Charles Emanuel instantly ordered his carriage; but the ministers and the queen advised against the visit. The king shed tears, but the father and son never met again. Charles Emanuel never alluded to the final catastrophe of his father's life without visible signs of the most painful emotion. Victor died at Moncalieri on the thirty-first of October, 1732, at the age of sixty-six.